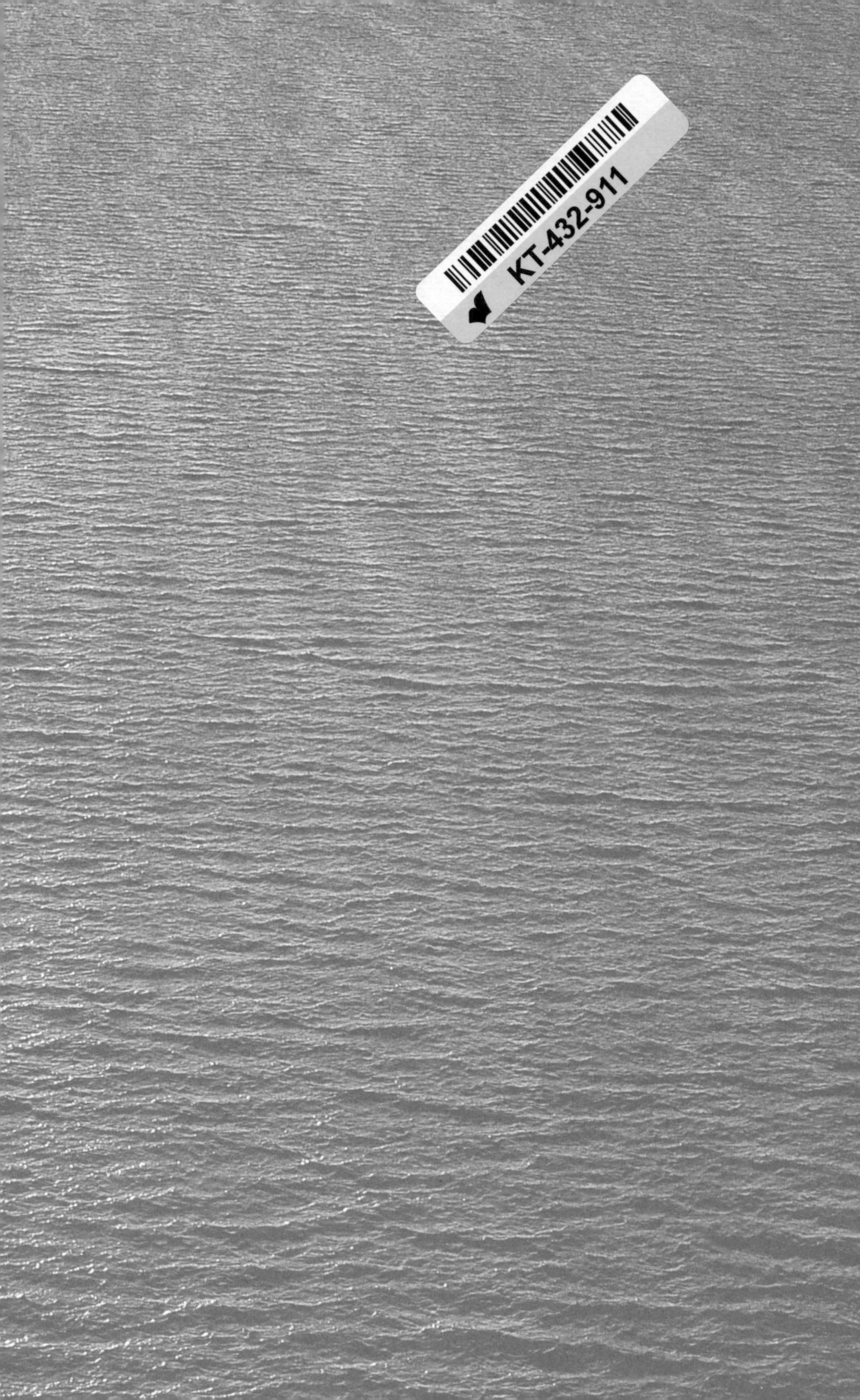

Taking On the World

Taking On the World

Ellen MacArthur

MICHAEL JOSEPH
an imprint of
PENGUIN BOOKS

MICHAEL JOSEPH

Published by the Penguin Group
Penguin Books Ltd, 80 Strand, London WC2R ORL, England
Penguin Putnam Inc., 375 Hudson Street, New York, New York 10014, USA
Penguin Books Australia Ltd, 250 Camberwell Road, Camberwell, Victoria 3124, Australia
Penguin Books Canada Ltd, 10 Alcorn Avenue, Toronto, Ontario, Canada M4V 3B2
Penguin Books India (P) Ltd, 11 Community Centre,
Panchsheel Park, New Delhi – 110 017, India
Penguin Books (NZ) Ltd, Cnr Rosedale and Airborne Roads,
Albany, Auckland, New Zealand
Penguin Books (South Africa) (Pty) Ltd, 24 Sturdee Avenue,
Rosebank 2196, South Africa

Penguin Books Ltd, Registered Offices: 80 Strand, London WC2R ORL, England

www.penguin.com

First published 2002

17

Set in 10.25/14.75 pt Trump Mediaeval
Typeset by Rowland Phototypesetting Ltd, Bury St Edmunds, Suffolk
Printed in Great Britain by Clays Ltd, St Ives plc

A CIP catalogue record for this book is available from the British Library

ISBN 0-718-14525-9
ISBN 0-718-14622-0

Contents

List of Illustrations

The publisher would like to thank the following photographers, organizations and collections for their kind permission to reproduce the images in this book.

MacArthur Archive 1, 2, 3, 4, 5, 6, 9, 10, 11, 14, 15, 16, 24, 53; Ken MacArthur 7, 91; Glyn MacArthur 8; Auntie Thea (Lewis) 12, 13; Maureen King 17, 18; News International 19; Ellen MacArthur 20, 21, 25, 28, 29, 30, 32, 33, 34, 35, 37, 39, 44, 46, 70, 71, 72, 73, 74, 75, 76, 77, 78, 79, 80, 81; Graham Percy 22, 23, 31; Steve Belasco 26; Carol & Derek Jones 27; Alan Wynne-Thomas 36; Peter Bentley 41; Thierry Martinez 42, 54, 55, 61, 64, 66, 92, 94, 95, 102; Liam Dryden 45; Merfyn Owen 47; Marie-Pierre Tricart 48, 49, 89; Jon Nash 50; Marten Yachts 51; Rick Tomlinson 56, 68; Jason Kerr Yacht Design 59; Jacques Vapillion 60, 67, 96; Kingfisher Challenges 62; Pat Ashworth 63, 88; Marie Cairo 65; Offshore Challenges 69; Michael Birot 87; Conseil General de la Vendée 90; Yvan Zedda 97; BBC Picture Archives 98; CEDM Visual Media, University of Derby 99; Penguin photographers 101

All the line drawings that are used as chapter headings in the book were drawn by Ellen.

Every effort has been made to trace the copyright holders of the images reproduced. We apologize in advance for any unintentional omission and would be pleased to insert the appropriate acknowledgement in any subsequent edition.

Round Britain 1995

North Sea

Lossiemouth
Whitehills
Peterhead
Inverness
Stonehaven
Montrose
Fort William
Kentallen Bay
Loch Aline
Port Appin
Kerrera
Oban
Loch Feochan
Craobh Haven
Seil Island
Crinan
Anstruther
Ardrishaig
St Abbs
Berwick-upon-Tweed
Largs
Troon
Amble
Girvan
Portpatrick
Hartlepool
Scarborough
Peel
Bridlington
(anchor)
Port St Mary
Hull

Irish Sea

Dulas Bay
(anchorage)
Port Dinorwic
Pwllheli
Aberdaron Bay
Lowestoft
Aberystwyth
Fishguard
Harwich
Solva
Milford Haven
Ramsgate
Southampton
Chichester
Poole
Newhaven
Eastbourne
Padstow
Weymouth
St Ives
(anchorage)
Brixham
Dartmouth
Fowey
Salcombe
Newlyn

English Channel

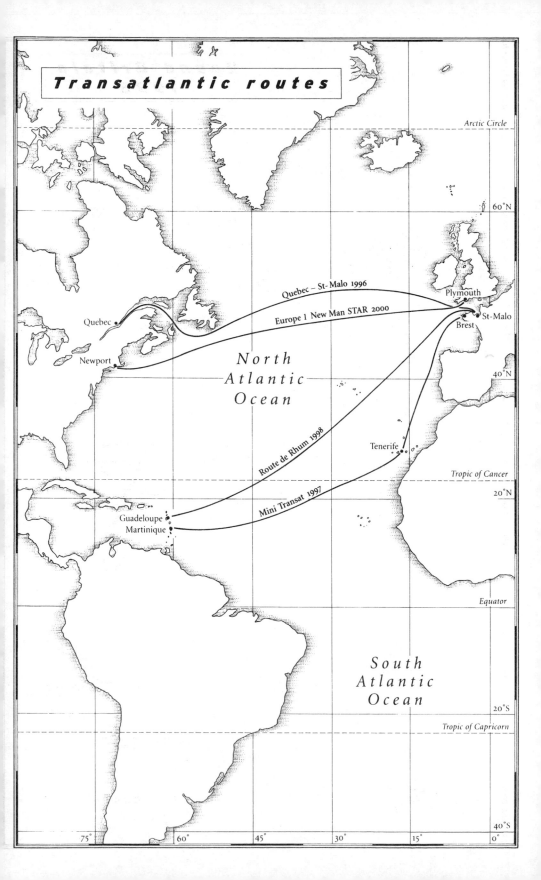

Transatlantic routes

Arctic Circle

60°N

Quebec – St-Malo 1996

Plymouth

Europe 1 New Man STAR 2000

St-Malo
Brest

Quebec

Newport

North
Atlantic
Ocean

40°N

Route de Rhum 1998

Tenerife

Tropic of Cancer

20°N

Mini Transat 1997

Guadeloupe
Martinique

Equator

South
Atlantic
Ocean

20°S

Tropic of Capricorn

40°S

75°   60°   45°   30°   15°   0°

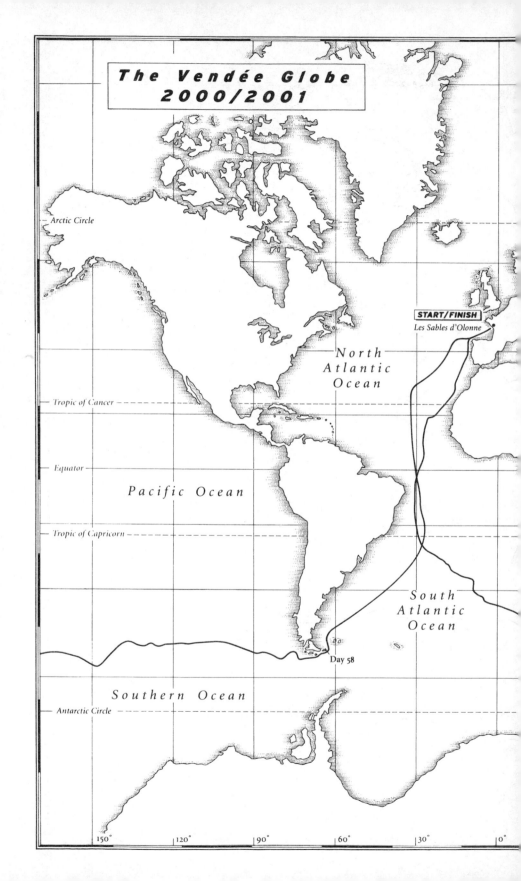

The Vendée Globe
2000/2001

Arctic Circle

START/FINISH
Les Sables d'Olonne

North
Atlantic
Ocean

Tropic of Cancer

Equator

Pacific Ocean

Tropic of Capricorn

South
Atlantic
Ocean

Day 58

Southern Ocean

Antarctic Circle

150°   120°   90°   60°   30°   0°

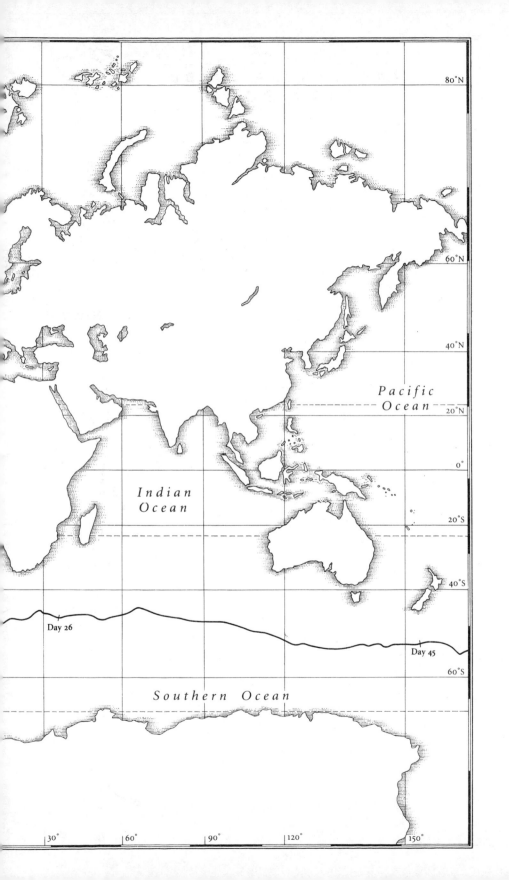

Pacific
Ocean

Indian
Ocean

Day 26

Day 45

Southern Ocean

80°N

60°N

40°N

20°N

0°

20°S

40°S

60°S

30°   60°   90°   120°   150°

I have always wanted to write a book for as long as I can remember, although when the time appeared right, the process was far harder than I could ever have imagined. As a shy six-year-old I'd won a writing competition on *Jackanory*, and when interviewed by the local paper I apparently said, *'Don't make it too long, just a few pages of your exercise book will do!'*

If only I had taken my own advice!

The reality of a naturally active person locking herself in a room to make a deadline has been a massive test in itself – never did I think that I would be able to spend three days in a house without leaving its walls.

I can only apologize for the fact that the book did not come out last year, the winter after the finish of the Vendée Globe, but I can't help but feel that it is a more complete story as a result of the extra year. In 2001 my life went upside down, with pressures from many directions – and it's been important for me to look back on it and reflect. Writing this account as seen through my eyes has been tough, but it has forced me to take time to try to understand everything that happened.

This book has been written and edited in the oddest of places, from the back of the car to departure lounges, at home and in hotel rooms. The long-lost depths of the loft have been explored for photos, and I think I may have visited some of the darkest recesses of my soul to transfer my experiences and memories as clearly as I could on to these pages. On the subject of pages I must thank from the bottom of my heart Rowland White, who must be the most patient and tolerant editor in the world. Without him, this book would have needed to be in at least two volumes!

I have included some early transcribed logs, correspondence, and more recent e-mails sent from the ocean in their original form, so you will find spelling mistakes or typing errors which are often a measure of the degree of roughness at sea at the time! I have assumed basic sailing knowledge in the text, but for those of you who have not yet experienced the feeling of the water beneath you, there is a glossary at the back.

The hardest part of writing has been the sheer number of people and experiences that we have had to leave out. The original text has had to be reduced by half, which has made it difficult to thank all those who have played such important roles in my life, from the time I began sailing up to our present projects. That is why there is such a mammoth set of acknowledgements at the end of the book!

But this book would not have been possible without the belief over the years of lots of people. So many have made such a big difference to our projects and have made them what they are so far, from Jim in Hamble, Lindsey who made *Kingfisher*'s beautiful tillers, BT for sponsoring years of communication, allowing us to share our races with millions, to the French boy with his 'Thank you Ellen' banner at my Vendée arrival – though much of the sailing I have done so far has been single-handed, I have not been alone. Mark Turner, in particular, and the extraordinary team around me really have made that difference: from those who prepared the boats for their voyages, to those who communicated the story hidden away in the office and without whom this would have been a *much* shorter story, if it could have been written at all.

I cannot finish this introduction, though, without thanking Kingfisher Plc. People often say '. . . and I would like to thank my sponsors', but I really mean it. Offshore racing as we know it would simply not exist without sponsorship. Kingfisher believed in us back in 1998 when we walked into their boardroom with a plan, and more passion and energy than you could imagine. In a pivotal year, when for us it was make or break, they made it!

When I was a kid I was inspired by books, and I would lose myself in a world of my own, huddled in a corner of the school library. One of my favourites was *Gypsy Moth Circles the World* by Sir Francis Chichester, published in 1967. When I visited my old school library just a couple of years ago I found that same book. The library card tucked in its cover still bore the name Ellen MacArthur several times – but there were no other names since mine and just one before!

I always try to give my all to any project that I undertake, and this book has been no exception. I have not tried to write a sailing book, nor a book about the Vendée Globe, but more simply a book about my life. I just hope that you enjoy it.

In the Vendée Globe section of this book, the e-mail logs sent back by Ellen start with log code of 'ellenmacarthur.com/dayX'. If you look up these links (e.g. *www.ellenmacarthur.com/day4*) on the web you will find a complete day-by-day account of the Vendée Globe, including weather charts, positions of the raceboats, full accounts of the race situation, photos taken during the race and a complete collection of Ellen's logs, impossible to print in their entirety in the pages of this book.

1 August 1995

Dearest Ellen,

Mum told me you had read recently a book by another young girl about sailing, and were overawed and convinced you could never write one as good. Of course you could.

Nobody wants to read a book which is almost a replica of someone else's. What they would be interested in, is how it feels to a young teenager in a very tiny home-worked on boat, to venture out around a coast she's never touched before, having to make friends as she goes. Don't use sentences everyone else has always used. Surely at your age, spurred only by your own ambition, everything is different to you from the norm. Recapture the feeling – of loneliness – of occasional panic – of irritation.

The thing to do is GET WRITING. Concentrate on that, and not on producing perfection. Get it written, then leave it to mature in a desk or drawer. Get it out and read it again in a month or two months' time. You will see its faults then, its badly written bits, its boredoms. GET WRITING . . .

Best of luck,

Love,

Nan

xx

'I'm not there yet, we haven't crossed the line yet.'

I spoke in French into the sat phone as I struggled to answer too many questions. 'It's not over till it's over' turned over in my mind. I was acutely aware that *Kingfisher* and I had not finished the race. Please leave us alone to concentrate on getting over that line.

Outside the fog was closing in, though until now the sea had remained calm. I was worried that I would hit someone or something over the last few hectic miles of the race. We simply had to finish safely; we had already seen what a fragile existence we were living out here. As far as a boat's concerned, more often than not it's the land that is the threat, and it was land we were approaching. The first support boat that came out to meet us was now almost out of sight, though only a few yards ahead of us, disappearing in the thickening fog.

I had felt torn over those last days of the race. Problems with the forestay had meant there was a constant risk of losing the mast, which was massively stressful. But despite this I wasn't sure I wanted to finish. Part of me quite definitely wanted to stay out there for ever.

The fog rolling in as the light faded felt like a sign, as if we weren't meant ever to see the finish. It was as if were meant never to come, or that we might be able to pop across the line and slip back out again silently under the cover of the blanket of mist. I thought back to my very first transatlantic crossing, in which our

I

first land fall after leaving America was Les Sables d'Olonne. Alone on deck then, seeing the shoreline for the first time, I'd wanted to turn back, imagining that the other side of the ocean would never come.

Five years later, right now, I have that same feeling.

Within the fog it was eerie. I could hear other boats around me, but all I could see through the grey denseness were the few square metres of dull water around us. The suspense gripped me. Small waves began to build as the wind increased, bringing a damp chill into the late evening air. My heart beat faster as with our growing motion my fears for the mast returned. I set about reefing the sail, reducing its area to lessen the strain. Moving through the darkness, I worried about a collision while I was busy concentrating on the sail. The support boat was out of sight now, blanketed in the fog, and I was worried she would lose me completely. With the reef in I was happier; although we were slower, we were safer. The ends of races are never easy, so why should the Vendée Globe be any different?

I popped below to the cabin to check our distance from the coastline; we were heading right for the shore and it was time to tack. Back on deck I looked up and could see more clearly and began to pick out a few lights around me. As the seconds passed the fog began to lift and I could see lights distinctly for the first time. My little world evaporated. I suddenly felt I'd been dropped into a Hollywood film set – there couldn't have been a greater contrast from the silent covering of the fog to the thousands of lights which surrounded me. There were boats of all sizes heading towards us, and helicopters above with searchlights sweeping as if looking to pinpoint an escaping prisoner. The noise dominated the moment – whenever the sound of the rotors drifted away on the wind, it was replaced by the radio chattering out information on our position and speed. I stood in the cockpit, took a few long, deep and calming breaths and looked up and around to try to take in the situation. It was breathtaking.

The water felt confused as the boats moved close around us, a choppy, fidgety motion which I hadn't felt once in months. I could hear voices on the radio, some in English, some in French, some of strangers, some of people I knew. I thought I heard the name of the boat that my parents had come out on at the start of the race. I knew they were near, I could sense it, but my world was blinded by the blazing searchlights. I had my own floodlight ready on board and tried pointing it at several of the large motor cruisers to see if I could spot Mum and Dad. No luck, just many waving figures and rolling cameras.

I had the photocopy of the finish line, given to all the skippers at the briefing before the race. I had put it in the waterproof folder, hoping then that the day would come when we could use it to find our way in. Everything seemed so different from our departure – even the lighthouses on the harbour breakwaters were lost in this artificial brightness.

I ran up and down *Kingfisher*'s deck making final checks as we glided towards the finish line, and could see every part of the boat, so there was no need for a head torch. I stood by the shrouds squinting to see the *Nouch Sud* buoy that helped signal the finish, but it was impossible. I returned to the chart table to study the chart. We needed to tack again.

I talked on the radio to the support boats, asking them to warn others I was about to turn. We had to make sure that we made space in the crowds so I could turn *Kingfisher* safely. I dashed below a couple of times to use the main VHF radio once the hand-held had gone flat. Although we were clearly not alone, it seemed so much quieter inside the boat. I tried to believe that the finish was not imminent, that I was just sheltering inside from a rough sea, still in the same world I'd been in for so long, but I couldn't. Our sole objective for over ninety days had been to cross the line as quickly as possible, and now it was less than a mile away. We'd sailed 26,000 miles, but I wished we still had 26,000 more to go.

As I peered into the cockpit of each boat I could see people, people I knew, faces I had not seen for over three months, tearful but smiling. Everyone hung on every second of every minute as we closed in on the finish.

Although I was desperate to see everyone again and to cross the line before we had more problems, I still wasn't ready for the race to end. Our focus on getting here had been so intense that it was hard to see to the other side of it. I had been through the experiences in my head a million times, but at the end of it all, something somewhere inside me knew that everything was going to change.

Things began to happen more quickly. The RIB with our support team on board was now almost alongside us. The flashing white light of the buoy was getting closer, and its enormous black and yellow superstructure became clear ahead of me. For a brief moment there seemed to be complete silence – we were nearly there. I looked around *Kingfisher* for one final check that everything was still OK. As my eyes refocused on the buoy, there was a deafening crack . . . the gun had fired, and at 1936 and 40 seconds on 11 February 2001 we had crossed the finish line.

Adrenalin surged through me. The RIB pulled alongside us, its passengers jumping aboard like a raiding party, and as the horns blew and the voices screamed I was embraced and wrapped up in loving arms – my first human contact for over three months.

Strangely, there were no tears, just the most incredible feeling of relief. As if a plug had been pulled, my concentration ebbed away in the time it takes for a gun to fire. No longer did I need to sleep for just ten minutes to recover, no longer did I need to look at the instruments each time I blinked. It was over, the race was over, and if it weren't for the adrenalin I'm sure I would have collapsed. We had made it. Together, *Kingfisher* and I had made it.

The whole team was soon on board and getting to work. As we pointed to the harbour entrance, I tried to say that the course was 055, but my voice was drowned out by the noise. Alain Gautier, a member of the *Kingfisher* team and himself a veteran of the Vendée Globe, came on board and placing his hands on my shoulders, looked straight into my eyes – he understood. He then handed me a rucksack like a radio pack connected to a pair of headphones. For the next hour I was interviewed live on at least two TV stations, but I found it difficult to concentrate, my first priority still being to get *Kingfisher* into the harbour. Alain asked what I had learnt about myself and how I had changed during the race. I tried to explain. But he knew, he had already been through this. We had lived through extraordinary and dangerous situations out there, and I reflected on how much people are capable of. But while it's tough, it's still our choice, and in that way we are very, very lucky.

Without warning, the mainsail dropped down as we approached the entrance to the harbour channel. I reacted without thinking before checking myself – for the first time in months, *Kingfisher* was out of my hands. I wanted to talk to the guys sailing her, I wanted to be with them, but as we neared the breakwater more and more boats closed in. Once in the channel you could have walked from one side of the harbour to the other across the boats. It was euphoric mayhem.

People were cheering, waving and calling my name. Through the smoke from the flares I could see whole families, people old and young on the edge of the harbour walls and along the water's edge. In the distance I could see thousands of people hanging over their balconies. I'd never seen so many smiles at one time. Overwhelmed by the welcome, I could only smile back, from ear to ear. I tried to smile for every single face in that crowd as we slowly crept up the channel.

I was handed a pair of distress flares, which I banged on the deck to light. The heat was intense and the fumes filled the air. Through the red light of the flares I could see more, and made out individual figures. 'THANK YOU ELLEN' was written on a piece of wallpaper held up by a boy and his mother – he was standing on tiptoe, trying to lift his message high in the hope that we would see it. People were waving flags and flares, there were scarves and torches. I felt every person in that crowd had been with us and that everyone there was sharing in the moment. It seemed as if I was enjoying a party, not a celebration laid on especially for us. I was smiling and cheering *with* the people.

The contrast from being completely alone to being surrounded by hundreds of thousands of people within a matter of hours, could not have been greater. It was such an intense situation that it was almost too much to bear. I wanted to jump high in the air to say thank you. The last time I had passed these harbour walls was when we set off for the start. I remembered the nerves, the reality of the situation, and the concentration of trying to focus on the race that was about to start. Although I had to believe we would finish the race, I was aware of the dangers to come. Every one of the twenty-four boats crossed that start line with the hope of finishing. I found it difficult to comprehend that of all of those, I was just the *second* to make it. As I thought of what we'd been through together I dropped to my knees and kissed *Kingfisher*'s cold deck, the two flares still burning bright and hot in my hands.

As the flares burnt themselves out I began to see the faces around the boat more clearly. Through the constant barrage of camera flashes I looked ahead and there, in a small RIB, was Michel Desjoyeaux, the Frenchman who had crossed the same line just over twenty-four hours earlier to win the race. I walked to *Kingfisher*'s bow and swung over her pulpit to climb below her bowsprit. In the shadow of the bow I could only see Mich's eyes as he approached; not a single communication had passed between our two boats while we'd been out there, but we had shared so much. Mich knew that too. We hugged briefly, then he was gone.

There was still another surprise in store for me in the channel; friends of the project had brought *Iduna* to les Sables d'Olonne. She was my first 'real' boat, bought with school dinner money saved over eight years. She had been laid up in Mum and Dad's garden for the last three years and I was stunned by the thoughtfulness of the gesture. At a little over 20 feet long she was tiny, and as I looked down into her cockpit from *Kingfisher*'s enormous bow it just emphasized how much life had changed over the last three years.

Seconds out from the pontoon we had left on the day of the start, Mum and Dad came on board for the first time, their faces showing sheer happiness and relief. Dad walked across and held out his arms, and as they closed around me the length of time I'd been away was suddenly apparent. Mum hugged me too and as I wrapped my arms around both of them, she kissed me on my forehead . . . now I was home.

As *Kingfisher* finally approached the pontoon, I felt like a child awaiting an exam. All I could see were the hundreds of journalists, their lenses and microphones pointing directly at me. When we touched the dock moments later, I was standing completely alone.

I talked but I couldn't concentrate. The situation felt unreal. How could it be me who was talking to these people? Questions were asked and I remember saying that it felt 'too much, both doing the race, and being here right now'. I was passed an enormous champagne bottle and stood there with my knees shaking. If ever there was a time I had to look like I could open one it was now! The whole world must be watching us . . . I shook the bottle and the cork exploded out above the heads of the crowd. As champagne sprayed into the air it sank in: we'd done it, we'd finished second in the Vendée Globe. *Kingfisher* and I had been out there for ninety-four days and we had done it together. I simply felt like her pilot – we had worked together but she, and she alone, had, at the end of the day, carried me home.

I was asked what had been the best and worst moments of the race. I replied, 'The best moment is right now, and the worst moment will be in five minutes' time when I have to leave and I don't want to get off.' I was dreading it.

Mark Turner, without whom we'd never have got this far, walked towards me, and I saw by the look on his face that it was time to leave *Kingfisher*. I felt a knot in my stomach and I wanted to run away, I wanted to turn back time, somehow to pinch myself to wake up, and be back out there again. But this time I knew that it was not possible, my time was up now.

Tears welled uncontrollably in my eyes and I could feel a pain burning inside me. I felt numb as Mark's arm touched my shoulder, and involuntarily my feet began to walk me to her bow to climb off. Like in a nightmare, my feet wouldn't do as they were told. I wanted to stop and stay put. I knew I wasn't ready to go.

I turned away from Mark and slipped out from beneath his arm, the tears blurring my vision. I was oblivious to the noise and the hundreds of flashing cameras. How could I leave *Kingfisher*? How could I walk away? Our trip was over, and I knew deep down inside that things never could or would be the same again.

I walked blindly to the cockpit. Never before in my life had I wanted to disappear like this. I stood facing *Kingfisher*'s bow and closed my eyes, my forehead pushing hard against her coach-roof. We needed time alone. I wanted to say thank you, I wanted her to know how sorry I was that it was all over, that I would have to leave her. Those few minutes felt like hours as I thought harder about one single thing than ever before in my life. Sadness felt so different from exhaustion. This was a pain in my heart, whereas before pain had only run through every bone in my body.

The last three months felt like forever and I could not remember what life had been like before the race. For the first time since I crossed the line my feelings were coming out, their rawness impossible to hide, I was about to leave my friend, and it was breaking my heart.

Deep down, I knew that I could not have done more to look after her. As I stood with my head bowed I could only say my last thank you as I heard the noise of the crowds once again. Just the fact that I was alive and standing with her was evidence enough to me that she had done her level best to look after me too.

Until this moment the finish had felt like a dream, the thousands of people, the yell from the crowds, and the bright lights continuously shining. But right now those images were blurred and distorted by the pain. I clenched my teeth and tore myself away.

I cannot remember those final steps to *Kingfisher*'s side, but as I climbed over her guard wires for the first time in more than three months I felt as if I was leaving a very large part of me behind. As I jumped on to the pontoon, I held tight on to her wires, then laid my head against her. My eyes were tightly closed as I reached out to stroke her hull, her rounded gunwale felt cool and calming, and for one last moment the world closed off.

Then I heard the gentle words 'Come on, Ellen' as an arm slipped around me, and as I turned to leave my hand slid silently away from *Kingfisher*. Our Vendée Globe was over.

I was clearly a stubborn child from the word go. I was not in the mood to come out, so Mum had to be induced three weeks after my expected arrival date.

I was very lucky with where I was brought up. Our house near Whatstandwell was in the heart of rural Derbyshire. We lived on a smallholding which had been growing slowly shed by shed and fence by fence over the years as Dad worked in his spare time filling our small field. The house was away from main roads, surrounded by farm tracks, fields and footpaths which scattered across the hills and woods as they disappeared into the distance.

The rattle of tractors and the mooing of cattle were more common than the sounds of cars and people, and we were always surrounded with things to do, whether it was converting an old motorized lawn-mower into a ride-behind, or building a flying fox from the massive sycamore tree. We would generally amuse ourselves outside and were never without a project on the go.

While I was young Mum was at home most of the time. She had left her job as a teacher to take maternity leave, though as I grew up she started working again as a home tutor. Dad was a teacher, as he had always wanted to be even as a small child, and taught craft design and technology.

Dad is a bit of a collector of tools and old machinery. What most people would consider junk, he treasured – but junk or not, it needed to be housed somewhere. In and around the duck yard were sheds of varying shapes and sizes, which sprang up year by year as I grew older. We had a small field next to the yard, and once the bull had been removed by a local farmer, the field became an outlet for our energy – an amazing playground.

I was fascinated by spy and survival books, and spent hours crawling around like a Commando in the long grass, which came well above my waist as a small child. I can still vividly remember seeing the stems waving gently above my head, dancing in the breeze as I lay on my back staring up at the sky and dreaming of being marooned on a faraway, hidden island.

As a kid I was full of imagination. I would play for hours with a few bits of cardboard, a pair of scissors and sticky tape, happily muttering away to myself as I worked alone on the kitchen floor. Failing that, I could spend happy hours swinging from the table edge, hanging on by my fingertips – just because it was there. I could not sit still.

I was always headstrong. From the age of three I was sent to ballet classes in an attempt to straighten out my pigeon-toed feet. I hated it. Dancing round a room in a leotard just wasn't my idea of fun.

It got to the point where I was so frustrated that one day I lay back in the car seat and simply said, 'Mum, I'd rather be dead than go to ballet.' Although I was only four years old, I think Mum understood that I really did hate it and had made my mind up, though I suppose I should grudgingly thank her for making me stay long enough to straighten out my feet!

When I was four my younger brother Fergus was born. Mum was worried at my initial lack of interest in him, so when I did show interest, asking if I could carry him into the house when they came back from hospital, she let me. Unfortunately I tripped and fell at the doorstep with the tiny Fergus in my arms. I immediately burst out crying, joined by Ferg once he'd bounced on the floor, then Mum came rushing in, crying too. I was clearly lacking doll skills! And I'm not sure Ferg has ever really forgiven me.

The extended MacArthur family all lived within walking distance of each other and therefore spent a good deal of time together. The villages in Derbyshire tend to be quite insular, so for most of the years of my childhood, our life revolved around the local area.

Nan was Mum's mother and lived alone. Gran and Grandpa were Dad's parents and lived with Great-Granddad, Gran's father. Gran still lives in the house where she brought up my dad and his brother, Glyn. There were sheds and fields there too, and a big orange Jersey cow that we kept for the family's milk. I remember sitting on Grandpa's knee on the old wooden three-legged stool, milking the cow and riding her in the field afterwards. Grandpa was a gentle, patient man who was very fond of his family. He was a stonemason by trade, working from home in his workshop down the yard behind the house, which was bristling with tools, saws and machinery. I would spend hours in there amusing myself by cutting and fiddling around with small chunks of local grit stone while he worked. Afterwards he would head inside to the cosy kitchen for orange squash and biscuits and, if we were lucky, we'd get a slice of Gran's fantastic sausage and egg pie, before settling down to listen to the football results with Great-Granddad.

We'd often play hide and seek in the yard, go climbing and build dens in the hay barn, or go on 'expeditions' in the attic. Grandpa was very keen on cricket and on a fine day we'd play a game together on the long flat lawn which had been hand-laid years earlier by Great-Granddad. He loved being outdoors and was an enthusiastic gardener, tending his vegetables with great care and joy or delighting in his brightly coloured sweet peas. He had an incredible affinity with nature, and as a child I was immensely impressed that he had a pet robin that often came and sat on his spade. I would spend hours sitting with him talking about his life down the coal mines, not realizing the danger he'd been in back then. He talked of the canaries they took down with them to warn of gas, and told me the names of every single one of his pit ponies, which he continued to reel off faultlessly at the age of ninety-three. There was a strange connection between Great-Granddad and me; somehow, even with a good eighty-five years between us, we were soulmates.

He had always maintained that he did not want us children to see him if he became very ill in his old age, and suddenly after he had a stroke we just did not see him any more. Mum told me that he was very ill but I didn't understand what a stroke was and when she told me that he wasn't eating, I felt sure that if I went over to their house I could make him eat. When he died I was sure my heart was broken.

Nan lived across the valley in a small cottage which was also where Mum and Dad first lived together. Lewis, my elder brother, spent the first few years of his life there too, before they moved across the valley to the family house where Fergus and I were also brought up.

I will always have the fondest memories of Nan – of going for long walks in the Dales with her wearing her woolly marmalade-coloured hat. From childhood her passion was for learning and her enthusiasm was rewarded when she won a scholarship to go to university. Tragically, her father forbade her to study further and forced her to go out to work as soon as she was old enough. She dutifully followed his wishes and worked as a secretary after taking evening classes in shorthand and typing at school. By the age of sixteen she was providing for the family. But fate intervened again when her husband died young. She was forced to stop pursuing her dream and worked ridiculously long hours to support Mum and her sisters, determined that each of them would have the chance to go to university.

We were lucky that Mum and Dad were at home with us in the school holidays which were generally spent as a family. In this close environment we did most things for ourselves. A great deal of our food was grown in the garden after Dad had specifically fenced off and cultivated an area of the field. He would always try to do all the car repairs and services himself, and our early holidays were generally in the caravan, bought when the little Fiat car which Mum won in a fish finger competition was sold.

Family walks would last for hours and hours in any weather. We'd pick bilberries in the summer on the moors, have snowball fights in the winter down the farm tracks, play hide and seek in the enormous rhododendrons, and be taught by Dad how to sharpen our penknives on loose bits of stone.

As a result of our father's love of machinery and antique engines we frequented the Crich Extravaganza each summer, taking along our Wolseley stationary engine and the little caravan. Dad loved these events, and as children we revelled in the chance to ride on the massive steam-powered, coal-fired traction engines, or feel the beating of the fairground generator steam engines which were run and looked after by friends of Dad's. I always thoroughly enjoyed being around the engines, getting covered in coal dust, oil and soot. The atmosphere was fantastic, with a real commotion when the engines moved around the grounds. The whistles would blow, breaking out above the gentle but constant throb of the moving pistons. Dad would spend hours chatting to his friends about threshing machines and old tools as the smoke and steam from the engines billowed up into the blue sky.

All of this could not have been further removed from the sea. None the less, this was an interest that showed itself early on.

Chapter Two

In 1980, Lewis went down to the East Coast to sail on *Cabaret*, my Auntie Thea's boat. I couldn't understand why I wasn't going as well and Mum's explanation that I was too young did nothing to console me. I was only four.

We saw Lew and Nan off on the train at Derby station and then Mum took me to the Derby Playhouse to see a puppet show called *Button Moon*. I was miserable. How could a puppet show ever take the place of an adventure of a lifetime? As I thought about what Lewis was doing I sulked until he returned.

He came back full of his trip, having loved every second of it. I think he might even have regretted being so enthusiastic, as I would not leave him alone, bombarding him with questions to find out something new about his experience, whether it was the weather, the number of sails *Cabaret* had or a detailed description of the interior of the boat.

My day came less than a year later. It was Easter, and for the first time I went with Nan and Lewis to see *Cabaret*. I remember nothing of the journey down to London other than intense excitement. I would not relax in any way, shape or form till I had laid eyes on *Cabaret*. I had dreamed of this moment for over six months.

I'd been told we were heading for Paglesham, and I had no idea what to expect. The word meant nothing to me, I was just dying to see the water. Face pressed against the cold glass of the window, the journey seemed never-ending. Buildings turned to trees, then to miles and miles of long, thick, wavering grass on the flat, marshy estuary. The land seemed to go on for ever, all the time ebbing away. Was this always the way to the sea, I wondered.

As I gazed out on to the river for the first time, the water was calm and muddy, with weed floating here and there. Lewis and I were hanging over the edges of the dinghy, looking at the boats on the river while Auntie Thea tried to answer my stream of questions. I just couldn't take it all in. I spotted *Cabaret* as she sat on her mooring and she was the most beautiful boat I had ever seen. She could, I was sure at that moment, take us anywhere in the world.

I was ready to burst as the little dinghy pulled alongside. Before we'd even tied on I was clambering up over *Cabaret*'s tall white topsides, trying to get under the guard wires and on board. The thought of climbing over the guard wire (which is the correct way of doing things) seemed quite impossible. The result was that, forgetting the size of my lifejacket, I got jammed beneath them. My head was on the deck and my feet were waving out over the water!

Once on board Auntie Thea unlocked the solid-looking wooden doors. I was right next to her, and as they opened I peered down into the deep, dark cabin. There was a smell of engines and timber, like Dad's garage, and the cabin seemed to smile at me. From that moment on, *Cabaret* felt like our little home.

Our first night on board was like a dream. I was tremendously excited as I lay there listening to the gentle lapping of the water on the hull. I could hear birds calling in the distance, I was so eager to get on with our adventures that I could hardly sleep. My world felt alive, and tomorrow we were going out to sea.

We went completely out of sight of land, and for the first time in my life I felt totally free. It would not have surprised me if I'd asked Auntie Thea if we could stay out at sea all week. I was hooked.

I became completely besotted with sailing and began to save every penny I could for a boat. Everything went into a money box which sat on my bedroom radiator for ten years. Above the radiator on a piece of graph paper was a hand-drawn box of 100 squares, and each time I made it to a pound I would drop it in and tick a square.

Once the 100 were ticked I would proudly ask Mum to pop the money into my building society account for me.

I would spend hours poring over *Practical Boat Owner* magazine, which Auntie Thea subscribed to, writing letters to companies in search of their latest brochures. Each one was filed in order of the size of dinghy. I also began collecting sailing books avidly. I kicked off my sailing library at a very young age with Arthur Ransome's *Swallows and Amazons* series. Mum and Nan had both been keen readers of these books and had passed them on to me.

I loved the spirit of adventure the books brought me, and dreamed of sailing on a lake to a secret island that had long been forgotten. I would spend hours and hours imagining what the secret harbour would look like, and how the firewood could be collected for the campfire. I dreamt of exploring at night with small hurricane lanterns, and of nights spent moored in a protected bay, or beneath trees at the side of the water.

Few children from the junior school in Wirksworth, our nearest main town, will remember me for anything other than being the girl who loved boats. I would draw a tiny optimist dinghy on everything from pencil cases and rubbers to exercise books – you name it, it had a boat on it!

I made three very good friends at junior school, Ben, Sarah and Simon. (Simon would become my boyfriend seven years later.) I was a bit of a tomboy, I guess, preferring to play with a good sharp knife and a block of wood than with make-up and dolls.

But Sarah was a bit of a loner too. She'd moved to our school from another one in Belper, and now lived across the valley from us and shared the same school bus. Though not as interested in the outdoors as me, she was, and still is, incredibly patient with my love for the sea. We would spend hours 'sailing' around the school playground pretending that the circles and squares painted on the concrete were islands and secret harbours. Poor girl!

I became friends with Simon when I was eight or nine years old. He'd just moved up to Derbyshire from Felixstowe on the Suffolk coast and he had sailed before. That was enough. On discovering we shared the same passion, we got on instantly. I can still remember the excitement of our first conversation.

Along with Simon and Ben I'd climb and abseil, play at being a Commando, go on expeditions and build dens in secluded woodland. Only more recently have I come to realize how lucky I was to be able to go out into the country and create a whole world of adventure.

I worked hard at school, though I did tend to spend every minute of my free time reading still more about boats and the sea, or I'd sit on the bus or in a corner at break-time with nothing more than a notepad and my imagination, designing possible new fittings to put on boats. The sky was the limit, but to make these dreams real I needed a boat.

For the time being, this meant *Cabaret* for a week each summer. And she was certainly no gin palace. Thea had bought her as a wreck and done her up herself. With seven, and later a dog, on a boat designed for four it was snug!

Cabaret was kept in a small boatyard at the end of a long, bumpy track. The main building was made of blackened weathered boards with the words J. W. SHUTTLEWOOD painted in white on a battered sign. This was a long way from being a marina. There were no floating pontoons to tie alongside, no fancy shower or toilet blocks, just mooring buoys scattered along the centre of the winding river. Creeks and gulleys crept inland from along the water's edge. I used to spend time looking out at the water, mesmerized by the movement around the buoys in the river, or dreaming of the adventures to be had aboard the rows of tiny dinghies lying in the marsh grass.

At just 26 feet, *Cabaret* was a small boat. Her cabin was dark and deep with a magnificent glow of varnished mahogany from her woodwork. She was not a beamy boat, therefore her cabin was narrow, and it was quite difficult for two people to pass each other below. On peering down into the cabin you could see the tiny two-burner galley on the left, and the chart table on the right. There were four adult bunks, two running underneath the cockpit, and one on either side of the main cabin. Beyond that was a door leading to the triangular forepeak where, along with the anchor and sails, we three children were stowed. I took the port side, Fergus the starboard, and Lewis, being the oldest and tallest, got the longest berth down the centre, above the toilet.

Nan was always the first to rise in the morning, with a thirst for her wake-up cup of tea. She was always slightly out of her depth in the galley as she found the paraffin stove confusing to use. We'd usually wake soon after she did to the sound of her cries as flames billowed up against the cabin roof.

For the first few years we cruised the local rivers around the East Coast, visiting new places like Brightlingsea and Walton-on-the-Naze, the evocative setting for one of the Arthur Ransome stories, before becoming more adventurous and heading across the North Sea to visit Holland, France and Belgium.

On our first crossing, Fergus and I were allowed to stay up long enough to see 'the galloper', which was a buoy moored near the coast, as we approached our home waters once again. After dark we saw phosphorescence for the first time – *Cabaret*'s bow wave churning up the plankton that responded by looking like a thousand stars twinkling in the water, before disappearing into the blackness behind us. I tried to take the phosphorescence home in a jam jar, but it died, and no longer shone when disturbed. I began to realize that the beauty of the water can't be taken away or captured. It can only properly be appreciated at first hand. I was also struck by how many sides the sea has to its personality. An angry sea on one crossing can be as smooth as silk on another. I was fascinated by how all this was possible and was desperate to understand much more.

I sailed alone for the first time in the French shipping port of Dunkirk on a sailing dinghy which my auntie had bought to be towed by *Cabaret*. I felt a mixture of freedom, responsibility and respect for the water – feelings which remain unchanged today. Each day that passed seemed to reinforce my love of the sea and photographs at the time invariably show me in knee-length shorts, with a royal blue peaked sailing hat and a little telescope which hung around my neck for years – just like the one from *Swallows and Amazons*.

We encountered our first real storm on the way back across the North Sea. I recall *Cabaret* being thrown around, but I also remember how solid she felt, and how much faith I had in her. I never felt scared in the storm, though I knew that something was going on in which we all had to be careful, hold on tight and clip on with our safety harnesses.

Sailing through the night was something else that left a vivid impression on me the first time it happened. Several times we had left early in the morning and anchored as the sun set, but sailing through the sunset and then the sunrise the following day was a whole new adventure. There was a feeling of constancy and endlessness about this kind of sailing. Why should we stop, why do we need to pull into port each night, why can't we carry on further? I had made my first open sea passage, and I'd loved it.

Following our North Sea crossings we returned to UK waters, and spent time cruising a little further north and south from our Essex home port. The first year we headed north and sailed up the Deben and the Alde rivers. We had the dinghy, so we children were able to do a fair bit of sailing too.

I was still desperate for my own boat, so when we headed south to sail on the Solent the following year, I decided to try to do something about it by busking in the street during Cowes Week to raise funds.

While *Cabaret* sat at anchor in Chichester Harbour I perched on the deck in the evening mist practising sea shanties on my tin whistle. I can only apologize to everyone anchored in the same harbour, as most of the shanties were learnt through trial and error – mainly the latter! Once we made it round to Cowes I lost my nerve. I felt intimidated by the multicoloured spinnakers and matching crew shirts. Everyone there seemed so much older and seemed to belong. I couldn't see any other children with sailing hats and telescopes round their necks. This was a type of sailing I really wasn't used to.

Lewis also enjoyed his sailing and started going to Ogston Reservoir with the school. I was still in the junior school and so, theoretically, not old enough to take part, but I would go with Mum to collect him and wait in the car looking out at all the boats. Eventually I managed to talk to one of the supervisors, and was lucky enough to be allowed to join in. I had found somewhere more local than the sea to sail.

But while I loved sailing there and learnt a great deal, I still dreamed of owning my own boat. I had in mind a tiny, varnished wooden dinghy with tan sails, though Auntie Thea was against it. She was sure that a fibreglass dinghy would hold its value better. The only problem was that a fibreglass boat was more expensive. I felt stuck, especially when I found an 8-foot fibreglass Blue Peter dinghy at a local boat sales yard a short drive from home. She cost £535, but I had barely £200 saved.

It was Nan who came up trumps. She knew how much I longed for a boat, and how hard I'd been saving. At the same time Lewis was trying to save for a BBC computer and Nan decided to give all three of us £300. It was a terrific amount of money and I am still amazed at just what a generous gift this was as it was a significant lump of her life savings.

After deep discussion I named the dinghy *Threep'ny Bit*, attaching the real thing, a coin found in the depths of one of our cupboards, to her hull. I used to spend my days rigging her up in the garden, making little tents for her, and working out how I could camp on board.

My bedroom at home was tiny. If I reached out I could almost touch both walls but I was determined to keep all *Threep'ny Bit*'s gear there. The ropes, oars and sails covered the whole floor and I could see that the only option was to keep everything on the bed, and move it when I needed to sleep. In the end, however, I came up with a simpler solution: when Mum and Dad went out, I took the bed apart and moved it to the barn. I slept in a sleeping-bag that I could roll up every morning, and the room felt as though it had more than doubled in size.

On the wall I had a 5-foot square map of a trout pond nearby. I'd walked there several times and was dying to get afloat on it. The owners of the pond couldn't have known how many of my dreams were realized when they told me I could keep *Threep'ny Bit* there. As she slipped into the water for the first time, the little wooden oars squeaked in her rowlocks and the water flowing beneath her bow made a bubbling sound.

Over the following months I spent many happy hours playing on the pond. I took *Threep'ny Bit* into the reeds, to hide from the savages. As I watched the moorhens going slowly about their business through my tiny telescope, I pretended that not a soul in the world could see us hidden away. I would land on the island and find perfect places to moor up, and the driest place to pitch a tent. I had the place for the campfire worked out so that I could hide the flames from anyone who tried to attack the island, and chose the tree in which to hang the lantern to show any allies the way in. There were passages behind the island which were difficult to negotiate with thick weed pushing its way to the surface, ready to catch unwary oars and leave them stranded in the weed beds till rescue came. There were fox tracks in the woods, and enormous holly bushes which opened out into tinder-dry palaces if you were brave enough to fight through the prickles. The pond occupied my thoughts and dreams day and night.

As my tenth birthday approached, I was just old enough to go on a race training camp at Rutland Water, a large reservoir at least ten times the size of Ogston. This was a long way from Derbyshire, but as soon as I knew that I was old enough to go I was determined to do so. The course was a week long, and I had asked for it as a birthday present from my family.

I learned a tremendous amount during that week. At ten years old I was one of the youngest of the sailors and was a bit too small for the boat. This wasn't helped by the weather we encountered during the week. It blew at least a Force 6 each day but one. I found keeping the boat upright incredibly difficult and capsized eleven times during the first day. I was so frustrated when I came last or second last in most races as I had imagined I would be able to get better results.

It was also the first time I'd been away from home by myself and I was homesick. I didn't really fit in with the crowds from the different sailing clubs, I didn't have a dinghy with new sails, or the latest gear. I had no wetsuit and sailed in a navy-blue anorak and tracksuit which I would try to dry each night over the dormitory radiator. It was the first time in my life I had felt lonely. I was surrounded by people but I might as well have been a million miles away.

On the journey home I decided that I would never let this happen again. I wasn't going to be last, no matter what it took.

A short while later, in a race at Ogston, I crossed the finish line first against the club sailors. It was a very satisfying feeling that made all my efforts there seem worthwhile.

My secondary schooling was at an old country comprehensive school with about 600 pupils. The Anthony Gell School was very independent in spirit. Half of it had been modernized, and the other half was fairly much as it had been when it was built in Victorian times. The old part had high-ceilinged classrooms with worn varnished wooden floors, the original blackboards and two beautiful globes suspended from one of the ceilings.

The school library was the central feature of the old part of the school, housing many rows of bookshelves. The shelves containing the sailing books were right in the far corner, opposite a window and beside a radiator. One of my favourite pastimes at school was to sit in the library, especially in winter, with my back to the radiator, my legs crossed and a sailing book on my lap.

The school was situated in Wirksworth, about fifteen minutes in the car from home. It had been a lead-mining town before switching to quarrying limestone, although that too was dwindling. Bare rock faces still show beneath the high conveyer-belt viaducts crossing the valley, whilst the fourteen pubs and the rows of tiny terraced cottages are also indicative of the town's history.

In the first years of secondary school I became aware that the girls and the boys were moving apart. I remember not understanding why Ben's mates were no longer keen for me to hang around with them. I had a skateboard like them, I could even hold my own in an arm wrestle, but things were definitely changing. At eleven there didn't seem to be a reason for it. Ben was always friendly, but I could tell that his credibility with his friends was threatened if I was around.

For the time being, life outside school continued much as it always had and Ben and I kept on exploring. Things were about to change for good, however, and for the best of reasons, when a girl from school phoned to tell me about some puppies which, if not found homes, would have to be put to sleep. At thirteen, I simply couldn't understand this. I'd always had a love of working sheepdogs, and I became a child with a mission. I discussed it with Mum and Dad long into the night. There were phone calls at midnight, promises made, tears shed. But the result was that I became the proud companion to one of my very best friends: Mac, a Border Collie cross.

Every evening on returning from school I would change into my scruffs, and Mac and I would head off into the fields together. At the weekends we would often disappear for the whole day, exploring every nook and cranny within miles of the house. Ben also had a dog, Ruby, who got on with Mac like a house on fire. The four of us went on den-making expeditions and fishing trips together.

At home Mac became part of the family and blended in well with the menagerie that surrounded us. I would spend hours helping Dad with the chickens and nurturing chicks which we kept warm in a cardboard box on the back of the Aga until they were strong enough to live outside. I also had a special friend in Paddy, a pure white pet duck, who would follow me round wherever I went. He hatched from an incubated egg, and considered me to be his closest family. I used to take him for swimming lessons on the pond with *Threep'ny Bit*.

It wasn't long before Mac came sailing too, joining us on our summer trips on *Cabaret* – which meant there were now eight of us on board! During that first summer with Mac, Sarah also joined us for a few days' sailing around Walton-on-the-Naze. This was the first time I was given the chance to navigate and try to handle things on board. I loved the responsibility and I was thrilled that Sarah enjoyed herself so much. If nothing else, it must have helped her make sense of my unstoppable ramblings about boats and the sea.

Chapter Three

When I was about fourteen, school organized a work-experience week. We could choose where we would go, and I already had an idea in my head. Earlier in the year we'd had a careers convention and I'd chatted to Simon Reeve, a local vet. He seemed to love his job and I found this enormously appealing. I felt I could relate to animals, having growing up around them, and I felt comfortable working with them.

I contacted his surgery and after a short wait they were able to take me on. It was a wonderful experience. I worked at the surgery and travelled round many of the local farms with Simon and the other vets in the practice. I loved it and made up my mind that I wanted to study veterinary science when I went to university. I was no genius at school, though, and decided to keep up my experience in the surgery, which I hoped would count for something in my university application.

One day when Simon arrived at the surgery he threw down a plastic glove and asked me to take a look at what was inside. It was a very strange fur ball which wasn't quite what it seemed. On closer inspection it looked like a long-haired guinea pig with no head, legs or tail. It turned out to be a 'thing' which was born alongside a calf. My task for the morning was to dissect it, pickle it and place it in a jar for preservation.

After surgery that day Simon was going into Chesterfield to look for a new car and I went along too as usual. We took the bottled thing with us and without thinking, left it on the seat of his old car as it was taken off to be valued.

As we waited in the garage foyer I realized where I had left the jar, but before either of us could do anything the man returned, with a pale green tinge to his complexion. Even after we'd explained that Simon was a vet, it took him a while to get over it.

During the time I was working with him, Simon took up microliting, and not long after I had moved away from home, he sold his business and flew solo from the UK to Australia. Perhaps there's something in the Derbyshire water!

My spare time was still spent either reading sailing books, designing bits for boats, or getting out into the countryside with Dad, going to farm sales. The sales were always different, never dull, and Dad's bearded face was well known. He rarely let a bargain slip through his fingers and as a result we'd end up coming home with anything from an old hay cratch to half a mile of electric cable. Often the trailer would be full and, as Lewis once pointed out, 'There's a lot comes up this drive, Mum, but not a lot goes down again!'

The faces of the other bidding farmers who returned time after time also became familiar. I developed a great respect for them all. More often than not farms were selling up, which lent an air of sadness to the sales. Watching the proceedings taught me an appreciation of time and persistence. Much of what was on sale had taken generations to accumulate. To reach a point where nearly everything which held a value could disappear so quickly reinforced my appreciation of just how hard some people work for things. There was an unspoken closeness between these people. Without words, a sentiment could be exchanged, respect could be shown and condolences given. This kind of mutual understanding was something I was to experience for myself when I entered the world of single-handed sailing.

I don't know why I resented being a girl when I was younger. It just seemed that what boys did was more fun. I wasn't cut out to play with dolls or gossip about boyfriends. Worn boots, numerous layers of old shirts, and a large knife hanging out of my back pocket showed that fashion was not a priority either! All I wanted was to be out filling my time with something adventurous and constructive – something I was sure was more worthwhile.

At school I never really felt I fitted that well into a group. I was attracted to boys now and then, but never really obsessed by them, although I do remember my first kiss, when I was fifteen, beside a phone box during a party of Ben's in Matlock.

I think lack of confidence played a big part in this. I was always quite shy of showing my feelings and of the reaction that this might prompt. On the face of it, there seemed to me to be little difference between being a mate and being a girlfriend. I felt I needed to be friends with someone in order to have a relationship, which was not a view I think most of the people around me necessarily shared.

I remember liking a guy who moved up to school from Leicester, though I never plucked up the courage to say anything to him. Once, in art class, one of his new friends, who was in my tutor group, turned to me as I walked past them and said, 'God you're ugly.' From that time on I just became quieter still.

Occasionally, perhaps for some special event, I would be persuaded to go down to the pub in Matlock. I rarely truly enjoyed the experience and had little enthusiasm for initiating conversation. I would never buy a drink and often took a yachting magazine with me. I didn't mean to be rude or to ignore people, but I did it as a defence. Bizarrely, it helped me feel more comfortable. Part of me also felt that if I took a magazine I could at least make the most of the time there and come home having learnt something, rather than feeling that I had talked about nothing very much for a whole evening.

It must all have been very difficult for the others to understand. They just didn't know what made me tick. Perhaps it's easier now that sailing has become my life. At the time, though, I can only imagine how weird my behaviour must have seemed.

I was never particularly unhappy at school, I just felt like an observer rather than a participant. My social unease, however, wasn't helped by a growing unhappiness at home.

Dad had always dreamed of being a teacher since he was a child, and early on in his career, I think he really did love his job. Over the years, though, things had changed, and he found himself being ground down by a job he had once lived for. He was promoted to Head of Year, with all the additional burdens that brings, and as a result was continually suffering from stress.

It was a time of cutbacks, schools were closing and merging, and Derbyshire teachers had to reapply for their own jobs. There was a very real chance that our circumstances would change. I could see the anger in Dad's eyes and how close to boiling-point he was when he came home late in the evenings. He seemed to turn to me to vent his anger on, maybe because I was the one who didn't hide in my bedroom upstairs. I remember once going to his school to see a production of some sort – it was rather a special occasion as it didn't happen often. More than any recollection of the production itself I vividly remember how happy and positive Dad was with his colleagues. It was a long time since I had seen him so jolly, and I could not see why he couldn't be like this at home. I felt I was to blame and was nervous when he came back in the evenings. Sometimes during these explosions I would run away down the field to hide, climbing into a tree, and squinting at the tiny glow from the kitchen window through my reddened eyes to see if Dad would try to find me. It felt unfair, but above all it was confusing. I could never have hated Dad for it, but they were difficult times for all of us, and each year I prayed things would get better.

There were always the good times together at the farm sales, however. On these occasions it was as if Dad was able, for a while, just to be himself again. We were like mates, discussing the machinery together or weighing up whether or not a tractor was a bargain.

While my strained relationship with Dad allowed room for the hope that things would one day return to normal, the death of my Grandpa had no such silver lining and hit me hard. I remember going to Gran's before the funeral service feeling confused. I was distressed that Grandpa was in the house: although I felt I wanted to say a last goodbye, I could not imagine what a dead person would look like, nor understand how I should react. I found it quite painful to see the whole family so upset too, fighting back the tears. For a brief moment I looked into the front room where Grandpa was, and although I could see little of his face, I saw his closed eyes and white skin. I was overwhelmed by the stillness in the room. The air seemed motionless, as if no person had entered for years.

I suddenly became immensely claustrophobic, as though I had to get away – I could not stay in sight of people. I ran into the kitchen, then out of the house and down to the yard where I knew I could hide. I felt people were watching me, but as I opened the tiny gate leading from the garden into the yard I knew that I was safe and would be more than able to disappear. Time passed very slowly from that moment on. My vision seemed to go into slow motion as I stepped down into the workshop where Grandpa's stone, tools and half-finished projects lay around me, the floor and windows, as always, covered in cutting dust. The machinery was all there, ready for action, and Grandpa's old black cutting apron and gloves hung ready, just waiting for him to pick them up. I was suddenly hit by the reality that Grandpa would never be within the walls of his workshop again. I felt empty, as if the breath had been drawn from my body, and tears began to stream down my cheeks. For the first time in my life I felt the awful hollowness of losing someone so close, and faced the realization that a figure who had been there for me every day of my life was no longer physically present.

It's impossible to say now whether or not events were connected, but as we struggled with our family sadness, I began to develop an intense interest in boats with tiny cabins. I think independence was what attracted me and these boats could be more easily lived on. They promised both comfort and escape. I found myself looking at every kind of tiny boat there was, trying to find the perfect one. I had attempted to be pragmatic about which type of boat would be best. I was still saving, and could afford something in the region of £900, plus the money from *Threep'ny Bit* which I had sold for £475. She had held her value as Thea had predicted.

When I bought *Threep'ny Bit* I had worked out that it was going to take a lot more than birthday and Christmas money to save for a boat. The only other source of income that passed through my hands was school dinner money, and once I was at secondary school, this vital source of cash came under my control rather than being paid in at the beginning of each week. I started a new regime which lasted until I finally left school. I would take a couple of slices of bread and a tomato or banana from the cupboard when I left home in the morning, then collect apples, plums or pears from the garden on the way to the bus. I would eat the fruit for breakfast, then save the banana and bread for lunch. My other option during the fruitless winter months was to buy mashed potato and beans, which cost just 8 pence, then smother it with gravy, which was free. A special treat would be jacket potato and baked beans (24 pence), though that was a fairly rare occurrence! Every night I would still religiously pile up the coins on top of the money-box, marking off a square each time I made it to £1.

By now, despite my imminent exams, I found it hard to concentrate on school work, or revise. I'd sit in my bedroom with my books open just staring at the Crich Stand Memorial that flashed like a lighthouse through my window from the hill opposite. And when the son of a friend of Mum's from Norway came to stay I was easily distracted. Robert was very interested in boats so a family trip to Nationwide Boat Sales was organized. As a break from my revision I decided to go along too. The truth is, it would have been hard to stop me!

While walking round the boat yard we spotted a man who appeared to be looking at the same type of boats as us. Dad wandered over to say hello and discovered that he was actually thinking of selling a boat. It turned out that *Kestrel* was exactly what I was looking for. A few days later she came home, towed behind the old Peugeot. I covered her in a tarpaulin in the field, forcing myself to leave her completely alone until I had finished my GCSEs.

As soon as my exams were finished, *Kestrel* and I became inseparable. I was constantly ferreting around for old bits of mahogany in the barn, then cutting them and sanding them to perform the perfect modification.

I worked on *Kestrel* during the two summers I had her, building everything into her from a chart table to a bilge pump-operated sink drain system. I learned about fibreglass work and mixing resin, and was regularly covered in bits of polyester and glass. Almost overnight all my clothes became covered in materials, but I was happy, I had launched myself into a teach-yourself boat-building course, and through trial and error it seemed to be working. Dad would often arrive home late from school to find special projects going on in the garage. I think I brought him close to despair!

The summers spent sailing *Kestrel* were fantastic. For the first time I really was in charge of my own ship and it inspired me to push my boundaries further. I wanted to be close to those whose everyday lives revolved around the sea. After my first week on board *Kestrel* we packed her away and were saying our goodbyes to Auntie Thea in the dark, about to drive back home. My eyes began to fill with tears, and either to hide my emotion, or try to understand it, I ran off as hard as I could along the long dyke by the side of the river. I wanted to stay there for ever, never leaving the sound of the pewits and seagulls for the drone of the motorway. This was special, there was something inside me that I felt sure no one else could understand. I stood still, wiping away the tears, and watched each of the little red and green navigation buoys flash away into the distance. I took long, deep breaths, calmed myself down, and told myself that it wouldn't be long till I was back.

With *Kestrel*, Mum and Dad saw me taking real responsibility for the first time. They saw how essential sailing had become to me and it convinced them it would be a good idea if I went to a sailing school to get some proper qualifications and real instruction. I shall always be thankful to them for suggesting this, as working on *Kestrel* had left me with no money whatsoever and, aged sixteen, I was stuck into my first year of A-level study and was acutely conscious that I was going to have to work very hard indeed to make the grades.

I searched through the back pages of yachting magazines to find a sailing school close to home. I rang a few, but found it hard to make worthwhile comparisons. I wasn't sure exactly what I should be looking for, but the decision made itself when I first spoke to David King. He obviously knew his stuff, and his friendly attitude appealed immediately.

I travelled to Hull not knowing what to expect and was very nervous as I walked up to David's yacht, *Alert*, to meet him for the first time.

'Who do we have here then?' he said as we shook hands. David was a small man with strong hands, a gentle smile and a tanned, weathered face. I didn't know it then but we were to become great friends. Choosing the David King Nautical School completely changed my life.

David's career began with the great shipping companies of the 1970s and 1980s. He had travelled the world during his years at sea and had been the captain of a cargo vessel when he decided to concentrate on sailing. I inundated him with questions, soaking up every tiny detail he mentioned. His knowledge and his ability to share it could not have been bettered. And for the first time I was studying a subject that I ravenously wanted to learn. The other guys on board *Alert* were great too. Sailing in the company of such like-minded, funny, friendly people, I had a powerful feeling that I couldn't have been happier anywhere else in the world.

The week ended all too soon. I was full of it, fizzing with enthusiasm like a birthday cake candle that can't be put out. On the unpromisingly grey-brown Humber I had found a place where I was immensely happy.

As I packed the last of my things away to prepare for the off, Mum and Dad chatted to David, discussing the week's events. Strangely enough, it was only recently that Dad told me what David had said.

'I don't know where your daughter is going, but wherever it is she'll go a long way on the water.'

It's nice to think that this, in even the smallest way, prepared Mum and Dad for what was to come.

Chapter Four

My confidence was sky-high as a result of meeting David. And just hours after getting home we'd packed up *Kestrel* and were on our way to Paglesham. Every hour I'd spent sitting on the school bus designing each tiny feature, and every moment spent grafting away in the barn was about to pay off.

After we'd launched her, the plan was to sail in convoy with *Cabaret*. I spent most of the trip with Mum, both of us sleeping on board. All space was used to a maximum, with the compartments under both bunks serving as handy food-locker space. It was wonderful to spend some time with Mum and to feel at peace, away from the pressure of exams looming at school.

It couldn't last though. I was back at school at the end of August and, as winter drew nearer, so did the 'mocks' which were crucial for successful university applications. (Bizarrely, students trying for veterinary science need higher grades than those who want to do medicine.) I used to sit on my bedroom floor, with folders and text-books everywhere, trying to cram photosynthesis or molecular structures into my head – often still battling at one or two o'clock in the morning. It didn't work though, my mind wandered and I knew I was kidding myself. I'd be constantly distracted by the sailing books on the shelves and the newspaper cuttings blu-tacked to the walls.

My thoughts frequently drifted back to the sailing course up on the Humber. Even months afterwards I often thought about that trip. I knew it had changed me. It would creep into my daydreams and conversations and provided a sense of quiet satisfaction. The effect on me of Dave King's encouragement was dramatic.

I began to be conscious of how precious time was and used every spare moment for thinking and planning. I would create situations in my mind and test myself – my brain always seemed to be preparing for the next project. For some, sitting in waiting rooms or on the school bus in the morning might have seemed boring, but for me it was free time, and it started the second the school bell rang.

I knew every course on offer at the Nautical School off by heart and I was back there again by October, this time for a three-weekend theory course. Dave had decided that I was of a standard to go straight on to the Yachtmaster shore-based course, missing out the stepping-stones like Competent Crew and Coastal Skipper.

As winter approached, Hull Marina was a grey place. The Nautical School was situated in the old lock-keeper's cottage next to the lock pit. For miles east and west on either side there were docks and oil terminals. The whole city seemed to revolve around the shipping industry. Dave had fired my interest in all that went on on the river, and I would spend every free moment standing by the window, my forehead pressed to the glass, absorbing everything.

Everyone on the course really wanted to learn and as a result, the atmosphere was quite different from school, but despite this I was beginning to feel the strain. I knew that every bone in my body wanted to be in Hull, learning, yet I was obliged to go back to Derbyshire to study for my A-levels. I couldn't give up on Hull, though, and I was determined to try to cope. But I couldn't.

In the early darkness of the weeks leading up to Christmas I'd run around outside with Mac after returning home from school. I'd chase her as fast as I could while she ran rings round me before the two of us would tumble to the ground. She always brought a smile to my face but too often this turned to tears. I was exhausted and felt pulled in opposite directions. I'd swing from happiness to misery with frightening speed. I would lie on the ground and sob, often watching the dim lights in the kitchen but feeling so far away from home that I might as well have been on the Moon. I wished I knew the solution, but I couldn't even figure out the problem.

The freedom of studying in Hull during the weekends and the weight I felt from the forthcoming exams seemed like black and white. So when my weekend course ended I jumped to fill a vacancy on a VHF radio course that came up in November.

As far as I was aware, school, exams and university were the only way ahead, and I struggled on, knowing in my heart of hearts that it wasn't right for me. Any alternative to taking the sensible, correct path forward was inconceivable. Moreover, by this stage Nan had not only attended our school, following her early desire to study, but was studying at Derby University for a degree in European Languages. She had clearly decided that it was never too late, and if at the age of almost eighty she could pass exams first time, then surely I should be able to as well!

Although I hadn't expected really glowing results, I certainly hadn't considered the possibility that I'd be advised not even to apply for Veterinary School. My grades had not been entirely disastrous but I felt embarrassed by my situation. Having worked for three years with Simon at the surgery, I felt that even without the very strongest grades I was in with a chance, but I took my teachers' advice. Despite what the rest of the world thought I was capable of, however, I was going to do my damnedest to get those grades, and if it meant taking a year out and applying the following year, I would. I was determined to prove the system wrong and began to work harder than ever. My bedroom light was often still on at three in the morning as I pored over the pages of biology textbooks. I was going to give this the best shot I could.

I remember quite clearly the day in the library when I knew I was going down with some kind of illness. I felt that something was wrong inside, and I could feel the glands in my neck were swollen.

I talked to Mum about it, sitting on the floor in the front room, realizing that although I didn't feel too ill at the time it was on its way. I don't know why I was so sure I was going to be ill, and it was a peculiar feeling. I wasn't scared, more worried about what I would be missing.

The following day I stayed at home while my temperature began to rise and the glandular fever I had contracted began to take hold. It was a month before I set foot outside the front door again. The next four weeks were filled with headaches and sweating. I would stick to my bedcovers, waking up from a fever feeling trapped. I would try to count the minutes making up the hours that would bring morning.

Just standing up was hard. And to go up and downstairs to the loo during the daytime I had to cling to the banisters. I had been ill before, but never like this. Mum was fantastic. She was working part-time as a home tutor but never failed to drive home between lessons to feed me, usually a lunch of bread and home-made soup.

When she went out to teach I would lie on the settee in the cool back room and stare out of the window for hours, just thinking. In the garden at the front of the house was a large eucalyptus tree, which became the focus of my attention, the pastel-green leaves dancing against the cool, clear blue of the sky. I don't remember any dull days, though a month could not have passed entirely without them. I would gaze outside and worry, tormenting myself about recovering the energy to complete those final weeks at school before the A-levels.

While I was ill the Whitbread Race was being shown on television. The Whitbread sailors travel around the world in hi-tech 60-foot racing boats. It's run in legs, and there are about a dozen crew aboard each boat. I had never really been excited by crewed sailing. I saw the Whitbread representing the 'macho' side of sailing, and found it difficult to identify with the sailors as the footage from the yachts rarely seemed to show any form of sensitivity towards the sea. Despite this, it grabbed me. Here were boats racing at sea, and back then it was a novelty to see any kind of sailing on television. It was also the first time I became aware of the sponsorship side of the sport. The programme came on at about 2 a.m. every morning and we'd record it using the video recorder we'd borrowed from Nan – she was away in Germany on a six-month exchange.

I practically held my breath during the opening sequence; the sharp editing, vivid images and dynamic soundtrack got me every time. I saw those guys out there, and all I wanted was to be on the ocean too.

Perversely, having glandular fever was one of the best things that ever happened to me. For the first time in my life I was really stopped in my tracks and inevitably gave a lot of thought to what would follow. And I felt a new sense of perspective. There are so many things we take for granted, especially our health, and I understood this for the first time. I realized that life is for living, and that I had to grab it with both hands. It's too easy to say 'I'll do that later', but the chance may never come.

It was as if I needed to burst out. With a feeling of most intense energy and clarity, I suddenly realized that there was another way. In an instant my exam pressures evaporated. The world was out there, and there was not a shadow of doubt in my mind that I was ready to take it on. I became desperate to recover, but from then on my illness was somehow different. Frustration was replaced by hope, and that sustained me and, I'm sure, hastened my recovery. The sea was waiting . . .

Just before I recovered I endured my worst night. I was virtually delirious and stumbled into the bathroom, collapsing in the empty bath at about two in the morning. It was cool there, and it helped ease the fever a little. I've no idea how long I'd been lying there before Mum found me, but she washed me in cool water and stayed with me through the night.

A day or two later I somehow knew I was on the mend. I put on a loose pair of black jeans, and a jumper of Dad's I'd adopted. My boyfriend Simon came round and we headed outside. The air felt crisp and fresh as it flowed into my lungs. It was still early, and I squinted in the morning sunlight.

We walked down the drive and began to head up the farm track adjacent to our drive. I felt so vital and alive. My legs were weak but I ran back down the track towards the house feeling brand new. The sky was the limit, I was so grateful to be better, things were going to be OK from now on – I was determined to sail for my living. Knowing where I was heading was priceless.

Just days after my recovery Mum left for Germany with Fergus to visit Nan and I was able to persuade Dad to visit friends in Grimsby, just the other side of the Humber from Hull. I had been thinking a lot about the Nautical School, and without doubt it was something that had helped pull me through. Just for the day I worked on the school's boats to help get them ready for the season.

It was a cold, northern winter's day, with a freezing breeze from the north following the snowy depression. As I gazed out over Dave's shoulder at the estuary, the massive grey silhouette of the UECC car freighter steamed into view, and the voices around me tuned out. I was studying the dim lights on the ship as it followed its careful path between the navigational buoys. I thought I could make out the bow thrusters' markings on the hull sides, and tried to peer up at the control bridge. There, a small figure dressed in an orange boiler-suit was wandering near the crew's accommodation. I realized I was grinning.

The need to get back to the sea had been the best medicine I could have wished for. There was a new life waiting out there and I was desperate for it to start immediately.

While I had been laid up at home I read sailing magazines. Although I found reading hard, I could manage small amounts of text. Looking through the back of a magazine, I spotted an advertisement put in by Nationwide Boat Sales, the yard where I'd first been introduced to *Kestrel*, and was excited to see there was a Corribee 21 for sale. I saw the Corribee as a fantastic boat, a big yacht with tiny dimensions, but definitely a real little 'sea boat'. Although reasonably priced, she was more than I could afford. But I kept turning back to the same page. I decided I had to go and see her as she'd been a great aid to my speedy recovery.

After my first visit I wrote in my sporadic diary: 'There she was, stern towards me like a scruffy heap. Her rudder was askew and one of her backstays hung lifelessly beside her mast . . . the word "Poole" shadowed into her faded and battered reddish topsides.'

It was love at first sight.

I think I fell in love with her because she looked unloved – but more than that, she looked as though she'd really achieved something. Her windows were strong, her forestay a massive stainless-steel fixing which would not have broken on a boat of twice her size. The little patchy-red Corribee was not a run-of-the-mill boat, but a tough little lady, with real character.

The second time I visited was with Simon. I was desperate to return to the yard and he agreed to come with me on the two-hour bus journey. I was not fully fit yet and the snowy conditions soaked into my bones, so that I had to jump around like a fool just to keep warm. The bus driver was clearly aware of my excitement because he made an unscheduled stop right outside the yard gates to allow us off.

We immediately made for the spot where I'd last seen the scruffy little red boat. I touched her hull to remind myself that she was reality. There was hardly anyone around so we found a spare viewing ladder and scrambled on board. The snow that covered her was speckled with dirt from the nearby railway line and made her look scruffier still. I began scraping the snow from her decks with my hands, and they were soon visible.

I'd spotted it before, but her decks were suffering from osmosis, a condition where water penetrates into the resin coating. It is treatable, but hard, time-consuming work. Inside there was a smell of damp and rotting wood. She had water in her bilges, and the floorboards were floating. On each side immediately below the hatch were the bunks, most of which slid behind us under the cockpit. Forward of them were the work surfaces; on the port side the chart area, and on the starboard the galley. There was little in the way of electronics – just a couple of strip lights, and an ancient-looking switch panel made of grey painted steel. The small brass switches should have shone through use, but they were dirty and corroded. Her cabin was tiny, but perfect.

After studying every inch of her, we wandered back down to the offices to speak to someone. Her sale price was £1,900, without the trailer – and my only asset was *Kestrel*. The outlook seemed bleak. I certainly could not buy her there on the spot but there was still some hard bargaining to be done!

The office was warm and our faces glowed as we asked to speak to someone. A man was sitting at a large desk beneath the far window, and it turned out to be him we should speak to. I was after a direct swap with *Kestrel* which I felt was fair, having spent hours thinking of why this was so. After all, they would *never* sell the Corribee – no one wanted a two-berth boat with an unretractable keel, so far away from the sea. *Kestrel*, on the other hand, was ideal, and I knew – though the neglected Corribee was bigger – that she was worth much more. I stood my ground in the office but in the end opted to quit while we were slightly ahead, saying I would be back. I think Simon was shocked by how totally single-minded and terrier-like I was in there. I was on a mission – and I was not going to let go.

Rather than being disheartened, I was fired up. I talked at length with Mum and Dad about her and they were happy for me to go ahead with things. I knew Dad was concerned about launching and storage, but we talked and between us came to sensible decisions about what was realistic. I think both of them realized that this was to be more than a hobby from now on.

Knowing she would share my enthusiasm, I had to phone Auntie Thea to discuss the purchase. Half an hour later, though, I walked into the front room devastated. Thea had fairly well trodden on my plans; she clearly thought it would be a great mistake and said so. She felt I would be far too dependent on Mum and Dad, and was in no doubt that I was too immature to handle a boat like this. I'd not seen Thea since I'd got better, but being ill had changed my outlook on life and perhaps she didn't realize this. It still saddens me though that I was unable to share my passion with her.

So Mum drove me back to the yard to try again. I was pleased that Dad had stayed at home and left me to go and do the bargaining myself. We passed by the boat to check that she hadn't been sold, then walked down to the office. I talked to the same man again, but this time I was not going to come out without a result. Twenty minutes later we walked out with a deal. He even threw in an engine and a jib, and he had not even seen *Kestrel*.

It took me three months to think of a name for the little red boat, but I settled on *Iduna* – the Norse goddess who held the apples of eternal youth. My plan was to give her a new lease of life – and keep her young forever.

I was now returning to Hull to sail most weekends, and little by little those weekends turned into long ones. By the time I had recovered from the illness, classes at school had finished ahead of the exams and so I was supposed to be spending my time revising at home. The determination to sail got the better of me even as the exams approached. Although I had decided that I would sit them, my focus now was beyond them. I'd be going through the motions.

Every now and then Dave's wife Maureen would call me from Hull to let me know if there was a space free on one of the courses, allowing me to take it up for just a small charge. I would leap at the chance, often packing my kit on the hoof as I ran for the door to leave, sometimes even trying to squeeze in a course between exams. On one occasion I had been sailing for a week, but had an exam the following afternoon in Wirksworth. We had been sailing all night returning from our last anchorage, and I had loved it. The journey home was usually a nightmare, and on this occasion the combination of trains and buses got me to the exam room just seconds before everyone sat down. Normally I got nervous before exams but now I just felt outside it all.

During my first months of travelling to and from Hull I was invited to sail on board a boat called *Panic Major*. Dave knew her owner, Robert Nickerson, and had asked whether I could sail on her. I had been told that she was a 'Class 1 Open 60 racing yacht', and though at that stage I didn't know what that meant, just the sound of it made my eyes roll and my heart beat faster.

When I was on her for the first time, she thrilled me. On board her deck stretched out fore and aft, with purposeful-looking ropes running in every direction. She was broad and sophisticated, with a powerful-looking mast twice the height of every boat in the marina. She also had a history. Not only had she sailed to the Azores many times, she had competed in a French single-handed non-stop race around the world called the Vendée Globe. I was in awe.

I was shy as I met the crew for the first time. Robert was the easiest to get on with initially. He was a larger-than-life character, with a sense of humour that could have you rolling in the aisles or wanting to jump overboard. Brought up on his family estate, he was not from a sailing background and had learnt to sail by sitting on the dockside till someone took him along. He was a doer, not a dreamer, who had forged his own path through building and modifying boats. He often sailed in a flat cap and overalls, and rather than buy yachting waterproofs, he wore a bright orange, one-piece, water-proof boiler-suit-type garment. He was a man who could afford to do or have anything he wanted but he chose simply to be himself.

Soon after our first sail on *Panic Major*, Robert asked me if I wanted to work for him. I would have worked for him for nothing if he'd asked. He had designed and built *Panic Major* himself, and I loved talking to him about her. His enthusiasm made him an inspiring teacher.

Long weekends began to turn into long weeks, and soon I was only returning home every fortnight or so. On those visits I would talk feverishly about all that had been going on in Hull – everything from RAF helicopter rescue drills to what we'd had for lunch when anchored off Hawkins Point. Once I'd finished enthusing, I'd go outside to where *Iduna* was laid up and make plans for her.

Every weekend Robert would come to the marina and we'd either take *Panic Major* out and sail, or work on the list of things which needed to be repaired or changed. I learnt to splice rope and use tools that I'd never even seen before. I began to learn about electronics and the use of specific custom-designed parts. I dismantled the boom with Robert, learning the best way to effect repairs, either at sea, or properly in port. Whether it was a new type of jointing compound, or advice on sailing her fast I was loving it all and learning a lot.

One night after a crewed race in Bridlington we anchored outside the harbour and after a quick pint, said goodnight to the rest of the crew. I was up early in the morning at first light, woken by the gentle lapping beneath my bunk, and wandered out on deck barefoot. I heard Robert stir. Minutes later he appeared. We grabbed some breakfast, then he announced, 'I'm going back to bed, you sail her back.'

I would love to have seen my face at that moment for it must have been a picture. Why the bloody hell was the fifty-five-year-old owner of this beautiful racing machine asking a kid barely through school to take responsibility for his pride and joy? I was speechless and I climbed outside to recover.

It took me over fifteen minutes to get the mainsail up, but I gritted my teeth and got on with it. Her mainsail needed at least eight people to carry it, so it was no mean feat getting it up that mast. I was determined not to be beaten by what I had to do. If one man had sailed her round the world alone, I sure as hell could make it 60 miles back to Hull. I felt hyperactive, but once the anchor was up and the headsail unfurled, we were off and I settled down. I put on the autopilot as we slipped along, and wandered around making sure everything was OK. I stood in the bows, checking for fishing pots, and looked back at her cockpit. For the first time in my life there was no one there. I could as well have been alone, and I loved it.

I felt very proud gliding into the locks as the evening drew in. I was on top of the world and anyone would have thought I'd just sailed across the Atlantic. I am so grateful to Robert for giving me that opportunity. I can see now that he knew exactly what he was up to and I wouldn't be at all surprised if he didn't sleep a wink during the trip.

The longer I stayed in Hull, the more I learnt. I was moving on, and a casualty of this, sadly, was my relationship with Simon. We agreed to call it a day. My hunger for knowledge was insatiable. I spent an increasing amount of time with David and his students, often filling any space during courses just to gain more practical knowledge. I learnt about instructing afloat and navigating in difficult tidal waters. We might head down to Skegness or Spurn Point where we would anchor, then row the little inflatable dinghy ashore, or sail into Grimsby and moor in the old Number Three fish docks, alongside the last of the trawlers. I loved Grimsby, and occasionally we would wander around the docks in the evenings, staring up at the enormous hulls of ships and fishing boats on the slips as they were lifted out for repairs. Old photos showed the same dock filled with fishing boats. It was almost impossible to imagine the atmosphere that would have prevailed here just decades before. Now there was just a handful left – a sad reminder of what had been lost.

I also sat in on a few shore courses during the early part of the season, before beginning to instruct in a small way myself. I had never taught before – I'd only just finished being taught myself! Standing in front of a class of adults at the age of seventeen was new to me but it must have been even more of a surprise for them. I was nervous to start with, but lucky to be in an environment where everyone was eager to learn.

Along with teaching there and working on the *Alert*, I started to camp out on the radio room floor. I would wake to the sound of the fog signals from the jetties and buoys, and smile as their low moans guided the ships to their berths by the banks of the river. I felt so close to the water, living and breathing the sea.

Just a few yards behind the school was one of the largest night-clubs in Hull. It amazed me to see the clubbers as I wandered back along the cobbled docks at night. It was generally fairly cold in Hull, and the howling winter winds from the North Sea were truly bitter. I couldn't decide if I was overdressed or they were underdressed as I compared my oilskins to their miniskirts and bare midriffs. I can't say I regretted missing out on all that. The state of the streets and doorways on the morning after was enough to put anyone off. As the evening drew in the noise would start, the back wall thumping with the music. I didn't really notice it though, I was usually so exhausted that I collapsed into my sleeping-bag.

I continued to work and race on *Panic Major* with Robert throughout the summer, juggling this with preparation for my Yachtmaster practical exam. After a short break sailing with Thea on *Cabaret* I headed back to Hull. I needed 2,500 miles at sea in order to qualify for the exam, which back then seemed like a massive amount. I was very nervous, but Dave told me, 'Just sail the boat, Ellen, you know what to do.' He was right, and once I'd relaxed the exam went well and I passed. It was a major step forward for me, but at the same time it was really just step one.

Talking through the future with Dave, I decided to bring *Iduna*, still in Derbyshire, to Hull. We worked out that I would be able to afford to put her in the shed for a while and I could then get the major jobs done under cover.

Once *Iduna* was in Hull I could tackle the really important work which needed doing. It was the first time I had seen her close to water and it fired my imagination, driving me on to spend all my spare time working on her. There were some massive jobs that needed to be done, so as a warm-up for this I went to work on the underwater portion of her hull. Despite the major work in treating the osmosis in the hull, I was soon to discover that problems with the deck were far more serious. She had extensive osmosis in the parts of it where rainwater had collected in puddles and thus had in effect rotted into the grey topcoat finish. She had been very badly laid up for a number of years and the damage was quite severe. I also endeavoured to make her more seaworthy by fibreglassing in a smaller hatch for her and increasing the size of the cockpit drains. David was kind enough to lend me some of his tools, and I tackled the work with great optimism – even though it was pretty gruelling, I was happy having the time to do it. I would often teach in the school by day before hurriedly changing to spend a few hours in the evening working on *Iduna*. I always seemed to be covered in resin, paint and skin-aggravating fibreglass dust, and with the wet weather in Hull the dust became embedded in my jeans and jumpers. Every day I'd scrub my arms clean with special blue gritty Swarfega and pick fibres out of the plughole. But working on her still felt like the night before you go on holiday. I knew good things were just around the corner.

When I started work on *Iduna* my sole objective was to try to make her as seaworthy as possible. When I bought her I didn't know what I was going to do with her. In the back of my mind, I had the vague thought of perhaps taking her to Norway, but once in Hull I realized that this would be very difficult. A trip there and back might not attract funding from sponsors. At that time I was more concerned about making her right. She was my dream boat and I wanted her to be perfect. But after all this major work I ran out of money again and couldn't afford to keep her in the boat yard any more. Dave saved the day, persuading a friend of his to let me keep her in his field near Dave's house. Whenever I was free I would stay with Maureen and work on *Iduna* in my spare time.

One day Maureen pulled me to one side and said that they needed a photo of me. Under a barrage of questions the truth eventually came out. Unbeknown to me she had entered me for the BT/YJA Young Sailor of the Year award. I was astounded that they had even put me in for the award but I'd actually won the regional title. I learnt soon afterwards that I'd made the final three and that the announcement of the winner would take place in London at the Boat Show. Maureen and Dave's kindness was to make a massive difference to me.

When I headed back home for Christmas my thoughts centred around preparations for going down to London for the awards ceremony at the beginning of January. Dave, Maureen, Mum, Dad and Auntie Thea all came to the event. Thea was in a lot of pain at the time as just days before she had slipped a disc doing some DIY. She was finding getting around hard going. We didn't know then that it was an injury which would lead to years of suffering. Despite her discomfort, though, Thea soldiered on and I was really glad she came along.

On the day of the awards we had an early start filming footage for the evening's ceremony, before heading to the Serpentine in Hyde Park for photographs. At this point I was told that I had won, and I was speechless. More than this, I was having my picture taken with Sir Robin Knox-Johnston – the first man ever to sail non-stop around the world. He finished his voyage in 1970 after 313 days at sea, and wrote a book, *A World of My Own*. My well-thumbed copy was one of my most treasured possessions. This year, though, he had won Yachtsman of the Year for the second time – for breaking the Jules Verne record, the non-stop circumnavigation of the world in any boat, with any number of crew. He had co-skippered his catamaran *Enza* with the late Sir Peter Blake, another of sailing's inspirational figures.

I was amazed at what an incredibly friendly and down-to-earth character Robin was. And yet I could not believe that I was there chatting to him. It was something I had never dreamt would happen, partly because I had never tried to win anything. We were given model sailing boats for the photos, and at one point we were asked to take our shoes and socks off and pose in the water. In January! I was finding the whole experience so overwhelming that I would have done anything I was asked, but Robin said 'No.' He had calmly but firmly shown me that you must make up your own mind about what you are prepared to do and what you are not and that you are not obliged to do whatever you're asked, however eager you may be not to let people down.

The awards themselves were a very nerve-racking experience. I could practically hear the sound of my heart beating within my chest, over the music that signalled the announcement of the award. I saw the images of the other finalists up there on the screen, I remember thinking how incredibly talented they were, having achieved remarkable results in dinghy racing and international competition. I felt that against my own achievements they seemed clear winners. The words 'And the winner of the BT/YJA Young Sailor of the Year is Ellen MacArthur' echoed through the ballroom, and I was instantly sure I would tumble and never make it to the stage. It passed in seconds as I tried to smile at the flashing cameras, and as I weaved my way back through the tables to Mum, Dad and Thea, the award clutched firmly to my chest, the words which resonated inside my head were 'Thank you' . . . the biggest thank you that an eighteen-year-old could imagine.

By February I was back in Hull when Mum telephoned me to tell me that there was a letter at home from Musto, a big manufacturer of sailing gear. I asked her to open it and read it to me. I was standing in a draughty pay-phone box in Hull Marina. The letter was from Keith Musto, one of the founders of the company. He said he'd like to meet me. I was so excited my feet hardly touched the ground as I ran back to the Nautical School. I needed time to think.

My only idea at that stage had been to sail *Iduna* to Norway and back. I was fascinated by the beauty of Norway and pored over maps of her coastline at Robert's house. I knew though that it would be hard to attempt a trip like that without a sponsor – for the safety gear if nothing else. I wrote back to Keith Musto saying that it would be great to meet and I would come down to Essex to discuss future projects. It was an odd reply. There was no hint of what those future projects might be.

By now I seemed to be forging two distinct but parallel paths. The first was gaining Royal Yachting Association (RYA) qualifications at David's school, the second was my still uncertain plans for *Iduna*. My meeting with Musto was approaching fast and I hadn't yet come up with what I was going to present to them.

I was back at the school teaching in full force by this stage, and I had put myself in for the next level of qualification, which was to be my Yachtmasters Instructor's endorsement. This would allow me to teach yachtmasters themselves out on the water. It was another water-based examination, this time of a week's duration, down on the South Coast. So I was sailing *Alert* as often as possible, as well as teaching courses in the school. I was very nervous about this course: not only was it the most difficult practical examination in the teaching of sailing, but it was also based on the Solent – where I had sailed only once as a child. It was going to be a tough one.

David's school was unusual because he taught commercial courses as well as the RYA syllabus. So the people I was teaching weren't always pleasure-craft users, but the men who worked on the river and on coastal barges and ships. These guys were in some ways heroes to me. I had seen the tugs and barges working the rivers in all conditions, the men tiny in comparison with the enormous machinery and power of the boats. I was intrigued to meet the people who worked them.

I remember shifting uneasily from foot to foot as new courses were about to begin. Until I got to know the students I was really quite shy. Someone would ask where the teacher was, and when I found the courage to pipe up and tell them, 'Actually it's me who's teaching you guys,' there were always looks verging on disbelief. It was strange, though, I never felt as if I was many years younger, nor did I feel that I had insufficient knowledge to do the job. The biggest hurdle was just the fact that I was a quiet, unassuming young woman and that many of the commercial guys didn't want to be there in the first place, having been forced into it by changing regulations.

During tea breaks, after 'smoko' we would talk together. I was transfixed by these men's stories. Often their fathers, and even grandfathers, had worked the river and the tales dated back several generations. It wasn't an easy life, they worked long, hard hours as if the tide was right they went with it, night or day, winter or summer. I was very conscious that they were already experts at what they did – skills to handle their kind of craft came mostly from apprenticeships.

Throughout my time in Hull I was blessed by many people's generosity of time and spirit. David's calmness and patience stayed with me. I respected him enormously, and we also got on famously. He was really the first person with whom I'd ever been able truly to share my passion for boats, the sea and sailing. There were others too whom I met through teaching. John Duckett was studying for his Yachtmaster, and his help in reviving *Iduna* was priceless. We became great mates, and he'd often buy me fish and chips and give me a lift with my gear in his dad's van. More than this though, I was inspired by him. He had been badly injured in a serious car crash and had been expected neither to come out of his coma nor, when he came to months later, to walk again. It took him years to recover properly, but he never gave up. Teaching him was immensely rewarding and he was the embodiment of persistence, good humour and sheer bloody-mindedness.

One other student also made an enormous impact on me. Don Hayes was a consulting engineer with his own business in the North of England who'd come to study for his Day Skipper qualification. He and I got on well from the start, his sharp wit and great will to learn making the classroom an even happier place. We talked a lot about *Iduna* at that time as I was still throwing ideas around as to what I was going to attempt next. After teaching Don for several weeks, I realized that we were becoming more than friends. At the end of the weekend teaching, we walked down to his car in the rain. I had been talking about Spurn Point in class, and as he got in to leave he suggested we both drive down there.

Over the following months we spent many happy evenings together. Before meeting Don I could have counted the number of times I'd ever been into a restaurant on one hand. Choosing from a menu – just understanding it – was completely alien. Even things as straightforward as 'rack of lamb' were unknowns! I was stunned at how expensive things were too. I was accustomed to scrounging food from anywhere and treating it as no more than fuel. This was a whole new world!

Don also opened my eyes to business. He talked about the agency he worked with to promote his company, and how marketing worked. I had never really been exposed to the reality of any of this before, and I began to think in a new way about how future projects could work. Don produced a massive marketing plan for me, looking at my strengths and weaknesses. It had all sorts of columns such as Projects, Contacts, Lectures and Speaking. I felt I poured everything I could into this chart. It became the blueprint for the future. Bearing in mind that it was put together well before my first significant sailing exploit, it turned out to be astoundingly accurate!

I was at home in Derbyshire in March when I hit on the big idea. I woke and rolled over in my sleeping-bag to see what the weather was doing outside. I glanced up at the collage of newspaper cuttings on the wall. Among them was a British Admiralty chart catalogue and as I looked at the map of Britain I thought, 'That's it.' It was as if the feeling had always been there and all I'd done was reveal it. Going round Britain suddenly seemed the most natural thing to do. In that instant I was sure I knew exactly what I was going to do next.

The timing was perfect too, as the meeting with Musto was coming up. I was not sure what that would involve, but at least now I was going there with a plan. Don had introduced me to Graham Percy, his marketing agent, and the three of us decided to go to Musto together. Don had agreed to support the project through Graham, doing all he could to help raise my profile.

As we walked into Musto's offices for the first time, everything seemed so smart and organized. We waited for a few nervous minutes before being met not just by Keith, but by a whole group of people. One of them was Brian Pilcher, Musto's PR manager, who took us to the meeting room. After a friendly preamble Keith asked me what my future plans were. I answered as if I had been planning the trip for years. 'To sail single-handed around Great Britain,' I said and promised to send a detailed plan to them by the end of the week.

They were genuine enthusiasts. Keith talked about his racing and proudly showed me a diagram of all the crew positions and jobs aboard his boat. I was struck by how much I had in common with these people who were clearly working with the professionals at the top of the sport. Brian was the real character, and a marked contrast to Keith, who while fiercely competitive was quiet and unassuming. Initially I found Brian a little overwhelming – I wasn't used to people who bubbled like this. I'd never met anyone quite as engaging as he passionately explained that the sailor on board the boat is the 'engine', and has to be looked after more than anything else. To be cold and wet is draining, and it can be very dangerous out there, particularly on long passages. Foul weather gear has to provide the right protection. Years later, I still think back to that conversation and find myself nodding in agreement. Brian would become a great friend.

We talked feverishly as we drove back to Hull, and I spent the next few days and nights buried in the *Almanac*. I looked up depths of water at all states of the tide, and the facilities in each port – whether there was water, fuel and food available and whether it was safe in all conditions. I found the telephone numbers of the yacht clubs and RNLI lifeboat stations, and worked out the exact mileage between each port. Then I split the journey into five stages, each made up of six or seven shorter hops. I planned to travel round anti-clockwise, to ensure that at the end of the journey I would have the wind behind me rather than having to face it. It was a mammoth task, but I attacked it with such energy and enthusiasm that it simply had to work out.

Two and a half days later I sent every bit of information I could pull together down to Musto and on 10 April they replied.

The letter, signed by Brian, outlined Musto's fundamental agreement to sponsor me. He'd gone out of his way. He'd found me a sponsor for autopilots and spoken to my insurers, to confirm that the project fell within *Iduna*'s current insurance terms. He also said he might be able to help provide a small outboard engine and weather information. There seemed to be less weight on my shoulders until I read his terms. There were two conditions for Musto's involvement: the first was to have *Iduna* surveyed, and the second to complete a single-handed voyage of 300 miles non-stop in her. This was a shock as at the time it suggested to me that Brian and the team weren't confident of my experience and training.

I had never envisaged sailing *Iduna* for 300 miles on any leg of the trip – with good reason, I felt I had limited my longest leg to just over 60 miles so that at worst it would take twenty hours and in good conditions should take no more than twelve. I didn't believe it was safe to have to sleep at sea in such a small boat, so close to the shore. There is a terrific amount of shipping in the North Sea, and this posed a threat. There was also the shoreline itself. Contrary to what one might expect, it's this which poses the greatest danger to ships, rocks being far more likely than waves to sink a boat.

After chatting to Dave, I wrote a long letter to Brian explaining how I felt. My view was that four sleepless days in the North Sea should be a last resort rather than a training exercise. I did however promise him that I would sea-trial *Iduna* in fairly serious conditions before I left, to ensure that she was up to the challenge.

I was sure I was right and I felt that we were going to have a stronger project if we shared our concerns openly. In the end Brian was persuaded and we ploughed on with the arrangements.

The first job was to get *Iduna* back to the marina yard, where I could work on her with electricity and light at hand. We had long discussions with Hull Marina who decided, to everyone's relief I think, to let me work on *Iduna* in the yard and keep her on the water free of charge. The deal was that I should carry a sticker from Hull Marina around Britain, and to be quite honest, I was proud to!

From January I worked all hours that God sent on *Iduna*. I broke off only to do a couple of courses on *Alert*, and to take my Yachtmaster Instructor's examination down on the Solent in April. On arriving at Hamble Marina, I wandered down to the boat we were sailing for the week-long exam. She was called *Hakuna Matata* – Swahili for No Problem! I wished I felt that relaxed. As soon as I got on board I climbed into every locker and inspected every hatch on board. I wanted to find out everything about this boat, from where the valves were in the hull to how I would switch the gas off to where the fire extinguisher was – and that was just below decks!

Our examiner arrived that evening, and all fears of being examined by someone I could not identify with were completely blown away! John Goode was a great character, with his spiky, greying hair and old reefer jacket, smoking his favourite pipe. He was incredibly sharp and had an acute sense of humour, and I warmed to him immediately. He was a doer, not a pretender. You will never meet anyone who calls a spade a spade to a greater extent than John. Nerves from the fact that I was out there doing an exam came back from time to time, but on the whole I tried to convince myself that we were just out there sailing.

On Thursday John jumped ship to another boat in the fleet, and another examiner, James Stevens, came aboard. James was the RYA's national cruising coach, and we were all very conscious of it. But the weather was easier now, allowing us to use the spinnaker for the first time, and James was only with us for the last day. It was refreshing to undertake new exercises scrutinized by a different pair of eyes.

When it was over, we returned the boats to the marina and received our debriefing from John and James. I was suddenly very nervous, feeling I was younger and less experienced than the others, though during the sailing I had tried to blank that out. My heart beat faster as I walked into the room when my turn came to be addressed. At least I knew the faces in there. Both James and John were complimentary, but frank about my weak points, the worst of which were my relatively few sea-miles and inevitable lack of experience in sailing in different geographical areas. I was expecting the great build-up so that they could let me down gently and say I was not ready. After all, if eighteen was young to take a Yachtmaster's ticket, perhaps it was just *too* young to pass the Instructor's ticket as well. When the verdict came, it was not as straightforward as it might have been, but I was thrilled. I was told that they would award me the certificate when I arrived in Southampton on my way round Britain. I slept for most of the train journey home.

I now had six weeks in Hull to get *Iduna* ready. There was still much to organize, from the electrics to a full set of the right spares. It was all incredibly hectic, and although I was doing most of the work myself, Dave, Don and John Duckett also put in the hours to get us to the start of our voyage.

On 1 June I was on the boat well before the sun came up, finishing the final wiring of the spare autopilot. People were gradually collecting on the dockside – Mum and Dad, Fergus, Lewis and Mac. Lew was going through a very difficult time at that stage. University had not gone as he'd hoped and he was trying to decide whether he should go back to complete his degree or look for something different elsewhere – perhaps a job. I was grateful to him for his presence. Sarah had come up to see me off too, along with Don, Graham Percy and others from Don's office. Dave and Maureen were there, of course, and Steve and Shamus who'd helped me work on *Iduna*.

I put on my oilskins and said my goodbyes. There was no sadness as I spoke to Mum and Dad on the pontoon. Saying goodbye to Mac was hardest as I couldn't let her know when I'd be back: she just knew I was leaving.

I hugged Lew. 'It'll be a walk in the park,' he said. And that was that.

Although it was going to be a long trip, I knew that all those people on the dockside would be with me in their own way and I was thankful to them all. I just wanted to stop time and restart it once I was on my way. I didn't cry until I had passed through the locks and was out on the river. I turned back to see Mac stretching high up over the seawall to watch me. A tear slipped down my face for the first time that day. I turned back to face the sea. We were off.

It was as if I'd left every part of my life up until that moment behind me on the dockside. Ahead was an unknown future, and suspended between the two were *Iduna* and I, waiting for the past to disappear over the horizon. This was the biggest single turning-point in my life and the intense anticipation was almost too much to bear. I'd been in Hull for just over a year.

Chapter Five

The wind was very light on our first day sailing out of the Humber, and progress was slow. The quiet, pale grey sky met the familiar brown-stained waters of the river and it felt like a very empty afternoon, the only sound the gentle slapping of the water beneath *Iduna*'s hull. Reluctantly, an hour or so after leaving the dockside, I switched her engine on. With the wind so light, we would have to speed up if we were going to make Bridlington for the tide. So we continued to the sound of the engine. It's hard to describe just how frustrating trying to sail is without wind. I was lucky that I had an engine I could run, but that feeling of quietness was just not there. When the engine is stopped and the bubbling sound of water under the hull returns, it's sheer bliss. As darkness fell the wind seemed to steady, and as I sat back in the cockpit I pulled out my dictaphone for a few words . . .

It's now 2115 at night, the sun's setting and we're sailing along at about three and a half knots with full sail, just managed to get the engine off for the first real time in days and it's absolutely fantastic and peaceful. The winds about Force 2–3 . . . it's what I've come for. I'm feeling in one of those moods where I wish I could jump off the boat, get in a dinghy and see what she looks like. She must look so beautiful sailing along tonight.

We approached Bridlington around midnight. I decided to anchor for the night, so that I could rest rather than wait for the tide at four o'clock in the morning. Though now exhausted, I was happy to be foraging around on the foredeck lighting my little paraffin lamp that Thea had given me. The lights of Bridlington shone over us and I climbed below and wrote up the log beneath the white glow of the little strip light above the chart table.

The following morning we pushed on up the coast. It was looking as though it would be a longer sail to Hartlepool, but due to the wind dying once more I decided to pull into the nearest port, which was Scarborough. I couldn't have had a more cheerful welcome in any port, let alone for the first of the trip. I was met by Tony, the harbour watch-keeper who lived in the lighthouse building on the docks, and I was soon invited into the yacht club to have pie and peas with the members. It was a perfect start and an early insight into the kindness I was going to encounter throughout my trip.

As we headed up the coast next day, the cliffs loomed up mysteriously. The breeze was too light to blow away the mist which shrouded the rocks at their base, but soon it cleared as the wind freshened from the south. I made my sandwiches as we passed Robin Hood's Bay, a beautiful cluster of houses sheltered in a tight little break in the cliffs. I had poled out *Iduna*'s genoa, so we had a sail out each side to pull along her little orange hull. For the first time in the voyage I could hear the water creaming at her bows. I wandered on to her foredeck and sat looking back into our wake, my eye drawn by her little red ensign fluttering away in the breeze. Scotland, here we come!

Our first real setback was Hartlepool. The forecast got progressively worse, and we ended up storm-bound there for two weeks. The waves were relentless and the wind blew angrily for what seemed like forever. Coincidentally, also in port but undergoing a refit was the Sea Cadets' training ship, the magnificent square-rigged TS *Royalist*. As I arrived she was in her final few days of making ready to sail, and I was invited on board for tea.

She was an incredible ship, covered in brasswork and weathered timbers. Though roughly my age, she was still an evocative link with sailing's past. We ate in the officers' wardroom in the aft of the ship, and I was made to feel completely at home; over the next couple of weeks I had great times on board her. I was invited to sail as Bosun's Mate when she went out to brave the mountainous swells. I was intrigued by the teamwork, seeing people function together so well. I climbed the rigging with the young Cadets as the wind howled through the ropes, the masts sweeping violently through the air as her hull pitched through the waves. I was very impressed by the way a job was done if it needed to be done and by how the Cadets were so willing to adjust to their newfound surroundings. I made some great friends there.

A more difficult part of my time in Hartlepool was when Don came to see me. I felt that what we both wanted from our relationship would not take us down the same path. Maybe I felt a little claustrophobic, having had time to think since setting off, and it seemed best to end it there and then rather than let it wither slowly and painfully. My final days in Hartlepool felt like a blur of sadness.

On my first attempt to leave Hartlepool I was piped out by *Royalist* with two blasts on her foghorn, but the swell was too large to motor safely and we were flung around so much that I reluctantly made the decision to stay another night.

When we eventually did break clear to continue on our way north the following day, the relief to be moving once again was overwhelming. From the iridescence of the water to the way the evening sun lit the hills of the Yorkshire Wolds as they rolled down to meet the sea, the sheer beauty of it all was breathtaking. I've never had so much time to wonder at my surroundings as during that trip. I sat in the setting sun writing up my daily log . . .

Puffins flying past just three feet away! Continued north then motored into Eyemouth roads. Anchored up in 5 metres of water, three hours before low water at 1215, then went to sleep. Up for the 1405 forecast – not too good. Eyemouth is a beautiful place, with a beautiful bay. My thumb has gone septic, so I doused it with TCP, pulled out the green stuff then plastered it up! Lovely! Departed Eyemouth at 1700. Sailed out! There wasn't too much wind but I was determined to sail, it's too quiet here to use the motor.

Almost missed St Abbs! I got my sails off and motored in – taking note of the pilot diagrams. As the entrance opened up I looked across and saw a chap standing by the lifeboat house – he showed me where to go, and chatted for a bit. He used to go to sea but is now in the building trade.

St Abbs is an indescribably peaceful and friendly port. I was so glad I came. I have had an eel feed on the weed on my keel and I can see starfish on the seabed – there was some confusion over where I should berth due to a rock – but everyone has been more than helpful. I am sitting in the setting sun writing this at 1948hrs.

On leaving I crossed the Firth of Forth, heading north past Edinburgh. It was a glorious day to sail across, passing the rocky but beautiful Isle of May. Once on the north side of the Firth I spent the night in Anstruther. It was getting late by the time we tied up, and I didn't feel like peeling the veg for the pressure cooker on board, so I popped out to buy fish and chips and wolfed it down as I sat watching the fishing boats.

The night, though, was anything but peaceful. I was kept up all night with agonizing stomach cramps. By the time the sun had risen the pain had completely gone, but I'd barely slept. By day I think I forgot how bad I'd felt. I cast off *Iduna's* lines, heading for our next stop – Arbroath. We had all day to get there, so I decided that even if the wind stayed light we'd probably make it under sail.

In the heat of the afternoon, the wind died completely and the pains came back, much worse than they'd been at night. I couldn't crouch anywhere and felt desperately uncomfortable – I was concerned that it might be appendicitis. Although Arbroath was only a couple of miles away now, I couldn't get in because the tide hadn't yet risen. I'd have to wait until evening before I'd be able to. I decided to carry on to Montrose – it was the only port I could enter, and with the tide still under us we would be there in a matter of hours. As time ticked away, though, the pain seemed to get worse. I tried calling home to let someone know what was happening, but got no reply. I then got through to Dad at school, but there was little he could do. I could hear the concern in his voice, but also his helplessness. None the less it was such a relief to hear him. Though I was close to shore I might as well have been out of sight of land. Trying to

57

think ahead, I left Dad to call Graham to let him know what was happening.

As I approached Montrose I called ahead to the Harbour Control Office to make sure they were expecting me and that there were medical facilities nearby. 'No problem,' came the reply and I was told that someone would come out to meet me. Montrose, almost exclusively a shipping port, was not really recommended for small yachts, but as it turned out I could not have made a better decision.

As I approached the harbour entrance, I edged my way into the cabin to call the port authorities to make sure that there was no shipping on its way out. As I reached for the VHF radio to change channels, I was startled to hear a very large vessel close to me. I peered out through the windows and saw to my relief that the pilot vessel *Southesk* was right alongside; she had come out to meet me.

They escorted me up the river where ships towered up above the concrete dockside. A shortish man walked out on to the *Southesk*'s side-deck and indicated where he wanted me to berth. The pain in my stomach was agonizing. It shot through me every time I moved, so tying *Iduna* up seemed to take for ever. The man I had seen on the deck of the *Southesk* turned out to be the Harbourmaster, Harry, and he drove me to the local infirmary. By the time I had arrived the pain seemed to be easing a little. I was assured by the doctor that I did not have appendicitis and that the pain would pass. I was feeling slightly better at this stage, so Harry ran me back to *Iduna*, where I collapsed in my bunk in an exhausted and sweaty heap.

I called home later that evening after trying to sleep. My parents had been talking, and Mum had decided she was going to come to Montrose. I was glad of this, though worried that her trip might be a waste of time. But I had been away for almost a month, and I knew it would be wonderful to see a familiar face.

That night began fine, but once the final cries from the settling birds and the noise of the traffic had stopped, I was again racked with intense pain. I was writing in my bunk, and *Iduna*'s cabin, which had always been comforting, now felt claustrophobic. I just wanted to curl up and scream, but I didn't have the space. I could hug one leg or the other to my chest, and I lay there whimpering the night away. I kept reminding myself that it was not appendicitis and that it would just go away, but it didn't. There was no relief till I woke with the first movements in the river rocking *Iduna*.

Harry came down to see me the following morning and asked how I was. I said that I'd had a terrible night but was feeling better, and that Mum would be arriving at Montrose Station at three o'clock. He offered to pick her up and handed me a key for the workers' shed. The guys who worked on the docks had asked him to let me have the spare key for their dock shed, in case I wanted to use the toilet, get hot water or use the kettle.

I slept all morning now the pain had eased a bit, and by lunchtime felt much better. It was wonderful to see Mum bounce off the train at the station, and as we hugged each other relief flowed between us. Harry dropped us back at *Iduna*, where we climbed down the ladder and I excitedly recited all there was to be told of the journey so far. That night I was ill again, doubled up in my bunk as Mum tried to sleep in the makeshift bunk we had laid down the centre of *Iduna*. It was no use, this pain wasn't going away, and by 0400 Mum was up to see if there was anyone around who could help. I was squirming again, and this time with a temperature. The night watchman on duty kindly gave us a lift to the infirmary in his van. The doctor was fantastic, but couldn't work out exactly what was wrong. He gave me something take, and we headed back to the dock. The medicine seemed to ease whatever was going on inside me and the following day I felt OK again.

Mum was worried about being away from home as so many people relied on her. Nan was struggling. She'd had to come home from her university placement in Germany because of illness. Mum now had to run her to places she'd always walked to. It must have been heartbreaking enough for Nan to have to break away from her studies, let alone cope with the frustration of being so frail. Auntie Thea was also staying in Derbyshire now. She'd had a crippling nervous reaction to a painkilling spinal injection after she'd injured her back and was being looked after by Mum. We talked a lot about what was going on back at home and it was clear that things weren't at all easy. Gran was also unwell and Lew was at home, still struggling to make a decision about his future. Poor Mum; as usual she was bearing the brunt, and not for the first time, being strong for everyone. I felt terrible that she had come up to Montrose. I can only hope that her break from home to look after me did her a fraction of the good it did me. She asked me if I wanted to go back to Derbyshire with her until she was sure I was better, and there was certainly some temptation to do that. But I resisted, telling her that if I went home I would jeopardize the trip and would not make it round. It was disheartening to have been storm-bound for so long in Hartlepool, but right now the weather was good and I was going to go for it, so the following morning Mum left.

We found ourselves walking back from town past the dock shed the following morning. On discovering it was locked, I realized I still had the little key tucked away in my pocket. As we opened the door, it was like entering a long-lost den. There were a few dark-coloured seats scattered around, several with the covers suffering a bit through wear. The windows were pretty dirty from the daily forklift and lorry movements, though shards of sunlight were still just about making it through. There were several rather unflattering pictures of semi-naked and naked women on the walls, and a large electric kettle with a few tins, mugs and spoons in the far corner. As I walked in I smiled, I don't really know why, but I felt right at home in a shed like this, and looking back, I think I was just plain chuffed to have been accepted into the dock workers' world. Mum commented, 'Goodness, this is well used,' which kind of summed it up really as we made ourselves a cup of tea and sat down for a great last chat.

We said our goodbyes, which in many ways was harder than in Hull. We both had a much better idea now of what I was taking on, although I think this just made me feel more determined. *Iduna* seemed too quiet that evening, but I consoled myself with the thought that the following day we'd be setting off again.

Monday June 26th
Got up at 0810. Spent the morning fixing the wind generator, making phone calls and washing up. Also spent quite a bit of time passage planning

– where to head next. Cut thumb – bad on the aluminium disc. Never mind. Sandwiches for lunch. At 1300 went to get water alongside SOUTHESK pilot boat. Big hassle – too strong a jet which burst my little water tank! Loads of water in the bilges. There was water everywhere, even in the battery box! Luckily I managed to fix tank, it had broken at the inlet! Decided water purification tablets needed. Went into town. Found mega expensive ones in Boots – so tried nearby chemist. Got some Milton! I'm sure it'll do the job. Got back to boat, handed in key to the shed – then departed as SOUTHESK was due to leave shortly. Still in jeans and T-shirt, started up engine and set off – waved goodbye. On way out called up Montrose port control. Thanked them for their hospitality and help and said I hoped to come back some time. The reply was 'Iduna – port control, no problem – you're welcome back anytime' – lovely.

The wind began to pick up soon after we'd left. As I sat in the cockpit with a cup of tea I could see fog looming up ahead, rolling towards us. Above the blanket the sky was clear and bright, and as the air turned grey there was a shimmering on the water as though it was coated in silver. I tried to stay close inshore to keep clear of the routes of any shipping that might be around – I had no way of seeing them other than by eye-balling. I hoisted my radar reflector into *Iduna*'s rigging, so that we might have a chance of being seen by the ships themselves, and listened hard for the sound of their engines. We tacked so close into the cliffs that they rose out of the fog high above me while the foaming waves broke on to the rocks beneath.

I called the Coastguard to let him know where I was and say that I was tacking up the coast in fog. I just wanted to let any shipping that was near us know we were around. There was someone else listening in to this radio conversation, though, and soon afterwards they contacted me directly. It seemed that a boat called *MRI 38* – a high-speed rescue boat – was keen to come out and test a new piece of technology on me. Once I was sure that their mission was in no way a 'rescue', I was happy to cooperate. Their equipment was designed to find a vessel purely with a radio signal. I carried on up the coast.

The boat loomed out of the fog. Asked over the radio if I could hear them, my reply was a loud and clear, but they meant engines! I said 'Hang on' stuck my head out of the hatch and saw their boat on my starboard side, they hung around as I tried to sail in. At approx 2030 I put on my engine and motor-sailed – gradually taking down sails – eventually motoring for the last half hour, very bumpy. Cut finger again!! – blood all over! Didn't want any on sails though. Waves breaking on rocks and sea eagles close, very eerie. Followed *MRI 38* into Stonehaven and moored up.

The skipper of *MRI 38* came up to talk to me as I was tying up. His name was Hamish McDonald, and he ran the company which had designed and built the boat that he had brought out to find me.

I needed to get something to eat, and on discovering that the local chip shop was closed, Hamish drove me straight off to his house at the top of the town. I was warmly welcomed by his family and his wife cooked me bacon and eggs for tea. We chatted till late and soon after midnight Hamish gave me a lift back to *Iduna*. I turned in straight away, lying back in my bunk with a big smile on my face.

Hamish came down with the weather forecast next morning and offered to send one of his engineers down to look at a small problem I'd been having with my outboard engine. He also handed me a copy of a book he'd written. Inside was a short handwritten note:

Live by this

Be at peace with nature
Be at peace with your place of work
Be at peace with your tools of work
Realize your capabilities – work to your limitations.

Very best wishes to Ellen, may all your dreams come true.

HM 27/06/95

After the engineer had fixed the outboard I shipped my lines straight away and departed Stonehaven, sad to be leaving new friends.

It was just minutes later that the dolphins came. I'd be hard pushed to think of another creature that has the potential to make people smile quite as quickly as the dolphin. I was grinning from ear to ear. I had never seen wild dolphins before, and laughed out loud as they swept past *Iduna*. Though we were moving quite slowly they leapt at her bow and dived beneath us . . . they would turn their heads on one side and look up, and at the same time I could reach down and touch them. This is what being out here is all about, I thought. If the trip was forced to end tomorrow, I would have already seen such a big part of what I came out to see.

The next stages were calm, a mixture of sailing and motoring. We stopped off in Peterhead, then after an early start, sailed round the headland to a tiny fishing village called Whitehills. I was starting to worry, though, because we were behind schedule: although we had covered a good distance, we were still below 400 miles of a 1,900-mile trip. We had had our two weeks in Hartlepool and three days in Montrose, and should have been nearer the top of Scotland by now. I thought about our options. The plan had always been to pass round Cape Wrath, between Scotland and the Orkneys, but now I was beginning to doubt that would be feasible. We'd had fantastic weather since Hartlepool and I'd been able to sail most days, but it was not going to stay like that – we had to get moving. I was worried about getting stuck in gales up there in the north – if we got caught, we would struggle to get into port at all. *Iduna* is a very small boat, and her outboard engine simply was not going to be something I could rely on. As our attempt to leave Hartlepool had shown, it could be practically useless when the propeller came out of the water each time *Iduna* went over a big wave. I had been worrying about this since the beginning of the trip, and reluctantly I decided to play it safe. Our other option, which would cut out those miles around the top, meant taking *Iduna* through the Caledonian Canal from Inverness to Fort William. I was angry with myself for having made that decision, but I knew it was the right one. No one else could make it for me, and I was determined we were going to do it.

29th June Whitehills

The Harbourmaster thanked me very much for coming to pay. He took my £6, and asked me if I liked fish and gave me 4 fresh haddock. He asked me if I could gut them, to which I replied 'No problem' which I was sure I could. I left the shed smiling and I had porridge for breakfast that I had cooked in harbour before my departure. I then set about cleaning and filleting the haddock. Great fun. I tailed and beheaded them first, which the sea gulls rather enjoyed! I then tried to get the fish off the bone. Which actually wasn't as hard as I thought. I then ended up with eight fillets, one of which I fried instantly, it was delicious. Three yachts passed going the other way to seaward. They looked like ghost ships. The horizon was hidden in the mist – they looked like they were floating on glass.

Next stop was Lossiemouth where Graham had arranged for me to meet some of the lads from the local RAF base. I was shown round the base and ended up going to the pub and chatting with the guys who worked the Search and Rescue helicopter. I made it back on board, almost drunk, just before midnight. It had been a long time since I'd enjoyed a big evening out!

I was still up early the following morning. The forecast was for quite strong winds but with advice from the Harbourmaster I decided to go for it – he thought I would make Inverness in time for the locks into the Caledonian Canal. He wished me all the best for my journey.

'Yacht Iduna, Yacht Iduna, Yacht Iduna this is *RAF 132* – do you read us, OVER', and before I knew it there was a Sea King helicopter flying over us! Wow! I spoke to them several times on the radio as they flew around, they said that it was great to see that I was OK, and that I was looking good down there. They circled round a few times, then did a fly-past at great speed – the noise was momentarily deafening . . . How cool is that!

It was a still evening as I tied up by the lock gates at the entrance to the Caledonian Canal. I closed up *Iduna* and headed to the supermarket which I'd been told earlier was not at all far from the moorings. By the time I returned I was surprised to see another mast just behind ours. *Iduna* is small but this was tiny. It was rare for us to dwarf anything bar small rowing dinghies. And the most astonishing thing was that this little thing had sailed over from Sweden. The guy on board her, Sebastian, was tall, slightly unkempt and wore a leather flying hat when things got cold. He'd built his boat, *Arrandir*, in his bedroom at home – he found he couldn't get her out again and had to remove a window! We left Inverness together the following morning and had a great sail down the canal to Fort William before going our separate ways. I was astounded by the sheer beauty of the Caledonian Canal. It took just under a week to sail through and I cherished every minute of it.

July 8th

I am realizing today that I am far more content alone than I first was. I am not worried that I am miles away from home with no one I know. I have *Iduna* and she has me and together we shall do just fine. My new home is with me and I have all I need, and more – I am very lucky.

We're moored up in Kentallen bay, a magical place. Tea is on the stove, and there is complete silence here. Haggis and vegetables, and maybe I'll try baking a cake in the pressure cooker for afters. Worth a try I suppose, even if it turns into a pudding with custard on – after all it's my birthday today!

Chapter Six

Two days later we reached Oban. The sailing from Port Appin at the mouth of Loch Linnhe had been wonderful. I felt like a character in *Swallows and Amazons*, exploring hidden caves and secret harbours. We moored across the bay from the town off a beautiful little island called Kerrara. I had decided to take a break for a day and catch the train to Edinburgh. *Royalist* was about to set off for the biggest event of her year, the Tall Ships Race. Virtually every square-rigged ship for thousands of miles around must have gathered for it and I was itching to wave them off.

Everyone aboard *Royalist* was on fine form, and the colour and noise couldn't have been more of a contrast to life alone on *Iduna*. There were water-balloon fights with the other ships as they entered the docks, and thousands of people. I also had the opportunity of talking to Barry Mattey, the commanding officer of the Sea Cadets, who raised the possibility of my taking a job with them as a yacht skipper. I'd had such great fun with everyone on board that the thought of being an official part of the organization was appealing. There were courses taking place on the Sea Cadets' smaller yachts later in the year and I had to think about what I was going to do next. It had been wonderful to see friends again, and a small part of me wished I could be sailing off with them. This soon melted away as my mind returned to my own journey. From Oban I had to make it to Southampton for the Boat Show.

From Kerrara we sailed through the stunning Crinan Canal, then beyond to Adrishaig, Largs and Troon.

July 26th

1055 I cannot begin to describe what a fantastic feeling it is to be sailing alone as Iduna is sailing now. She is alive, and I am convinced she is aiming to please in every way. We are in harmony! She gracefully flows over the waves parting the water at her bows and leaving just an indent, a slight disturbance at her stern, the only trace of her presence. God has blessed us with fair winds at last.

We were out of sight of land for the first time in the voyage as we sailed for Peel on the Isle of Man and rather than making me fearful, this actually filled me with a greater sense of freedom than ever before. *Iduna* and I were off, and I had the most incredible urge just to carry on south and out across the Atlantic. The day was stunning, we were hammering along, and I got the wind-vane self-steering, feeling as if it was in control of us for the first time. I laughed aloud at the waves that splashed my face.

Just two hours from Peel things changed dramatically, however. We were downwind of the island, which normally means that the sea flattens behind the shelter of the land. I was looking forward to that final blast in flat sea. Then the wind changed direction and started to increase in speed. I reefed down *Iduna* as she had begun bouncing around in the waves, and struggled to get things sorted quickly. It seemed everything was against us at that moment. As the winds grew in power they were also turning, blowing us away from Peel. We were experiencing extreme catabatic winds as the air funnelled down the island's hills and out to sea. I felt vulnerable but knew we were just going to have to hang on and battle it out. The waves grew dramatically, and I feared we might even have to change course and head for Ireland – and safety. I tried running *Iduna*'s engine to help us claw towards the harbour, but I could only run it on one tack as the propeller came out of the water on the other. I tried to stop and start it as we changed tacks, but each time we fell down a wave the engine would scream in complaint as the resistance from the water disappeared below it.

It was the big test for me and *Iduna*, and although the ordeal lasted only two hours, I learned a lot.

27th July

Iduna and I belong together. She provides me with a home and shelter while I give her direction and adventure. I feel proud to be associated with such a wonderful yacht. How could anyone have abandoned her like they did? She is willing to please if given half a chance. She has carried me through rough and smooth. She has never given up, maybe tested me a little, but we held our own.

My excitement rose as we headed down towards Anglesey and prepared for our passage of the Menai Straits. The goal was to arrive safely in Port Dinorwic where I would be met by my friend Sarah and her Mum and Dad, and then, the day after, by my own family.

I was looking forward to seeing Sarah but found it difficult to relax. I did not feel in holiday mode as I could not get my mind off the trip. I enjoyed our time together but I did feel a little bit outside it all. It was a shame – I probably could have done with letting my hair down!

It was similar when Mum and Dad arrived with Ferg and Mac the following day. I wanted to see them and to introduce them to my world, but I also felt distracted. I was definitely not my normal self and was still too absorbed in my trip. It was a shame. Dad, having just retired from teaching, was more relaxed than I'd seen him for years. I was tired, and concentrating hard on not making mistakes. My focus was on making sure that *Iduna* was OK. I had set out to make it round, and that was what preoccupied me. My family had come out to have a holiday but, in my mind, I was working. I tried really hard to relax and enjoy myself but sadly failed pretty miserably.

After just one day in Port Dinorwic I decided to continue on my trip to the next scheduled stop – Aberdaron Bay. We had chosen it on Graham's recommendation as he holidayed there every year. Mum and Dad had brought their tent and I would meet them there.

With Aberdaron Bay virtually in sight, the wind shifted, forcing us to spend two hours tacking in towards the beach to reach water shallow enough to anchor in. It was a struggle – the wind was all over the place as it swept into the bay from around the hills and cliffs, one moment strong, the next very light, leaving us at the mercy of the current. The waves picked up by the current were small inshore, but quite vicious, short and sharp.

We had agreed that Dad would row out to me in my inflatable dinghy which he had brought over in the car from Port Dinorwic, though I dismissed this as a possibility with these waves in the darkness. I could see very little as I tacked from side to side in the bay. I could just make out the silhouette of a high skyline to windward, and saw the dark blue-white of breaking waves on the rocks at the far end of the beach. It was not going to be easy to anchor here. Slowly we edged our way further in towards the beach, watching the depth gauge constantly to know when it might be shallow enough. *Iduna*'s motion was horrible, and it took all my concentration to navigate her safely in these conditions so close to the land. Preparing her anchor was difficult, and as I finally let it fall into the water and felt it biting on the bottom, I sighed with relief.

But it didn't hold, and we were being dragged out of the bay by the wind. The deck swayed from side to side as I pulled up the anchor. The wind was stronger now, and the cold was penetrating my wet clothes. I just needed to make sure we were safe for the night, get dried off, and wait for tomorrow's light.

I glanced towards the shore and picked out a tiny torch beam. It was easy to lose it against the lights from the village. My heart sank when I realized I was watching Dad and Ferg rowing out towards me.

My first reaction was to drop the anchor chain I had just lifted in an effort to slow our drift, but it looked as if nothing I could do would stop us from moving further and further from the dinghy and its passengers. I put the engine on to try to hold ground, and as we swayed around in the darkness of the night, the howl of the outboard as it was lifted in and out of the water only increased my anxiety as I watched and worried.

They looked so exposed and I was afraid for them. I could not understand why they had come out in such grim conditions. The wind was blowing off the shore, and they would have to row hard to get back to land against it. I knew they'd come to collect me, but I could not leave *Iduna* tonight, and while part of me loved them for coming, their recklessness frustrated me beyond reason. Soon their faces came into focus, and I reached down to them as Dad grabbed at *Iduna*'s sides. Incredibly, he was still wearing shorts as water sloshed around the bottom of the dinghy. Neither of them was wearing a lifejacket. I couldn't contain my anger.

'What the bloody hell are you doing out here now?' I yelled.

'We saw your signal . . . so we came out.'

'There was no signal – it's too dangerous, I have to move, I have to re-anchor – I'm staying here tonight,' I shouted. 'Come back in the morning, call me on the radio first.'

'OK.'

And with that one-sided exchange the little inflatable boat ended its squeaking up and down in the waves against *Iduna*'s topsides, and there was quiet except for the splashings of the oars and the noise of the weather.

'Signal when you're on the beach,' I shouted after them and sat in a trance for what seemed like hours as I watched the silhouette of the dinghy edging its way to the shore. There was a flash, and I could see figures moving in front of the lights on the beach. They were safe.

I hauled up *Iduna*'s anchor once more, and moved further along the beach to try to find better holding ground. On the second attempt things were better. The anchor seemed to hold, and I switched off the navigation lights and lit the little paraffin lamp which I attached in her bows. I climbed down below, foraged up forward for dry clothes for the night, stripped off and swapped my clammy wet ones for a wonderful layer of warmth. Though exhausted, I could not sleep. There was the constant banging of the wires within *Iduna*'s mast as she rolled in the waves, and knowing the tide would change in a few hours I worried that the anchor might not hold. I couldn't dispel the thought of waking to the sound of breaking fibreglass as her hull was washed up on the island's rocks. I thought of Dad and Ferg in the dinghy, and had to keep telling myself that they were OK. In reality *Iduna* and I were fine, though sitting in uncomfortable waves; I think I'd just been shaken by the dinghy coming out to meet me.

I must have slept eventually, as I stirred when dawn arrived. I clambered on deck, which was covered in dew, and everything was clear: there was still an orange tint in the sky. I sat outside with my jacket wrapped round my shoulders. I looked up and saw the tents on the hillside, and recognized our little murky yellow one with the car parked next to it. Last night seemed a long time ago.

That evening we all ate on the beach with Graham and his wife Penny, but before the sun set it was time for me to head back to *Iduna*. It had been hard seeing everyone in the middle of the trip, and pulling myself away to set sail once again was a wrench. Graham took a photo of us all on the beach. In it, Mum is looking at me, and, although she is visibly holding back her emotion, her concern is clear to see.

After passing the spectacular Pembrokeshire coast, I stayed becalmed for five days in Fishguard where close friends of Dave's, John and Margaret, took me under their wing. I stayed in a bed for the first time in months and talked to John for hours about his grandfather's experiences on the clipper ships. While there I carefully studied the charts to Solva, an ancient fishing port which was the next stop along the coast. The entrance was tricky and I would have to dry *Iduna* out when the tide went out, leaving her standing on her keel out of the water, leaning against the harbour wall.

It was a choppy sail round to Solva, but on securing *Iduna* in the harbour I joined Tony Rees, of the Solva Boat Owners' Association, and his wife Joy for dinner. While we ate, I was concerned for *Iduna*. I wanted to be there while she dried out. Half an hour after Tony and Joy dropped me back she touched the bottom, and with a rope attached to the top of her mast to stop her falling away from the quay, all seemed well. I changed into my jogging pants and a T-shirt and slid into my bunk, listening to the water slip down her keel as the tide fell away. Our angle began to feel excessive, however: *Iduna* was sliding away from the wall. I got up slowly, moving gingerly to prevent her from slipping further, and climbed the ladder up on to the dockside. I could see that in a few minutes' time her wire rigging would be taking her whole weight as the keel slid further away from the harbour wall. This would wreck her. I dashed around looking for a piece of wood to jam between her and the wall to try to keep her upright but found none. I ran back, my bare feet stinging on the loose tarmac. Her rigging was already touching the wall. I reached out over her and pushed her mast away. It looked as though I might be able to hold her.

I tried to calm myself down and assess the situation clearly. On the one hand, the rigging was safe and she had stopped slipping. On the other, I knew that I couldn't let go – I was stuck there. With a wave of relief I realized I had my mobile phone in my pocket, and fumbled to get it. Don't drop it, I thought, for God's sake don't drop it! I pressed a key to illuminate the screen – no signal. I tried calling the Reeses anyway, but without success. It was now well past midnight and getting colder.

I tried sitting down, but that was no good as I couldn't reach far enough to hold her mast, so I resolved to stand there till about 6 a.m. when the tide would float her once again. I tried counting the stars, then singing songs, frustrated that I could not remember the words to Kylie Minogue tracks I must have listened to a hundred times. I couldn't help but laugh – here I was standing in joggers and a T-shirt, freezing, singing half-remembered snippets of Kylie while I held up a boat.

It didn't seem funny for long, though, and I wondered whether the mobile might be worth another try. When I held it as far away from me as possible I got a glimmer of a signal. I dialled, held the phone to my ear and lost it again. I called again and again, knowing full well that even if I could get Tony and Joy to answer, I would only be able to shout into the phone at arm's length. Thankfully the plan worked. At 4 a.m. I saw their headlights sweep into view. Tony held *Iduna*'s mast while I scouted further afield to find something to wedge her hull. Once this had been done, they bundled me into the car and took me back to their house where I gratefully enjoyed a sleep for the rest of the night.

Our next fixed rendezvous had now been announced by Graham. Robin Knox-Johnston was to make a TV programme sailing his famous yacht *Suhaili* from Plymouth to Bristol. I had been asked if I wanted to be a part of it and I jumped at the chance. We now had four weeks before we had to be in Southampton for the Boat Show, and getting to Plymouth for the end of the month seemed realistic. We made good progress from Solva, sailing into Milford Haven and then making our biggest hop so far, across the British Channel into Padstow.

The early stages of the crossing passed quickly, and I worked hard on my navigation with shipping around. As the sky lost its azure blueness it softened and melted into delicately layered pastel colours, and the water was as smooth as glass, disturbed only by *Iduna*'s bow wave, until a pair of dolphins joined us. I sat on the cabin roof and sang out loud. There was phosphorescence that night, lighting up each fish like a dart as it fled through the water, startled by our progress. The bow wave seemed alight and I turned off the navigation lights for a couple of minutes, just to enjoy it at its most vivid.

I woke the following morning in Padstow to the hustle and bustle of people, the barking of dogs and the squeals of children, and when I popped my head out of the hatch I saw that the quiet little harbour had become a gathering-point for holidaymakers. The yacht I had tied alongside began to sway a little, and after a few minutes a scruffy-looking head appeared in the hatchway. The sailor, who was quite young, smiled instantly and asked where I had sailed from and when I was heading off.

'Tomorrow morning,' I answered as he jumped into his tender.

'Do you want to have dinner on board then?'

'Cool, thanks,' I replied as he paddled away to the dockside.

As I sat in the sun, I reflected on the journey so far. It was incredible how far away glandular fever seemed, as if that experience was years before rather than just eighteen months. I could not believe how my life had changed. I was doing everything I'd ever hoped to and had been the recipient of enormous kindness from virtual strangers. But I thought of Thea, and how she was doing. She was still flat out suffering from her nervous reaction. I had called her from time to time to discuss where I was, or let her know what was happening, but she should have been out here sailing on *Cabaret* as she had been for the past fifteen years. I knew how it felt to be lying unable to do anything each day, and knew too that it would come as unnaturally to Thea as it did to me.

The sound of oars brought me back to the present as my new friend returned and invited me aboard. The cabin was dimly lit, and the first thing I remember seeing were pots and pans, books and bits of fluffy carpet on the floor. The boat was a tip! In stark contrast to the clutter of the main cabin, the forepeak held the lovingly well-tended items on board. As I peered into the forward cabin, the setting sun highlighted two thriving cannabis plants.

We got stuck into a Chinese takeaway and opened beers; and with the little oil lamp lighting the cosy cabin, we chatted passionately about heading out to see the big wide world. He was as chilled out as you'd expect and we had each other in stitches till the early hours of the morning.

August 20th – St Ives
Felt a bit down when I got up this morning! – probably due to bad night and the lack of sleep! Anyway it's now 0922. – have spent 20 minutes fiddling with fishing tackle to catch some mackerel. The rocking of the boat should do the job!! Not having much luck though but it's the thought that counts I guess. The forecast is crap, and the visibility bad – just over one nautical mile. I won't see much of Land's End. Continued fishing and planning . . . Just waiting for a nibble and the tide . . .

In the end Land's End was fairly uneventful, but the Longships lighthouse still felt like a major turning-point. Since Scotland I had been clawing my way west to round this rock, and now we'd done it and were heading east to that final corner. We were on the home straight.

We arrived in Plymouth on the evening of the 22nd, with a great feeling of triumph. I was so proud as we sailed into Plymouth

Harbour, I could have been at the helm of the *Cutty Sark*! That evening, however, I discovered that my sail with Robin Knox-Johnston aboard *Suhaili* had been cancelled, and that the filming was not going to take place. I remember that evening well, sitting on the head of my bunk with a mug of hot chocolate and the rain beginning to come down outside. I suppose I'd got myself quite excited about meeting up with Robin properly after our introduction at the BT/YJA awards, and felt low about those plans falling apart. The forecast was appalling too, with gales for the next few days – good enough weather for us to be able to leave would take a miracle. I checked my diary and reminded myself that Nan's birthday was in two days' time. I was going to have to send her something tomorrow. I fell asleep wondering what it might be.

Next morning I set about making a little card for Nan myself. I drew a small map of the UK, painted in the land and sea, and annotated it with a little flag for Plymouth, marking Nan's eightieth birthday next to it. I finished it off with pictures of our adventures in Scotland, the dolphins and the storms on the East Coast. Then I wrote: 'So sorry I can't be with you.'

And as I did so I thought, I *can* be. I could just catch the train and go up there for a day. Suddenly I became very excited. I rang Mum to ask what everyone was doing and where everyone was going, though I gave no indication that I might come home. I was determined to try to join them. Sarah agreed to pick me up and take me to the pub where they would be eating.

When we moored in Plymouth I'd been struck by two boats branded with company logos. I recognized them as 67-foot BT Global Challenge boats. The Challenge was set up by Sir Chay Blyth, famous for his own solo circumnavigation against the prevailing winds and currents. The race crews follow the same route. I had read that a woman called Samantha Brewster, having taken part in the last race, was going to be sailing a Challenge boat single-handed around the world. I realized that hers was one of the two moored on the same pontoon as us, only about 100 feet away. I watched the commotion on the pontoon and felt I understood a little of what was going on after my efforts to get *Iduna* ready for her trip.

Brian from Musto had told me that he was working with Sam on clothing, and he must have said something as she came over for a chat that afternoon. She was small and strong-looking with a high-energy smile. She was very down to earth and happily took me on board her boat. It made a huge impression on me.

As the sun went down I sat in *Iduna*'s cockpit, sipping a mug of hot tea. I found it hard to stop looking in the direction of the boat, and I kept thinking about what Sam was going to be undertaking out there.

Sarah met me at Matlock Station and drove me to the pub, where to my horror, there was no sign of the family car. There was no point in going in as it was obvious we must be in the wrong place, so we headed back home. Sarah left and I let myself into the house. Soon after I heard the sound of the car engine and hared up the stairs. I could see everyone getting out of the car from my bedroom window. Suddenly I felt embarrassed. I heard Mum go into her bedroom and decided to follow her. She was on the far side of the bed, getting something from a drawer, and as I walked in she looked up, and for a second I thought she was going to faint.

'Ellen!' she cried, and I ran round the bed to hug her, both of us with tears in our eyes. Nan was quite speechless as I appeared in the doorway. It had been well worth the effort.

My next log entry was for the following day when I made it back on board *Iduna*.

25/8/95
1328 Back in my world!

I was stuck in Plymouth for a further three days. Each morning I would get the forecast and decide whether it was possible to leave or not. It was frustrating when each forecast seemed just to hold me back and we spent another day tied up. I was pretty happy to eventually get going again.

1700 :   Speed over ground 6.5 – racing another yacht – have sat in bow ECSTATIC!! – I love Iduna. THOSE WERE THE MOST EXCITING 7 MINS OF MY LIFE – IDUNA WAS OFF!!!

1 Mum and Dad at home in Derbyshire

2 Home in Whatstandwell, Derbyshire

3 With older brother, Lewis

4 (below left) From an early age I was always busy

5 (below right) Fishing as a child

6 On the beach with my sailing cap on and telescope round my neck

7 I went to farm sales with my dad, who never missed a 'bargain' . . .

8 . . . which is why his garage looked like this!

9 With Lewis, younger brother Fergus, Gran and Nan

Family expeditions ere common

11 Auntie Thea's boat, *Cabaret*, under sail

12 Sailing aboard *Cabar*

13 Nan on *Cabaret*

14 Dinghy sailing

16 Sailing *Kestrel*

15 In the garden with Mac in my first boat

17 On board *Cabaret* with David King and Auntie Thea

18 Sailing with *Alert* out of the Nautical School

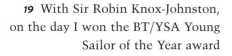

19 With Sir Robin Knox-Johnston, on the day I won the BT/YSA Young Sailor of the Year award

20 Home aboard *Iduna*

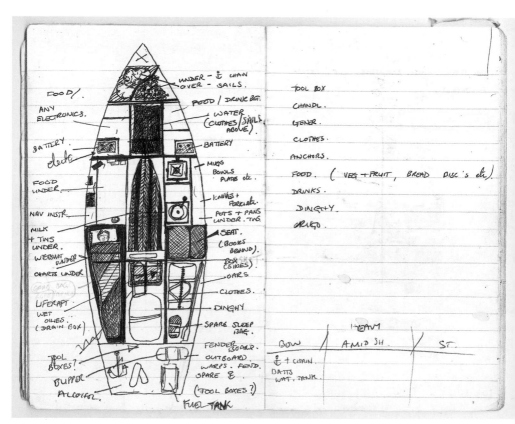

21 My plan of *Iduna* drawn in preparation for sailing round Britain

22 Saying goodbye before setting sail on the Round Britain

3 'Let out at last' in *Iduna*

24 'She knew': Mac watching *Iduna* leave Hull

25 Welcome company while sailing round Britain

26 Sailing *Iduna*

27 *Iduna* at se

29 Mooring for the evening on the Caledonian Cana

28 *Iduna* dried up in Peel, on the Isle of Man

We had the most incredible time, stopping in ports such as Salcombe, Dartmouth and Brixham. I was looked after by the Island Cruising Club in Salcombe, welcomed by the glorious castles at the mouth of the River Dart, and built up quite a chatty rapport with Brixham Coastguard on the radio. Each time I left a port and arrived at another I would let them know my passage plan, and by the time I left their coastal region they'd generally guessed I was sailing around Great Britain. One of them even asked me to send him a postcard from Weymouth.

The longest passage on our way along the South Coast was the trek across Lyme Bay to Weymouth, which, although just under 60 miles, seemed like a major crossing for a 21-foot Corribee. What made the passage even more tricky was the rounding of Portland Bill, a massive natural spit of land leading to a headland. Portland Bill is renowned for its dangerous overfalls and terrifying seas in strong winds. I'd sought advice from several people during the trip, and one piece that particularly stuck in my mind was 'Sail round the point close enough that you could touch the rocks with a boat hook.' I couldn't wait!

Time passed quickly once I'd rounded the Bill and left Weymouth. I made a stopover in Poole to sleep for a few hours, then an early start to sail straight up to Southampton.

That afternoon I arrived in Ocean Village, and in the grey drizzle tied *Iduna* alongside the pontoon in our new short-term home. As I stowed everything away down below, I heard the sound of an engine coming closer. I peered out of my hatch and saw the BT Global Challenge boat that had been tied up next to Sam's in Plymouth pull gently alongside the dock. There were five or six people on board, and after tying up, one of them came over to say hello and tell me I'd be more than welcome if I fancied popping round for a cup of tea later.

Nervously I climbed on board a few hours later, feeling a little self-conscious. The noise of my feet echoed around, and for a moment I just stood there feeling stupid. I didn't know whether to leave or not.

'Hello,' I called. No answer.

Remembering the layout of Sam's boat, I peered down into the living space below the cockpit and called one last time. Still no answer.

Creeping back, I was stopped in my tracks by the grunt of a sleepy giant. A man dressed in very unflattering thermals appeared through a small door just opposite me.

Merfyn Owen had clearly been sound asleep, but having extended the invitation was adamant that I should not leave. He suggested that I put the kettle on while he got dressed, and five minutes later as the kettle began to boil, a new man emerged.

Merv was tall and well built, with wild, curly black hair and the loudest laugh you could imagine. It soon became clear that he was a gentle giant, and one who was more than prepared to give a tremendous amount. We got on famously from the word go, and he explained that he was in Southampton with the BT Global Challenge as at roughly the same time next year he was going to skipper one of the boats sailing around the world.

Merv, like me, had been brought up in the country, but had not begun sailing until he was eighteen. I talked of *Panic Major* and Hull, and discovered Merv knew Robert. He talked of the places he had sailed to and the boats he had sailed on, of skippering Open 60s across the Atlantic, of the job he had as shore crew for the BOC, a single-handed round-the-world race that stopped in ports. He'd even sailed on 60- and 80-foot multi-hulls around France and the rest of Europe. I lapped it up, and as our conversation unrolled I learned that Merv now made his living as a yacht designer. One of the designs was in the marina and he suggested we take a look.

Maverick was a unique, incredible boat. Her wide decks and funky-coloured hull gave her an almost dinghy-like appearance. She had no visible cabin like a cruising boat, just a small hatch that went below decks where there was a tiny bay for a gas stove and four very basic bunks, which were no more than aluminium frames with plastic mesh stretched over them. The rain began to hammer down, so we climbed inside. Merv leaned back against her hull on one of the bunks, as he could not even sit upright inside, and I sat on the step, entranced. He began talking about the reasons why he designed *Maverick* in the way he did, and he described a race called the Mini Transat. The Mini is a single-handed transatlantic race which is sailed in high-performance boats the same size as *Iduna*. I was fascinated by what he told me and began to think again about my next step. It had been a long time since I'd had a conversation which appeared to open so many doors.

The Boat Show got off to a whirlwind start as Brian Pilcher whisked me away and seemingly introduced me to everyone he had ever known. We called at TV stations and show stands and went and had lunch together when I poured out stories of every adventure I'd had on the trip so far. Graham Percy was there too and between them they set up interviews with local radio, TV and the yachting magazines.

As they'd promised, the RYA presented me with my Yachtmaster Instructor's endorsement at the Royal Southampton Yacht Club, and I met up again with James Stevens and John Goode. It was odd seeing them on home territory, but I was really pleased to have lived up to their expectations with the miles I had covered on board *Iduna*.

I also got back in touch with the Sea Cadets while I was in Southampton. They'd offered me a week's sailing on one of their smaller yachts out of Gosport immediately after the show. I was unsure whether to accept at first, as I was keen to finish the trip, but I knew it might lead to opportunities for the future. I had thoroughly enjoyed every minute of sailing on board *Royalist* and I realized I would be crazy not to say yes.

After a week in Southampton I was itching to get moving again – I had a week to get as far east as I could before joining the Sea Cadets back in Gosport. So *Iduna* and I left Southampton before the end of the show and headed for the rising sun.

23rd September
1924 hours. Sailing up Chichester Harbour. Fantastic. Beautiful sunset – red sky and complete silence! Amid this peace and tranquillity, Iduna creams along, feeling almost motionless!

28th September
Depart Northney Marina at 0530. Ran aground on way out of Chichester Harbour. Very shitty feeling! However, managed to clear her. There was a

starboard mark out. But an ebbing tide!! I'm writing this at sea on passage to Newhaven just found out £10 per night there – no free either! The cliffs past Brighton look rusty along the tops! passed one anchored ship and I trapped my thumb when disconnecting the Navik. Looe Channel was a piece of piss! (right now 1317) I feel very tired! keep thinking about Mini Transat, Merv and Maverick . . .

After a five-day break sailing with the Sea Cadets, the rest of the trip passed very quickly. The goal was just making it back, and although we stopped in several ports, I was so focused that I almost stopped taking it all in. I knew I had to make it to the mouth of the Humber at exactly the right time. The Humber is such a fast-flowing and powerful tidal river that if I got it wrong, even by no more than half an hour, I would stand little chance of making it to the marina. I could be in sight of it, but if the tide turned against me before I made it through those lock gates, I would be carried back out of the river.

The last night was a testing sail and it passed slowly and foggily. I was grateful as the night crept past that the fog was lifting bit by bit and I was relieved to be able to see the lights of the ships once again. I smiled, then laughed out loud at 0257 when I heard the familiar voices of VTS Humber on the radio. I knew I was home.

As the dawn broke on 12 October the most incredible light was shining through the light mist and gradually crept up into the sky. Everything seemed tinted with silver, almost as though a blanket of moonlight was covering us. *Iduna* was sailing perfectly, heeling over and making good speed, the muddy Humber waters once again washing past her tiny hull. I picked out those all too memorable sights on the skyline as we sailed along – the huge Tetney Mono-buoy, Grimsby dock tower and the structure of the Immingham oil terminal. As we crept past each buoy it flashed us, and I picked out its name. I felt as though I was being silently welcomed back.

All my friends from Hull as well as my family, including Nan, were there to see me in. There were cameras and journalists, and Robert had come down with a bottle of champagne. I shall never forget Nan's smile as she came up to give me a kiss, she seemed so proud. I was surprised by my reaction to seeing Mum and Dad too. Of course I was excited, but at the same time it felt as though the spell had been broken. I had been desperately looking forward to telling everyone what had happened since I left, but now I felt numb that it was over.

After a day of celebration it was sad to see Mum and Dad leave that evening. Mum had asked if I'd return home but I had to stay in Hull. In forty-eight hours I'd be joining the Sea Cadets again. *Royalist* was in Dundee and I'd be sailing her south to Great Yarmouth over two weeks.

As the sun set that evening I wandered back down from the Nautical School to *Iduna*. She seemed so peaceful as she sat there alongside the pontoon, the radar reflector still hanging in her rigging, her starboard spreader slightly drooping with the load.

'It's over, lass, thank you,' I whispered quietly as I rubbed her dewy cabin top.

I went up to the marina bar for tea that night, and joined David and his new crew for his weekend sailing course. The familiarity of the scene was reassuring but I knew that I'd changed. I was still the same person, but now I could see further. The trip had broadened my horizons, and my need to explore them further had intensified. I thought about Merv and the race called the Mini Transat, and about the Sea Cadets and the wonderful work that they do. I didn't know which way to head yet, but I realized at that moment that I was not going to be happy visiting that bar every night for the next thirty years.

I grew up on that trip around Britain. When I set out to do it, I was going to give it my all, just hoping that we would make it back into the marina in Hull. I had seen the most beautiful, memorable places, and more than anything else had enjoyed the company of people whose openness and generosity never ceased to amaze me. But deep down I was driven, driven not to stay in a place longer than was necessary, even if great people had invited me to stay. I found myself frustrated that on so many occasions I was sailing slowly, or that the winds had simply not come and we'd had to motor. I forced myself to make decisions which I'd never taken before. I had sole responsibility for myself and for every move we made. I knew now that there are no magic methods of making a situation better, you just have to stay calm, do all you can, and *believe* that things will improve. You can't really anticipate that feeling sitting at home alone. It's not just the fact that you are on your own, but the safety decisions: do I go, or do I wait? There is never an unquestionably right answer – except, of course, with hindsight.

When I listen to my tapes of that trip I heard such intense unease in my voice. Only now can I understand why I was stressed. There's such a contrast between the highs and lows: I can hear such desperate anger in my voice when conditions were not as they had been predicted, when I was soaked to the bone, hand-steering because the autopilots would not work properly. At eighteen you look for someone or something else to blame but I grew to realize that there is no one to blame, that anything can happen and the reasons can never be completely anticipated. Preparation can eliminate some but never all of these problems, because so much is the unpredictable, and it's the unpredictable that you have to learn to handle with flexibility and pragmatism. You simply have to take it in your stride.

I can see the differences in me then, but I can see the similarities too. I was learning to be philosophical when plans have to change and also the extent to which that can and will happen. Good and bad will be thrown up in equal measure, and while enjoying the former is easy, you can't let the latter drag you down.

Chapter Seven

I immediately felt at home back aboard *Royalist* in Dundee. The sunrise was stunning, with the wisps of cloud forming ornate silhouettes in the beautiful orange sky, and the water so still as we slipped along past the tiny craft dwarfed by our imposing presence. Standing there on *Royalist*'s deck, I had responsibility, shared with the rest of the crew, for the Cadets on board.

I loved seeing how they grew in confidence over the week that they were with us. It was constantly rewarding, from the initial days where they saw peeling potatoes in the morning as purgatory, to finding them singing and joking while they did it by the end of the week. What always struck me was not so much how the week would bring people together as how it made them realize the value of their own contribution.

At the end of the first week we said goodbye as a new group of Cadets embarked. The next leg, though, was sailed in very different conditions. On the way from Hartlepool to Lowestoft, we got stuck in difficult weather, in the shape of a much stronger than predicted south-easterly which peaked at a Force 9 gale. The North Sea is relatively shallow, resulting in waves that get short and steep very quickly. The motion aboard *Royalist* was dreadful as she pitched and rolled. Each time she punched into a wave, spray and water hurtled over her decks. It was a constant job to make sure that the kids who were off watch were harnessed to the boat as they made a dash for the rail and threw up into the churning water. *Royalist* was unable to sail into the wind in those conditions. The result was that we had to motor, and even that was a struggle as we managed only a few knots before the night closed in on us, the sky appearing barely high enough to let our masts pass beneath it. I had never been at sea in such bad weather before, and was fascinated by its wildness as foaming crests crashed again and again as they passed the porthole next to my bunk. I watched as the world outside was submerged with each roll.

Adrenalin surged as I woke from a difficult sleep to the sound of the fire alarm. I sprang from my bunk, grabbed my jacket and the fire extinguisher and made my way to the deck. The kids were flowing out of the hatches, all with their harnesses on, and were calmly marching to their muster stations. Some, already green with sea-sickness, now had anxiety etched on their faces. We soon tracked down the problem, which was not actually fire, but smoke and steam from the port engine which had begun overheating. We shut it down but were now in danger of not making our destination at all as we could only just creep forward. As a precaution, we lowered the anchor in an attempt to secure the boat in its position while an assessment of the damage and repairs was made.

We had to wait several hours for the engine to cool before Dave, the engineer, could attempt to fix it, and as it looked like an awkward job, my offer to assist him was accepted. *Royalist*'s anchor was dragging and we were starting to drift slowly towards a nearby gas field. Luckily I was able to restrain her enough to keep us safe while we worked on the engine.

Dave and I climbed down into the engine room, and as he opened the watertight door, the heat surged out into our faces. I took my last deep breath of cool, sweet air, and clambered inside the diesel-smelling sauna. Every creak and groan from *Royalist*'s structure seemed amplified down there and certainly made the situation feel more urgent than it actually was. The problem was with the water-cooling impeller, which, because of where the engine was mounted, was very difficult to get to. I lay on the engine, stretching to reach the impeller cover, while Dave slid beneath it to reach the bolts from below. The heat was extreme, and I had to move slightly every few seconds to shift the hot spots and remain bearably comfortable as our bodies rocked back and forth with the boat's continued violent motion. I am fortunate that I have never suffered from sea-sickness but am sure that if ever it was going to happen, that would have been the time. Sweat streamed down our faces but around an hour later we finished the job and Dave tentatively started the engine. Upon emerging back on to the deck, thankful the job was done, we realized that it was not over yet, as we still had the anchor to get up and were now approaching the exclusion zone around one of the rigs in the Rough gas field. It was time to get out of there, and so began the laborious task of bringing in the anchor, which seemed an unusually slow and difficult process. The hydraulics would only winch when the bow was falling into the trough after a wave passed beneath us. The bow then seemed heavy as *Royalist* began to climb the next wall of breaking surf, and as the two met the sea exploded over us, sluicing unyielding walls of water down along the deck.

Eventually the final feet of chain appeared and then the anchor emerged at the surface, but they were not alone; we also had an old cable which we must have dragged from the sea bed. With skill and a few years' knowledge, Paul, the skipper, managed to flip the anchor, using the trip point at just the right moment to release the cable. *Royalist*'s bow popped up like a rubber duck in a bath as the restriction was eased and once more we were able to ride over rather than through the waves and continued our passage to Lowestoft.

Ashore in Lowestoft at the end of my trip, I phoned home. Lewis answered, said that Mum and Dad were out and told me to call back later. I couldn't linger on the phone and got no hint of what was to come.

I called again that afternoon, by this stage on the train on the way south. I was bursting to tell them all that had happened on *Royalist*, but my enthusiasm evaporated the second I heard Mum's voice. It sounded empty.

'What's happened, Mum?' I asked.

'Your dad's had an accident, don't worry, we think he's OK, he's here at home now.'

She continued, explaining what had happened. At the weekend, Dad had offered to chop off a few branches from the trees in the school car park, and while working with his chainsaw he was struck in the chest by a falling branch that knocked him out of the tree. He must have fallen about 20 feet on to rocky ground. Luckily someone ran to help him, but in typical, stubborn Dad fashion he said he was fine, just winded – this was the same Dad, after all, who had dropped lump hammers on his head and had fallen through ceilings. But he wasn't OK, and an ambulance was called anyway. Finding nothing other than bruising after he'd been X-rayed, the hospital sent him home, but he couldn't walk and virtually crawled into the car when Mum came to pick him up. That evening Uncle Glyn, who was the local GP, quickly discovered that Dad had lost some of the feeling in his lower body.

On re-admission to hospital he was X-rayed again. The first X-ray had missed the fact that he had smashed one of his vertebrae. It was now thought sufficiently worrying for him to be sent immediately to Sheffield Spinal Unit, where for the following three months he remained strapped to a bed, unable to move his back in any way. It was a real shock to see him looking pale, helpless and in pain in a hospital bed. He was always such an active, healthy character.

Throughout his ordeal he showed no anger, or at least not in front of his children, but it must have been a real trial for him. A day never passed without Dad working in some way outdoors. He could see trees outside his hospital window, and they reminded me of how much it helped me when I was ill to look outside at the eucalyptus. I was glad he could see trees too.

1995 was a horrible year and Mum really bore the brunt of it. She's the most honest and gentle person you will ever meet and has seemingly endless reserves of patience. She seemed to be carrying the world on her shoulders that year and I felt acutely aware of how little help she was getting from me. As well as the aftermath of

Dad's accident she was helping Lew to decide about his future. By this stage he'd dropped out of university and was struggling to cope with the added pressure of Dad's accident. And the illness that had marred Nan's university exchange in Germany was diagnosed as a form of fibrous cancer in her lungs which had led to mild pneumonia. Mum was taking meals over each day and trying to look after her, but it didn't stop there because she was still caring for Thea as well, who by now had moved up north into my old bedroom. I'm sure that walks with Mac were pretty much the only thing that kept Mum sane through those dreadful months. I told her I would stay at home and help her look after everyone, but she was adamant that she was OK and that I should do what was best for my future. Although I decided to carry on sailing, it wasn't a comfortable decision to make and one that I still look back on with unease.

My own life at that time was a whirlwind. I was travelling around the country, writing and answering letters to everyone I had met on the trip, and to those who had sponsored me for it. In mid-November, just two weeks after my trip on *Royalist*, I received a letter from Barry Mattey, the Offshore Commander of the Sea Cadets, offering me a post as a small-boat skipper. I was sufficiently tempted to arrange a meeting with him just before Christmas. I was also receiving requests for talks about my trip with *Iduna* from various yacht clubs, along with the incredible offer of a space in the pool at the London International Boat Show.

Brian Pilcher, once again, was my guide through the coming weeks. He encouraged me not to sell myself to people for nothing, and to write letters in the correct way. I would have run across the country at my own expense to give a talk or have a meeting, but Brian taught me to realize that I held some value. That made a massive difference between having very little or, worse, nothing. The plain fact of the matter was that I did not have any financial reserves. I had spent my last savings in trailing *Iduna* to Derbyshire and was subsisting on a small amount of money from my first painting commissions, including one of Merv's boat, *Global Teamwork*.

In December I had my meeting with Barry Mattey. I knew I loved the Sea Cadets and I wanted to work with the kids, but I couldn't stop thinking about the Mini Transat and single-handed races. I had just seen a long article about the Mini in *Yachting World* which I'd read and re-read. I didn't know which way to jump.

I arrived down in Portsmouth and, before the meeting, was shown the boat I would be skippering, a Morgan Giles 43 called *Petrel*. As I walked into the shed she towered above us. I went on board and it soon became apparent that she was very much in refit. Most of her interior had been removed, as fittings were accessed and the engine serviced, but even in this less than perfect state I could see she was beautiful.

I talked about the position with Barry and with one week in four off, allowing me to pursue other options, I was convinced it could work. I wrote accepting the job and was due to start at the end of January.

Dad wasn't around for Christmas. He would normally fuss about in the kitchen with Mum, or ferret around in the fields for holly and mistletoe to hang in the rooms. He loves Christmas and his enthusiasm had rubbed off on his family.

Thea managed to come downstairs on the day, even though she was forced by pain to lie flat on the floor. Mac, Ferg and Lew, who seemed to have grown from the responsibility that came from our father's absence, were also there, and Nan came over. In the evening we drove to Sheffield to see Dad. Mum, as ever, had been a trooper and again I felt guilty about leaving, this time to head south for the job with the Sea Cadets.

All too soon our Christmas was over and I had to go down to London to prepare for the Boat Show. I knew the show would be a golden opportunity to meet people who might be important to furthering my sailing career.

Each day of the show I would sit on board *Iduna* and talk to passers-by who showed an interest, or go to functions held by some of the sponsors that had helped me get around Britain. I spent a lot of time with Brian, who was revelling in the fact that I had made it all the way round and was talking enthusiastically about it to everyone.

I'd invited Mum down to London in the hope it would be a welcome break from life at home and she came along to the show. One afternoon I left her alone briefly to man the boat and when I returned she handed me a card left by someone called Mark Turner. Intrigued, we went to meet him on his stand but missed him – a less than successful start to a relationship that was to become one of the most important of my life.

We did meet the following day, however. Mark was an athletic-looking guy who I guessed was in his early thirties and at the show because he worked in the marine industry for a company called Spinlock. He had heard that I had done my round Britain trip single-handed and wanted to talk about the race Merv and I had discussed, the Mini Transat. Fluent in French, Mark had contributed to the article about the Mini in *Yachting World*, which I had read so avidly and so often. In it he'd mentioned he might be interested in doing the race himself, and they printed that. That was enough for Mark, who is not one to dodge a challenge, and the Mini in 1997 became an unbreakable commitment. We parted on the understanding that if I decided I might be doing the race, we would talk again.

For the rest of the show I wrestled with a dilemma that had become increasingly clear and I knew that I had to make a difficult choice. I began to doubt whether I could manage further projects alongside the Sea Cadets job. There was no shortage of reasons why I shouldn't just carry on with the job, and move *Iduna* to the South Coast to live on her in Gosport. But the morning after my first meeting with Mark, I had woken with a start. I could sense that burning feeling inside me once more, and was certain deep down that I had to choose racing.

I knew from my own trip around Britain that a venture demands 100 per cent commitment to be successful. I couldn't take the Sea Cadets job without such commitment, nor would I be able to pursue racing if I lacked it. I needed to seek advice and once again I turned to Brian.

He helped me to clarify things. Although he thought the Sea Cadets offered a great opportunity to do something I loved, he saw the danger in starting something I was not entirely committed to. I drafted a letter to send to Barry Mattey, explaining that while at the Boat Show, my exposure to new options had meant I'd come to a decision:

These options will allow me to get a foothold in the short-handed trans-ocean racing field, which is where my long-term ambitions lie . . . it would be inappropriate to instruct Cadets if my heart could not be 100 per cent devoted to that task.

I concluded that I had 'a very real opportunity of fulfilling dreams which have driven my enthusiasm for sailing for some years'.

I hoped with all my heart that Barry would understand.

Just four days later Mum called me to say a letter from Gosport had come for me and asked if I wanted her to read it over the phone. I was petrified of what I was going to hear, but asked her to none the less. Barry began by saying he'd had mixed feelings when he read my letter. He was disappointed that I would not be working with them, but went on to say, 'However I am very pleased for you and if there are any opportunities out there for you as a yachts-woman then grasp them with both hands.'

The relief was unbelievable. I could not imagine anyone could have written a more sensitive or supportive reply. He finished by insisting that I should be neither too proud nor too shy to let them know if my plans went awry for any reason in the future.

Things moved quickly after the show. I needed to make my home on the South Coast because this was the only place I could learn to race. I had everything to learn, and my limited experience of racing *Panic Major* out of Hull only emphasized that. I decided that I would base *Iduna* on the Hamble, the river I had sailed from for my Instructor's examination; and yet again Brian helped me out, finding a marina that would let me leave *Iduna* on her trailer for a few months for free. We were about to begin a whole new adventure.

*

Meeting Mark at the Boat Show had fired my imagination, and by the beginning of February I was on my way to the Isle of Wight to see him. He appeared at the door of his office in jeans and a rugby shirt. He smiled as he welcomed me in, but seemed distracted by other things. I followed him up a flight of winding steps.

'I've just got to finish this, are you OK to wait for a while?'

'No worries,' I replied, and pulled out my notes I'd printed on Nan's word processor, and sat down at a desk to the side of the room to work. I flicked through a few documents and calendars I had been working on to help make the Mini Transat project work over the months ahead. It was very much on the list of 'things to do', but it was an ocean race, a transatlantic ocean race. I'd never crossed the Atlantic before and I was desperate to get more experience. I read through the two-page agenda I'd prepared. There were fourteen items, to show Mark what I personally could bring to any project, but in truth there was little concrete on offer.

11. I have a problem in that I am trying to make a living out of all this, so it's just slightly important to get sponsorship! I would be quite happy to belong to a company! Do you reckon I'd make a successful mascot!

Exclamation marks were a common element in any text I put down on paper. I was a bundle of energy, just desperate to get on with things.

The list read on . . .

14. Finally – *We must go sailing together!!* – Who knows, we might not get on?

I peered over my papers through the window, and caught my breath on seeing the view. I could see beyond the river, all the way out to the Solent. The navigation marks were flashing in the channel, and I could hear the Red Funnel ferry engine as it docked just a few hundred yards down river. Mark was oblivious to all this and was typing away as if his life depended on it. Anyone could have walked in and dropped something on his desk, and I swear he would not even have noticed. I had never met anyone who seemed so confident in the use of computers. Mark had so many projects going on professionally, but also clearly on a personal level – I saw his collection of posters from the races he had done. He virtually lived in his office, and I guessed from the futon on the floor and the duvet in the cupboard that he worked some long nights. It was immediately obvious how industrious and dedicated he was.

Although his present job was primarily office-based, he was visibly someone who just went out there and got on with it. Incredibly, at the age of twenty-one, he had already sailed in the 1989–90 Whitbread Round the World Race. I learned that he had been to university in Exeter before joining the Royal Navy, where he stayed for six years but left after feeling quite simply like too small a cog in a big machine. It turned out that he had raced in 1994 in the two-handed Round Britain Race on Merv's boat *Maverick* when she was fresh from the yard. They had encountered problems and had not done too well, but one thing was for sure, I was sitting in the same room as someone who had exactly the same interests as me – short-handed ocean sailing.

It is difficult to place your finger on what it is about short-handed sailing that is so special. The guys that race single- or two-handed are not necessarily the best at any specific job on a boat but do have to be the most resourceful and widely knowledgeable about all aspects of sailing. Unlike racing round buoys in an estuary, short-handers tend to be good on longer events where stamina and the ability to maintain an even level of good performance are more important than flashes of pure brilliance. Above all there is an unwritten bond that ties the skippers together along with the sea, all realizing how they depend upon each other.

Mark was new to single-handing and though very positive, was clearly nervous about the prospect of racing in the Mini Transat. We talked about other events using the same boats – the Mini Fastnet and Trans-Gascogne the following year and basically just about every Mini race there was or ever had been. The Mini is an unforgiving but ultimately very rewarding race; it hits home hard that you're sailing thousands of miles of open ocean alone in a truly tiny boat.

It's impossible to hide from the dangers of the Mini and tragically there has on average been one entrant lost each time it's taken place.

We broke off briefly to eat a Chinese takeaway and then worked on until about 2 a.m., when he gave me a lift to my guesthouse in his old Fiesta. It had been a brief but valuable insight into the life of Mark Turner.

Dad was out of the spinal unit by now and back at home with us, but he was far from recovered. He had to be very careful moving around and had great difficulty walking. As a result of lying flat for so long his legs were swollen and uncomfortable, but the hardest part must have been not knowing if the feeling would ever return – only time would tell. The rest of us were just relieved to have him back but it was upsetting to see the frustration in his eyes at not being able to do all he could previously. But he wouldn't give in, and it was that spirit which kept him positive. I think Mum and Dad were also very conscious that I was in the process of leaving home. They knew now that sailing would be my career, and had accepted that it was highly unlikely I would ever go to university.

In mid-March the day finally came for my move south. I collected together my clothes, bike and the other personal belongings I needed to move on board *Iduna*. We planned to drive down in the evening and spend a full day organizing everything before Mum returned to Derbyshire the following day.

We arrived late at our B&B near the Hamble and went straight to our room. As we laughed at shared memories and with relief at having Dad home, I talked to Mum about her worries. We topped up the tea, and Mum spoke about Nan, Gran and Lewis. By this stage Lewis was looking at moving down to a different part of the South Coast to live with his new girlfriend and it was wonderful to see him so positive after the disappointment of leaving university. Nan and Gran, though, were very ill: Gran had lost a terrific amount of weight, and had been at her worst while Dad was in hospital. We had recently discovered that it was her thyroid which was causing the problem and at least the diagnosis meant there was now a possibility of treatment. Nan, however, was not really improving.

The only glimmer of positive news was when the consultant at the Chest Clinic suggested she went back to university to finish her degree. I think it was his way of gently acknowledging that Nan would not get better. For her, though, it was the best news possible and something to get her teeth into it once again. She would return in September. Although Mum was happy for her, I couldn't help but feel she was a little apprehensive at having to run Nan to college and back each day. But Mum was Mum, and she would go on trying to please others till she dropped.

We had a frustrating time looking for a marina to berth *Iduna*. Moorings were expensive and much sought after, but I could no longer keep her where she'd been sitting on her trailer since I brought her down after the Boat Show. With each visit we found the fees still out of reach, and, weary at the end of the day, we reluctantly got back into the car and headed for the last marina on the list. I had been told that it was the most expensive, so we drove in feeling gloomy. It certainly seemed like one of the places to be. There were all sorts of boats around, racers and cruisers, all sizes – some absolutely enormous. If I was going to meet people to race with this must be one of the best options, but I simply could not afford to keep *Iduna* here. I had managed to save up just over £2,000 – that would not even cover the mooring fees in a marina like this. We drove past the brokerage, bar and the offices and at that point I couldn't help but feel that it wasn't the place for us, but we continued on past a sign saying Hamble Yacht Services. The clinical feeling that had put us off the other marinas vanished. There were enormous sheds and another pontoon. It was a hive of activity, a working boat yard. There were so many boats everywhere, in travel hoists slung above the ground or chocked up across the yard that we could not even make out the other side. I now had a good feeling about this place.

We found the dock office in a small Portakabin by the walkway to the pontoon. I knocked on the door, which was slightly ajar. 'Come in,' said a voice on the other side and as we entered we were immediately greeted by a smile.

'How can I help you, my love?' he said, and I began to explain that I was looking for an annual berth. He didn't hang around with his quote for very long and said it'd be £1,000. I could have hugged him to say thanks. Though we didn't know it then, Jim was to become one of the very few friends I made on the South Coast.

We returned to *Iduna* after shopping for essentials in Southampton. It was getting dark now and had been raining on and off for hours. We piled everything out of the car and put it on board. It suddenly dawned on me that Mum was about to leave. In the half-light the yard was grey, damp and empty except for the two of us standing by the tiny boat and the car. As we hugged goodbye I heard the wind whistle through the forest of masts. Mum's door clunked shut for the last time and I cried as I watched her rear lights vanish in the rain.

I climbed on board *Iduna*, trying to take my mind off Mum's departure by stowing the remaining gear in the cabin. Everything was damp and I was exhausted. When the only torch I could find began to die, I decided to get some sleep. My bunk was full of gear which was virtually impossible to move, so I wrapped myself as comfortably as I could around the outboard's propeller on the cabin floor and pulled my sleeping-bag over me. As I lay there on my belongings and listened to the alien sounds of my new home, I felt more alone than ever before. 'You've got to make the best of this, kiddo,' I whispered, and closed my eyes.

The first weeks in Hamble were difficult as I tried to settle into my new environment and work out how my life in the south was going to take shape. I was shocked at how few people I was meeting. When I was in Hull, strangers would come up and introduce themselves and ask what I was up to. In Hamble it just never happened, the only faces I knew were the guys in the yard, and Jim of course, who was always happy to have a friendly chat. I suppose a scruffy-looking little 21-foot boat with a handful of stickers on her side doesn't really look that cool next to a stunning collection of pristine race boats. I felt very out of place. Everyone else seemed to belong to this boat or that team and it's not something you can easily break into.

Without company in the evenings, after seeing the sun set along the river I would often walk to the end of the pontoons and sit watching the flashing navigation lights and the water flowing round the boats. Sometimes I would even do handstands and cartwheels along the planked pontoons – it felt fantastic to be able to stretch out after spending so much time working in *Iduna*'s cramped cabin. But the freedom to enjoy this release was restricted at the weekends when the character of the yard changed completely. The weekend racers would descend on the village, lining the streets with their expensive cars. The commotion would start early in the morning. Gaggles of people would file past *Iduna* while I sat in her cockpit, sometimes writing, sometimes reading, hoping that someone might come up and ask if I was free because they were one man down. But that didn't happen. By mid-morning the pontoons would be silent again while the boats raced before returning in the after-noon, everybody rushing in eager to fill the bars. I hated the weekend evenings, Hamble was buzzing, but I was never a part of it. I eventually plucked up the courage to visit a pub in the village where I knew the racing crews hung out, but I felt like a fish out of water. My face must have been beetroot as I edged my way to the bar, overhearing their tales of the day's racing. I bought a beer and sat at the bar, slowly sipping away. People crammed in alongside me but I felt as though I was just observing what was going on and regretted having come. The high point of the evening was when someone I'd seen in the yard came up to buy drinks and recognized me. We spoke briefly before he returned with his drinks to his friends. I finished up and left, thankful for any friendly human contact.

It was weeks before I got to sail as part of a crew racing around the 'cans'. It was organized by Ashley Perrin, with whom I'd made contact after the last Boat Show when she was described to me as someone who 'has a similar determination to yourself'. She was planning to compete in the 1997 two-handed Round Britain and Ireland race and we'd stayed in touch. We arranged to meet at the Royal Ocean Racing Club and I remember being a little fazed by Ashley's confidence; though just over a year younger than me, she seemed mature for her age and clearly felt quite at home in the

Yacht Club, which along with the surroundings made me feel self-conscious.

I found my first race pretty difficult. I wasn't used to playing just one role on a boat. Everyone on board seemed to know exactly what needed to be done, well trained to the point where it seemed they had been doing this all their lives. Every manoeuvre was like an army drill. It meant each person learned a sequence of events in an almost robotic manner and the raised voices on board just reinforced the military feeling. My kind of sailing had never been like this. I was used to sailing off the seat of my pants, using common sense and feel. I handled things as they came along, which meant being aware of wind, tide and boat speed, and a hundred other things all at the same time. This was very different; on this boat we had specific, inflexible roles and I found it difficult to fit in.

As the days rolled by I worked on my computer, writing new proposals for sponsorships and a newsletter to let people know what was happening to me, as for many it must have seemed that I had disappeared off the face of the earth. I knew that if things became financially impossible I could attempt to get a job as a sailing instructor, but I wanted to hold back on that. If I was going to give racing a fair crack I had to hang in there longer and try harder to gain experience and contact more sponsors, and be ready to grasp an opportunity if it arose.

Not long after returning to *Iduna* from my first race across the Channel to Le Havre, I received a phone-call from Merv that was going to shape the year 1996 completely. Merv had been in Hamble for a while, preparing his crew for the BT Global Challenge, and had often supplemented my meagre rations with food left over from his weekend's sailing. This time, though, his help was to prove much more significant. He'd recommended me for a preparateur's job on an Open 60 which had been chartered by his friend Alan Wynne-Thomas. I asked what 'preparateur' meant and he told me it was a French term for the people who prepare racing boats. Merv wanted to make sure that I was interested. My job would be to prepare the boat in Plymouth for the Europe One Star (Single-handed) Transatlantic Race, then sail her back from the US with her skipper Alan Wynne-Thomas, before getting her ready for the ultimate: the Vendée Globe. I tried to sound calm on the phone, but I'm not sure I managed to. I had only dreamt of sailing on a boat like this. Simply to be around one was a thrill.

I arrived in Plymouth a week later on 1 June 1996 – exactly twelve months since I had set off to sail around Great Britain. The sun shone as I checked over the boat. There was no sign of Alan on board, so I put my bags in the cockpit and, as Merv had suggested, went to find him in the bar.

Alan was a short, stocky man, with a weathered face, a twinkle in his eyes, an infectious grin, and curly brown hair. He was wearing a red and black lumberjack shirt and jeans, and did not look in the least bit like a sailor. I liked him instantly. He was laughing with friends in the bar so I grabbed a drink and sat down. Once Alan and I were alone, we began to discuss the programme for the boat, newly christened *Elan Sifo*. I must have asked Alan a hundred questions about his life. He was a natural single-handed sailor, and at over fifty had a wealth of experience. He seemed to have raced everything across the Atlantic from his own 40-footer, *Jemima Nicolas*, to a 40-foot trimaran, and above all he had already competed in the Vendée Globe, although the last time he took part had almost led to disaster for him.

We talked and worked on board for the rest of the day before Alan returned home to Scotland for the last time before the race. I had to organize the collection of sails for repair and replacement, clean the boat, check the ropes, fix some of the electronics. At times I was out of my depth but knew it, so sought advice from people in the yard, learning as I worked. I absolutely loved it. I kept reminding myself that Alan was about to cross the Atlantic and that everything had to be right.

Alan returned from Scotland in time to make final preparations for racing before we finally moored her up with the other boats competing in the race. I looked out at a marina packed full of the world's most innovative and hi-tech ocean-racing boats and felt inspired. Each one was going to set off across the North Atlantic with just one person on board. As we tied *Elan Sifo* up among them,

I could only think of sprinting off around the marina to look at them all.

Everything about being in Plymouth seemed to seal my fate, from the marina full of Open 60s and space-age multihulls to, more importantly, the people. This was what I had to do, I was in the thick of it and felt like I had really arrived. Alan was the best guy I could possibly imagine working for; he would take me to the receptions that were held for teams at the Yacht Club, introducing me to many of the other skippers and preparateurs, people like Yves Parlier, skipper of the extraordinary *Aquitaine Innovations*, or Vittorio Mallingri, who'd competed in the same Vendée Globe as Alan. Although we met only briefly, Vittorio gave me his brother's telephone number and said that if I wanted to race with him in the Quebec–St-Malo race in August, I should give him a call.

The single-handed racing scene was a small world and I was overwhelmed by how welcoming everyone was. Even the competing skippers seemed really close-knit and, although they were clearly highly competitive, there was no visible aggression between them or their teams. If anything, the opposite was true, as tools were shared happily if a rival was missing something; it was a wonderful atmosphere. I felt embarrassed by my very rudimentary French which sometimes made communicating frustrating in what had become a French-dominated sport. This was never a problem with Gerry Rouffs, a French-Canadian skipper who, like Alan, was aiming to take part in the Vendée Globe later in the year. He too made me feel at home immediately. Ironically, despite the differences in language and culture among the teams and my own inexperience, I was already beginning to feel like a part of this incredible world.

When start day arrived I think I was more nervous than Alan, and as he went to the clubhouse for his final shower I checked over the boat time and time again, switching on all the electronics and starting the little generator for a final battery charge. There was no room for error, Alan was going to be out there for over two weeks, sailing through everything from storms to icebergs to calms. I checked through the water and food we'd put on board, the spares, the fuel; this was my last chance to make sure everything was ready and on board.

I had asked Mum and Dad if they would come down on the day of the start so they could see what I had been up to. Dad was mobile enough now, though still a little unsteady on his feet, and this was to be his first trip of any distance since his accident. Alan had arranged for them to watch the start from his friends' catamaran, which we thought would be more stable. They'd seen me in Hull and sailing *Iduna*, but this was completely different. I wanted them to know that this was where I hoped my future would lie. The weather was beautiful and they couldn't have seen it in a better light. I hoped they shared my pride in watching Alan's departure.

He seemed relaxed as we were towed out of the marina. There were a few cheers as we left the dock, and once clear of the first breakwater we unfurled the headsail. Our towboat departed for its next customer, and we slowly headed out to clearer water. It felt wonderfully quiet all of a sudden, with just the distant applause in the marina still within range.

There was just time to hug Alan goodbye and jump off *Elan Sifo* into a support RIB before the ten-minute gun fired. And although I could feel the tension in the air and sense the strain these sailors would be under for the next few weeks, I knew that one day I wanted to take that same start line myself.

Then the start gun fired and they were off.

Chapter Eight

After the start of the race, I went home to *Iduna* and followed Alan's progress as often as I could through the RWYC. Two weeks later I flew to Boston to join him for the sail home. It was the first time I'd been to America and I hadn't timed my arrival very well. I was due in at eight o'clock in the evening but Newport was a two-hour drive away and I didn't have a driving licence. Even more cleverly, I'd managed to land on 4 July – Independence Day. Well done, I said to myself as I walked rather nervously round to Customs and Immigration. I was fortunate to catch a night bus to Newport.

Alan had had a hard race and finished tenth in his class. It had been eighteen days, eighteen hours and fourteen seconds since that gun had fired and I had watched him sail west from Plymouth.

We had only three days in America and they flew by. After restocking *Elan Sifo* from the supermarket and making the few necessary repairs, we still had some time to spend enjoying ourselves. I'd hoped to find Vittorio to talk about racing with his brothers, but had no luck. I would have to ring when I returned to Europe. And anyway, I needed to see how this crossing went first.

Our departure was on 8 July, my birthday. Alan took me to a bar on the High Street, not far from the boat. Though now twenty, I was still too young to drink in America – but we celebrated anyway!

It was five o'clock when we left. The sky was foggy and there was an air of caution around. A hurricane was developing a long way south, but as it was predicted to be five days away, we decided to cross ahead of its path. Whilst there was some nervous anticipation of the crossing to come, I did not worry. I felt comfortable with Alan and I knew I'd be safe with him. We saw little of the harbour or coastline, just the last outlying rocks as we slipped away, knowing that if all went to plan our next sighting would be the French port of Les Sables d'Olonne. As our world became the ocean I stood on the bow, and looking back at Alan across *Elan Sifo*'s enormous deck, I knew that he would be my only human contact for the next two weeks. We were on our way, and it was the best birthday present I could possibly have had.

I learned fast on the trip, through both advice and experience. On day three I had to climb to the top of the mast to retrieve the main halyard. I had only been up tall masts in the harbour before; and as the sea was relatively flat I jumped at the chance to let Alan hoist me up it. I returned to the deck completely exhausted; I had found it hard enough just to hang on, let alone bring the halyard down.

On one occasion we also lost all the instruments, including the autopilot, which meant that someone had to steer her all the time. We took turns trying to work out what was wrong before I discovered that a loose piece of antenna aerial in the pilot compartment had shorted and was fizzing away. It was straightforward to fix but drove home how easily one tiny thing can cause such a massive problem. If it had happened during Alan's race, it would probably all have been over for him – nobody can helm for more than a couple of days without any kind of break.

Alan and I got on famously, regularly falling into fits of laughter. He had an incredibly engaging way of telling his stories, which left you no option but to laugh as his face slowly broke into a wide smile and his key words became completely over-pronounced in his eagerness to get the point across. I would question him endlessly, and he would talk patiently for hours about his experiences. We spoke about his last attempt at the Vendée Globe in 1992–3. He had been in fifth position in the Southern Ocean when he was hit by storm-force winds, and his boat was lifted and rolled by a freak wave. Alan was flung across the cabin whilst asleep in his bunk, landing on the cabin sole face down in bilge water – that was where he woke, choking and starved of breath. Although he did not know it then, he had broken six ribs, one of which had punctured his lung. A lesser mortal would have drowned there and then in the bilge water, but not Alan. He spent hours lying exhausted, trying to collect together enough energy to sew his sails, which were badly damaged after his roll. After several weeks of fighting for his life he struggled into Tasmania – his survival was a mystery to the doctors who could not understand how his body had coped. No one really knows how he did it; I'm not sure he does himself, but it wasn't just his determination I had respect for, it was the fact that although he had been through what can only be described as a worst night-mare, he had not only picked himself up, but retained the ambition to get back out there and do it again. I was so lucky to have a teacher like him on my first ocean passage.

After a week at sea we were caught in the tail-end of Hurricane Bertha, which since our departure had swept up the Florida Keys towards Newport. This was my first real storm at sea, and the memory of watching the clear skies disappear quickly behind a solid-looking blanket of black clouds remains vivid. The water changed from bright blue to dark grey, and the evening lost its yellow warmth as it was suffocated by the advancing front. Though afraid of what might happen, I was comforted by Alan's composure. He was alert but relaxed, still effortlessly bringing a smile to my face.

It was two days before the storm relented. I was transfixed by the sheer size and power of the waves, and fascinated by the way *Elan Sifo* would weave her way through them, so rarely faltering even under autopilot. She would regularly fall off the waves, slamming uncomfortably into them, which sent a shudder through every one of her 60 feet. I had felt myself stepping up a gear; and though this was clearly time for calm heads, I was excited and enjoying myself. I would helm for hours as we sped along, trying to carve our way through the waves. Looking back in our log book, I saw that I had reached a surfing speed of 19.54 knots, which was by far my fastest ever – as much a result of the big waves as the 40 knots of wind we were experiencing. Even with the tiny triangles of sail we had hoisted we were powering along. Alan seemed frustrated by the storm and tired of the slamming, whereas I was raring to get back up for my next three-hour watch, and was actually revelling in the challenge of it. One night-time watch when I was sitting on the helm, I realized just how exhausted Alan must be. After all, he had just done three times what we'd been through, alone, and in a race situation. On reflection I felt particularly responsible.

I was on watch on the morning when the French coast loomed into view. I knew it was coming but had tried to imagine it wouldn't. When I could make out the chimneys of Les Sables d'Olonne through the gentle haze, I couldn't help but feel sad. I hadn't wanted the trip to end, and toyed with the idea of saying nothing to Alan and turning back out to sea. Although we had been out there for two weeks and sailed through testing conditions, I had absolutely loved it. We really had sailed across the Atlantic and I knew I was doing what I'd been born to do.

Alan left at dawn the following day to get back to Scotland, leaving us with just a few hours the night before to say our goodbyes and collect our thoughts together. It was a still evening with a clear sky and we sat in the cockpit for a while chatting before turning into our bunks. I felt quite inadequate that evening, and desperately wanted to tell Alan just how much the trip had meant to me. Too soon by far it was time to turn in, and as we stood up to climb below he reached over to hug me.

'Thanks, kiddo, you've done a great job.'

'Thanks too,' I said, 'it's been fantastic.'

With tears of joy hidden by the darkness I knew there was no need to say more; in that moment I realized that if there was anyone in the world who understood, it was Alan.

Chapter Nine

I stayed in Les Sables d'Olonne for a few days after we finished the transatlantic crossing. It's a very special place for single-handed sailors. As the start and finish town for the Vendée Globe it definitely has an aura. While I was there something seemed to trigger inside me, and each morning at dawn I'd get up and run to the empty beach, strip down to my underwear and dive into the sea. I was so happy to be there, so happy with everything in my life and maybe, even then, deep down I was thinking I'd be back just four years later to start the Vendée myself.

I knew at the end of my crossing with Alan that I had to call Vittorio's brother. The start of the Quebec–St-Malo was two weeks later and I was going to have to get my skates on.

I still had to raise the funds to get out to Canada, though, and while catching up with Merv and hearing about his preparations for the start of the BT Global Challenge at Ocean Village, an opportunity arose to make the plane fare. My paintings of the fleet were going down well with the BT crews and Mike Golding had asked if I could do a large one. The fee was just right and soon I was on a plane heading back across the Atlantic. I could think of nothing but the race which lay ahead.

I stared for hours at the maps in the in-flight magazine, looking at the route we would be taking. Though I knew we were sailing out of the St Lawrence River, I hadn't realized that it would be 600 miles before we cleared its mouth and over a third of the trip before we sailed past the south-eastern tip of Newfoundland. The shortest route from Quebec to the English Channel actually takes you to the north of Newfoundland, and even though we would be keeping to its south, this was going to be nothing like the Transat with Alan. We would be venturing into iceberg territory.

On arrival I cursed myself for not trying harder to learn French during my Transat with Alan. I managed to get on the right bus, but when the bus driver pointed to the various stop names in Quebec I had no idea which was my destination. I said, 'Bateau, bateau de course,' and he nodded, though I'm not sure he understood as when he signalled that I should get off the coach after a journey of several hours, the water was nowhere to be seen. After years of family holidays planned with military precision I felt I had let the side down – I'd just flown into a country I'd never been to before without so much as an address. And on top of that, I had met the skipper I was sailing with for less than five minutes and had no idea of who else might be on the boat!

Heading downhill seemed like common sense and I was relieved to stumble upon the marina after just over an hour's walk. Exhausted and apprehensive, I wandered along the busy pontoon in search of Vittorio Mallingri's boat *Anicaflash*, just glad that I'd made it to the marina before sunset.

Vittorio had designed and built *Anicaflash* with his father, the goal being to compete in the same Vendée as Alan; he failed to finish the race due to steering problems, and then, in true Vittorio fashion, chose the port of Tahiti, 3,000 miles away, as his port of refuge! He was tall and thin, with wild, adventurous eyes, jet-black curly hair and an almost permanent smile. His brother Enrico, known to all as Toto, had a similar complexion but was short, strong and solid and, with a business career, had a less wild character and was far more organized. Claudio, six foot and built like a gladiator, had a gentle, friendly nature and, as it turned out, was competing in the Mini Transat the following year. Of all the Italians on the boat he was the one who spoke the least English, which was a shame as I would have loved to have chatted to him about the Mini. Andrea, a hydrodynamics expert who had worked on several boats' keel forms, was around the same age as the rest of the guys but kept himself pretty much to himself, and as a result I was more wary of him. Finally there was Giulio, a small, charismatic man who'd recovered from an almost crippling accident in an earlier career as a freestyle windsurfer. Vittorio explained to me that we would work in two watches of three. Giulio and I would be in his watch, while the other would consist of Toto, Andrea and Claudio. I could not wait to get going and set about checking lockers and fittings under the amused gaze of the crew.

The few days in Quebec preparing *Anicaflash* for the race seemed to be dominated by stocking up on food – fresh coffee, fruit, salami, bacon, eggs, tomatoes, garlic and of course pasta. This was a real eye-opener for someone who considered a ketchup sandwich a treat and thought that racing meant you were only allowed weight-saving, freeze-dried 'fuel' without worrying about how it might affect your soul.

On our final night ashore we all sat around in the cockpit, talking and drinking cans of beer. It was still warm, and our faces were lit by a faint glow from the cabin entrance. I felt happy, truly content, and calm in the presence of these guys who were making every effort to include me. As I glanced around the cabin from my sleeping-bag that evening I felt I would develop some very good friendships over the following weeks.

Once the stress of the start was over, we began to take in the beauty of the area we were sailing through. It was unlike anything I had seen before, the gradually widening river with its lush green banks scattered with little villages that turned to clusters of fairy-lights at night. We were demoralized by mistakes at the start which had left us well adrift of the rest of the fleet but as each of us, one by one, cracked some kind of joke, our spirits lifted and we began to bond more tightly as a team. By morning we were in the lead of the monohulls, and though only briefly, we had made remarkable progress to catch up with the leaders; it was reassuring to be back in the match! It was a whole different atmosphere out there in a race situation, we had been in sight of another boat virtually all the time from the moment we left, and the strain of balancing on the knife edge of pushing as hard as you could, but not too hard, was really tiring. When I had sailed with Alan on *Elan Sifo* we had sailed with the autopilot on virtually all the time, and just steered for fun, but this was different, we were steering for speed, and if that meant spending two or three hours at a time at the helm during your watch, so be it.

On day three we left the mouth of the St Lawrence Seaway, and although I was looking forward to the Atlantic Ocean once more, I was sad to see the beauty of the mountains disappear into the distance. Over the following few days we passed south of Newfoundland, so were not out in deep water. The Grand Banks and Flemish Cap are renowned for horrendous seas in bad weather, and for the next couple of days we would be crossing it.

14/8/96 (Day 4)
Vittorio made breakfast, bacon eggs and toast.

Strange day. Toto not too good at all. Spent day in bed with flu-type symptoms. Feverish in the night and a painful back. We think he maybe caught something in the water in Quebec when fixing the keel. Saw sharks in the evening – I saw two. It was a quiet evening. Our world had shrunk by dusk, as the famous Newfoundland fog had arrived. Visibility down to about quarter of a mile.

A ship loomed out of fog, not too far away. Light airs, with many sail changes. Hadn't eaten since breakfast, so mixed salad made by Giulio very welcome! Turned in at 2000 after sunset. Had a chat with Vittorio about what it was like in the Southern Ocean – enlightening, but I still feel I have to go there myself!

Our watches were particularly tiring and I could often be helming for hours as Giulio, who did not steer, and Vittorio spent a great deal of time down below communicating and navigating. At the end of my watch I would collapse with exhaustion into my bunk or on to the floor. I soon realized that the two, three or sometimes four hours of helming I would do on the trot would become quite commonplace, and relished the challenge.

Vittorio finally came on deck after another hard watch at the chart table where he had been studying the charts so closely that he had the Grand Banks imprinted on his forehead. I immediately handed him the helm and dashed to the back of the boat for a pee – I had wanted to do that for a good two hours!

The wildlife further north in the Atlantic was like nothing I had ever seen before. We'd seen the albino-looking Beluga whales as we crossed the St Lawrence entrance, and Pilot whales once we were away from the coast. Now we were seeing massive pods of up to fifty dolphins firing alongside us, whatever the weather. As we passed Newfoundland we saw several sharks silently slipping along just beneath the water's surface. I was hypnotized by the wildlife, looking out across the waves for any hint of movement, and amazed at how many species were around us when we moved further away from the land into colder water. Even the seagulls were still around, swooping in and out of the waves, their wingtips a paper-thickness away from the wave tops. I wrote a great deal about the wildlife during the crossing, just to try to capture the impact it had made on me.

During helming this morning I had dolphins for over an hour! In the end there must have been at least fifty, you could see them coming from all directions. About twenty swam under the bow, and the rest alongside. As the waves fell away, they jumped clear, and into the trough of the wave ahead. Giulio took photos but I couldn't (because helming!). As the dolphins left the water you could see them looking at you, as if to say 'Hi, guys, we haven't seen anyone around here for a while – we'll keep you company for a bit.' From the stern their grey bodies glimmered in the white light of the rising sun ahead; another grey but beautiful day.

Life inside the cabin was not too comfortable, particularly after the water ballast tank holding 2 tons of water sprang a fairly rapid high-pressure leak and left us with its contents slopping about on the floor. Claudio and Vittorio were working away, trying to fix it with epoxy resin, so, exhausted after a serious lack of sleep I made the most of the light winds and dragged my sleeping bag on to what was thankfully a dry deck. I had slept no more than three hours in three days, and had no idea why. I can generally sleep on my head if I need to but I was struggling here. At last, though, with the cool afternoon air blowing over my face, I fell asleep.

'Hey, Ellen! Iceberg!'

I leapt up and made for the leeward side so I could look under the boom. I expected to see a small floating lump of ice but what greeted me was a colossal ice mountain that had formed into three peaks, two of them the size of tower blocks. The cold radiated off them as if we had sailed into a fridge. I knew I could never capture anything so dramatic with my throwaway camera so I made coffee for everyone while they took pictures of each other with the berg in the background. By now Claudio and Vittorio had finished repairing the ballast tank, and I gratefully took my sleeping-bag down to a bunk.

On waking there was bad news. We'd run out of gas and although we had spare canisters on board, they had the wrong adaptor, so were completely useless. The prospect of having to do without a cup of tea for the rest of the crossing was bad enough, but the thought of having to try to fashion something cold out of all that pasta made me wish I'd brought some of Mum's flapjack! The lesson was well learned, though, as I've always sailed with a box of her homemade treat since!

A more significant cause for concern came through on one of the weather faxes. A big storm was on its way. As if that was not enough, we had just discovered that the ballast tank repair had given up and, once the mess was cleared up, faced up to the fact that we would not be able to use the ballast system. We had already experienced the problems of handling *Anicaflash* with no water ballast and in a storm the lack of that added weight to help us punch through the waves would be far worse. That night the clouds became more dense and the wind began to build.

I took over the helm as the first hint of dawn washed into the sky, wearing the 'full metal jacket' of protective kit the conditions would demand. Only my eyes were visible. I was immediately struck by how much harder it was on the helm. We had a lot of sail up and it was taking all my strength to hold her on track as she was taken by the gusts and desperately tried to turn up into wind – a boat instinctively wants to do this when overpressed. My arms were throbbing and pains shot through my elbows. I could only relieve the tension by straightening my arms and using my legs like hydraulic rams. This was sailing on the limit, and much as it hurt, I was in my element. For the first time ever I sailed at over 20 knots through the water and there is nothing to beat it – absolutely nothing!

At about 0100 there was a loud crack, the speed dropped instantly, and the helm died. I shouted for Vittorio, as I didn't dare leave the tiller. The spinnaker halyard had parted and we had a 90-foot-long, 3,000-foot-square sail dragging in the water.

Everyone was on deck to pull in the material, bit by bit, over the guard wires, but as well as getting the sail on deck we also had to retrieve the spinnaker halyard. We only had one and Vittorio had no choice but to climb the mast to feed another in. I was steering, and tried desperately to stick to as 'rock-solid' a course as possible, but the boat still rolled in the waves, which I knew would feel horribly magnified at the top of the mast. I felt that if I made any sort of over-aggressive movement of the helm I risked shaking Vittorio off – a danger made more real because he had to climb the final few feet without a line to his harness; the only halyard to the top was the one he was to fit.

It was dramatically evident that night just how responsible we were for each other and how much trust we placed in each other. On *Iduna* I had only myself to look after, but I knew now that I was worrying far more about the others. It was obviously more of an acute feeling when Vittorio was literally hanging on for his life, but whether you are helming the boat or making decisions at the chart table, you are doing so for the others too, some of whom will be sleeping helplessly below. I felt enormous responsibility.

That night had only been a mild indication of what was to come, as the weather deteriorated further. The hard thing was that the watches were not getting any shorter and I was really beginning to feel it. *Anicaflash*'s steering system is basic to say the least, as she'd been designed to take a wheel, then crudely modified to be helmed with a tiller. The tiller itself was quite long, but almost inaccessible being so close to the deck, so we relied on the tiller extension. On top of that the steering position was appalling. There was nowhere to sit other than in the seat part of a legless plastic chair on the deck. My problem was that I was too light and my legs were too short, so the chair always slid at the crucial moment and I found myself steering on my knees, where I could brace myself against a lip on the hatch. After twenty minutes of this, with the blood-flow restricted behind my knees, I'd lose the feeling in my feet and I also had no way of stopping the water which came rushing down the deck from sluicing up my trouser legs. I would finish a watch soaked beyond my knees and past my elbows. It would always take ten minutes of pins-and-needles hell before I got my sensation back.

'There'll be some really big ones when the bow just drops away, try not to fall down there, but go across – and hold on!' said Vittorio as he passed the tiller across. He then left for the cover of the cuddy. The waves were now immense, they were long, and very, very steep. Looking behind was like looking up at a mountainside, but jet black fringed with lighter water. The breakers were also getting bigger, some tumbling in behind, in *Anicaflash*'s wake. Within 60 seconds I had surfed, stalled and was soaked completely up to my elbows in icy water. As my body moved I could feel the water working its way up inside my oilies! Very soon my feet were numb, not so much from the cold, but from sitting on them! But it's tricky to even shift slightly for relief as this means a moment when you are not 100 per cent ready to react with the tiller. When cramp sets in it's nasty but the helm's more important. The wind died a little, followed shortly after by a strong rain squall. The stars disappeared, and the sheets of driving rain were illuminated by the navigation light at the masthead. Through the distorting perspex window, I could see the figure of Vittorio in the candle-like glow from the cabin lights, clad only in a yellow fleece, compared to my total protection. My feeling of exposure was emphasized – like looking through a pub window on a cold, wet night!

Never before had I been in so much pain from aches and bruises, without an opportunity to stop and relax. I was abusing my body and as a result it was starting to let me know. I had a very painful leg and elbow, and with the boat's violent motion the cabin was even harder to get around. By now the normal procedure for eating in the galley involved feet on work-surface edges and head pressed against the cabin roof, and even that was beginning to really hurt. I guess the feeling you have out there is of continuous physical exertion, to such an extent that after saving the boat from a gybe on one occasion you thank God that you've done it, not believing that you physically managed it. I felt I was pushing myself to a point where I could do no more, then having to find twice that strength seconds later. The wind was now blowing up to 55 knots, the top end of Storm Force 10, and it whipped the spray horizontally off the tops of the breakers.

I'm sitting on the windward bunk, with cold feet and wet thermals! Giu's put some music on, which is occasionally drowned out by the drone of the surf. I have so much salt on my face from the spray that it feels like it's covered in sand! A cargo ship has just passed in the other direction. You can only see its lights for about five seconds in every minute – that's how rough it is! It even hurts to move about in the cabin now – it's like trying to walk around in a rollercoaster,

Time 0614hrs. Just suffered a KNOCKDOWN!
I was in the windward berth. We were over well past 90 deg, as the skylights went blue – sea, not spray! The propeller shaft flew across the cabin, and hit the roof! The prop shaft is 10 feet long, 1½ inches diameter, with a bronze propeller still attached! It is mounted on the floor/hull of the boat, right down the port side – it is not in the water because of the drag it causes there when racing. We really must have been over a long way!! When falling sideways down large waves, it is possible to roll to well over 90 degrees without the mast going in the sea. Our mast was not in! (although I must check with Toto!)
Under my berth cushions were the solar panels, which flew out. My wellies hit Giu, and all the remaining veg went under the pipe berths down

her stbd [starboard] quarter. The Weather-fax and electric panel, high on the stbd side are soaked with bilge water! Something we could have done without! I shall try again to sleep!

As the storm was beginning to abate I came out on watch and clipped on as usual into the helming position. Toto had just finished and was sitting behind me, removing his gloves and passing them to me. Without warning we were hit by a huge freak gust and the boat just took off uncontrollably.

I yanked the tiller extension towards me as hard as I could, legs jammed against a rim, the handle at my chest. 'Toto!' I called, but he was already there, reaching down to grab the tiller extension; we had just managed to settle her when the extension ripped away from the tiller. The boat was now out of control. We both dived towards the tiller and pulled it hard, forcing the wind aft of the beam, and she heeled less and leapt forward through the heavy seas. Spray flew from the bow and off the tops of the waves like snow in a blizzard. Both of us knew she was in charge now, the two of us and our passengers helpless against her massive sailplan. We were going to gybe violently, now irrelevant and powerless to stop it. Vitt was up from below now, his face creased in a look of total concern. Almost as if in slow motion, *Anicaflash* heeled over on top of us, the boom slamming across the centreline, its crash like a starting gun for what followed.

Suddenly our lives went into fast forward.

Before we could even let go of the tiller, Toto and I looked forward to see a mountain of water bearing down on us. The boat was already on her side at 90 degrees, her decks vertical above us, like a wall waiting for the wave to break into it. I slid down the deck, my feet jamming on the toe rail, which offered a tenuous foothold from which to leap as the wave approached. Almost as soon as my feet stopped sliding, I grabbed at the mainsheet traveller ropes.

I held on with both fists clenched, as high up as I could, and as my fingers gripped tighter around the ropes, the force of the wave hit me, carrying my body away from the deck as if I were being sucked down a plughole. I tightened my grip on the ropes as smothering water sucked my breath away. I was completely submerged.

Desperate for breath, I scrambled up the traveller, using all the strength I had in my arms to make progress. I didn't know how far over the boat was, or even whether heading up promised escape. I struggled until I felt the air on my face, and gulped a lungful. My next thought was for Toto, and as seawater turned to daylight, I saw his red figure clinging to the pushpit. Thank God!

He was up to his waist, but signalling to us that he was all right. He had been swept about 8 feet along the deck before hitting the pushpit. Getting back to the cockpit was impossible along the deck – it was like a cliff – so he climbed through the toilet hatch, which was just above the water level, and came to us through the hull. As I hauled myself over the cockpit edge, I could feel a burning sensation in my left knee. I caught it but it was the least of my worries. I helped Vitt to furl the genoa, mind and body working like clockwork. It was not easy, as most of the sail was in the water.

Once the genoa was furled on its stay, we gybed her back and got back on course with the autopilot. Once everything seemed a bit more settled, Toto and I struggled in the fading daylight to relash the tiller extension while the tiller bucked and spat to the autopilot's commands. As we worked, Toto said that if his back had not hit the pushpit, he would have gone over – a sickening thought and the first time I had really confronted the full force of the sea and its mortal danger.

The plastic chair, which was tied on, had been pulled over the side. It was now flapping against the stanchions like a box blowing down a street.

Next morning I discussed the incident with Toto. He had been in real trouble and said that when he hit the pushpit, the force of water was so great on his body, that 'Any more and . . .' He crossed himself. I felt cold and just stared for a moment, unable to focus as I thought about what might have been.

As the French coastline drew closer, the houses gradually became more pronounced and the sunlight picked out the rocks, trees and roofs with a warm glow. Many of the houses were built high on the rocky outcrops, narrow and tall with pointed roofs and walled gardens full of dark vegetation. A couple of cruising yachts passed as we drew closer and, shortly after we crossed the transit of the outer pillars, the Emerald Line Seacat left the natural shelter of St-Malo. It slowed and gave a long blast on its horn as if in recognition of our crossing. There was a great feeling of achievement at that moment, and looking up towards the bridge wing, I saw the captain raise his arm. I returned the gesture. Without even having seen his face, I knew it was a sincere, meaningful congratulation.

At the start in Quebec I had been sure that I would develop some truly great friendships and I was right. After just fifteen days I felt that we all knew each other, cared for each other and really loved each other. The sea had brought us together and through our shared experience we'd forged strong bonds which in a normal situation would have taken years to emerge, if ever. It had been a far from easy trip, but one thing was for sure, we'd each finished with something special – a small but significant fragment of life which we would treasure forever.

Chapter Ten

I called Merv. There was less than a month now till he set sail, so things were hectic in Southampton. He had some bad news. Alan had contacted him while I was at sea and told him that he wouldn't be racing in the Vendée Globe. Unable to raise the finance, he'd had to pull out – my first real experience of just how crucial it is to find sponsorship.

I called him straight away and could hear the disappointment in his voice. I knew how much it had meant to him and felt awful for him. Having just finished my own race, I felt particularly aware of what he would miss, and I knew nothing I could say would change that. I felt terrible for him, but there was nothing I could offer.

Back in the UK, I went straight to the Southampton Boat Show and dumped my bags on *Global Teamwork*, Merv's boat, before going off to find Merv. I'd just had the best time of my life and was bursting to share it with someone. Although Merv was incredibly busy, with just weeks before he left to sail around the world, he still managed to find time for me. It was great to catch up with him, but watching his team stow their food on board for the race made me realize how desperate I was to get out there again.

While wandering at the show I spotted yacht designer Nigel Irens. I'd met him in Plymouth with Alan but I was nervous he wouldn't recognize me. I needn't have worried though – as soon as he saw me he said hello. He was a big man with a warm smile and could not have been more gentle-natured. He wandered over to the boats he was exhibiting and I was bowled over by how beautiful they were with their low, sleek back hulls, cream decks and teak rails. Nigel had been designing and sailing for years, winning races himself back in 1983 with boats built from his designs. He was a purist and loved not only the high-performance racing boats but also the older traditional yachts. I discovered that at my age he too had lived on a 20-foot boat on the Hamble, albeit thirty years before. From the day we met at the Boat Show he became a firm friend, and I think he could justly be described as one of the nicest guys in the world.

By the time I finally returned home to *Iduna* in Hamble I felt differently about the crowds who descended at the weekends. I did not feel the same desperation to speak to them, nor did I feel alone or excluded. I had found others who shared my passion and I'd made some close friends. Still, Merv's imminent departure would be tough, and typically, one of his last acts before leaving was to take me around the other boats in the fleet getting painting commissions. I managed about twenty before he sailed, and while not everyone remembered to pay, I'd made enough money to survive until winter.

As I'd expected, things felt very empty after he'd gone. I had become used to having him around and cherished his friendship in a place where it had seemed very hard to come by. But any sadness soon evaporated as Alan rang to ask if I was interested going to Les Sables d'Olonne for the start of the Vendée. My answer was never in doubt!

Alan and I reminisced about our experiences in the Transat, but in those quiet moments I could do nothing but think of the race that was about to start. Alan must have been hurting but I was pleased he would be there for the start as I was equally sure that in the long run he would have regretted missing it.

On our arrival that grey, November day, Les Sables was packed. When we eventually made it close to the pontoons I instantly recognized *Elan Sifo*'s mast. I discovered she had been chartered by a woman called Catherine Chabaud and renamed *Whirlpool* when Alan had to pull out, to make a late entry into the race. The tension was entirely different to what I'd experienced in Quebec and I think I realized for the first time what these skippers were undertaking. This was in no way a cruise around the world. It was a race, and that was going to make one difficult task a whole lot harder.

I was mesmerized as I walked along the pontoons, stopping to look at every boat as I ambled along. I stood on tiptoe to peer into cabins, and eyed up every piece of rigging termination in an attempt to learn what was going on in these guys' worlds. I smiled at skippers I knew and sometimes chatted to them if they had time, reeling at the enormity of the whole event. There were thousands of people around, some hailing skippers asking for autographs, some simply watching and talking about the boats to each other, some just touching the hulls of the boats that they knew were about to set off on an almost incomprehensible challenge, a non-stop race around the planet. Englishman Pete Goss was there with his state-of-the-art 50-footer. I chatted briefly with him and though he looked tired he was clearly elated to have made it to the start of the race against the odds. I saw Gerry Rouffs, Tony Bullimore, and Yves Parlier with his space-ship-like *Aquitaine* – it was fantastic just to watch what was going on.

I came across Mark Turner on the pontoons, there with Spinlock. We met only briefly but it was a reminder of my big question: what next?

Watching the boats from a flat by the harbour as they sailed away the following day was an emotional experience for me. My heart was pounding before that gun went; for reassurance I looked over at Alan who was putting on an admirably brave face. He had an uncanny knack of being pragmatic at some of the most difficult moments. I wanted to be alone as I watched the boats disappear into the distance, and pressed my face against the window to watch the tiny sails on that grey seascape. I had to be here in four years' time, I thought; no matter what it took, I had to be on that line. I could not put my finger on what it was about the Vendée Globe, but back then, standing in a window watching a cold and open ocean, I knew it would be the ultimate.

*

After returning home from France I discussed the future with Nigel. He spent most of his time there and was very well aware of the races that I was interested in. The Mini Transat seemed like the best option, although I knew I had to find a sponsor. Nigel was a wonderful support that winter, at one point taking me with him to Paris to a conference at Disneyland Paris to discuss a new event called simply: The Race. It was a new concept for competition, using boats of any type, any size and any number of crew to race non-stop around the globe. As I looked around, I spotted sailing stars I would normally only see in magazines. It turned out that the majority of them were people Nigel had known for years, and as a result meeting them felt entirely natural to me. It was not until years later that I wondered what they must have made of me. I was twenty years old, and probably the youngest person there by at least fifteen years, but Nigel gave me confidence.

Later that evening we were approached by a man who introduced himself as Hugh Morrison and asked us if we had any plans for dinner. He was involved with the business side of Disneyland and, in an indirect way, The Race. I sat very quietly through the beginning of the meal, but when Hugh asked me a question I talked feverishly about *Iduna*, my transatlantic crossings, and in particular my plans for the Mini Transat. I think that my mind was made up in the course of that discussion – little did I know that it would change my life.

I was back on the South Coast in mid-December, when I began my first-ever official job working at a boat yard. At the Boat Show I'd been approached by a man called Mark Orr, General Manager for Bowman Yachts in Southampton. He had worked with Pete Goss, who had just left on the Vendée Globe, and, having watched Pete's struggle to get to that start line, wanted to help others to do the same. He offered me a job at Bowman primarily so I could earn some money, but also to have the use of the office facilities out of hours. The yard, with its large boat sheds and complete woodwork shop, had been there for years. Bowman's reputation was based on tradition and quality, employing many craftsmen who had been building boats all their lives.

After I'd spent a couple of weeks cycling to and fro from Hamble to Southampton, Mark suggested that I bring *Iduna* to the boat yard and moor her on Bowman's own pontoon. This made longer hours possible and I was able to use the office in the evenings for both warmth and letter-writing.

Often the electricity cable I had running to *Iduna* would trip out at night, and rather than climb back up the long rusty ladder, I would resign myself to having no heater, a covering of ice on the decks, and waking with freezing feet. I exhausted myself during that time in the yard. I was still getting up at 6 a.m., writing letters or planning before everyone came in, then working as many hours as I could by day at Bowman's to earn enough money for the batches of stamps I was getting through with my letters. I would then work in the offices at night, sometimes until two, three or four in the morning, trying to write as many letters and address as many envelopes as I could for the following day. I would finally wander down the yard away from the buildings clutching another pile of post, hoping the next day might hold a reply from someone. I still wince when I think of posting in one drop letters bearing £300-worth of stamps. The reality was that it was a fairly grim life, although at the time I didn't see it that way.

The possibility of teaming up with Mark Turner was still nagging away at me. I knew that right now he was searching for a sponsor and we'd talked several times about working together.

At the London Boat Show in January I had a decision to make. Was I going to go this alone, or try to work with someone I hardly knew? Everyone I talked to spoke very highly of Mark. This was reinforced by what Merv had said after Mark had raced his boat *Maverick* in her maiden event. Brian Pilcher once again provided a sounding-board. I trusted him implicitly and he could usually reason my worries away in no time. With this issue, though, we were struggling. I explained that I was worried about jumping in with someone else. I knew my own strengths and weaknesses, but I also knew that if I decided to go with something, unless things went seriously wrong, then I would stick at it, and I did not want to make the wrong decision. I knew that we would be stronger as a team, but at the same time we were going to have to raise twice the money. Mark did have an incredible number of contacts in the marine industry, though, and had already tried, unsuccessfully, to compete in a mini race the year before, and we had discussed how we could work together to our mutual benefit. I think I knew that whatever the decision it wouldn't be easy – almost like marriage, I guessed.

I decided to go for it, and although I found Mark's reaction incredibly businesslike, he too seemed even more motivated. But despite the importance of making the decision to team up with Mark, my strongest memories of the Boat Show were of the stories that emerged from the Vendée Globe. In December of the previous year, Isabelle Autissier had limped into Cape Town with a broken rudder, but now people I had seen with my own eyes just weeks before were clinging on to their lives deep in the Southern Ocean. Tony Bullimore and Thierry Dubois had both turned upside down, and no one knew if Tony was alive and on board, in contrast to Thierry who was waiting for rescue literally clinging to his upturned hull. We had already seen the dramatic rescue of Raphael Dinelli by Pete Goss shortly after Christmas, and were lucky enough also to see the rescue of both Thierry and Tony. But far less publicized in the UK was the loss of ARGOS transmission on 7 December from Gerry Rouffs on board *Groupe LGII*. Several boats from the fleet diverted to his last reported position, but no trace of the boat could be found. The sailing world hung on, hoping Gerry would miraculously reappear, but the tragic reality of his death was confirmed on 17 July when the wreck of his boat was spotted by a ship off the coast of Chile. He remains sorely missed.

A few weeks after the Boat Show Mark and I forged our new partnership by taking a weekend trip over to France to see which Minis might be available for me and get a greater sense of the scene. Even today, France is very much the heart of the Mini Transat. We were to meet a man called Thierry Fangent who ran a yard, AMCO, and whom Mark described as the 'all-time guru' of Minis. Mark talked about his first visit to the yard when he'd unsuccessfully tried to compete in a Mini race the previous June. I could tell that he was frustrated at not having pulled it off and this was being channelled into getting this season right. There was something about Mark, some inner drive which pushed him to do everything he did as well as he possibly could. I was sure that this was also in a small way his downfall, as he would work himself into the ground to complete things. He was also a risk-taker, to a far greater extent than me, though I was beginning to realize that I would have to stick my neck on the line too, as the life I had chosen was not going to fall into my lap. I asked Mark questions about his childhood, trying to find out what made him tick. I felt that in many ways we had a lot in common – his parents sounded quite down to earth, and I sensed that we'd had a similar upbringing. But I knew deep down that there were some fundamental differences. It has to be said that back then many of these stemmed from my own lack of experience and exposure to the big wide world in contrast to Mark's early Navy career. I must have been a nightmare to be around, continually asking questions about anything to do with the Minis, the ocean-racing fleets and Mark's career. As we drew into AMCO's car park, I don't think there had been five minutes' silence during the whole journey.

Not speaking French, I felt fairly helpless once we'd arrived and wished, once again, that I had devoted time to learning the language. Mark, though, appeared fluent and he spoke with confidence. Thierry was tall and wiry, with piercing eyes and a mop of tightly curled black hair. He stood talking to Mark holding a half-smoked, unlit roll-up in his hand. I was wary at first as it seemed he was keeping us at arm's length and their conversation appeared to be going round in circles. Eventually, though, Thierry reached down, relit his roll-up, and wandered over to another door in his office. He took us down a dark and dusty corridor and I instantly smelt the fumes of acetone and epoxy resin. When Thierry opened the door I had to hold my breath; we were standing in the doorway of a shed at least 100 feet long and 50 feet wide – full of Mini Transat boats. I grinned at Mark, then up at Thierry, elated to see him smiling back. In that instant Thierry's character changed for me from being a cool Breton who quite rightly did not want to waste time letting his shed be used as a museum into someone proud and passionate about what he was doing. He became a comrade.

I wandered around the shed, in and out of the keels, looking up at the hulls, running my fingers along them. I could see *Omapi*, the boat that had won the previous race, and the boat that finished second, Thierry's own *151*, sitting looking immaculate in her cradle. But there was another boat there, looking back at me as I looked at her. She was distinctive, her entire hull covered in painted fish scales and her bow decorated with eyes and a mouth; she was called *Le Poisson*. Without having so much as set foot on board, I knew that I had just found the boat I was going to race. It was love at first sight – literally.

I made my decision that I had to leave Bowman Yachts when I returned home. It was grinding me down, trying to work in the yard all day and toiling in the offices all night, although the big plus was that I was managing to save some money. But during our trip to France Mark had talked to me about working for him on his boat for the Mini, which he was completely refitting, and when he offered to pay me £5 per hour I decided to run with it.

Within a week of arriving back in Hamble, and at Nigel's sugges-tion, I moved up in the property world. I rented a 12 × 9-foot Portakabin and moved most of *Iduna*'s contents into it. I needed a land-line to make phone-calls to potential sponsors as attempts to use the mobile were proving financially crippling.

I bought a scrap of carpet, the cheapest futon I could find, and plugged in the sandwich-maker and kettle. I had no running water and had to carry bottles across the yard – but I reckoned I had the best home in the world. After all, I had a heater and I could stand up – it was palatial!

Working life settled into a pattern. I divided my time between working on Mark's boat and phoning companies and preparing documents to try to attract sponsorship. The boat shed was cold, draughty and empty at night, though the sound of my sanding would echo around and keep me company. Sometimes I would have the radio on, knowing full well that when the DJs went off air, it was time to stop, but I didn't, I just kept at it – after all, the job had to be done. As I worked on Mark's boat I would drift off, dreaming about preparing *Le Poisson* for the race. Then reality would intrude – don't be stupid, you haven't even bought her yet, I'd remind myself.

Occasionally in the evenings and at weekends Mark would come over from Cowes to see how things were going. He would join me on the night shift. I would teach him how to laminate fittings on to his mast, and we'd go through the latest developments on the boat or any positive contact I'd had with sponsors. Mark too was on the search for sponsorship and was sending out proposals to several contacts he had. His situation was different to mine though. He had begun his struggle being able to buy the boat himself, and stood more chance of attracting support with a material object around which to base his proposals. He was also able to borrow money, which was something that I knew I didn't have a hope in hell of doing. When I'd tried to buy a mobile phone, I'd been turned down because of my credit rating. I don't think I even had one!

I applied to organizations such as the Foundation for Sports and the Arts, and had a meeting with the Royal Yachting Association. That morning I put on my smartest shirt and trousers and scrubbed myself red-raw trying to get the paint and resin off my skin, but the verdict could not have been more stark. I did not qualify in any way for grants or support. In fact I was told that they were unable to support single-handed sailors in any way whatsoever. I had been an RYA member since I went on my first dinghy training course on Rutland Water ten years before, and I had trained up through their schemes to Yachtmaster Instructor. I couldn't help but feel disappointed.

After approaching a number of companies from outside the marine industry, I have come to the conclusion that unless there is a representative within
the company with a passion for sailing/racing I am very unlikely to get the
chance to convince the Board that their involvement with this campaign
could provide unique benefits. These range from international and national

media coverage to corporate opportunities (Cowes Week, Martinique, etc.) as well as internal company incentives related to the stimulus of adventure – through talks (see CV), and following the race, etc.

Funds to support, programmes to follow and schemes to assist are not available for sailing of this kind. It is for this reason I write, as I feel the truth from my position is that I have to build my own ladder before I, and others, can climb it. I only hope that in doing this, I can inspire others, showing that it really is possible.

If you are involved with or know of a company which might be seriously interested in this campaign, or feel that you can help in any way, PLEASE get in touch ASAP. Either call me, write to me, e-mail me or fax me (details below) – I'd love to arrange a meeting to share a little enthusiasm!

Although the response to various letters was disappointing to say the least, I had in no way given up hope. But before long the lack of replies made me realize something; if I was going to find the money, I was going to have to buy the boat first. For me there was no income of any sort, other than the money from Mark – and I soon realized that that too would soon run out. I took my time-sheet off the wall and stopped counting; I knew all too well that Mark had no money either, and while I had joined as an employee it was obvious that we were in it together – we were partners. I had to content myself with the fact that when my money ran out he could pay me subsistence, and he was still paying for the phone bill. I had no house to sell, no car to sell. All I had was an old bike that was too knackered even to give away since it had been vandalized at the railway station.

Mark and I would talk through most of the night about our thoughts, contacts and ideas, while I would attempt to make us something to eat from what I had in my food box under the table in the corner. It was usually cheese and rather sickly-looking broccoli shoved into the sandwich-maker. The choices were slim really – it was virtually impossible to keep food without a fridge or cook without a ring or an oven, and I limited myself to no more than £10 a week on food.

In the not so early hours of the morning we would crash out on the futon. I only ever opened it out when he was there; the rest of the time I just left it folded, lay down and stuck a bean-bag under my feet where they hung over. I know that many people thought that Mark and I were emotionally involved, and I guess in many ways they were right. But it was more like a brother–sister relationship than anything else. We were inseparable, bonded together by the burning, sometimes seemingly impossible goal of both making it to the start line of a race.

At the end of March Mark took a trip over to France to see Pete Goss and Catherine Chabaud finish their Vendée Globe. He was completely blown over by the intensity of what he saw. Once he'd returned he described the atmosphere and emotion displayed by the huge crowds that had turned up to see the boats. I wished then that I had been there, and while I'd convinced myself it had been better to stay in the UK, I made a pact to myself that I would be there myself in four years' time.

The future, while daunting, wasn't all bleak. I had been in touch with the owner of *Le Poisson* several times, and had had a survey carried out on her. There was also, at last, the prospect of a loan from a businessman who'd been a supporter since my Round Britain trip. The only condition was that we brand *Le Poisson* with the company logo. Mark, Brian Pilcher and I arranged a meeting to discuss the details and planned our trip to France to buy her.

The afternoon that I'd arranged for *Le Poisson* to be trailered back to the UK, I received a fax from my friend's solicitor that caused my world to fall apart. The terms and conditions were just impossible. I slammed my fist on the desk and sobbed with frustration. I couldn't believe we'd got so far only to have our expectations shot down. The fax set out the amount I had to sell the boat for, and by what time. It stated that they had to remain the prime sponsor, and that the costs of the rebranding had to be covered by me. I was sorely tempted just to sign the thing, and to hell with the terms, but I knew that I couldn't. I relied on the value of the boat when I had finished and to have to sell her by an arbitrary date crippled the chances of her holding her value. Selling a boat can rarely be forced, especially when the race she'd been specifically built for only takes place every two years.

In desperation the following morning I looked into borrowing the money some other way, and tried to find loans companies who might allow an unguaranteed loan. Things looked likely to get very messy. While I was at my lowest ebb, Mum and Dad called to ask how things were coming along, and when I built up the courage to tell them about the offer falling through, it was impossible to mask the disappointment in my voice. I told them that I was going to borrow the money and asked them if they would be prepared to act as guarantors. It was as much of a shock for me to ask them as it must have been for them to hear this. I never imagined I would end up in debt, and in fact had always been determined to avoid it. But now I felt as though I was in a position where it didn't matter any more; I needed the money and hang the consequences. Then Mum and Dad said that between them they could raise £15,000 – Dad had been awarded some compensation after his accident and said that in these circumstances they would be prepared to lend me the money. I felt giddy with happiness, while knowing that it wasn't as straightforward for them as the simplicity of the offer had made it sound.

I'd got on the ferry to France still uncertain that I would be able to raise enough money to bring Le Poisson home, and despite a massive leap forward, thanks to my parents, I still needed a further £2,000 before I could buy her. As I was standing just a few yards away from her owner in La Trinité, a call to Mark Orr saved the day – he lent me the final amount. The belief and faith in me that Mark and my parents had shown were the next critical stepping stones towards that dream.

That evening we arrived in St-Malo too late to make the evening ferry and went to look for a hotel, finding one in the outskirts of town. It was dark by now and Nigel, the truck driver, hovered by the entrance waiting for me to go in with him. I looked over at Le Poisson.

'I'll stay on board,' I said.

In truth, I couldn't afford the hotel. I found a comfortable place on the cabin floor, put on an extra jumper and buried myself in an old spinnaker. I woke up half frozen but I was over the moon.

*

The next month was spent checking over *Le Poisson*'s equipment, and working on her as much as possible before she went into the water. The jobs I decided to do were those I could afford and attempt myself – not necessarily those I would have liked to complete before the race. For a start, my mast was shorter and heavier than the others; and all the sails I had were to fit my smaller mast, so if I changed the mast I would need all-new sails, and I could never afford this. I had to stick with what I had. Mark's contacts within the marine industry were proving vital; it was their trust in us which often allowed us to change essential fittings.

Hamble life was becoming more enjoyable by now as I had made some friends with guys from a boat preparing for the 1997 edition of the Whitbread race. They provided good advice on setting up her rig, but beyond that were just fun to be around. I was surprised how friendly they were, and astonished at the difference from others' reaction to me only a year before. Two of them, Jez Fanstone and Jan Dekker, came out with me on *Le Poisson*'s first UK sail. It was a fantastic feeling, and an emotional release as well. We ended up becalmed off the mouth of the river, and accidentally splashed her sails with red wine as we celebrated her maiden sailing. I laughed more in those few hours that evening than I had since the project began. I felt as though we were on our way.

Mark, meanwhile, had received his first really positive news on the sponsorship front. Charles Dunstone from Carphone Warehouse had decided to sponsor him. Mark immediately threw the money into *our* project. With a sponsor behind us, we could announce our launch on 23 May.

This took place in Cowes. Although it was a small event, we'd got the boats ready in time and branded them with our new sponsor's logo. It was also an opportunity to thank everyone who had helped us. Seeing the two boats side by side was a very proud moment, and although we were stretched to the limit financially, both of us felt we had already achieved a great deal in just getting them both this far. That evening we relaxed for the first time in months, with the Pier View pub being the main beneficiary!

Two weeks later Jez and I took *Le Poisson* out to compete in the

Round the Island Race. We didn't do terrifically well, but it was a great sail and a very worthwhile test-bed. Jez was not only a great guy to sail with but made more difference to my sanity over those months than I'm sure he ever realized. He had organized for a friend of his, Keith Willis, to race with me in June on one of the two available qualifying races for the Mini Transat. It turned out to be a race to be reckoned with, setting off from Trebeurden on the North Britanny coast, round the Fastnet Rock on the southern tip of Ireland, then back to Trebeurden. There was the inevitable struggle to get the boats to the start line, not helped by the dreadful gales. As neither of us was really ready to sail the boats there and risk damaging them on the way, we opted to take them by trailer. Working until the very last minute, we made our ferry with only ten minutes to spare. With fittings still being attached and the mast needing work, we were lucky to make the start. Mark's boat too, though now beautifully painted, was far from ready. We worked frantically to prepare them, knowing that the start date of the race wasn't negotiable. Dark depressing skies, horrendous wind speeds and the relentless rain seemed an appropriate backdrop to our efforts.

Somehow, and I shall never understand how, we both set off on the race. A photo was taken of Mark on the morning of the start, and in all the years I've known him, it is by far the most revealing – his eyes are sunken, and he looks as if even keeping them open was a struggle. He looks as though he could give no more. And he hadn't even started the race.

Thankfully there was a light patch in the weather for the start, but it didn't last – another gale was on its way. Mark and his crew, Fred, and Keith and I set off knowing it was going to be tough, and we were right. We ended up spending several hard, stressful days fighting through Force 7 winds on our way to the rock before turning round to weave our way through the steep Atlantic waves. The conditions were physically some of the hardest I had been through, and the Minis are not your average boat. They're light and flat and surf like little skiffs. The big difference is the size of their masts, and the absurd amount of sail they carry. *Le Poisson*'s mast was well over twice the height of *Iduna*'s, and the boats are pretty much the same size. Being racers, they offer little protection from the elements. The cabin was wet, as were the clothes we were wearing, and when we tried to sleep, exhausted, we would lie against the hull down below without removing our waterproofs in an effort to keep the freezing cold at bay. The motion was horrendous too – we were pounding into the wind and massive waves in a boat the size of a large dinghy. We would hold our breath on deck as waves passed over us, and close our eyes down below as *Le Poisson* fell off the top of one wave and into the next. With her heeled over – up to 45 degrees or more as the gusts hit – doing anything on deck became brutally difficult. There were simply no creature comforts, just an empty fibreglass sandwich shell which resonated like a loud-speaker, amplifying every squeak and groan on deck for the benefit of anyone in the cabin. Keith was sick on the worst day, so I found myself on deck longer, feeling the cold that bit more. After the first twenty-four hours I'd virtually given up the possibility of feeling my feet again, and with every wave trying to wash us backwards, progress was painstakingly slow. We dreamt of getting round the rock, and charging back towards Trebeurden at three times the speed with the spinnaker up.

Sadly, the return leg wasn't the long down-wind sprint we'd hoped for. After several incredible hours we broached, damaged the spinnaker and broke the boom before finally finishing in eighth place. But we'd had it good compared to Mark and Fred. A few hours after rounding Fastnet they'd been dismasted, and as we sailed towards Trebeurden we saw them limping along with just half their mast – a large part of the transom had actually been ripped away. Better now than in the Atlantic, anyway, I thought. At least they were both safe.

I returned to Derbyshire for my twenty-first birthday at the beginning of July. Having missed being with the family for my eighteenth, nineteenth and twentieth birthdays, it was time to go and see everyone. It was very much a double celebration as Nan had just passed her European Languages degree with honours – an astonishing achievement at eighty-three. After her long struggle, not least recently against illness, it was precious to see her eyes sparkle as she spoke of the lecturers and staff who worked in her department. The degree ceremony itself was still a long way off, at the Playhouse in Derby after Christmas. I hoped I'd be there.

After my brief break at home I was back with Mark in France to prepare for the Trans-Gascogne Race down to Spain and back across the notorious Bay of Biscay. The race would fulfil the single-handed part of my qualification for the Mini Transat. I was really nervous about racing alone – it would be my biggest test so far. Any chance of Mark competing had been wiped away by the extensive damage to his boat, which was still at AMCO being repaired.

The race got off to a terrible start, with a collision after only an hour, just when I had everything settled down. We were heading up to the first mark when a boat tacked beneath me. I saw the tip of his mast just a fraction of a second before the splintering crack that stopped us dead in the water. The damage to the bow was ugly but did not look structural. I decided not to retire from the race but to keep checking the damage regularly, and I was fortunate that things did not get any worse.

I finished eighth overall in the race which I was happy with, especially after our prang. Spain not only offered the chance to effect a temporary repair but ironically also marked the first time I managed to hold a conversation in French, bumbling and slightly alcohol-fuelled. It was a wonderful feeling to be able actually to communicate though, and to realize how keen people were to help you speak their language.

After a tiring return across Biscay to Port Bourgenay I sailed on to La Trinité where Mark was back with his boat. I was ready to drop, but on arrival in La Trinité I turned straight round again as Mark had arranged a photo shoot with a helicopter for publicity images. I was absolutely shattered and spun around beneath the helicopter in a fury, oblivious to how necessary getting the shots was to our efforts. Their worth was soon confirmed though when Mark's boat appeared on the cover of the next Carphone Warehouse magazine.

I woke drowsily to the sound of church bells the following day. I remembered driving somewhere with Mark the night before but as I opened the shutters I was taken aback. Below me was a market bustling with people. The church was just across the street, and to the right, just beyond the little market-place, was one of the most beautiful stretches of water I had ever seen – the Golfe du Morbihan. The house belonged to a photographer friend of Mark's called Thierry Martinez, and his generosity meant that it was to become home for the next two months.

There was still little cash, and we were getting through the sponsorship money quickly with race entrance fees, travelling and eating. But setting aside time to find a sponsor was almost impossible. Mark had his job to do, and I was in France trying to repair my boat. Things were going to be really tight.

Just days after arriving in La Trinité, *Le Poisson* was out of the water and in the sheds at AMCO. I would often stay there working away till eleven or twelve at night as there were always errands to run during the day to the sail loft or to the machine shop where I had some pieces made. Often I would go into the little room by the offices, make myself a cup of potent coffee and sit there, with my head in my hands, trying not to let myself fall asleep.

To make matters worse, I also knew that I was missing important equipment. In the last two races I'd found a few creaks and leaks in my four-year-old kit. Safety-wise we were OK, but from a competitive racing point of view we were struggling. What options did I have though? I was maxed out, financially and mentally. I suppose all this was building up inside me while I was working like crazy to repair my boat in a stinking hot shed. Watching the magnificent progress of Mark's boat next door – financed, it has to be said, by the insurance money from his Fastnet disaster – just seemed to be rubbing my face in it. As it neared completion it looked like a totally new boat, with a new rudder, bowsprit system, mast and sails, and every little detail done and dusted. All the ropes were beautifully coloured while I had to make do with what was left. I was angry that things appeared so one-sided. Mark's boat had the best of the new kit we'd received and I just felt like the kid tagging along. We'd set out to work on this together, and in my book that meant we should have been sharing everything.

One Sunday afternoon when Mark came down to the yard to see what was going on, I lost it. I felt like the underdog, and I had to let him know.

Mark's reaction only fanned the flames when he said that he was the person who had to worry, that bar the Mini Fastnet he had hardly sailed his boat. That tore it. Desperately needing to let off some steam, I yelled, 'That's it, it's always Mark f*****g Turner!'

A few no more elegant sentences later he was gone. He did not even appear to be listening. He just walked out.

A few hours later, and with both of us feeling we'd been dragged through it a bit, we were fine. The bottom line was that we needed each other, and Mark actually had a fair point: he *was* in a weaker sailing position than me and although he had more race experience in general than I did, he had far, far less experience of sailing alone (he was to start the race with only eight days' experience solo). I was the kind of person who would simply charge headlong at something and I relished being alone at sea. Mark, in contrast, seemed to be pushing himself into racing single-handed, challenging himself. It wasn't until then that it sank in – the sailing itself held a fear for him that I'd never previously understood. For Mark, this was the coming-together of a ten-year campaign and, as he saw it, his boat just had to be as right as possible for him to succeed.

I was doing all I could to save money. Lunch would be a baguette and a couple of tomatoes, and dinner was more often than not out-of-date freeze-dried food packets we had kicking around in boxes on the floor.

I grew to love the French. Their way of life and passion for sailing were second to none. I talked with Thierry, learning new words, understanding more as he generously shared his knowledge. I would often watch him at work, laminating rudders for the Open 60s, or working on Mark's Mini, so meticulously and accurately that anything he did was an absolute work of art in my eyes. My French was coming along in leaps and bounds, although it was by no means classical. I was learning French boatyard slang – phrases like 'A donf', 'A+' and 'Ça roule (ma poule)': 'Go for it', 'See ya', and 'That rolls my chick' – or more literally, something about hens!

We were getting ready to leave La Trinité. Mark's boat was finished and he had just completed an extremely hairy single-handed qualification to Spain and back. We were on board his boat, having tied alongside, discussing his trip and bailing out water that had collected in her bilges, when we noticed some small water droplets on the inside of her hull. They were the first signs of total disaster.

As a safety precaution we had her lifted out of the water, then asked Thierry if he would come down to have a look. He climbed down into the tiny cabin and spent a few silent minutes examining the hull. He then shook his head slowly, before looking at us with a pained expression on his face. When he spoke, we could tell by the tone of his voice that it was serious. His verdict was that there was virtually no inner skin, and what there was, was not bonded well. Basically Mark was in danger of losing his keel, and with the foam core being wet, there was no time to repair it safely before the start. A second verdict from Nigel Irens was the same. We had no money, and one boat between the two of us in which to race. It was going to take a miracle to get us to the start line.

As we wandered back along the pontoons to *Le Poisson*, we were joined by another competitor, Thomas Coville, whom we'd met through Thierry Martinez. Thomas had heard what had just happened, and he walked up to Mark and simply said, 'You have to make the start, Mark,' and handed him a cheque for 10,000FF. Mark has never cashed that cheque, but its message has never been forgotten.

In the evening we returned to Thierry's house and sat on the sofa together. Mark was emotionally drained, his eyes tired and sad, but there was still a spark of defiance in him. We talked late into the night. It couldn't all stop here, not after what we'd been through. The only way to race was to find another boat, and the only way to do that was to find more money. We knew the cost of chartering a Mini and it was totally out of reach. Without money we didn't stand a chance. We just kept coming back to the same place. At

2 a.m. we typed out an e-mail, really no more than a cry for help. It explained what had happened and what we were going to have to do in order to make it to the start line.

Both Charles Dunstone and Hugh Morrison contacted us the following day. Hugh, to whom we had barely spoken for six months, bar the odd updating e-mail, called asking what our bank details were, offering to transfer £10,000 immediately. Charles agreed to up his original £10,000 to £15,000. This generosity was awe-inspiring but it didn't solve everything by any stretch of the imagination. We could move forward, though, and while it was going to be a real struggle, we were driven by the challenge of making it happen. While my boat was renamed *Financial Dynamics*, taking on the name of Hugh's company, the money itself was used to try to get Mark back into the race.

The few days until the start in Brest seemed like months. Mark managed to find and charter another Mini not already taking part in the race and hired a wonderful preparateur called Jeanne to transfer much of the equipment, including the mast, electronics, boom and sails, from his old boat on to the new one. It was going to work. Meanwhile, Mark also laboured away on the publicity side. He was a natural at making sense of this. He knew instinctively what needed to be communicated, when and to whom.

Meanwhile, I returned to the UK to make a flying visit to Southampton during the Boat Show to collect my final equipment from Hamble. By pure chance I remembered to check my mail as I called by to thank the yard staff for all their help. A life-changing letter had arrived that very morning. It was from the Foundation for Sport and the Arts. They had considered my application, and stated 'that it would be their desire to offer a grant'. They had offered me a grant of £6,000.

I called Mark, unable to tell him fast enough. After all the bad luck someone must have put in a good word for us! They couldn't have known just how crucial their backing was. I now had the chance to buy that much-needed equipment for the race and spent a frantic afternoon at the Boat Show, sprinting from stand to stand, picking up everything from an extra sail to the autopilot I needed so badly. In the end I just managed to make the ferry but only because the man who sold me the generator gave me a lift.

We were only a week from the start when I arrived back in France, and with a whole hoard of new equipment to fit, I felt woefully ill prepared. Work on board *Le Poisson* – now *Financial Dynamics* – was hectic, and the race had come down to the amount of gear each boat had lying on the pontoon. We had the rest of the fleet licked.

Every single skipper on that start line had struggled in some way. Most had been living on board their boats for months. Those struggles brought people closer – there are few races where skippers will donate their unwanted sails to other competitors who are struggling, or discuss their weather tactics with each other in such detail. Everyone in the Mini shares something and everyone gives something. There were fifty-two boats in the fleet and it was one big family.

Over 70 per cent of the boats in the race were French, and most of the rest were Italian. But as the only two English competitors in the race Mark and I had our following too. It made for a busy time as we were not only preparing the boats but trying to give interviews to all who asked for them as well. I was unprepared for how many there would be and how time-consuming they became. More unsettling, though, was being continually asked about what it felt like to be the only girl and the youngest competitor in the race. I wasn't sure how to answer. I had never considered it and had never known what it felt like to be anything else; the question drew attention to me for all the wrong reasons and I hated being singled out. I just tried to play it with a straight bat: 'It's an impossible question for me to answer. I don't know how it feels to be a guy or ten years older.'

I thought a lot about it afterwards though. Why should I be any different? Of course I was happy to be there like everyone else. I was nervous, excited and impatient for the start – but so were the rest of the fleet. It was the first time I had even considered being any different. I had not thought of myself as the fleet youngster, nor the token girl. I had never felt that I was being treated any differently from the way Mark was, for example. Yes, fine, I was a girl, but I had sailed and worked with guys for the previous four years, and I had always considered myself to be absolutely one of them. I had my own strengths and weaknesses but so did every other skipper. Ultimately there could be no difference. We'd be in the same boats, in the same race, in the same seas. And no storm would make any distinction between us.

Mum and Dad had come down for the final day before the start, so that they could send me off with home-made flapjack, and they were surprised to find that they too were a target for interviewers. We had begun working on film of the race ourselves, so they were also filmed and interviewed by Dick, our cameraman extraordinaire. Mum said far less than Dad, but was clearly nervous about the race. Dad tried to be braver, although as he finished his sentence I could sense his voice was breaking. 'If I worried about Ellen in the same way I probably wouldn't sleep. I don't think it's logical to worry, we've tried to understand what Ellen is doing, and we've helped her as much as we can, and as Dave King at Hull, where she did a lot of training, used to say, "The sea will look after her," and if it does, then what more can we do?'

On the morning of the start I felt anxious. People tried to talk to me, but I struggled to communicate. My mind was elsewhere and all I wanted was to be away. I wished that I could just have been transported out to sea. I had my last real chat with Mark: almost mechanically, we went through the weather situation and discussed our tactics. It was a comfort to know that no immediate storms were forecast; we were due to have a fresh, but not tempestuous, start to our race.

When the time came to leave, before saying my final goodbyes, I had to see Mark again. We had not really parted earlier and I could see that further along the pontoon he was preparing for his tow to the open water. I wandered along, acknowledging many other skippers as I went. The French just say 'Merde' as their equivalent of 'Break a leg', so there were many 'Merdes' as I walked along. I could see that Mark was standing with his father, and the first thing

I noticed as he looked over at me was how red his eyes were. He didn't appear to be finding it easy to say goodbye. I stood back for a while, just watching. It struck me again that I did not share the fear that Mark appeared to be wrestling with. I did not for one instant think that I might never return to those who loved me. For me, this was an incredible moment.

I walked over to Mark. I have no recollection of the final words that passed between us before he stepped on board his boat and left, but I felt I had to be the stronger one, and I remember his arms wrapped tightly around me and the look in his eyes as he let go, which said it all. Whatever happened over the next weeks out there, we had already achieved an incredible amount together.

Mark slipped away and as his concentration focused on the boat I walked back to say a final goodbye to Mum, Dad and Dick who were waiting by *Financial Dynamics*. I didn't feel like crying at all as I prepared to sail away. I still felt oddly detached, being more focused on getting out and over the start line safely. I hugged Mum and Dad. I looked Dad in the eyes and he smiled back to tell me he was OK.

'Take care, Mum,' I said and jumped on board. I was off.

Almost as soon as I arrived in the start zone I had a call from Mark on the radio. It looked as if his autopilot wasn't getting a reading from the electronic compass. I told him what to look for and where I thought it might be, while assuring him that I would sail round to him while he was down below to make sure there was no collision. I stayed with Mark for over half an hour while he tried unsuccessfully to fix the problem, speaking to him every couple of minutes on the VHF to reassure him that he was in no danger. I guess it was good for my nerves at this stage to be worrying about someone else's problems!

I soon had my own to occupy me, however. As I turned the windward mark after the start, I went up to the mast to hoist my new spinnaker. In the rush of preparing for the race it had been overlooked and this was the first time I'd used it. As I pulled the halyard through the clutch I watched it flow out of the bag. I couldn't believe it – it was too short, a long way too short. I cursed myself for not having had the exact measurements when I ordered it at the Boat Show. The guys had been good to build it and get it to us in time, but I was still angry – I'd thought I'd given them enough information.

I knew I had to live with it as without it I'd be a sail down. It was just a shame that we weren't allowed to modify our sails when we stopped in Tenerife after the first leg. My only large spinnaker was so damaged that I could breathe through it. I gritted my teeth; it was simply going to have to last.

As I headed away from Brest, I was badly placed. The wind was dying, the sun going down, and day one was drawing to an end. By this stage I had changed my spinnaker for my older and now largest. The last of the support boats had turned home, leaving me very quiet and almost deflated, slowly creeping out to the west through the silhouetted rocks. All movement, sounds and thoughts seemed very small against the magnitude of the ocean, as the sky gave up its gentle orange for an inky black. The sleepless nights, financial worries and sheer bloody-mindedness over the previous nine months had all been for this. I had a video camera that Dick had given me and a small Dictaphone and that evening I made my first comments.

It's not half good to be out here. This is it, this is the Mini Transat. I can't believe I'm here, I can't believe it. It's almost too good to be true . . . Incredible. I just wish the people who've helped me to get this far could be living it with me. I'm doing about 12–13 knots, kite up, and after all that's happened it seems like magic that there are three dolphins with me right now.

The following morning I heard on the radio that many people had broken bowsprits or spinnaker poles. We were required to call up by VHF radio at a set time each day; these 'scheds' were only possible if we were in range of one of the four support boats that followed the fleet. We also had ARGOS beacons, which informed satellites of our position, allowing the organizers and then supporters to follow where we were. These positions were sometimes broadcast on Radio France along with our weather bulletin.

30 Choppy weather off the West Coast

31 Congratulations from Nan on finishing the Round Britain sail

32 *Iduna*, my 21-foot Corribee, winters in the garden at home

34 Alan Wynne-Thomas's *Elan Sif* which I prepared for his Europe One St transatlantic rac

33 The Sea Cadets' T. S. *Royalist*

35 Alan Wynne-Thomas

36 My first transatlantic crossing with Alan aboard *Elan Sifo*

37 Vittorio Mallingri aboard *nicaflash* during my first transatlantic race. Notice the badly designed tiller, which caused endless problems

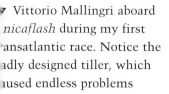

38 Mark Turner, without whom things would have been so different

39 Home in the Hamble was the bottom Portakabin

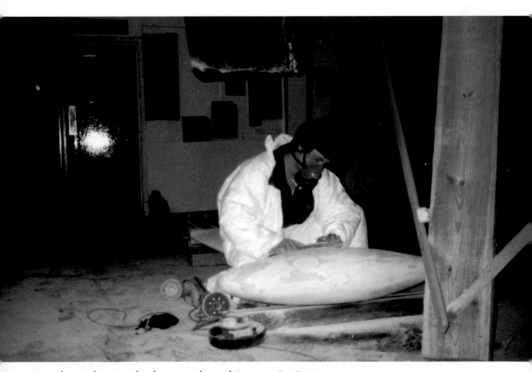

40 Lonely nights in the boatyard working on *Le Poisson*

41 Sailing *Le Poisson* – the small size of the Mini Transat boats is evident here

42 Saying 'Thank you' to *Le Poisson* at the end of the Mini Transat

43 Exhausted after the Mini Trans

44 Liam and Chris show off their new clothes in Bermuda before our delivery voyage aboard *Great Circle*

45 Sunset aboard *Great Circle* . . .

46 . . . and the storm

47 Hearing the news that Kingfisher were going to sponsor the Route du Rhum

48 Pete Goss's *Aqua Quorum*, renamed *Kingfisher* for the Route du Rhum

49 Very sunburnt and tired at the end of the Route du Rhum

Even when I did manage to get some sleep the following day it was only for ten, or at the absolute most fifteen minutes; and generally it would be lying on the cockpit floor in full thermals and waterproofs. I would stretch out with my head on the liferaft, watching the speed as my eyes closed. It's incredible when you dream, wake and look at your timer, to find that you've been asleep for only eight minutes. I think it has something to do with the comfort factor too: at the end of the day, not even having a bunk in *Financial Dynamics* didn't really allow my body to lull itself into the false thought that it was tucked up in a nice warm bed. For the four weeks I was at sea, I didn't climb into a sleeping-bag once.

In Biscay I was joined by a little bird like a yellow wren. He didn't seem to know where else to go. That night the little fellow hopped into my tiny cabin and roosted for the night in a small loop of cable I had hanging loose. I was devastated when in the early hours of the morning I startled him and he flew off in a panic. He never returned, despite my efforts to guide him in with a torch.

Further south, as we approached Finisterre, the wind died and we all had to really fight to keep the boats moving. It's even harder when the fog comes down, as the worry of being too close to another boat or, worse, a large ship is completely consuming – sleep is virtually impossible.

There are a few ships quite close. Luckily I can hear the fog signals, which makes things quite a bit easier. But there are whales too. I'm floating around with no wind doing about 1.5 knots, and I can hear a 'blow' just 20m away on my starboard side . . . That's quite scary . . .

When conditions changed and the wind increased, things did not improve. The following night we were surfing along at 10 knots, not even able to hear the fog signals through the sound of the waves. I felt pretty helpless, unable to see anything and just ploughing on into the unknown. But then, what are the options? It's even worse to be slow – at least keeping a constant course and speed gives a ship's radar operator a better chance of seeing you.

I managed to call Mark up on the VHF radio and we discussed conditions and experiences. He too had been through the shipping lanes with no wind, which he felt had been far too much of an exhilarating experience. He told me he'd spoken with Thomas Coville, who was narrowly ahead of him. He had missed a cargo ship by feet, slamming his boat into a gybe to miss it. His spinnaker was lost as it snagged on the side of the ship. He must have been seriously shaken by this and it preyed on my mood for the rest of the day.

During the final part of the first leg we approached and finished on the island of Tenerife. The lack of sleep was beginning to take its toll though – I could not have been getting more than three hours in every twenty-four. The last miles of the race resulted in a desperate struggle to find wind, and for the first time I was close to cracking. I sat off the island for hours, caught in its wind shadow all night, and had to endure the sight of three boats sailing past me just a little further from the coast. I knew that I had to come in wide, but when the wind had died the current had taken me closer to the shore and I was stuffed.

I crossed the line in twenty-sixth position. I was bitterly disappointed with my result and vowed that no matter what I had to do, I would do it to achieve a better result on the second leg. I spent hours trying to analyse every move and where I had gone wrong. I knew that I had struggled at the start and that my spinnaker had lost me miles that I'd really struggle to regain, but I worried about my weather knowledge; although I understood the weather systems themselves, I felt I needed to know more about the tendencies in specific regions.

I was upset that Mark hadn't been by the waterside to see me in, but quickly learnt from the other skippers that after finishing ninth, he'd literally fallen into his hotel room, completely exhausted, and couldn't be woken. By the time he came along the pontoon I was glad my anger had blown itself out. It was great to share and celebrate his impressive performance!

We spent just under two weeks in Tenerife preparing for the next leg. It was a long break, but one which was engineered more around the weather than anything else. September/October can still be quite an active time for hurricanes on the other side of the Atlantic; so the longer you wait, the less chance there is of getting caught up in them.

By sheer coincidence Sir Chay Blyth was in Tenerife while we were there, for the start of the first edition of his transatlantic rowing race. We'd met before at the Boat Show in London which I'd attended with *Iduna*. He'd been quite rude about her, calling her a cockleshell, and I vigorously defended her honour! He recognized me and called my name. We also discussed the round-the-world record against the prevailing winds and currents which Sam Brewster had sadly failed to beat. It was still held by Mike Golding and there were still cuttings from that attempt blu-tacked to my bedroom wall in Derbyshire. During a meal later that evening Chay surprised me by offering me the chance to skipper an attempt to challenge Mike's record. He had a sponsor lined up and said I could choose any designer to have a boat custom-built. The offer was extraordinary, but I tried not to show my excitement. In effect he'd just offered me the complete package – the chance of a lifetime. At the same time, it would still be Chay's project. My gut feeling was that I should do my own thing, though I knew I needed to think hard about his proposal.

The restart was a nerve-racking process. All the skippers agreed to it being delayed for twenty-four hours to allow one of the competitors to finish repairing his mast, during which time the wind built steadily. Everyone was nervous and the atmosphere in the port was almost subdued as each boat slipped out and was towed to the entrance of the adjoining harbour. There was another question too – the weather. Mark had been in contact with an American weather-router who had sent a fax offering his present synopsis and views on the leg. The stable area of high pressure which normally causes the trade-winds was simply not there, meaning that the trades were much weaker. Although he recommended that we headed south to sail close to the African coast before crossing, there was another option: to follow the more northern, but direct, route. I was still not really confident in my knowledge of the Atlantic systems as Mark and I discussed the options.

I decided to go south. *Financial Dynamics* was not by any means an efficient boat upwind, so the northern route would be a meteoro-logical and also a tactical risk. Even if there was less wind south, I would have to run with it . . . by the looks of things, this was going to be a tough leg.

By the time we started, the wind was really blowing, making it hard going and reducing much of the fleet to two reefs and a storm jib. The radio was wild with voices as several boats were dismasted; one was run down by a ferry and another lost a rudder. It was carnage as we fought our way between the islands in the choppy weather, watching out for one another. That night I had my own nightmare when I caught a 60-foot, 2-inch rope round my keel; not so easy to remove with a boat hook in the darkness. In the morning I was worn out from lack of sleep and frustrated as the wind had dwindled to nothing. It was murder trying to keep *Financial Dynamics* moving, knowing that each time I closed my eyes the tiny puffs of wind might change direction by 10 or 20 degrees, and I would occasionally wake after my twenty-minute snatches dead in the water. Again I kicked myself for not buying new sails for the race. My big old spinnaker was in a terrible state now, its fabric resembling tissue paper and fraying at every seam. My gennaker was even worse – knackered, and flying from the bow rather than the bowsprit, it never set well and rubbed against the shrouds. I'd have been faster if I'd thrown it over the side.

I managed to raise Mark on the radio. He was currently in first position and had a light but steady breeze. I knew also that once the wind had died we would not be able to contact each other again. Our only form of communication was VHF radio, which has a maximum range of about 60 miles, and once this distance separated us we would be on our own and would only have the French weather reports for company. The Mini is unique in leaving competitors so isolated.

As the wind filled in bit by bit from the north-east, my hopes grew with it. We crept up from thirtieth position to nineteenth.

Even if I am not breaking any records and my speed is not as fast as I would wish, it is wonderful sailing! There are fantastic flying fish, one that seemed to glide for simply miles. I have just realized that it is 1 November and that it will be Bonfire Night on the 5th. It feels very strange to be at sea on Bonfire Night. I think of everyone back in Derbyshire, fireworks and toffee apples. It is all a very long way away from here.

The breeze was a false dawn and over the next achingly frustrating windless days we slid back down to thirty-ninth place. As I sat in the cockpit clutching my radio, I was further discouraged to read that the wind was not forecast to improve and that the boats to the north were barrelling along – the leader was 250 miles ahead but after only a week's racing. Conditions on board were sweltering, and it was racing her in these airs that was hardest to cope with. Each time we had the weather, we had the position reports. They were all equally bad. I felt as though I'd been kicked in the guts each day. I was exhausted, pushing myself harder and sleeping less to keep us moving in the desperate heat. There were no options though – you just had to dig as deep as you could and get on with it.

There can't be many boats in this situation, this is crazy just crazy, you can't do anything; just helpless . . . [pause] . . . Anyway just got to keep plodding on, and keep trying and when a little bit of breeze comes take it, make it have it, and get the boat moving, then eventually we'll arrive.

I calculated that at the current rate of progress it would take us forty days to reach the finish. I knew that this wouldn't happen, and the wind would come, but when was the big question . . . it was a depressing thought.

The windless days ended abruptly with an enormous electrical storm. It was a daunting afternoon before it hit. I'd heard on the weather report of an area of high electrical activity with its epicentre just a few miles directly in front of us. I slept as much as I could before nightfall when I knew a storm like this would intensify with the cooling of the air.

What began as a low line of dense cloud in front of us slowly enveloped us, its slashing lightning strikes becoming increasingly vigorous. I was soon in its centre and I'd never experienced anything like it before. The sky lit up as if it was day and as I worked reefing and changing the sails in the squalls I could see everything I was doing. The air was dark with rain, like a cloak around us, snatched away with each fork of lightning. The thunder was felt as much as heard and the wind snapped from nothing to 20 knots and back again as it whipped in from constantly changing directions.

Following the storm, though, the heat returned. This time the barometer read 98 per cent humidity in a temperature of 33°C. I didn't care, the wind was back, and we were eating up the miles.

It's so hot that the sweat is pouring off me and when I sit down in the cabin I leave behind a little pool. The skin on my legs has come up in little spots, which although they do not hurt and are not even sore, look pretty horrible. I also have sores on my hands, but even if a little battered I am in good spirits. We are sailing well, averaging about 7–8 knots thanks to this precious breeze . . .

There was even better news when it turned out that the boats to the north were becalmed – albeit temporarily. When the next position report came through I leapt so high I was lucky not to crack my head on the deck head. We were in thirteenth position – I'd overtaken seventeen people in forty-eight hours! I was back in the match and the gloom of the preceding days was forgotten completely. On a high, I felt as if nothing could stop us; it just went to show that you can never give up.

I am surfing at 12.4 knots. I have clouds behind me and in front but they do not look vicious. It was a long night but I should now be west of the storm area. I have better weather, a good wind, and I am averaging 9 knots. I have 800 miles to go . . . I've been thinking about Chay's suggestion. But it does not thrill me at the moment. I know that all I want to do is to race like this.

I slept for no more than a total of an hour or so in the final few days and the last 500 miles was a hard grind. You can smell land when it draws closer – the French call it 'smelling the stables' – but you just have to keep going and not let your concentration slip at the final hurdle. One mistake and it could all be over. I thought a lot about my option to the south and whether or not it had finally been the right choice. My verdict in hindsight was that I *had* done the right thing – with the boat I had. I had less sail area than most others and our poorer upwind capability meant I just wouldn't have been competitive if I'd tried to stay with them. But then, if the wind had come in a day later – or, indeed, if it had arrived days sooner – it could have been a very different story.

I now feel so wonderfully in tune with the boat and the sea that I know I shall really miss this once the race is over. At night I watch the sun go down and in the morning the sky is there above me, a wonderful feeling of space and timelessness. Today the sea is blue and ahead of me the sky is clear and so very fresh. I shall be very sad to leave all this behind.

My feelings were mixed as the lights of Martinique appeared – I even regarded their presence as a bit of an invasion of privacy. As I approached the tip of the island, I had to turn and could see just one boat astern of me. This turned out to be Number 333 who, though I could not see it, had just lost the top half of his mast. We were in for our fair share of problems too, though, as whilst we were almost at the headland the wind changed violently and we broached. *Financial Dynamics* was lying on her side and as I blew off her spinnaker halyard I realized that finally our precious 'tissue' spinnaker was completely in tatters. I dragged the sodden mess out of the sea and changed as fast as I could to the smaller, bright pink spinnaker, though I took that down shortly afterwards when the wind changed once again.

Our final straight-line course was along the southern coast of Martinique and, though only short-lived, it was awesome. We were reaching a high speed with waves washing over us as we sped along. I sat on the side-deck and steered with the warm, scented air blowing off the land into my face. Below me, in the water, a pod of dolphins played, and the sky above was littered with stars bright enough to silhouette the island.

I crossed the finish at just after 3 a.m., after almost twenty-four days at sea; relief surged through me, and satisfaction that we had clawed our way up through the fleet from way, way behind. My goal to do better in leg two had been achieved. As before, and it was less unexpected this time, there was no sign of Mark on the dockside as I arrived; he had finished the afternoon before and was no doubt enjoying his first real sleep. I threw my lines to the guys on the dock, who swiftly tied *Financial Dynamics* up. I spoke briefly to Dick's camera as I began tidying my little world. I popped down below to drag out my sodden spinnaker, and smiled as I looked up at the electrics panel: no need to check that the batteries were charged tonight!

I was alone on *Financial Dynamics* now and I wanted to say goodbye. I had no urge to leave her, but I knew it was time to go – Dick was waiting for an interview. 'OK,' I said, 'I'm coming.' I stepped on to the pontoon; I slid my hand along her guard wire until I reached the bow, kissed her gently and then patted her goodbye, silently wiping away a tear. She's a pretty cool boat, that one.

My position coming in tonight, 13th, I was very pleased with. I know there are many boats out there faster which is a big thing and I couldn't have pushed any harder I don't think . . .

The feeling inside is one of nervousness, of being aware all the time and trying to make the boat go. It's very hard to describe; but you're doing a job out there, you are in a world where you have your 6.5m by 3 metres and you are in control of it, and that is it.

After our interview Dick took me back to the hotel. He told me that as he'd come out to meet me in he'd banged on Mark's door trying to wake him, but he was dead to the world so Dick had had to come alone.

When we eventually managed to wake him, Mark and I talked as if it was the last time we could about all that had happened to us out there. Mark described hallucinating on his trip which scared me a little. At one stage he was sailing along with a team of guys on board who were trimming the sails for him, but more worryingly on another occasion he had actually taken his spinnaker down without really wanting to, after cursing his imaginary companion for not taking it down himself. Twenty-four days is a long time when you're exhausted and pushing yourself harder than ever before. Mark spoke of the weather front he had sailed through, battling with high winds, and his time spent sailing close to Thomas Coville, the conversations they had had on the radio and of his second-night disco. Unable to contain the excitement he felt at hearing he was in the lead, he pressed transmit on his VHF radio, then yelled out in a very uncharacteristic DJ fashion, 'Yo, get down . . . it's Carphone Warehouse party night,' then played some of his favourite tracks. He hadn't thought there was anyone to hear him, but he was caught and, of course, word spread quickly!

Mark and I talked a lot about the future during our time in Martinique, and it was great to have some time together without the pressure that had been so overwhelming pre-race. He was going to return to his job at Spinlock, whereas I had nothing to go back to other than a burning passion to progress with my racing. There were a number of options, but I always knew that the Vendée remained the primary goal. The debate was about how to get there. To be ready I needed more experience on bigger boats. The Open 60s that competed in the Vendée were nearly three times the size of *Iduna* or *Financial Dynamics*. I was also keen to have sailed in the Southern Ocean before tackling the Vendée, and there was a race which could take me there – the single-handed Around Alone – round the world with stops. But there was no time to raise the finance to charter or build a boat for such a long race which started in less than a year. We couldn't risk being badly prepared.

Another option, though not one that would take me into the south, was the Route du Rhum, a race that I knew little about before meeting Mark and being introduced to the French scene. For a single-handed sailor the Route du Rhum is probably the most competitive trans-ocean sprint in the racing calendar. It runs from St-Malo to Guadeloupe and attracts the best of the best, sailing single-handed in Open-Class trimarans and monohulls, most of which, like *Elan sifo* and *Anicaflash*, are 60 feet. Mark had been to the start of one of these races and was sure that it was the right move. I agreed, and the Route du Rhum became our immediate aim: not only was it high profile – we felt sure that after training for and competing in it I'd be ready to challenge for the big one, the Vendée.

In the end, Martinique was far from a holiday paradise for us. After those initial days fuelled by the adrenalin of finishing, we knew we faced the enormous task of getting the boats freighted home. We were badly let down by our first shippers when a written quote for this turned out to be nothing more than a barefaced lie. After the agent reneged on the agreed deal I ended up paying double the price but thankfully at least it was to a different company found at the last minute. I was furious.

Since finishing the race Mark and I had become listless and tired and after this knock-back the consequences were beginning to show. Emotions were inevitably running high after the race but my frustration overflowed on the final night when Mark asked me to pay for our hotel. I left the room where he was working on his laptop and wandered off barefoot into the hotel complex. My blood was boiling and I didn't know where to turn. Anger was consuming me and I hated it. I knew I had to get over it, but had no idea how. There was resentment and fatigue, frustration at not standing my ground, lots of bottled-up emotions too. The fact that we were staying in a smart hotel, while many of the skippers were living on their boats or in cheap hotels in town frustrated me. We had no money, but Mark viewed the end of the Mini as the end of a ten-year campaign – his last big single-handed race. He felt he'd earned a reasonable rest and knew that in the grand scheme of things the cost of a couple of nights' decent sleep was unimportant. At the time I just couldn't see how much sense that made. All I knew was that we had to stick together in order to make all this happen. I gritted my teeth, and hammered my fists a few times into the concrete steps I was sitting on. After a long think, and time to cool off, I returned to the room feeling deflated, but a million times more positive. Mark and I were fundamentally different in this respect but it didn't mean that we couldn't or shouldn't continue working together. Mark was completely unaware and the following morning

I just gritted my teeth again and put the entire hotel bill on my card.

With the boat delivery sorted I was finally able to put all this behind me when we caught a ferry to Guadeloupe, from where we would be flying home. We were staying for a couple of nights with Mark's friends Pipo and Marie Cairo and their daughter Mathilde. They couldn't have made us feel more welcome. Mark and I decided to make the most of our time on Guadeloupe and hired a small car for twenty-four hours, which we took over to the mountainous side of the island. I'd never seen lush scenery like that before. Strange animal calls and steam rising from the dark green slopes made it seem impossibly exotic. I was fascinated by the isolation and density of the forest. I felt intensely alive, savouring all the new sights, smells and sounds. Mark travelled with a less obvious sense of wonder, having seen the world with the Navy by the time he was my age, but still his curiosity and appetite for living were undimmed. It was all so far removed from the rest of my life.

As we drove back to Pipo and Marie's, relaxed after a wonderful day, we discussed the Mini. And I began to understand more the differences between the two of us. We had teamed up by trusting our instincts and that decision was dramatically shaping both our futures. Mark was competing to challenge and test himself, whereas I was there primarily to be out on the ocean. For me the racing side was a bonus which made it tougher and without a doubt made me push myself further, but the reason was not the race itself. I relied on my natural competitive instinct to push me harder when I was out there. I didn't need it to force myself to the start line.

I was intrigued by the difference in our views, and saw why our partnership worked. Mark had needed my support as much as I had needed his; he was looking for someone with whom to share this experience. He had known that his drive and knowledge of the racing world would help me get to the start of that race and most probably make something happen which could otherwise have taken years longer. But equally he knew that in order to get to the start line of that race himself, he needed someone there too.

Mark told me that the skippers of the top three boats had all said that by the time they arrived they were dying to get off their boats. I hadn't wanted the race to end and I wondered if this meant that I would never be a winner because I might not have put in enough to hate it. I knew though that greater success in the Mini wouldn't have changed the way I felt at the finish. I thought about everything that I had done, every decision I had made, and about what had gone right and wrong for us. With hindsight maybe I would have done better in the north, taking the same route as the winners, but since *Financial Dynamics* performed less well upwind I was convinced that I would have really struggled up there. I had put in everything I'd got and relished every second, good and bad. And I told myself that what I'd felt was not a fault or a weakness but a strength.

Chapter Eleven

Life was hectic on returning from the Caribbean, and it seemed strange to come back to a Portakabin in a quiet boat yard in the cold of winter. Mark and I brought back some of the best memories of our lives from the Mini, and a list of great new friends, but we were financially drained. Both of us owed large amounts of money, but Mark at least had the income from his job, while I was in a more difficult situation. It was then that Mark asked me if I would like to become a joint partner in the company he had set up a couple of years before. Although it had done little up to that point, it seemed a good idea to become part of an operation through which we could run our future projects. After what we had been through together my mind was quickly made up and I decided to go with it. Working with businesses was a big part of our projects: I was having to learn fast and a few weeks later became joint owner of Offshore Challenges.

I wasn't long on the South Coast before I headed home to Derbyshire to see everyone. It had been a long time since I'd managed to visit Gran and Nan, both of whom were unwell. Gran had been into hospital for a heart operation and, though there had been some complications, was improving; but Nan was struggling. She had finished her degree course by this stage and had just about given all she had left in achieving it. She seemed so happy to see me, but while her eyes still shone she was clearly very frail and weak. Dad was getting stronger and was wearing his back brace less and less.

But even as he recovered and was spending more of his time outside in the yard and around the barns, he remained incredibly frustrated that he was still not fit enough to do half of the chores he loved.

That Christmas was wonderful, really normal. Dad played his Scottish pipe music extra loud on Christmas Eve and was more than making up for the fact that he had missed out the year before. On Christmas morning he went over to collect Nan and we all sat around for a fantastic Christmas lunch of turkey, rounded off with one of Gran's famous Christmas puddings looking splendid with the sprig of holly on top. Dad poured on the rum and lit it, then after lunch we sat down around the fire and opened our presents. Thea came down from her bedroom and we talked about all that had happened in the Mini and the conditions Mark and I had experienced. We talked about the Route du Rhum and reminisced about our fantastic adventures on *Cabaret*. I walked Mac in the hills, sometimes alone, sometimes with Mum. I was relaxed and happy and the time at home did me a power of good.

The break ended all too soon, however, and I returned to the Porta-kabin to prepare for the London International Boat Show, starting on 9 January. It was a crazy show for us, meeting yet more people, and I gave a presentation in the seminar room about the Mini Transat. I had done several presentations by this stage, but none with quite the same pressure of venue. Several people approached me afterwards, asking about the race and whether I had any secret tips on how to make it to the start line. I was embarrassed not to be able to offer more help, saying only that learning French and spending as much time as possible on the water before the race was important. What people really wanted to know, though, was how to find sponsorship; a difficult one to put finite detail on and prob-ably the hardest aspect. I knew well enough from my own experi-ence and couldn't help but think that Mark and I had set ourselves a new impossible task in finding sponsorship for the Rhum.

The most promising development for me at the show was the possibility of a new challenge on board an Open 50. The boat was about to be bought by a family called Rowen and I was asked if I would be prepared not only to manage the boat but also to co-skipper with David, the son, in the Double-handed Round Britain and Ireland Race. I was reluctant to commit myself long-term, but their offer made sense. Not only was it a great race to compete in – clockwise round the UK and Ireland in short sprints – but more importantly, I would also gain valuable hands-on experience in the Open Class world.

The boat the Rowens were interested in, *Jusq' au Bout du Monde*, was lying in Brittany, and soon after the Boat Show we took a trip down there to look her over. Merv, who was now settling into life after the BT Global Challenge, joined us to do the survey. He was living and working in Cherbourg managing the building of a new Open 60 for Mike Golding, which was his subsequent project to winning the BT Global Challenge. We all chatted away like a bunch of old schoolfriends, which was good news as David and I would be going through a tough race together. David seemed quite shy at first, but he had a wicked sense of humour and a very definite passion for sailing.

Things then happened quickly. David and his father bought the boat, and on Merv's recommendation we sailed her to Cherbourg for the bulk of the work to be carried out there. So by the end of January we had her in a new base, had sorted the cradle, had her out of the water and had begun the list of works to be done. She was to have a new engine and a new water-ballast system and we were going to repair her keel which was not very symmetrical. Merv suggested that I could stay with him during the three months I would be there in the beautiful cottage he had rented, about half an hour's drive from Cherbourg.

On 23 January, while I was still in France, the rest of the family joined Nan, now very ill, at Derby University for her graduation ceremony. She was understandably thrilled not only to be receiving her degree but also to be asked to give the thank-you speech on behalf of all the graduates. It seemed a fitting recognition of a lifetime's determination.

As she finally collected her degree she got the loudest cheer of the day and when she gave her speech she held the 2,000-strong audience in the palm of her hand, mixing humour and warm anecdotes that kept everyone in the hall transfixed. Her final line read: 'I was glad to have been made aware that life holds a lot of treasure – still to be mined in one's eighties!' She had been living for that day all her life. At long last she had achieved her goal. Just three months later she died from the cancer she had been fighting.

The springtime after Nan's death was bleak, but while we were devastated to lose her, we were comforted by the fulfilment of her dream and the end of her suffering.

I travelled home as often as I could and whenever possible met up with Mark to discuss any leads on sponsorship and progress on trying to find a boat for the Route du Rhum. There were few around, though, and we knew that without sponsorship the task would be virtually impossible; with Mark desperately trying to catch up at Spinlock, and me with my head buried in the Round Britain and Ireland project, it was difficult to make headway. At least by April I would be back in the UK for a month to prepare for the Round Britain and hoped that being nearer, things would be easier to complete and achieve. Just to complicate things even further, Mark had decided that he was going to compete in the race as well, but in a 40-foot catamaran called – ironically as it turned out – *Fingers Crossed*. It really was all go once more.

The only break I had from a life revolving around the dockyard was a five-day trip on one of the BT Global Challenge boats. Two of these had been chartered by a company called TMI and I had already met one of the directors, Antony Lane. Antony had sailed with Merv on one of the legs of the BT Global Challenge, and had always been a sailor, as had his brother Chris. We had a rough start to our trip – a race against other Challenge boats around the Fastnet Rock. Every boat in the fleet turned back, though we were the last to, and when we finally called it a day the majority of the crew of twelve were seasick, and the rest too inexperienced to carry on safely. Below decks was carnage – items of clothing slopped around with bits of revisited breakfast from one end or other that had failed to make it into, or had fallen out of, the buckets. Rather than continue the punishment, we spent the last few days cruising in the West Country, and laughed so much we didn't know what to do with ourselves! The memory that really sticks with me, though, is of a fourteen-year-old girl called Hemma. She had been asked along by an educational trust created by TMI that aimed to provide youngsters with otherwise impossible opportunities. Hemma, from inner-city Birmingham, had never been on the water before, let alone lived on a boat with a bunch of puking adults, but as our trip drew to a close and she stood at the helm, in complete control of the boat, I don't think I had ever seen anyone's eyes shine so brightly.

Back in France it was hard graft. I never seemed to leave the dockside until after dark. Although *Jusq'u au Bout du Monde* was out of the water, making it easier to work on her, the docks near the ferry terminal where we worked were horribly exposed to the bitter Cherbourg winter. While I felt sure I would lose my fingers through frostbite, I never lost my enthusiasm and was never more than a couple of minutes away from a quick hot chocolate and a warming chat with Jean-Marie Vaur, the manager of the JMV yard, about the work that was going on. In the evenings we would talk about the Open 60s and he would show me around the yard, explaining what each piece of machinery was for and how it functioned. He showed me the types of construction and the various materials that were used in these modern racing machines. His pride in the yard was transparent and I was fascinated. Merv was still there too, working on the final stages of Mike's boat, *Team Group 4*, and when we both had a few minutes to spare we would wander around talking. I also got on well with the guys working with him and would sometimes join them after hours for a beer laid on by Merv. He was sensitive to the guys' feelings and had built a great relationship with them. He was aware that a boat's eventual level of performance would be a direct reflection of the amount of energy and care put into building her.

During the final stages of my time in Cherbourg Merv and I both realized that we were becoming more than just the close friends we already were. We shared so many of the same passions and dreams.

In the evenings we sat in the cottage tapping away on our laptops and chatting about Open Class boats and the Southern Ocean. We had lived together for two months, gone running in the evenings and cooked meals for each other (though mine rarely stretched to anything more glamorous than crêpes) and saw that this could be something longer term. It was a wonderful feeling, almost a relief, to start a relationship with Merv. He understood me, watched out for me as I did for him, and took me for what I was. I felt like the luckiest girl on earth. He was a caring, loving man, who would go out of his way to help people. He was as solid as a rock and wore his heart on his sleeve – both qualities I warmed to immensely. After only a few precious weeks, it was a wrench to leave him behind in Cherbourg and head for Plymouth with David to prepare for the race.

It was an odd time in Plymouth. I felt nervous and very responsible as for the first time my work was important directly to David too. There was a real mixture of boats in the race, from our 50 to the monster 60s, and several trimarans around 45 feet in length. It's a special race, run in stages giving us exactly forty-eight hours in each stopover, which though busy normally end up as quite social occasions with the other skippers too.

David and I had a great time on the Round Britain and Ireland Race. We not only had some hard and tactical racing, but also laughed a lot. We got on famously, and it showed once again the incredible spirit it is possible to have on board when people are compatible and really have to work hard together for something. Mark, on the multihull *Fingers Crossed*, was desperately unlucky when the catamaran's mast began to come down just 60 miles into the race, which forced them to turn back before they ever really got going. But for the lucky ones the route was beautiful: the Outer Hebrides were stunning and we were blessed with wonderful weather and light winds – eternal daylight was breathtaking as we headed further north. It was not without its problems though. During a rig check in Lerwick I discovered our forestay was breaking, so we set about a laborious and rather chilly day removing it.

It wasn't half nippy spending hours up an aluminium mast as far north as Cape Horn is south!

It was a foggy passage through the North Sea and past the River Humber, before a real bashing down the English Channel where we developed problems with our other forestay, which led to an incredibly stressful final night in a very black and vicious storm. We made it back to Plymouth though, and the icing on the cake was that we won our class in the race.

But it meant there was a lot going on ashore while I was racing. Mark made a big life-changing decision; he resigned from Spinlock, having decided that he had outgrown his post there. There was no doubt that the Mini Transat had changed his outlook; in fact, it had changed us both – and my goal of the Vendée Globe was sitting there just waiting to be seized. The Mini had taken us a long way towards that. At the time of the start it was the unimaginable culmination of all our hard work; by the finish it had become the foundation on which we could build the campaign for the Vendée. The biggest step forward for both of us was simply our decision to work together.

On our return from the race I sailed back to Hamble with David, where the boat came out of the water. I made a quickly filmed BBC *Waterworld* programme about my plans for the Vendée Globe, then, in a car the BBC were kind enough to hire for me, I drove to Falmouth with some parts for Merv, who by this stage was preparing *Team Group 4* ready for her first race. It was great to see him again, and I even got a few hours' sailing on the boat, which was fantastic. Mike Golding was going to race over to America in the feeder event for the Around Alone, the same race we had looked at; but with stopovers, it meant that Merv would be following him – I would be seeing little of him.

After my brief trip to Falmouth, Mark and I once again set about looking for sponsorship and a boat in which I could race in the Route du Rhum. A seemingly obvious option for the latter was the 50 that I had just raced on. She had been bought very much as a boat for a single purpose, and now the race was finished. I also knew her well, and since several discussions touching on the subject had already taken place, we thought we should ask the question properly.

We had several meetings with David, his father and their business associates, and contrary to what we had initially thought, they seemed quite keen to take it forward as a project. We came to an agreement whereby I would be able to sail the boat in the Route du Rhum. The boat itself would be further enhanced by work that we would do over the rest of the summer, ideally including a new mast and new sails. Her profile would be significantly raised in France and along with that, the prospects for selling her would be greatly improved.

We were over the moon to be working with people whom we had got to know and trust over recent months, and as we had learned with the Mini project, having a boat meant we were on far firmer ground in our search for a sponsor. Finding main-name sponsorship was undoubtedly going to be hard, but using the success we had had with our Mini sponsorship, we explored every avenue. Dick had already made a programme on the Mini Transat using footage I'd shot, and Mark and I set about producing a sponsorship video with him, which we could show at meetings. Along with this we developed a computer presentation with more particular talking points which could be shown on a big screen.

Every billboard or poster seemed to suggest a new opportunity or sparked an idea for the sponsor we were looking for. As I curled up in my Portakabin I would close my eyes and drift off to sleep, always keeping a notepad on the floor next to my pillow as nine nights out of ten I would switch the light back on and scribble down a thought or idea, whether in pursuit of finance or for modifications to the boat.

The pressure was definitely mounting. As each day passed there was more and more to organize. Mark was in the process of completing his three months' notice at Spinlock, we still owed serious money on our Mini Transat boats and could not risk spending the money I had earned working on the 50. I decided to move out of my Portakabin, which was costing us over £30 per week, as while *Team Group 4* was out at sea, I could stay with Merv, who was staying with friends in Cowes. Some nights I would stay at Mark's mother's house on the other side of the Isle of Wight. Meanwhile, Mark and I arranged to share an office with a good friend, yacht designer Chris Stimson.

I saw Cowes Week in August as an opportunity to meet people who could be potential sponsors for the Rhum. I'd met one of my sponsors for the Mini Transat this way, so the omens were good.

In the end Cowes yielded fewer contacts than we'd hoped. It hadn't helped that I'd been ill for most of it, sleeping on the floor of Chris's office right in the yard where the nightly celebrations in the beer tent took place. Not only did I hear the commotion of thousands of people enjoying themselves outside, but at about 10 p.m. the nightclub started up for the all-nighters in the giant boat shed adjoining the office. I would lie there on any cushions I could find from the chairs and, in a fever-like sweat, try to block out the thumping bass by listening to music on a portable CD player. I knew that I was not supposed to sleep up there, so I would keep the lights off when darkness fell, and if I was working, rely on the glow from the computer screen. It was a small office, and as it was a basic single-skin brick construction and had only single-glazed windows, it got cold at nights. But I could work and live in the same place, which saved time and energy. We were able to meet up with and interview a French girl, Marine Crenn, with a view to her working with us at Offshore Challenges. She was young, very outgoing and a good dinghy sailor. She had grown up in a world of single-handed sailors on the north coast of Brittany and spoke good English. Now having a base meant that we were able to be more than just Mark and Ellen, and as Marine spoke French she would be perfect to take over from Nick, the student who had been helping us as a summer job. We made a hasty but life-saving decision to go with it: she joined us on 14 September and could not have worked harder for us.

I kept in regular contact with Hugh Morrison at the time, and kept him up to date with the latest developments. He has always been an incredible ideas man, constantly coming up with different suggestions or a new angle. Having people like him helped keep us going. I know that enthusiasm on our part was not lacking, but when the chips were down – and we were about to discover how that really felt – his support was priceless.

Hugh,

I had a phonecall the other day from Antony Lane the Chairman of TMI (UK). He had a fantastic offer, which needs a little explanation . . .

His brother Chris, the Chief Executive, was one of the founders of the company and during their first years, when they were really quite small, Chris managed to get British Airways to take them on to train 38,000 staff in 18 months! At that time TMI had five employees! They did it, and the company has never looked back.

Now, there is a story behind their offer to help me that I must tell you . . .

A friend of Chris's, a musician at the Royal Shakespeare Theatre in Stratford-upon-Avon, had a teenage son who was an incredibly talented flautist. He was winning competitions all over, and was accepted into the finals of the Young Musician of the Year award. His flute was good, but certainly not up to award standards . . . He said exceptional talent will only take you so far, you also need an exceptional instrument . . . true, I suppose!

Chris was having this discussion with the boy's father in a local pub, and after a few beers he suggested that TMI could sponsor a top-class flute made specially for the young man at a cost of about £10k. The boy's name is Julian Cawdrey and he has never since been parted from his flute. He now plays as a soloist for the world's top orchestras and is much sought after as a teacher. This was the 'ethos' behind their offer of help.

Chris and Antony set up an 'education' trust fund, which is what they want to use to help me. Their solution to the problem is to pay some of my 'billed items', and they are not asking to have their name on the side of the boat. They simply want to get me to that Start Line . . . fantastic . . .

Their company is a training company, with courses

predominantly on team building, time and stress
management, customer service, etc., etc. The courses are
fantastic, inspirational, really hitting home. Their
intention is to send me on some of these courses, and
for me, in a few years' time to work with the company
delivering messages. I will take this on as a challenge,
I enjoy speaking . . . who knows what this might lead to?
Their courses are for companies such as Esso, ICI etc.
so could lead (and I know they're considering this) to
some great opportunities, and an income of sorts . . .

Wonderful, wonderful news . . . with their intention
that I can still find a main sponsor!

Feeling quite run down right now, I'm homeless as the
Portakabin was towed away last Friday . . . My life is in
a lockup, and I'll be free till the beginning of
October! What a story . . .

Will be in London for meetings next week. I'll mail
with more details . . . Thanks for all your support Hugh,

Ellen

Antony had been fantastic in giving us a break that we so desperately needed to survive. Despite this, however, we still had few financial reserves left. What we lacked was hard cash. The support from TMI was very much a reality, but as it was a trust fund, we would only be able to refund from receipts. By now we were really facing trouble – we had still not been able to pay the £5,000 entry fee for the race.

We suffered what felt like a knockout blow immediately after Cowes Week. Mark called and I knew instantly from the sound of his voice that something was wrong. He had received a fax from the Rowens, stating that they had had advances from a potential purchaser for the 50. With those few words, we knew they had withdrawn the offer of the boat and we felt devastated.

I forced my eyes shut so tightly that I could feel the blood withdraw into my head. I wished I could turn back time five minutes, and just be getting on with the project: why had we not had a face-to-face meeting a month earlier and been told? Although we had still been waiting for the contract, we had had the verbal agreement for weeks.

In anger and frustration I hammered out my thoughts for a reply on paper. I knew I just had to get it out of my system.

I honestly believe this is your loss . . . and unfortunately, as a result . . . our pain, and our explanation to those who have helped us get so close . . .

My teeth were gritted together firmly as I wrote.

Now we have only our own enthusiasm, and that of those who believe in the project to make it happen . . . and who shall see it to the end. We shall find a solution, but for now our work has been made far, far harder.

Finishing the letter, I let my head fall into my hands. What was the use? She was their boat, not ours: their call. If we were going to make it to the start line we would have to find another boat. I think we both knew that with less than ten weeks to the start of the race this one was going to hurt. I was confused too. David and I had got on so well during the race and I couldn't help but take their decision personally. (Ironically, the 50 didn't sell for another three years.)

Mark and I got to work immediately, contacting every person we thought might know of a boat, but with two massive ocean races in progress we had our work cut out. It looked as though there were just two options in the whole of the northern hemisphere: a 60-footer called *Coyote*, which could be ours to own for more money than we could ever dream of attaining and *Great Circle*, a 50-footer lying in Bermuda, charter price negotiable.

In the end Merv turned out to be our saviour when he e-mailed Brian Hancock, the owner of the boat in Bermuda – e-mails were soon flying back and forth between us. Brian had been planning to race his boat *Great Circle* in the Around Alone Race, but after a fruitless and frustrating search for sponsors was reluctantly accepting that it wasn't going to be possible.

It was mind-blowing to see the support we had from people at this point in time: the Lanes for a start, Merv for his time spent on trying to find another boat, Ashley Perrin and her family for offering me companion passes for the airline so that I would be able to travel at a fraction of the usual cost – very handy when a trip to the States was in order.

In a few days' time Mark was due to fulfil his final commitment to Spinlock – a series of meetings on the East Coast of the States. Ironically, this was where Brian Hancock, a South African, was now living. I could join Mark a few days later. Brian had said that he would fly to Bermuda and sail *Great Circle* back to Marblehead – we would therefore be able to see her there the following weekend.

Before this, however, I'd promised Mum and Dad I would join them in Scotland on holiday. My plan was to pass through London to see Hugh Morrison, then catch the train north to Derbyshire. As usual, Hugh was full of enthusiasm, bundling me into a cab at the end of our chat with a packed lunch from the canteen. He really did understand.

I spent a night in Derbyshire before driving north with my parents. As we drove, a million things spun round in my head, and I could not help but feel that I shouldn't have been there. I desperately wanted to spend time with Mum and Dad, but it was very stressful. Each day we would go out in the car, and I would connect my laptop to my mobile to read e-mails. I was waiting to hear from Brian. Although I knew that he would be at sea for a few days, I needed to check all was well before catching the flight to the States. I was stumped when I received an e-mail from Brian, clearly sent from the boat's e-mail address – short of characters as each message is paid for by its length.

Date: Tue, 25 Aug 1998 00:31:39 +0000 (   )
To: Offshore_Challenges_Ellen@compuserve.com

HiEllen Cant GETthro2U from here. Here isTHE situation asICit. Letsmeet inMarblehead ths weeknd & sort allBOATdetails I will SAIL2Azores from here W/U. Boat

willB redy2leave whenURredy. Please GIVEme somedates
4depart BDA that work4U soTHAT I can makeMY flt res4
return 2 BDA. Please understand that by yourREPLY Iam
finally givingupon my campaign&working w/U & willHOLD
U2 our agreement outlined invarious e-mls.Pls reply
ASAPvia eitherMYWIFE orMERF. LK fwd2seeingU Brian

This was odd – Brian was still in Bermuda and was suggesting sailing back to Europe from there. I was getting worried by this stage and it was impossible to reach Mark to discuss the situation. I felt as though I had the weight of the world on my shoulders.

Although I was distracted, I think that ultimately the trip to Scotland allowed me to carry on with that year. I was absolutely exhausted when we arrived there, although I'd slept for most of the way up in the car. I felt drained, and on the second day developed very swollen glands in my neck. I worried that my glandular fever was coming back. A blood test by a local doctor put my mind at rest on that one, but I was forced to slow down – I had two days to get stronger before leaving. As I lay in bed that night I began to breathe deeply and slowly, and I closed my eyes. Mac was lying on the floor next to me, and I let my hand fall to stroke her. I simply had to get better, I could not let everyone down. On the last morning I woke and wandered into the living area of the cabin. I could see the Monroes disappearing into the distance, and the light mist softening each feature. I could see the shepherd in the farmyard preparing to leave for the hills, and the rabbits that had come out for their first lollop. Mac sat by the window, ears pricked up, watching every move outside, while I made a cup of tea and curled up in a ball on the sofa with a thick scarf round my neck. I loved that time in the morning. I reckoned I'd be OK.

I queued nervously at the gate at Heathrow, the last person to board and lucky to get a standby seat. Mark picked me up at Boston and we drove north to meet up with Brian Hancock. We talked feverishly in the car – I felt better now, relieved to be back on form.

Brian had boundless energy and it was evident just how much effort he had put into his campaign. He seemed to live by its slogan, 'Goals are just dreams with a deadline'. He had bad news, however, which made sense of the e-mail I'd read in Scotland. He had attempted to sail *Great Circle* back to Marblehead for us to see, but on leaving Bermuda he'd got caught up in a tropical storm and gone on to the reef. The boat had been damaged – the forward fin ripped out, the keel scraped and the rudder broken. We now had even more on our plate. Brian could see that we were struggling and had decided that if *Great Circle* could not race around the world, she would be far better off racing in the Route du Rhum. He let us charter her for a fraction of the cost of other boats.

The plan was to fly to Bermuda just two weeks later. Things were going to be very, very tight and there seemed an impossible amount to do back home.

Hugh Morrison was trying to set up a meeting with a company he had been thinking might be a potential sponsor for us. In the UK, Kingfisher Plc owned well-known brands like Woolworths, COMET, Superdrug and B&Q, and Hugh explained that they had similar brands in France and Europe. He felt that it would be a great match for us – we were English, wanting to compete in a French race but in no way going out there to 'take on' the French; both of us felt European, and Kingfisher was a pan-European company – perfect. Hugh might give us the opportunity to walk through the boardroom door and make our case.

We worked with Dick on the sponsorship video and put together a new presentation for the meeting. Although our most pressing battle was simply to get to the start of the Rhum, our strategy was to present a campaign culminating in the Vendée Globe; while that remained the ultimate, we planned to present the Route du Rhum as an imminent trial run for both us and our sponsor. We would offer main sponsorship for the Rhum at a tiny price, but enough to give us a chance to show the sponsor what we were capable of. We simply had to give the meeting our best shot.

At the same time we prepared for a press launch at the Southampton Boat Show, now just a week away.

Mark,

I've spoken to Hugh, and he was great . . . As usual, more helpful than imaginable . . . I said we could (just feasibly) have the Video done for next Friday . . . He said I must let him know if we're really scraping for money, and that he'd be there to try to 'unstick us' if we got 'stuck!' He also remarked how experienced we were at getting these projects together at the last minute! He's such a great person . . .

He said he's likely to have an answer from the KF group by the end of next week.

I desperately need to get practising 'close racing!' . . . This, plus the weather routing . . . needs to happen . . . I've got to get some things right!

Hugh's final words were to contact him without any hesitation whatsoever . . . if there was anything he could do, or we were stuck . . . His final words were . . . 'no worries mate, I think you're worth it!'

It's priceless to have people like this around . . . never doubting, never pausing . . . always, supporting, helping and encouraging . . .

And Mark, you are the same . . .

There is always a way, we can always succeed, and we will get there . . .

Thanks for everything . . .

see you later . . .

and smile!

e

xx

I had also been asked to give a speech at the opening lunch of the Southampton Boat Show. Once again it was going to be a busy show and we had a lot of ground to cover in our time there. We borrowed a tank test model of an Open 60 from Thierry Dubois, a French sailor who has always keenly encouraged newcomers into the sport. We painted it silver and had stickers announcing GLOBE 2000 put on its side. We had to give out the right message and we wanted no one to be in any doubt about the ambition and substance of our plans. Our first press release together under the banner of Offshore Challenges read:

GLOBE 2000 – SINGLE-HANDED, NON-STOP, AROUND THE WORLD – TO WIN

Today Ellen MacArthur announces her campaign for the Vendée Globe single-handed, non-stop, round the world race in the year 2000. Whilst there are nowadays a number of round the world events, the Vendée Globe clearly remains the pinnacle of human challenge – and nowadays as professional and competitive as the Whitbread/Volvo Race.

Short-handed racing is growing fast in popularity in the UK, with as many as ten skippers signed up for the next Mini Transat, and for the first time British born and based professionals entering the professional French Figaro circuit.

Teaming up with fellow solo skipper and marketeer Mark Turner, and his company Offshore Challenges, the search has begun in earnest for a business partner and sponsor. The objective is clear – to win the race, but also inspire as many people as possible along the way, whether from their armchairs or for their own campaigns. The budget for Globe 2000 is £1.5 million.

The path has been a fast one for 22-year-old MacArthur – and the learning curve steep – but the results prove her incredible ability to learn, and her competitiveness. With more than 30,000 miles in Open 50s and 60s, a victorious two-handed Great Britain, and the tough 1997 Mini Transat under her belt, she is moving on to the next stage of Vendée Globe preparation, the Route du Rhum.

Departing from St-Malo on 8 November this year, this the most famous of French races (an event recognized by 30 per cent of the French population as a whole), will provide the first solo big boat test for MacArthur. The 4,000-mile race includes some of the top names in the single-handed circuit, and takes the solo skippers from the north of France across the Atlantic to Guadeloupe in the Caribbean.

The Boat she will be sailing is a lightweight all carbon Open 50 previously named *Great Circle*. She was built in the USA by Concordia Yachts for over 1 million dollars, and has since never raced competitively, narrowly missing the qualification date for this year's Around Alone race . . . maybe she has something to prove?

By the end of next week MacArthur should be at sea on the delivery of the boat back from Bermuda, ready to change sails, and fit an engine in preparation for the start. The programme is charged, but the participants motivated to overcome the hurdles!

From a small beginning just three years ago - a round Britain solo voyage in a 21-foot Corribee - Ellen MacArthur has progressed way beyond most people's expectations. There will be no change of pace. With her are a fantastic group of sponsors and supporters - from inside and out of the marine industry - without whom this would be impossible.

On the day of the launch we got a call from Hugh Morrison to tell us that we had our meeting with Kingfisher – the meeting that we hoped would allow all our plans to become reality. It was arranged for the following Friday, just seven days away.

That evening I went back to Ashley Perrin's place. Ash was brilliant, keeping me fed while leaving me to get on with writing. This time I just got in and collapsed on a bean bag in the corner of the room, but snatched only a couple of hours' sleep before getting up to prepare my Boat Show speech.

I knew that it had to be a good one. The show was launching a new campaign called Big Blue, aimed at inspiring kids to get on to the water. I wanted to show support for that cause, and to demonstrate that things really are possible if you really give them your all. I knew that I had to communicate my passion. I would have to stand up there and wear my heart on my sleeve.

I was incredibly nervous as I stood alone at the microphone, hearing my heart-beat pounding away in my chest.

Normally when invited to lunch, I would politely decline, and ask if I could please have the money instead. For ten years I collected my lunch money, on a mission to save for a boat, each day placing the 70 pence in my tin! When I asked Denzil if this was possible today, he cunningly suggested I made a speech instead . . . maybe I should have kept my mouth shut!

Since then things have moved on. I have spent four solid years working on projects, racing, crossing oceans . . . and really living. The decision to sail full-time was, and I always hope will be, the best decision of my life.

Many of you will remember the Mini Transat, the biggest project for me until this year. Over 4,000 miles of 'hard-core' racing in 21-foot skiff-like boats, Cabins resembling the interior of washing machines (size included!), no bunks, no sleeping bags, freeze-dried food, and the ocean. A wonderful race – I learnt so much about campaigns, racing alone, myself, the world and about others. I made some fantastic friends, and through this race have teamed up with Mark Turner, with whom I now work on future projects. Not only for ourselves – Offshore Challenges is a company designed to help and inspire others, and to work with them to achieve their goals.

As with any industry, we face huge hurdles. Just eighteen days ago, and weeks from the start of my next race, the Open 50 we'd had promised for the Route du Rhum was withdrawn. Since then we've travelled over 8,000 miles in search of a new boat. Having found one in the States, I fly out next weekend to sail her home to a race start just three weeks later.

Tiny things can make an immense difference, and people's kindness and support in whatever form is priceless. But this is not about asking for charity, it's not about pleading for help. The bottom line is business. Single-handed sailing in particular has the potential to break through the barrier of people's perceptions. It can dismiss the elitist image, bringing passion, emotion and feelings into people's homes. If someone is exhausted, happy or emotional, anyone can understand, anyone can relate. You don't have to be a sailor, or have even set foot on a boat before.

Eight hundred thousand people will descend on St-Malo for the start of the Route du Rhum in two months' time. The event is covered extensively, the start shown 'live' on national TV and radio, and is virtually as popular in France as Formula 1 Grand Prix.

Their sailors are heroes. They are setting goals, they are winning. Young people in France believe that they can do that too, because they can see, and have access to this success. Each and every one of them feels a part of it, and I believe their nation feels this.

Exactly three years ago I was here at the show. I knew no one in the industry but was so quickly supported and accepted. I have been lucky – I was a wide-eyed teenager, finding my feet during a single-handed round Britain sail. I was young, naive, and soaking up the atmosphere. People have helped me, supported me and believed in me. The BMIF took me under their wing, and gave me chances to speak, to talk to people and to learn more. I hope that in time I can not only just return this, but put more back in.

I do not know where my motivation has come from, but I feel it is my goal to pass it on, to help and encourage others, and to sow the seeds of inspiration, which transform dreams into reality: to race, to compete, or simply to enjoy the water.

In the next ten days I have to find £25,000 to make this race happen. New sails, a new engine, travel and a roof over my head. This end of the sport is expensive, but so vital for the future. The football industry will not promote sailing, the Formula 1 industry will not promote sailing. It is down to us.

One thing I've learnt over the past years is that if deep down in your heart you have a goal, you CAN achieve it. Getting to this stage has pushed me hard, harder than I ever imagined, but I have experienced moments more rewarding and more beautiful than in my wildest dreams. Yes, it's true, luck does play a part in it. But if you believe, and are determined, you can build your own luck ... and realize that vision is really NOT so far away.

As I spoke my final words there was silence. I had to pause for breath between the sentences to try to calm myself. I was exhausted, completely exhausted, and letting all that out in one hit had just about finished me off. As I sat down in my seat the world closed around me – I could make out faces, but their words didn't connect. I suppose it was the relief of having shared so much. The bottom line is that we could not have coped without the support of all those who rallied around us.

After the show, work on both the race and our crucial sponsorship presentation continued at fever pitch. The speech had immediately resulted in offers of everything from free berthing for *Great Circle* to a free engine and other bits of kit for the boat.

Date: Wed, 16 Sep 1998 02:21:39

We were working on the promotional video tonight . . .
still up as usual! 0059. We have a meeting on Friday
with a sponsor we hope will come in for the next three
years. However, there's a fair bit of persuading to do
on this front, and we've never met him before . . .

We're in a bit of financial strife here! We're cleared
out with sail deposits, charter fees, insurance premiums,
flights and 'everyday bills' . . . All fairly stressed.

We should have had the entrance fee in by the end of
last week. but they've given us till this weekend to
come up with the money. £4,500 . . .

Later that day I called Mum, and though I had kept her up to date in sporadic phone-calls with all that was going on, I don't think she realized quite how bad things were until that moment. I was desperate, and just needed to share the burden. I had held back before as I didn't want to worry my parents, but right now I just had to call. We had less than twenty-four hours before, without the entry fee, we were out of the race. Since the holiday in Scotland they had clearly been discussing things between themselves, because after listening to me without saying a word, Mum said quietly that there was some money available. I was puzzled, I still owed them £15,000 for the Mini Transat.

'Your Nan left you £5,000 in her will.' Oh, Nan! My eyes welled with tears – she was still making the difference. It may have been last minute, but we'd be on that start line now. I gave Mum the race organizers' bank details.

The surprises didn't stop here though. That same evening I was asked if I would present the prizes for Cowes Week. I was supposed to be with Mark and Dick working on the video, but I decided to go anyway.

I arrived in a terrible state. I'd bailed out of Ashley's that morning and had run from the Boat Show with all my bags. As I arrived I was flushed and sweating. I took a deep breath in an attempt to make myself look presentable and as the lift headed to the top floor I leant back against its cool wall and took advantage of the brief moment of peace to drift away.

I was shown round by Bill West, whose company was behind the awards, and recognized Johnny Caulcutt, who'd supported our Mini Transat campaign. We all talked and I couldn't hide the fact that things were pretty dire. How we'd just managed to charter a boat and just managed to pay the entrance fee. How we were still in the race by the skin of our teeth.

Our conversation was cut short by the prize-giving, and after a brief introduction by Bill I handed over each prize in turn.

As things were drawing to an end, Johnny leapt up on stage without warning and began to recount our conversation, finishing emphatically, 'Now, this girl needs support right now! I pledge £1,000, Bill, you'll pledge £1,000, won't you?' and within five minutes we had raised almost £5,000. I've no recollection of what I said when Johnny encouraged me to say a few words. I just know that they ended with the most heartfelt thank-you. I only hoped that each person who had supported us had just an inkling of what a difference they had made.

I wanted to hug everyone in the room. As soon as I could, I raced outside to call Mark and tell him not to despair. He immediately ran off a string of problems with the video and sounded very depressed. The computer had just crashed and they were having to start a whole section from scratch.

'Mark,' I said, 'I've got some good news. We've got £5,000. Johnny Caulcutt just stood up and raised £5,000.'

I'm sure Mark thought I was winding him up as he failed to react at all, saying little more than, 'I have to go, see you later' before hanging up.

Date: Thu, 17 Sep 1998 23:11:03

Another fairly full on day. Found out today that the rudder for Great Circle is being rebuilt, and will not be flown out (nor will the owner, as he's coming with it!) till Monday 21st!!!!

The more I think about the problem, the stronger I feel. There is such determination inside me; I can feel it ... We will not give up, and we will get there ... and NOT just for me.

There is a way, and I shall run and run until I find it.

Friday was suddenly upon us. Since starting on the video we had worked non-stop, snatching no more than eight hours' sleep between us in three days. At nine in the morning on the day of the presentation we were still getting documents bound.

It felt like all or nothing. The following day I was flying out to Bermuda and we were heading for the meeting that held the potential to change everything. Mark and I met Hugh in London and we all jumped in a cab to head for Kingfisher's office. He was a calming presence. If he was nervous it was impossible to tell. He'd obviously done a lot more of this than we had.

It was intimidating to walk into an enormous boardroom which we felt so unaccustomed to. But we felt the meeting went well, and by the end I think that the CEO Geoff Mulcahy's interest had certainly grown for the project. Hugh had sat down on the opposite side of the table from us; it was really Mark and I who were there to sell the project.

We talked predominantly about the Vendée Globe, showing the video we had produced with Dick, and talking through slides we had created. We were passionate about the fact that a project like the Vendée Globe could work and that we were not asking for the money so as to enable us to stick their name on a boat's hull and go sailing. We wanted to work with the company to make the sponsorship work for them, both internally and externally. We felt that some sailing sponsors had been used in the past, and we emphatically were not going to allow this to happen. As far as we were concerned we were in it together and were going to work as a team.

What was initially a chance meeting on leaving the boardroom was later to become a critical factor. Geoff left the room to answer an important call, and briefly greeted a man who was leaving the lift. Hugh whispered to Mark, 'You should engage this guy.' Mike Hingston was not only a keen sailor, but a perfectionist with vision.

Three months later he was the Director of Corporate Affairs and a key decision-maker when it came to sponsorship.

Chapter Twelve

I don't think that Liam or Chris had a clue what they were letting themselves in for when I met them at Heathrow. They were willing volunteers for the delivery from Bermuda. Liam had been working at Ocean Village on the trimaran *Spirit of England* at the same time as I had been working on the 50 David and I had sailed in the Round Britain and Ireland race. We had kept in touch since and both Merv and I thought he was more than up to the job of helping with the delivery of *Great Circle*. He was from Liverpool and had a great sense of humour; his laughter proved to be a very precious commodity in the weeks that followed.

I barely knew Chris at all. He was hoping to do the Mini Transat the following year and had already bought a boat. He was about to take part in the Atlantic Rally for Cruisers (ARC) to get miles under his keel, but before that the trip back from Bermuda was a great opportunity to gain open ocean experience. I think he got a bit more than he bargained for!

When we arrived in Bermuda the weather was deteriorating. We headed for the Customs House in St George's where the boat was lying. Once on board we made ourselves at home and I was impressed with how well built *Great Circle* seemed. Everything was clean and tidy and there was even enough food from Brian's trip on board to fashion a meal later. There was a bunk on each side of her and in the centre she had a canting chart table facing a Recaro race seat. I dropped my sleeping-bag on it and gave the guys the bunks – I'd need to get used to sleeping in it anyway.

We soon jumped off for a swim. I wanted to see what state the keel was in as we knew that she'd suffered damage on a reef last time she was sailed. Besides, we'd been travelling all day and it was stinking hot.

```
Hi Mark,
     Just to let you know the situation with the boat.
     We're alongside in Bermuda. The boat is relatively
OK, although the mainsail and rudder are a large
problem. Brian has not arrived yet, he should be flying
in today. Apparently he had problems with getting the
rudder stock through Customs. The new one is fairly
heavy . . . like three times the weight of the old one!
No choices on this one now though.
     The mainsail will, I hope, last the trip but we
haven't had it up yet. So far things have been very,
very hot, very, very windy, and very, very, very wet.
We've had squalls so strong the aircraft have not been
able to land!
     The rudder is another problem. There's a lot to do on
it. We literally have some foam shapes here, that's all.
They're not even really rudder shape! A big job, and
more I will only know when Brian arrives. It seems a
little suspect to me. The thought of glassing foam
fairings on to an aluminium stock does not fill me with
a feeling of security! I will mail Merv and Nigel now to
ask for advice.
     As far as life in Bermuda is concerned. Great people,
extremely hot, warm water, but very, very expensive.
Food is at least twice the price of in the UK. We have
cooked for ourselves here, but each meal is costing at
least 40 dollars! Money is going quickly here. I am
worried about stocking up for the trip back. I guess I
just have to go for it, but it will be hundreds . . .
```

The generator will not start at all right now. We've played with it a little, although I'm loath to play with it too much, as Brian obviously knows the systems much, much better. The Ockham electronics are 'half working'. Heading works, but no wind-speed, wind direction etc.

Fitting the engine will be fun too. If we change one for the other, we'll have the sail-drive leg sticking through the rudder tube! Problems . . .

The mast leaks like mad around the base. Minor problem right now though.

Hope all's well there, thanks for everything,

Please mail back with any news. We'll be at least another three days here . . . a bloody expensive three days at that.

Ellen

xx

As planned, Brian flew in for a couple of days with the new rudderstock and we immediately rose to the challenge of preparing the boat with enthusiasm. But as the whole thing began to take shape I realized that the key-way at the top of the rudder was back to front. This meant that we could only fit the rudder in the boat backwards – which was worse than useless. This was disastrous: we were already delayed, and had now to find a machine shop which might be able to mill out a flat area on the other side – which we could only hope to goodness would be a solution. We made a number of inquiries and managed to find a machine shop where the stock could be ground down to fit, and at least the time it took for the stock to be milled gave me and Brian a chance to go through the electronics and instruments on board, and spend an evening together on the dockside discussing the sailing side of her. The day after we'd collected the rudderstock Brian flew back to the States.

We were on our own, but throughout, the warmth of the local people and their willingness to help were priceless. One of them was the retired harbourmaster, Bernard Oakley or 'Bitzy', who would come down to see us every day on his moped – a lovely and unbelievably helpful guy who deserves a medal for his services to sailors. His brother owned the local hardware shop and as there was no real yacht chandler's we became very dependent on Bitzy's brother.

Cannon Ball, a big friendly guy who wore his baseball cap under his crash helmet, also made Bermuda feel like a different place. He came down on his moped just to ask, 'How ya doing?' A measure of how bedraggled we must have looked was when he arrived with a bag of clothes for us from the local charity shop. Chris was particularly taken with a pair of bright green trousers which needed the ankle cuffs cut off and the waistband folded down just to fit.

I felt immense pressure during our days in Bermuda, and though I desperately wanted just to have a laugh with the others I felt completely detached from them. On a couple of evenings they went off into the town for a few beers but I could not go with them as I dared not spend more money than we had to, and my mind was completely preoccupied. I was worried, really worried – we had a rudder to repair, there were three hurricanes tracking towards us, and we just had to get out of there. As they recounted their tales the following morning I smiled, but felt a million miles away.

Still, the guys ground out the day's work, although I think that Chris in particular wondered what on earth he was doing there. I don't blame him. They were both amazing and it made a massive difference to have their help and support. They both did it all for nothing. We had paid for their flights, but could not pay them for the work that was necessary just to make *Great Circle* seaworthy.

The rudder was a massive job which had taken the best part of a week to complete and when finished it was by no means perfect but it had to work. However, getting the stock up inside the boat might well have turned out to be a hellish task as she was moored alongside the dock. I envisaged the 120-kilo stock sinking to the bottom underneath the boat. As it turned out, once we had actually repaired it, it floated despite its great weight. While this made fitting it easier it also created its own set of problems, however.

Amazingly, local people appeared from nowhere to watch the event – they all came to see what was going on. We couldn't have wished for a more helpful audience. With the rudder floating we had to find a way of sinking it, so some of our audience disappeared in search of something appropriate, returning later with an enormous piece of cast-iron drainpipe. This we tied to the rudder in a way that allowed us to control the depth the whole weighted arrangement sank to, and Liam and I swam beneath the boat, diving under, holding our breath, making sure that it was aligned with the hole. When released, the rudder floated up underneath the boat, and I think everyone was amazed when this strategy worked and the stock fitted exactly in place.

We were told that the old sails on the boat were adequate to deliver *Great Circle* back to the UK where we planned to replace them. As it happened, they were rather less than adequate – particularly the mainsail – in fact they were barely in one piece – one side of the main had even been completely covered in sticky-back sail cloth in an attempt to hold the whole thing together. The existing inboard engine was also in a shocking state and could only be started by shorting it out with a screwdriver. We got it going but once it was running, it made a variety of frightening rattling sounds.

On the final morning we started the little emergency outboard engine (our only propulsion as the inboard engine was for charging batteries only) to make sure all was OK. We'd tested it a couple of times and had got it going, but weatherwise we were looking at sailing into a large high pressure, which was good news on the hurricane front, but bad news on the wind front. With this in mind Liam suggested it would be a good idea to check over the outboard to clean the spark plugs. A loud Scouse 'F***' told us that the spark plug had sheared off inside the engine. My heart sank.

The nearest machine shop was a taxi ride away and we used our last $20 to get the engine there. I walked in and told the guys what had happened. We fought with the engine for three hours, but the thread was completely corroded to the cylinder. The engineer shook his head. If it had not been for the incredible help that we were given in there we might never have left – they called up every outboard engine supplier on the island, and on their last call found a man who had a suitable engine costing $2,500. I knew full well that only one of my cards might work, and that it had already been refused a $600-dollar transaction. I phoned Mastercard in a final attempt to beg for a higher limit. I began to explain the situation, but as soon as I mentioned Bermuda I was told that there had been a problem with the lines and that my earlier attempt should have been OK. I had barely enough, but enough. Thank God.

This piece of good news was followed by a much greater one. Just before we left Bermuda I called Mark. His news took my breath away. Kingfisher had confirmed that they were going to sponsor us for the Route du Rhum. Absolutely elated with the news, I ran to tell Chris and Liam. Although it didn't make much difference to our immediate plans, it lifted all our spirits and we left Bermuda on a high. I knew that our quest for the Vendée Globe was starting to come within reach.

As we left we hoisted the sails behind two cruise ships. We were elated. On several occasions problems had looked insurmountable and it seemed that there would be no option but to fly home. We hadn't showered in ten days, had lived in clothes covered with carbon, grease and resin, and the conditions in St George's had been pretty miserable. Only the wonderful support of the people in Bermuda had made things possible. Now at last our destiny was in our own hands again.

Most days on the *Great Circle* epic from Bermuda, as it was soon to be dubbed, we worked on the sails, fixing holes and just trying to get them to stay together long enough to see us home. As we helmed there was a regular shower of glue and flaked-off particles falling on us – the sails were literally disintegrating before us.

But as though the sails were not a big enough problem, the weather was also about to test us. Hurricane Lisa, instead of following the normal hurricane track, heading west and then north from the Caribbean, came charging up the Atlantic towards us before reaching the Caribbean. Roughly 1,000 miles into our trip we had to turn back towards Bermuda for two and a half days to avoid the storm. It was massively frustrating but it would have been idiotic for us to continue on and try to battle it out, especially with the mainsail in its fragile condition. We just wouldn't have managed it. We fretted about the possibility of breakages, from the rudder up, but our major goal was to get back across the Atlantic to Britain and then sort things out. We were not racing but we had to make it to the other side, that was our sole aim. We had provision for replacing the rigging once back in Southampton – new sails were being made as we sailed – and back in Cowes a lot of effort was going into the project. Mark was spending all his time trying to work out a schedule for us, and the list of jobs to do was growing by the minute.

We were sailing as conservatively as possible but even so, I remember that at one point we were sailing in a fair amount of wind with three reefs in. We were under-canvased but we did not want to go back to two reefs because then we would be carrying slightly too much sail. In the end, though, we were forced to go back to two reefs simply because the third had all but pulled out of the sail. The second reef appeared to be the strongest of all the points. I could say that things were far from ideal but that would be something of an understatement. We had to do the best we could in the circumstances. Despite everything, humour on board was outstanding, I don't think we were demoralized, the guys were fantastic – we all just got on with the grim situation, which perhaps just seemed too farcical to be anything but laughable to them, and certainly they always tried to see the funny side of what was going on. We occasionally trailed a line, never really expecting to catch anything, but one afternoon Liam and I caught an enormous Dorado off the stern deck. Our on-board diet was fairly basic and it was great to enjoy fresh food – we had eaten the whole thing by sunset.

Great Circle didn't perform as I had imagined she would but I hoped that with her new sails and faired rudder her performance would improve. The stakes had been raised greatly with the news that Kingfisher was sponsoring us, so while I needed to learn more about the boat I also had to deliver in the race to secure our future. It was a real concern to think how unprepared to race she was.

About a week into our trip, the luff of the mainsail was ripping apart, tearing at the seams of the battens. Everyone's patience was tested to the limit as virtually every stitch had to have a bradawl hole made first, or someone else at the other side to retrieve the needle. We ended up sewing webbing straps around in an attempt to hold it together. We sewed for days on end and that was the most demoralizing thing for Chris and Liam. They'd signed up to sail across the Atlantic, not limp across as tailor's apprentices. I felt guilty but they never complained.

We made a decision to put into the Azores where we could replace the mainsail. But as we approached the islands my mobile came back into reception for the first time in just under a month and I spoke to Mark, uncertain of which course of action would be the best to take. We would have to wait two days for the sails to arrive so I suggested that we head for Spain instead – it would be much easier for Merv and Sam Davies, a new member of the team, to transport the sails there. I found it hard to tell the guys. We were a mile off the entrance to Horta in the Azores and could practically taste the ice-cold beers!

The disappointment was exacerbated by the next few frustrating days, probably the most difficult of the whole trip. We had no wind and I wrote in my log:

Battered and exhausted. Mentally tested and just 'hanging; hanging in'. If there were ever a test of endurance as far as I've ever been tested anyway now is it. How late can this RUN? It's never time to give in, we're almost on European shores and we shall not give in until she reaches them with the three of us on board.

When we finally arrived in Spain it was far from over. That evening I planned to set sail once again to the UK with new sails. We had just thirteen days before we were due in St-Malo for the start of the Rhum, still with a million repairs, an engine to fit, and a delivery to the UK, then France!

Another new priority was to take a few promotional photos that needed to be sent back of me wearing my first Kingfisher shirt –

the only clean piece of clothing I now possessed! I'd spoken to Merv a few times from Bermuda but it was wonderful to see him again.

Late in the afternoon, Merv took a call from Mark. Even recalling it now makes the hairs on the back of my neck stand up. I was lying on the gravel car park floor trying to attach one of the batten fittings. Merv handed the phone over to me, and I knew something important was about to happen when Mark said, 'Make sure you're sitting down.'

'Don't worry, I'm lying down,' I replied.

He then told me I needed to get on the next plane home to Britain. It took a long time for his words even to register. I told him he must be nuts. I still had to sail the boat back for the qualifier and I didn't have time to fly home for some meeting.

He had difficulty making me understand, as my mind was racing at such a pace that I wasn't really listening. He told me I wasn't going to race *Great Circle* in the Route du Rhum. I feared the worst and felt sick deep in the pit of my stomach. I was light-headed and confused. Entirely without my knowledge, Mark had negotiated some additional funds from Kingfisher to charter *Aqua Quorum*, the boat in which Pete Goss had competed in the Vendée Globe, and had just had confirmation seconds before calling. There were no more flights to the UK that day so I had to spend a night in Spain. With no necessity to work on *Great Circle*, it was the first time I had relaxed in months. There was nothing more I could do. Indeed we all talked and enjoyed each other's company, laughing about things which at the time had seemed obstacles beyond belief.

Next morning I jumped on the first flight back to Britain while Merv and the others finished the final jobs on board *Great Circle*. As I sat on the plane I felt a pang of regret that after all we had been through *Great Circle* and I would not be racing together. But I couldn't help but feel it was our only choice. We had been delayed so many times now that we would only have been able to spend a few days in the UK – not really enough to complete the jobs that were necessary for her just to qualify. It was sad for Brian Hancock too – after being forced to pull out of a race, the glimmer of hope that the boat might race in another had gone. I wrote him a letter, which finished:

I am sorry not to have taken GC. I was sad as we drove off to the airport. You do develop a relationship with a boat over a period of time. I was never worried about her strength. She lives for the surf, and is very easy to sail.

Life works in strange ways . . . Goals ARE dreams with deadlines. That's the problem! It's a shit fight out there.

Brian, thanks for all your support.
Will be in touch.
kind regards
ellen

When I landed in London I took the train down to Southampton, spent a few hours in the office in Cowes and met up with Nigel Irens who was driving to the West Country that evening. This was a happy coincidence, and it was wonderful to chat about all we had been through to someone who understood the situation. We drove down through the night, arriving in the early hours of the morning at Nigel's office in Totnes, where I slept on the floor after he dropped me off.

As I woke the following day I was tired but excited. I had read Pete Goss's book on the way back across the Atlantic but the possibility of chartering *Aqua Quorum* from him came as a complete surprise. My understanding was that Andy Hindley was going to sail her in the race. However, Andy, a member of Pete's team, had not been able to find sponsorship. He was there when I arrived in the boat shed and was organizing getting her ready to go. I felt for him, and could only imagine the sorrow he must be feeling at being unable to race.

The boat had been laid up for some time so there was a tremendous amount still to do if she was to be ready in time for the race. The mast wasn't in, the keel wasn't on and some of the electronics were missing, but somehow we got everything done and when the logos were finally applied she looked fantastic. I was desperately trying to get some rest as well as being down in the yard for the important jobs that were being done. There were interviews too. A French TV crew came over to Plymouth, wrapping up by asking, 'So tell me, Ellen, what is your favourite French phrase?'

I thought about it briefly, then replied, '*A donf!*' Slang for 'Go for it', this was seized on by the French public watching the programme and has become the slogan for all our campaigns.

We were hampered by gales all week but just before we left for St-Malo, *Aqua Quorum*, now renamed *Kingfisher*, and I went out for a test sail in Plymouth Sound with Pete. It was blowing about a Force 7, and I doubted that we would be able to make it out against the wind, but Pete knew her well, and we had a cracking sail for an hour or so. Ashore, the team were fantastic and Pete's team couldn't have been more helpful, which meant I was able to take a little time away from the boat. Although I found it difficult not to be there all the time – and particularly not to be doing the jobs myself – I knew that the next weeks were going to be tough, and that this really was my last opportunity to check over charts and weather tactics and to spend a couple of mornings with Merv before I sailed off to St-Malo. Merv himself would be flying to Cape Town in a few days, for Mike Golding's next stop on the Around Alone. I would have loved to have had him there for the last week before the start of the race.

Nothing could have prepared me for St-Malo – and the atmosphere before the start. I was aware that the Route du Rhum was a massive event but the thousands and thousands of people who came to see the start still took me by surprise. By the start cars, all facing into town, were parked bumper to bumper for miles on every approach road. The dock held thirty-six of the most beautiful boats I'd ever seen, lined up on the pontoons, decorated with flags and lit by floodlights. I felt very privileged even to have a slot there.

I had never before been asked for my autograph, but here I could not leave the cabin without hearing my name called out. I spent hours signing autographs, and found it difficult to walk away when so many people were still holding out their programmes and pieces of paper. It was quickly apparent that sailing in France is far from an élitist sport. People were coming to see us not because it was their hobby, but because they enjoyed what we did and wanted to show their support by wishing us 'bon vent'.

As the week slipped by I found I was talking to journalists for hours on end. St-Malo was wearing me down. I found it increasingly hard to spend time anywhere other than hidden away. And as the number of people coming to town increased, so the number of interviews seemed to explode exponentially. I was still very wide-eyed and keen to soak it all in, but there is only so much of this you can do before becoming saturated. Luckily the euphoria of being there kept me going and Mark was in the same position. His brain was working overtime as he tried to juggle the demand for inter-views with time with the team, discussing final adjustments that needed to be made to the boat.

I spent what free time I had learning about various emergency procedures, the electronic systems and the hydraulic keel with Jim Doxey, from Pete's team, who had worked on the concept of the boat. There were always solutions to find on a boat designed with a 6-foot marine in mind – I could not even reach some of the cleats on the mast and had to jump up to them each time. I spent several evenings poring over the weather charts with Andrew Cape, the new team expert, but I was so tired I could hardly keep my eyes open. Most of them, it seemed, contained bad news – big depressions, and a string of them – and it was obvious that this was not going to be easy. One weather fax had 'bomb' plainly written on it. Even Capey said he'd never come across that before. Great, I thought, that's all we need!

That day we had our first visitors from Kingfisher when CEO Sir Geoff Mulcahy and Mike Hingston, who had both been present at our initial meeting, fought their way through the crowds to come aboard. I didn't know whether to shake their hands or hug them as I knew it was only through their support that we'd got this far. Geoff was very tall, but despite his imposing presence remained very approachable. Mike, responsible for corporate PR, was also a passionate supporter of ours. You knew that once he was committed to something he'd give it everything he'd got. Geoff asked about how I put the spinnakers up and as I described the process, I was conscious that I had only ever seen one of the four spinnakers out of its bag. I was confident, though, because this was our big chance.

I felt sure that Kingfisher had said yes to our project for a reason and I drew strength from that thought.

That evening, as we took *Kingfisher* through the locks ready for the start the next day, the crowds went wild, and I tingled from head to toe at the warmth and encouragement they showed. I waved back at them and shouted inadequately, '*Merci, Merci.*' It was now nearly midnight and there were literally thousands of people jamming the sides of the lock and the docks. It was early in the morning when I eventually crawled beneath the sheets to sleep. I made a quick call to Merv and drifted off. I was tired, but still relaxed.

At 1302, the gun went off.

Just ten minutes earlier all the team had clambered off the boat. It was a powerful moment, the reward for months of determination. Mark was unable to articulate the intensity of how he felt. He didn't need to, his face said it all. We had succeeded. We were on the start line.

After the gun, as the boats jostled for position, I was more concerned for our safety than anything else. There were race boats everywhere, and I didn't want to have a collision so close to the start. I was out there now racing with a large proportion of the best single-handed sailors in the world. This was it; my turn.

It was hazy and drizzly, but thankfully there was wind. I was further out than other boats and so I spent the first hour more alone than with the fleet. Mum and Dad, who'd arrived the day before, came alongside in an RIB to say goodbye before watching their daughter sail off into a gale. I caught my last sight of them before they turned for home, their faces betraying a mixture of pride, happiness and concern.

They very nearly failed to make it at all when the boat they were in broke down right in the path of Mike Birch's trimaran, and understandable abuse flung their way during his avoiding manoeuvres is surely among their most vivid memories of the day.

As Cap Frehel approached we were still surrounded by spectator boats, from tiny fishing dories, to family cruisers and cross-Channel ferries. All shouted encouragement. The clifftops of Cap Frehel itself were also lined with excited people, all cheering '*Allez Ellen!*'

or 'A donf!' There were tears in my eyes, and the emotion inside was hard to contain. Both praise and support were relentless. These people were proud of us too, it seemed that they understood the strain of the past months, and their smiles and good wishes were telling me that all would be well and that it had all been worth it.

By midnight on the first night it had blown up. The barometer fell and the wind howled through the rigging. Changing sails on the foredeck was lethal. *Kingfisher* tried her best to cling to the water's surface while I just tried to cling to her. I was being pounded, thrown again and again on to the deck as her hull flicked up to hit me while I was slammed down by the motion of falling from the wave before – it was unrelenting. With each impact I closed my eyes and gritted my teeth, hanging on as tightly as possible. I tried everything to calm her, but the waves were enormous, and whether we charged over them or fell down them, it was going to hurt.

A hard lesson learned though – Pete's boat was unusual in the fleet as it did not have furling foresails which allow the sails to be rolled around the forestay by a control line worked from the safety of the cockpit rather than requiring a sailor to manhandle them on the foredeck. Foredeck work in heavy weather is fairly full on, and Pete was clearly stronger than me. He had gone for the reliability option in the Vendée by not taking furling sails – it was a shame we had not had time to fit them before the start of the race.

The wind continued to rise during the first few days, and by the third I was changing down to the storm-jib on the foredeck, and was thrown off my feet before cracking my head hard against the inner forestay rod, resulting in an instant lump and a strange nausea. Soon afterwards, the front passed, only to bring even stronger 55-knot gusts in a steady 45. It was an unreal, crazy situation; just trying to hang on inside the boat took every ounce of strength. Food was hurled around the cabin along with water containers and spares, while I tried to scrape things up and put them back in the boxes. My hands stung, my eye was swollen, and my wrists were already covered in open sores. The Quebec–St-Malo had been very tough physically, but nothing like this. In fact, conditions were so bad that Mark Gatehouse, an experienced English single-handed sailor and a friend of Alan Wynne-Thomas, had been thrown across the cabin and smashed his ribs, forcing him to head home just days into the race.

Dawn brought some respite. My core temperature warmed after the freezing night, but if I sweated through the physical exertion of a sail change, when I stopped I'd once again cool to a shiver. Sleep proved virtually impossible – just snatched ten-minute bursts ended by cold.

Sent: 9/11/98 2:50
Received: 9/11/98 6:34
From: Kingfisher, 423420410@c-link.net

M. FullOn but allOK bar unbearable shddering. Survival
suit s godsend. 45 knts plus. Fredeck is hell!
Lst night was bad, so very cold. If my eyes closed to
sleep They would opento find me shvering. Decsion making
hard, getting strm jib ondeck yestpm felt like climbing
everest. Fightingthis cold and enrgyless state. Can
hrdly type, thnkx fr messges. V welcme! Love to M&D.
Love from a batered e! (glad 2 be off tho!) Exx

Just two days later conditions began to worsen again. Doing anything was not only difficult but painful. My hands were red-raw and swollen, and my head was aching – even more so when the freezing water washed breathtakingly over it each time I went forward to change sails. It became more obvious that the boat had been designed for Pete Goss. Shifting the sails was hard, brutal work. Each time it was time to change one I would pull it forward, clipping myself on and hanging on for dear life. Waves would continuously power down the side-decks, often washing me and the sail back several feet, and I had to hang on and tighten my grip on the sail tie even further. I would often cry out loud as I dragged the sail along; it was one way of letting out some of that frustration and of finding the strength to do it. Once forward, each sail had to be clipped on hank by hank with freezing fingers. After each sail change I would collapse into the little cuddy seats out of the spray, close my eyes briefly and try to recover.

After a week things finally began to calm, and with my backside red-hot and sore, and my wrists and fingers swollen, I finally enjoyed the first opportunity to remove my survival suit. Though the relief was wonderful, the smell was not!

Sent: 14/11/98 15:23
Received: 14/11/98 17:50
From: Kingfisher, 423420410@c-link.net

HI .. OK my words, but first. . . . An overwhelming thankyou. There is noway in thisworld I could be here without you, I have been doing a lot of thinking over the past days, and can offer little more at this time other than offer my eternal thanks, and win the bloody race!
. e xx

4 hrs at 12-19 knots! Great to have KINGFISHER going like a train. WE're hanging in there in the 60 fleet, and proving our own as being 2 of the smallest in the fleet! Herself and me!

Its been fantastic tbe able sail her rather than simply survive! The storms of the first week were horrendous, and now, after I had a chance to walk on her decks rather than crawl, and place someing on a surface without it ending up in the bilge! Today I removed all the food I could fnd from in the spares boxes, underthe anchorand behind the bunks. Each of the food boxes crossed the cabin at least 6 times each during the storm, dispensing hteir cotents eerywhere they could!
Got to go.
exx
love
e
xxx

After a frustrating, windless time around the Azores, worse was to come, however.

Survival suit back on. It was the fourth depression – ten days into the race. We had winds reaching 65 knots over the deck, and as the front passed a constant 50–55 was not welcomed with open arms. Tacking the boat was interesting in such strong breeze, the swing-keel timing playing a vital role in her somewhat wave-driven dance. The wind was to switch to NW with the front, and this was the debut of our sleighride to Guadeloupe (or so we thought).

It was after this fourth depression that disaster struck. I was having a rather bad time, as I'd spent five hours of a 35-knot night resewing the leech on the staysail. A piston hank had come undone, allowing the leech to flog. I was exhausted as the crashing waves slowly became visible in the approaching daylight, and my fingers were now bleeding with punctures. Elated that I had finished the job, I went below to grab a snack – it was almost time to put the staysail up again. As I foraged in one of the food boxes I noticed there was some water on the floor, and although there was usually a small amount from drips, this seemed like a bit more. I checked forward to see if there was water there, and was shocked to see there was. It was ankle-deep, so clearly the forehatch must have come undone over the last few hours.

I decided a complete bail-out was in order before I changed sails, so I started the process of drying out each compartment in turn. I sealed the fore-hatch, and while trying to balance with the horrendous motion I took a good few bucketfuls out of the forepeak.

I thought that I should check the aft compartment too, in case water had leaked on through the rudderstock seal. I'd already had this a few times, so before finishing off in the forepeak I decided to bail out the back. There were a few bucketfuls in there, but it was a frustrating job with the horrific motion. With the new wind direction we were sailing straight into the waves, which makes it hard for the boat to stick to the water. I was being flung up at the deck-head and then back down on to her hull, which made keeping the water in the bucket virtually impossible. I was sliding around and cursing at myself as the bucket's contents repeatedly ended up in my face before I could get it out of the hatch, and if it wasn't the contents of the bucket it was a wave coming down through the hatch as I opened it to empty.

I suddenly felt something was very wrong. *Kingfisher* began leaning more and more, and I heard the motor that controlled the swinging keel whining uselessly. I scrambled out of the hatch and across her now precariously steep deck to the cockpit, hanging on to anything I could as I went. I bore her away from the wind to bring her as upright as possible, reset the autopilot and went below to begin my crash course in advanced hydraulics.

My first slightly panicked call was to Mark. He answered from a marine equipment show in Amsterdam: 'I know you'll work it out.'

He hadn't said much, but his confidence in me was reassuring.

After I'd closed the 'last-resort lock-me-in-place' valves, the keel was still swinging as freely as ever, and after a tedious session removing at least 40 bolts I at last got the appropriate section of the keel box lid off. The problem was immediately obvious - the box was swilling with litres of oil. The hydraulic pipe had burst and the system itself was drained and lifeless. I called Merv, who was with Jim Doxey in South Africa on the stopover from the Around Alone. Jim had designed the system, and discussed with Merv what to do. Although we had been through the system before leaving, this was clearly a more critical problem, and it was difficult to understand exactly what went where, especially as I was already so tired. At the end of the day, though, what were the options? There was only the one, so I just got on with it.

I began to refill the 10-litre reservoir spoonful by spoonful with the spare oil I had on board. I was lying on my back on a rolling boat wearing a survival suit. I was covered in hydraulic oil and had denzer-tape grease from the valves spread all over my hands. There was still some water in the cabin, and the contents of my food boxes were swimming around in it. It all seemed so bizarre I could only see the funny side. What a state we were in!

Five hours later I had the keel jammed in the centre and was in a position to race once more. And despite the now inefficient keel and relative lack of stability, we enjoyed the fastest average in the fleet over the next four position reports.

After this disaster I did the usual full check through the boat and was alarmed to find a crack in the forward bulkhead, stemming from a drain-hole at its base. I went on deck and slowed her down, sitting next to the damage for an hour or so to see if it moved. I could see nothing, but the slow movement through the water was causing the boat to slam more. I marked the ends of each crack so that I could keep an eye on it, and gradually increased sail until she felt comfortable. I had been in the forepeak before the storm to check all was well, so it couldn't have been there long before I found it.

Before the keel had gone I was just a few miles behind one of the newest Open 60s in the race. But it's easy to lose miles and a damn site harder to pull them back. The tiredness and the heat were a problem, but most difficult of all was when the wind disappeared between depressions. One day we would be in a full-blown storm, the next we'd have a boat speed of barely 3 knots and mere whispers of unreliable wind. I found it frustrating beyond belief and I had to learn a more pragmatic approach to this kind of weather. It was up to me to understand better why and how the wind dies, then work to use that to my advantage. Races really can be won and lost in light airs.

```
Yesterday was awful. Really light breeze. 23 sail
changes - from kites to jibs . . Hard work in the
windless scorching sun, time when it becomes obvious I
am 50 not 60feet. FOr 4 hrs there was literally nothing
as the trough passed over us. I wonder if the rest of
the fleet have had personal clouds too?
   Helplessly sitting, as the position reports showed
othersmoving. A time to reflect on things far, far
away . . .
```

My hands were still raw, painful and riddled with salt sores and scabs, and in the still heat, sweat stung as it found its way into every abrasion. Even the easiest task such as sitting on my backside became an uncomfortable chore!

196

Thank goodness we had a good breeze for the last few days on our run into Guadeloupe. Just a few miles out I was told I had a call from Robert Nickerson, my old friend from Hull. I wondered what on earth he was calling me on board for. I phoned the number I was given, and he answered.

'Where are you?' he said in a familiar, friendly way.

'In a race called the Route du Rhum.'

'I know that, I've heard – what's your position?'

On his Round the World sail with *Panic Major*, Robert was coming to meet me! He joined me early on during the final painful day as we drifted around without wind in the lee of the island. Most get caught here with the finish just out of reach, and we were no exception. We eventually crossed the line that evening after dark.

There were horns and sirens, and a flotilla of boats of all sizes came out to greet us. After the becalmed final day the noise and colour were overwhelming. And we had not only won our class – the 50-footers – but only four of the twelve Open 60s that started had beaten us. Adrian Thompson, *Kingfisher*'s designer, and Pete Goss had built a 50 which was quite at home racing among the 60s.

All the same, the end this time felt very different to the Mini. I was ready to leave her. Although I patted her goodbye and said thank you, I was acutely aware that I had been sailing Pete's boat. I had felt a little like a guest on board – albeit a lucky one. She was a great boat. I climbed off her still sticky with sweat from our final hours of fight. Except for the rain, I had not washed for over twenty days and my face was sore with sunburn. But I knew I was glowing not just from the heat, but with relief.

As soon as things began to die down I crept off with Mark and sat in his rented car for five minutes while he made a phone call. I was almost delirious with fatigue, but my eyes were wide open, just soaking in the atmosphere around me. Mark said that we were going to a hotel for the press conference, and I rested my head against the car window as we sped through the streets in the dark.

Chapter Fourteen

We spent less than a week in Guadeloupe after the race although we did manage to catch up with Robert and Marie and Pipo. The response to our performance in the Rhum was extraordinary. The number of e-mails and fax messages of congratulation we received really opened my eyes to just how many people had been following us out there.

To: e.macarthur@rhum98.com
Subject: congratulations !

You are the English girl in the race.
We don't know you but are happy to tell you 'bonjour'
Sincerely Yours.
Famille Macabies
(We live in the Alps)

And

From: AMCO
To: La Reine Ellen et le Roi Turner

Well done the Glaouchs [Breton slang for the English] - you have really stuffed the French, and the rest of the world!!
Good luck for your future projects.
                    A+ Thierry

There was also a handwritten fax message sent from a small office services company in Derbyshire:

CONGRATULATIONS
WELL DONE!
WITH LOVE FROM ALL AT
HOME INCLUDING
MAC
MACARTHUR TRUE GRIT ALL
THE WAY AND FROM HEAD TO TOE.

The race marked a significant turning-point in so many ways. Both our futures had rested on how we performed but now we were faced with starting again from scratch. To compete in the Vendée we needed a boat, a team and sponsorship, and Kingfisher were not committed beyond the Rhum. We had proposed the Vendée project to them initially and were wondering if we had done enough to convince them to continue working with us. After the Route du Rhum a photograph of *Kingfisher* finishing appeared on the front page of *The Times*. I don't think in our wildest dreams we had thought that the race would get that kind of recognition. We knew that we had a powerful story, but that was never any guarantee. We felt this was an incredibly positive sign. It showed us that we were communicating what we were doing in the right way, and that sailing could reach the front pages for the right reasons. Sadly, since the arrivals of Sir Francis Chichester, Sir Chay Blyth and Sir Robin Knox-Johnston, single-handed sailing in the UK had more often than not been covered when things went wrong. We were in no doubt that Kingfisher would be over the moon too. As a stepping-stone for the future the Rhum could not have served us better. Mark and I believed that with *Kingfisher* we had something special: the relationship worked well, the formula worked well, the publicity had been an outstanding success, both in France and in the UK.

I could sense that one of the biggest difficulties facing Kingfisher was that they felt responsible for me and were concerned about sending someone in their early twenties out to race around the planet. I understood their point of view and knew that an article quoting a top single-handed sailor who said I shouldn't be going for the Vendée Globe hadn't helped. I had talked to other sailors who had taken part in the race and I knew that some of them felt I should be racing in a 50 rather than a 60. But I had sailed two transatlantics on 60-foot boats and knew that the size simply wouldn't be a problem. I also knew deep down that whatever happened, I would be in the next Vendée, with or without Kingfisher. The race was just waiting to burst out of me. But if things were going to happen they would have to move ahead very quickly – we would have to be building the boat by the summer.

It was time for me to write an honest letter that would let Kingfisher know in no uncertain terms that there was no way I would do it if I wasn't ready, and that there was no pressure on me to compete in the Vendée other than the pressure I put on myself.

Dear Geoff & Michael,

I have spent my life dreaming of the ocean, since 1994 I have done nothing but sail. It is my passion, my life, and undoubtedly is my future.

The Route du Rhum was a demanding race, both the conditions and the boat made it very testing, but it became the most incredible proving ground . . .

It is firmly cast in my own mind that I can do this. I had sailed the boat very little before the start, was learning the whole time, despite getting thrown around somewhat, I never felt out of my depth. I am a tough cookie, not someone who gives up. That is why I am ocean racing alone at 22.

There are real dangers, we all know what has happened in the past, but I believe I have a very level-headed approach. I will be getting around not only for Kingfisher, but also for my family and friends.

From a non-sailing point of view, the work with both

Mark and Gwenola on the Public Relations side has also
been a success. I have proved to myself that I can
communicate, even when things are tough, and the world
outside has been able to actively follow our progress.
This has led to an explosion in both UK and European
press. It has amazed us all, and I can see no reason why
this should not amaze us all again.

Being part of such a fantastic team, working with such
enthusiastic people has been a real pleasure . . .

I may sail alone out there, but without a committed
team it could never happen. I can do this – just as we
can do this.

It is inside me to compete in the Vendée Globe . . . I
will be on that finish line.

What more can I say, than,

Thank you to all at Kingfisher for the support so far.

Ellen

I had never written a letter trying to sell myself as confidently as this before, but I knew it had to show that I was sure I could do it, and was determined. We would have to wait and see what the response would be.

Our stay in Paris following the race was notable for a couple of reasons. I was astounded and touched to be told I had been awarded the 'Jeune Espoir de la Voile' or 'Sailing's Young Hope'. I gave my first speech in French with a little help from Gwenola on the translation front, addressing hundreds of people during an enormous dinner. Every other name on that trophy was French. It was a further measure of the impact we'd made with our campaign for the Rhum.

More significant, however, was a phone call from Kingfisher confirming that they would sponsor us for another two years. Mark and I were crossing a busy Paris street as we took the call on the mobile. By the time we'd reached the other side, both our lives had been changed for ever by the news. The new sponsorship meant that both of us were now by any measure professionals. And with this status came obligations. We'd always maintained that we had more to offer any sponsor than simply the opportunity to display their logos on the boat. We wanted it to be a partnership and this meant that our commitments to Kingfisher were to form a vital part of preparation for the Vendée.

At Christmas I returned to Derbyshire while, as usual, Mark headed to Australia on a one-month work contract and to compete in the Sydney Hobart Race. Although I had bought a Christmas card for him, I was too late to send it, so I included its message in a festive e-mail:

```
Mark,
    Just wanted to say the biggest thank you I can
electronically!
    It's been bloody hard this one, and we're both tired.
    You can't believe in half the things you hear,
You can't believe in most of what you read,
But you CAN believe in all of what you do . . .
We WILL get there . . .
    Message from Xmas Card I bought for you! . . .
'I was going to give you MONEY for Xmas . . .'
(TURN PAGE)
'But the Police dragged me out of the fountain before I
could gather together a respectable amount!'
    NOT FOR MUCH LONGER!? . . .
Love and best, best wishes,
sail safe, keep well,
    E
    Xx
```

Mark's Hobart race turned out to be a tragic reminder of the sheer power of the Southern Ocean at its most raw. A freak storm intensified, smashing many of the boats and causing a terrible loss of life. Mark was one of the lucky ones.

Christmas was cut short for me the day after Boxing Day when I drove down to Plymouth to the marina where *Aqua Quorum* was now lying after her delivery home. I spent a day on board trying to clean her, remove our belongings and leave her ready for handing over to Pete. I did all I could there and took away our belongings with her engine running to heat the cabin a bit. It was a sad final goodbye to the boat as I struggled along the pontoon in the drizzle with the last boxes of kit. Pete was upset about the crack I'd discovered in the forward bulkhead as well as external damage from having hit something at night, but I was hurt by his suggestion that I'd pushed her too hard. I could only reassure myself that I'd been as protective of her as I have of any of the boats I've sailed on – thinking of the boat before myself even. I understood Pete's instinctive reaction to the damage caused by the extreme conditions. I too would have felt wounded by it. It was a shame, though, because we should have been celebrating together, and I hoped that day would still come.

On the first day of the London International Boat Show in January we announced on centre stage that Kingfisher was sponsoring a fully funded Vendée Globe campaign. As I stood there and spoke in front of the journalists my knees shook. This was really it, this was the start of our dream. Our relationship with Kingfisher was building day by day in the planning, preparation and organization for the project and I found it both stimulating and rewarding to be involved in the meetings. We also made presentations to various different parts of the company, the first of which took me and Mark to Germany to talk to an audience of senior management. My right knee shook again and my mouth became so dry with nerves that I could hardly finish. Their support and belief in us were overwhelming and the implications of our relationship took a while to sink in. It simply changed everything – what we could do, how we could do it and what we could aspire to. It was important to us that they knew this – that we were able to convey how offering an opportunity can change people's lives. And that we'd never take it for granted.

Mark and I soon had to make our biggest decision of the year so far: who was going to design the new *Kingfisher* 60. It's more than just a question of finding who can design you the fastest boat. The

Vendée is notorious for its duration and remoteness, and any boat taking it on has to be strong, safe and reliable – your life is in their hands.

Initially we sent out a tender document to a host of designers, and reviewed them once the replies were back. All the responses were credible and it was a difficult decision to bring it down to our final two. One of these was Marc Lombard, a French designer, and the other a team comprising the Owen/Clarke Design Group, Rob Humphreys and Giovanni Belgrano. It was a tough decision but the team approach with its wide base of knowledge to draw on appealed enormously. Our only concern was that the Owen of Owen Clarke was in fact Merv, who had set up the company years before with his partner Allen Clarke. But we knew that there were few people available with such extensive knowledge of modern Open 60s, and in our final decision we felt that our personal relationship would help to make her a better boat. Merv was committed to his work and had already suggested he would be prepared to project-manage the build of the new boat. This was a big plus. We strived to do something a bit different, and though it was not our intention to take too many risks on the development front, we did not want a clone of the other boats. With the addition of former Vendée winner Alain Gautier, the team became the 'Kingfisher Design Team'.

The design decision-making process had been stressful. I had not discussed my views with Merv at all outside the office and this wasn't made any easier when we moved into a rented flat together. I think that even at this stage the project had begun slowly to grind us down. And although, perhaps, our relationship contributed to the care and incredible attention to detail so evident in *Kingfisher*, at the same time she put us both under the first signs of pressure.

We also went with the decision to build *Kingfisher* in New Zealand. I had made a brief trip out there to see Merv at the end of January. He was there as part of Mike Golding's Group 4 campaign before he'd run aground off North Island, which ended his race. I fell in love with the country and its people instantly. Another attraction was New Zealand's incredible sailing industry. Thinking aloud, Merv said that it would be a great place to build an Open 60 and we realized it would be great experience for me if I sailed the boat back to Europe.

Initially we'd considered New Zealand to be too far away from Kingfisher Plc's interests, but on further reflection it began to look like the right idea. If we could build within the build schedule, it made sense to use the journey back from New Zealand as a sea trial for the boat and a chance for me to gain experience not just with her but of the Southern Ocean. There was also the added bonus that New Zealand was hosting the America's Cup. This would not only be fantastic to be around and watch, but the country would also be buzzing with journalists from all over the world.

By April there were a couple of new faces on the project team. Mary Ambler joined us to take on some of the media work which, with the launch of the Vendée campaign, had grown enormously. Dana Bena came to take some of the logistics, while Ian McKay, a graphic designer, began to work wonders with logos and press packs. Back in January we'd announced that I would be competing in the Vendée, and now we were launching the whole project in detail, announcing our design team, build location and training pro-gramme, and we brought journalists over to the UK from France. We wanted the whole launch to be as professional as possible.

We were asked many questions about our hopes for the project and what was possible in the race, and here our emphasis had changed over recent months. We'd set out just a year before saying we aimed to win, and of course that had to remain our target, but we knew we had to prove the boat before we could make any real predictions. The competition out there was going to be the best in the world and, as had been seen in past races, anything could happen at any stage. Leaving in November always poses a threat to the fleet, with the winter gales beginning to roll in. In order for the campaign to be seen as a success for both us and Kingfisher we couldn't allow it to hinge on winning alone.

From a personal point of view, one of the most important parts of the launch was announcing my own intensive training pro-gramme. It was designed with one clear objective – to plug as many holes in my knowledge and experience as possible. I knew as I stood on that stage in April that I was not ready to take on the Vendée Globe, but I also knew that twelve months later I really could be.

The programme contained a number of different elements, including offshore racing both single-handed and crewed, dinghy racing, meteorological instruction, first aid and straightforward fitness training. All of this would be supported by Kingfisher's sponsorship, which meant we could include what was necessary rather than simply what was possible. We were able to approach things professionally, albeit in a somewhat compressed manner.

Training began back in France aboard boats called Figaros. These are small racing boats just over 32 feet in length, which are used for highly competitive single-handed racing in France. A Figaro campaign is not so expensive, and with so many stop-overs gives great return to the sponsors. It would be my first real immersion in French pro sailing. In my first race with Gael le'Cleach, a teacher at the Figaro training school, we were taken apart by the rest of the fleet – a real baptism of fire and a shocking reminder of just how much I still had to learn. In the few days I spent at the training camp I realized just how different my life was compared to these other sailors. They focused each day on their physical ability, weather strategy and sailing skills; and though my training was more spread out geographically, I was impressed by the thoroughness of their approach. I felt quite uncomfortable there, even nervous. In their world I really was an outsider. And the culture there was completely at odds with the crazy life I was leading, literally running from event to meeting. While I was there I really had the chance to think and take stock of where I was. Sitting around the dinner table each evening talking about their courses or race tactics, I knew that I could not drop into a life like theirs, but I could also see the real benefits of focus and studying in one place.

Mark decided that he also wanted to compete. He had all but given up his own sailing to project-manage the Vendée campaign and it must have been tough seeing me out there on the water. He chartered a boat he named *Offshore Challenges* – the racing took no account of office hours, so we struggled to keep up to speed with the 'Project' as our pursuit of the Vendée had become known. He had raced Figaros before but he too failed to find a winning formula, although I have to say he finished ahead of us!

Perhaps the most obviously vital part of the training programme was the offshore racing. This was to culminate at the end of 1999 with a race called the Transat Jacques Vabre. There was no way that the new *Kingfisher* would be even remotely ready for this, so I needed to find another boat to sail on. We decided to approach Yves Parlier, who had raced the spacecraft-like boat, *Aquitaine Innovations*, that had made such an impression on me at the start of the last Vendée Globe. Rig and rudder problems had forced him to drop out of the race and then, soon afterwards, he had a massive accident while flying a paraglider and had badly damaged his legs. Though still struggling on crutches and with one final operation to go, he was well on the road to recovery – although a question mark still hung over his foot, in which he had lost the feeling.

Mark and I went to Bordeaux to visit Yves with some trepidation. I was aware he was a rather headstrong character, but knew little about him beyond that. Our saving grace was that Yves had followed the Route du Rhum very closely and was aware of my result there. In the end, though, I think the strongest bond between us came from the discovery, much later, that we had both grown up far from the sea and spent our early years dreaming about it. Yves was tall and thin, with short-cropped grey hair – it seemed to have been that colour since he was in his twenties. He also comes across as one of life's great thinkers, his background in engineering leading to an almost scientific but always creative approach to problem-solving. Yves had an incredible track record: he'd competed in two Vendée Globes and won the Mini Transat in 1985 and the Transat Jacques Vabre in 1997 with French sailing legend Eric Tabarly.

Kingfisher would part-sponsor his boat for the race that autumn, and we discussed the programme in great detail. Far from just competing in the Transat Jacques Vabre, we would train together in Arcachon where *Aquitaine* was based, and I would also sail on board her in the Round Europe Race in June.

I fitted in quickly with the guys aboard *Aquitaine*, and soon thought of them as family, but one of my first trips with them turned into a classic demonstration of the pace of the life I was now leading. Sailing to Italy for the start of the Round Europe Race, we were delayed badly by storms. I was concerned about missing a presentation I'd agreed to make to one of Kingfisher's operating companies in Nice. I ended up being dropped off in a bay off Majorca where our enormous Open 60 was circled by German and Spanish holidaymakers in pedalos. Eventually I hitched a lift ashore in a tiny Spanish rowing boat, with a man who understood enough English to know that I had a plane to catch! I flew to Barcelona, hired a car for a twelve-hour mind-blowing taste of the Pyrenees, then flew on to Nice.

Geoff Mulcahy, Kingfisher's CEO, was at the presentation and asked what my plans were. When I told him I was returning to the UK first thing in the morning he asked if it would help to get back that night. This was incredibly useful as we were tank- and wind tunnel-testing models for *Kingfisher*, and as far as I was concerned, the earlier the better. A couple of hours later I was boarding a private jet for the first time. I was so excited that the pilot asked me if I wanted to sit in the cockpit, from where it looked as if we were chasing the setting sun all the way home. We landed at Luton, and Geoff's chauffeur gave me a lift to my aunt's empty house in nearby Hertford. At about 1 a.m. I assured everyone I would be fine, and walked off into the darkness. Only then did I realize that while I had a key I didn't have the code for the new burglar alarm. I tried phoning everyone who might know but got no reply. Admitting defeat, I made a nest in the garden and went to sleep with a smile on my face. From executive jet to sleeping in a garden – great!

I was soon back with *Aquitaine* in Italy for the Round Europe Race. A surf-filled first leg in which we were in our element led to an eventual race-winning lead, but our celebrations were muted by the news that a crewman aboard the trimaran *Biscuits La Trinitaine* had been washed overboard and killed during the strong downwind conditions that had served us so well – devastating for the crew and his family.

Along with the Figaros and sailing with Yves there was one further aspect to my training on the water: racing laser dinghies with Paul Brotherton. Paul had represented Great Britain in the Barcelona Olympics and was an incredible natural sailor. Originally from inner-city Manchester, he had discovered sailing almost by accident and we hit it off immediately. Each time I sailed with him I realized how talented he was. I was on a near-vertical learning curve, but we were sure that the skills I picked up on racing dinghies could only make me more competitive offshore in an open 60.

Paul and I had hoped to actually start a race together before competing in the Laser Eurocup Regatta in Milan, but as usual, lack of time stopped us and we were able to complete just a few training sessions on the Solent and a day in Italy. The atmosphere on Lake Como was fantastic, however, and tired as we were when we drove into Gravidona, relaxed people and warm weather kept us going. It seemed odd for me to go into a race environment and know so few competitors – especially while Paul couldn't walk three paces without someone spotting him.

I was completely unsure of how I was going to find the racing. It had been a long time since I'd competed in such close quarters and this time there were over seventy boats in our class! Paul was great to sail with. There were stressful moments and it must have been particularly frustrating for someone as experienced and skilled as Paul to crew while I, a novice in this kind of sailing, took the helm. We were therefore fairly amazed at sailing into third place on the first race. And while our results were an absolute team effort, I fear that the importance of our contributions were weighted in favour of Paul! He must have been hoarse by the end of the regatta as he frequently had to employ his very verbal approach to collision avoidance:

''kin hell, Ellen!'

Throughout the intense sailing programme I also had much to learn ashore. Training for an event like the Vendée is nothing like training for athletics. We have to learn everything about the function of the weather and the boat. That ranges from being able to repair the sails to perhaps changing hard disc drives and replacing circuit boards or relaminating broken fittings. We can have no outside assistance whatsoever with our weather routing either, so have to make all those decisions on board ourselves. It is outside the rules of the Vendée for sailors even to pick up the phone and ask what someone thinks of their ideas, which in turn puts an enormous strain on the skipper who has not only the welfare and speed of the boat to think of, but also its position on the ocean which is critical to its success. I completed a course on engine repair and maintenance in Oxford and was fascinated by the knowledge I was gaining on everything from changing oil to stripping down diesel-injection pumps. By the end I was stripping the engine down and putting it back together again with some aplomb. And in La Rochelle, I spent two days of intense training with Jean-Yves Bernot, a French weather expert, covering a whole range of subjects from weather fax interpretation to the use of weather-routing software. Previously, particularly on the Mini Transat, I'd felt that I lacked confidence in this aspect of my racing and was keen to address it. Jean-Yves also worked with me on weather training as I sailed back to Europe from New Zealand during *Kingfisher*'s sea trials.

As crucial to success as understanding the boat and weather is looking after yourself. Fatigue is always a potentially huge problem in long-distance single-handed racing and I started working on a sleep training project with a chrono-biology expert, Dr Claudio Stampi. This involved wearing a monitor on my wrist which looked like a watch and recorded when I woke and slept. I never took it off and the data we collected about my sleep patterns would help plan a sleep strategy for the Vendée.

Immediately after finishing the regatta on Lake Como, I undertook a three-day commercial first aid course at Warsash Nautical College with a mixed bunch of people from all sorts of vessels – I was unique among them in that I would be sailing alone: not everything was useful – mouth-to-mouth resuscitation, for example! In the past there have been serious medical emergencies too – from Alan Wynne-Thomas limping into New Zealand with his smashed ribcage, to Bertrand de Broc who had to sew his tongue back on deep in the Southern Ocean. Being independent is not just a desirable attribute for the Vendée Globe, it's essential.

It was a taxing schedule, but somehow sheer eagerness to be out there and take things on fuelled my enthusiasm and kept my wheels turning. People would often ask me what I was up to and when I gave them a typical sample they were usually fairly aghast. Though I showed a brave face and would not have chosen to change what was going on, I knew deep down that I was now running not far from empty. The sporadic training sessions and snatched moments on the water, or even a brief moment looking at the hills out of a train window were just enough to keep me going. There were moments of desperation in there, though – one in particular was filmed by the French crew when I was training in a Laser with Paul. I was knackered, and finding it virtually impossible to concentrate, particularly in the strong winds – it was almost as if I wasn't there.

Part of the problem was that I was beginning to feel a lack of control. I was concerned that I had not been as in-touch as I would have liked to be with the general running and design phase of the project. I was used to being that person who was around and about putting in 'hands-on' time, but now I was away from both our office and the design office nearly all the time, my input often being on the phone, making a motivational call when I sensed things were at a slightly lower ebb. I began to feel more like a pawn in a far bigger system and it seemed as though there were many aspects of my life that I had little or no control of. A couple of years before, as I had been sailing the oceans, I had made every decision for myself – but now things were different. On the grand scale of things they were small though, and I knew full well that I could not have done more or been in more places. At the end of the day I had a great team, and they were doing a great job.

I still pushed myself to try to be involved with just about every stage of the design process of *Kingfisher* and was rewarded with the most incredible feeling, almost day by day, of a dream come true. I felt part of her from the moment she was the first line on the computer screen; it was almost like watching her grow. We made a computer-generated virtual 'Ellen' which we could slot into various areas of the boat, although unfortunately we had to modify some areas as when we tried to drop in a person of more normal dimensions (I am 5 foot 3½ inches tall) there were a few problems with space!

On 18 September 1999 I flew to New Zealand for a couple of days to see the first stage of *Kingfisher*'s build. Walking into that shed for the first time and looking up at the curve of her gigantic hull, I was in awe of her beauty. The feeling of enormity was like realizing the sheer size of a whale in the wild for the first time – almost spiritual. Only this being, I knew, was going to become a close friend.

We had a scare too, though. On our final night we heard the phone ring, and a car leave the drive very soon after. We were staying with Steve Marten, the owner of the yard, and discovered that he had been called out due to a fire there. The oven next to *Kingfisher*'s had caught fire while cooking some of her bulkheads and had set off the burglar alarm. The guy on duty there had run off to check the alarm system, not knowing that it had been triggered by the oven that was on fire – the temperature sensors measured heat of up to 130°C, and the wall between the two ovens had collapsed by the time the fire was extinguished. Miraculously, *Kingfisher*'s mould was completely unscathed – how a tinder-dry wooden mould could have survived so close to such an intense fire we shall never know, but in a way it proved to us from the start that she was a born survivor.

I was back in France by the end of September to prepare for the Transat Jacques Vabre which started on 15 October. Life continued to be hectic, but although they were no less time-consuming, I was now a little more used to the endless interviews and photo calls that accompanied the build-up to a major race.

The night before the start we all went for a meal, organized primarily for Yves' sponsors, Aquitaine. There were a number of guests from the Kingfisher side of the project too. Although it was good to catch up with sponsors and the team, it was not, perhaps, the best night for it. I left early and slept in the car before heading back to the hotel for our final night's sleep.

We left Le Havre on a hot, still afternoon, and after at least fifteen hours at the helm we were in second place and already well down the track. It felt wonderful finally to be off. There had been some friction between Yves and me on shore as he was very much the kind of person who had to run things his way, but we both knew that on the water our primary objective was survival – and of course the race. As we crossed that start line any differences ashore melted away and we bonded well, but while our start was clement, there was a massive depression heading across the Atlantic: Hurricane Irene . . .

```
3am. Freezing, soaking, and impossible to stand. Its
been a bit full on last few hours. We're under deep
reefed main, storm jib. Just got slaughtered whildt
chaanging to storm jib - THrowm up and doen on deck,
washed sideways so many times. She mght have a wide
open flat deck f;r'd, but it's very ecposed! Rightnoe
trying to thype, warmer than before as put survival
suit on, very tired. eyes trying yoi shut, and stinging
still from salt. DeCk . . . virtually lifted off seat
here . . slamming is bad. and40kn . . the slower, the
worse.
xex
```

During the storm we broke all the rigging on the starboard side – which when simplified means every single cable holding our mast up on one side of the boat was slowly breaking. Hour by hour the mast was leaning over more and more and at any time the whole lot could have fallen over the side. The fibres with which the mast was supported were quite a new development, strong and light – PBO. Though we knew that these fibres degraded with sunlight, no one was really sure how long they would last.

We had over 60 knots at one stage, and because of the rig problems we had just a tiny piece of sail up and had to wait, agonizing, for over forty-eight hours before we could repair the rig. This was not as easy as it sounds as it involved me climbing up several times and completely replacing each cable, one by one. *Aquitaine* was the first of the Open 60s to have the deck spreaders that made her look so unusual; the objective being that they allow a large section of wing mast to rotate – they were never designed with climbing comfort in mind. It was complicated further by having to make the replacements on deck first and use any rope we could find on board. We spent days scrambling about on the decks trying to remove covers from ropes and splice them together – all made difficult and dangerous by the aggressive waves and horrific motion, and not helped by the fact that we sailed entirely in the French language. Although by this time I was fluent, I certainly lacked various words in the French vocabulary. It was pretty hard working out what an 'anneau' was when hanging 50 feet up a mast. It turned out to be a loop! I was incredibly motivated though, and the morning after our diagnosis I was out there working as soon as there was the first glimmer of light in the sky.

```
Pretty exhausted . . Started at 4am , and still up.
Feeling lucky to be alive after hours up the rig, one of
the hardest physical challenges ever . . . Waves after a
big storm, came down in 30 knots after dark, just after
a rain squall. . . . A lot of bruises, very sore. But
lucky. It's hard to describe how it feels to hang on up
there. Like trying to grip on to an enormous shiny pole
(which for me is just too big to get my arms around
properly), with someone continually kicking you, and
trying to shake you off. At least the mast is still
sitting there vertically though - the other option does
not baer thinking about.
```

Although we had massive problems in the storm, nearly resulting in us losing our mast, there were others far worse off than us. We received a message stating that one of the multihulls, *Group André*, had capsized and one of its two crew was missing. Later we found out that Paul Vatine was on deck when they went over – and tragically was never seen again. As I sat on deck in that raging storm I thought of what his co-skipper and family must be going through – it was a dangerous life out here, and sure as hell, one which we have little or no control whatsoever over.

We finished in eighth position after twenty days of hard racing. Mentally it had been a tough race, both tactically and living with our disappointment and frustration, but once again I knew I'd learnt a lot, not least how it is possible to overcome really serious problems. The odds had been against us all the way, but we had made it to the end, and although eighth was not first we still felt we'd achieved something. As we crossed the finish line in Cartagena Mark and Yves's team jumped on board; it was fantastic to see them all again. But aside from the knowledge I'd gained from the situation we'd been through, the biggest gift from that race was confidence.

It was a great relief to head back to New Zealand after the race. It was now summer down there, the America's Cup was in full flow and Auckland was buzzing. By this stage we had a great team working on *Kingfisher*; Marie and Pipo had moved from Guadeloupe with their two kids to live in New Zealand for five months. Pipo was responsible for the deck gear and above-deck equipment, and Marie, with her new industrial sewing machine, was making sail covers, cockpit covers, seat covers – and just about anything else you could imagine! Others, like Frenchman Marc Dutiloy or South African Mikey Joubert each had their own area of expertise, be it dagger boards or rig. On the organizational side, Martin Carter, as well as being responsible for everything below decks, took over as team leader in New Zealand, ably supported by Dana Bena. Back in the UK, designer Ian McKay produced designs for *Kingfisher*'s distinctive yellow bow, sweeping into her blue hull, which we all thought was beautiful. She reflected the passion and dedication of everyone involved and there was no doubt in any of our minds that she was going to be the best Open 60 in the world. And although ultimately I would be the one who would sail her, there would be a piece of every one of them on board with me.

Whenever I walked into the yard there would be another part attached to her, or a new piece built. *Kingfisher*, because of the work and graft of every person there, was coming to life and I can only describe it as wonderful. Every day our delivery home was getting closer.

I made a big effort in New Zealand to try to get my life in order, and although one of the best things that's ever happened to me was taking shape, I was at the same time struggling. Being in New Zealand was a stark contrast to the frantic schedule I had become used to in Europe, and although things were very busy there was more time for contemplation. I was concerned about my relationship with Merv. We were living away from the rest of the team, away from Auckland and the others. I don't think it helped to be apart from them, but I'd hoped that when I settled in over there with Merv, things would get better. But they weren't. I was becoming more and more frustrated with myself for feeling frustrated with Merv; the more I tried to drag myself out of it, the more I felt distanced from him. He was putting every ounce of himself into the project, which was wonderful, but he was putting too much in, and I could see that his reserves were getting dangerously low. Even if we grabbed a day to try to get away from the city he would sleep in the car rather than running on the beach or playing in the surf. On the few occasions when we did get away, I didn't feel I was with the same man, and I remember leaving him collapsed in the guest house while I sprinted down to the beach and flung myself into the surf to vent my frustration. I tried to talk to him, and tried to be strong to help him, but often I felt as if I was talking to a wall. He had no energy, no time for anything; long gone were the days when we would talk of exciting plans for the future. We seemed to be sharing less and less. He would crash out in the evenings while I would stay up at my computer going through my weather notes, or checking e-mails.

At 0515 every morning I would get up and go to the gym – it was half an hour's drive from the farm, and I would make a start there for six. It was a great way of getting rid of that pent-up energy. I'd often be joined by Allan from the yard, a great bloke whose easy manner and sense of humour helped me relax. Sometimes, instead of going to the gym we'd thrash around in kayaks on the river. It was great to have a mate to mess around with, but made me realize how much I missed doing this with Merv.

I desperately needed to get away and think, and when Christmas came round, knowing I wasn't going home to Derbyshire, I bought a tent and a pair of hiking boots and headed off into the bush.

Merv dropped me off at the end of a long wooded track on Christmas Eve. The road we had hoped to take was closed, so I spent the evening finding my first campsite at 2200hrs in the dark.

The following morning I unzipped the tent door to be greeted by a beautiful day – Christmas Day – and headed off up the Twin Peaks track. I managed to get a signal on my mobile and made a quick, successful attempt to wish close friends and family a happy Christmas, before switching it off for the first time in months. I had mixed feelings making the call – this was my first Christmas away from Derbyshire, and I couldn't have been much further away.

The track was incredibly steep. As I clambered up some of the slopes, the gradient and the weight of my pack forced me to climb using my hands and feet together. By afternoon I had climbed over the top of the hill and was heading back down to the water. I was thrilled by the sight and sound of a Red-crowned parakeet: I'd dreamed of green parrots in my adventures as a child and this was the closest I'd got to seeing it become a reality. I filled my water pot from a tiny trickling stream before stumbling across one of the most beautiful campsites I could imagine: a tiny grassy glade under the trees, right by the water's edge with a view the full length of the water. I stood watching grebes diving and herons feeding.

I pitched my tent and heated a Christmas dinner of chicken curry pasta and Christmas pudding on my little stove. As the sun dropped slowly over the wooded slopes, I lay back in my tent, doors wide open, and drank in the atmosphere.

Next day, after a lazy morning making porridge and berry tea, reading and paddling amongst shoals of baby fish, I packed away my home and by about midday headed on along the track, determined to spend my next night by the sea. At one place I came across a patch of long lush grass. I happily walked straight into it – it reminded me of walks with Mac as a kid and I missed not having her with me.

As I headed up to the ridge the views were breathtaking. I glanced down the steep sides to see gulls circling over the water hundreds of feet below. I spotted a kingfisher on a branch in the nearby woods – a good omen for the night's camping, I felt.

It was as if I'd climbed out of my skin and could take a bird's-eye look at my worries before returning revitalized to the yard and the team. But it was hard to admit to myself that in some ways I was unhappy. After all, how could I be? I was about to see the launch of *Kingfisher*, about to sail her half-way around the world. But blanking out my true feelings would not help me or Merv in the long run. He was tired, and I wanted to support him; but however hard I tried, I just didn't seem to be getting through. Maybe I just had to try harder; we had both put so much effort into the project and I thought that perhaps once she was in the water things would change.

I woke the following morning at 0530, and as I opened my eyes I saw the orange glow of the rising sun appearing behind the cliffs through the open tent door. I could have sworn I was in Narnia, and as the morning warmed up, the steam from the damp grass emphasized the magical atmosphere.

Either side the beach stretches away for miles, not a soul to be seen, just my solitary set of footprints . . . This seems almost surreal; if this were England the beaches would be packed and noisy. Over the past three hours I've even seen an endangered species, washed in a freshwater river, and perched on a solitary log . . . all out of sight of man, and miles from the nearest house.

I was ready to get back to *Kingfisher*.

Although the days that followed began on a more positive note, things were not getting any better with Merv. I had been kidding myself to think they would. Our millennium celebrations were spent together in the house. After an early night, it took me hours to fall asleep. I lay there feeling sad and I hated myself for it. These should have been the happiest times of my life. Early on New Year's

Day I tiptoed outside into the fields past flocks of sheep to the edge of the river. It was peaceful there. I knew that I had to leave Merv. It might even jog him out of this insane lifestyle he had slipped into. I thought back to our first conversation on that wet day in Southampton, when he said that his boat *Maverick* had cost him a seven-year relationship. I had thought that having so much in common, things would be different for us. But I could not carry on like this, and nor, I felt, could he.

Soon after New Year I returned briefly to Europe where I spent a week in London for the International Boat Show. We had organized a live webcast and a press launch for the Vendée Globe itself, trying to stimulate awareness of the Vendée in the UK. We had invited Pete Goss, Tony Bullimore and Catherine Chabaud from France as competitors from the last Vendée. Each spoke of their experiences, Catherine talking of her plans to circumnavigate again in the next Vendée with her new boat *Whirlpool*. She talked of her experiences in the last race, and how this time she was raising her sights, putting the sport aspect above the adventure. Pete talked of his position in the previous race, saying that he was an adventurer and not a sailor, and that rang a bell in my head. No matter how geared up for racing you are, you can never take that aspect of the Vendée Globe away. As a result of its conditions and the hardships out there, the adventure part is almost crucial. And as Catherine said, there were a million people in Les Sables d'Olonne to see the start of the last race. Tony said that the Vendée was the ultimate in single-handed racing, and that if that's what you love then you can't really miss it out. I then went up with Mike Golding, whose ultimate goal with his *Team Group 4* project had always been the Vendée. He had so much more experience than I did as well as a reliable and well-tested boat. He was one of the favourites and I felt nervous while he spoke.

While I was in Europe I also had time, however little, to spend with friends, which made a massive difference to the state of mind I'd got into in New Zealand. Ian McKay, the graphic designer who had worked on the project since earlier in the year, proved as usual incredibly supportive. He was a kind man who always had time for people and had become a popular person for the whole team to turn to when in need of someone to talk to, which is what I did in London. It was an immense relief to unload some of my worries. In New Zealand I was close to the team, but could not really talk to them about what was going on with Merv, as it wouldn't be fair on them or him. Ian was great though, incredibly patient, and as he was verging on workaholic himself I think he understood Merv's predicament. I felt about a ton lighter for sharing things with him.

I didn't sleep a wink on the flight back to New Zealand, however. While I was thinking about every aspect of sailing *Kingfisher* home, my mind drifted to Merv. I was desperately trying to work things out in my head, but time was running out. If things did not get any better in the first few days then I would have to end it.

Kingfisher was in her final stages now, and it was wonderful to see her almost ready to launch. She would be in the water in less than two weeks' time. On the Friday after I arrived we had an evening of beers for the boys, and it was great to see the team again and the smiles on everyone's faces despite the final grind to the launch, and to catch up with what had been happening while I'd been away.

But the situation with Merv hadn't changed. If anything it was worse – to the extent that I was really worried about him. I was getting up earlier and earlier; now I would sit for an hour on the beach and watch the sun rise before going to the gym. It was becoming ridiculous, and I finally decided that if I didn't call a halt we would probably both go mad.

Several days later, when everyone else had left the yard, I went to talk to Merv. I wished I could have broken it more softly but the truth was too painful. He was not the same man that I had known twelve months before. I'm sure that the break was harder because we both knew how much he was putting into the project, but the trouble was that this was the root of the problem. I felt desperately sad, especially as Merv disappeared to spend time alone and I could not even talk to him. I cannot imagine what must have been going through his mind during the time he was away.

At the same time *Kingfisher*'s launch was approaching, and the pressure mounted accordingly. It was a difficult situation without

Merv and I was so glad that everyone else rallied round. Martin took over the final organization and Mark assumed a bigger role too. *Kingfisher* left Marten Yachts for the first time on a lorry, and at 3 a.m. on Wednesday, 9 February the gates parted for her. Mark and I followed in the car, and I stood up out of the sun roof filming her enormous hull weaving in and out of the Auckland streets. It wasn't really a time for words; I think we were both struck by just what a milestone it was to see her leave through the gates of the yard that had given birth to her. Five months of effort and care emerged as *Kingfisher* – a work of art. I felt so proud of everyone who had got us this far.

She went into the water several days later. Mum and Dad had arrived the evening before, and apart from Brest before the Mini, it was the first time they had ventured to one of our foreign events. Merv was now back too, and I was glad that he was there to see her touch her new home, the sea, for the first time. Mum poured some champagne over her keel for good luck and as *Kingfisher* was lowered into the water I stood on her keel bulb until I was able to wash those first splashes of real sea water over her keel.

Seeing her afloat for the first time was our dream come true – now she could really show her character. Strangely, bar the rumble of the hoist, it was a quiet moment, though incredibly intense. I think we were all close to tears. Mark spoke to a camera, saying, 'I think that from the outside it's very hard for people to appreciate just how much work actually has to happen, and how much commitment goes into getting a boat like this into the water.' He was absolutely right.

We were in the water for about five days before her official public launch, and we had time to test all her systems. A boat is not just about the obvious pieces like the mast and sails; the network of hydraulics and electronics inside is incredibly sophisticated, from solar panels to computers to autopilots and two enormous hydraulic rams to cant her swinging keel, each weighing more than I did and not only holding but moving the most incredible loads. Everything has to be fitted, checked and tested. To see the first hoisting of her enormous sails was nothing short of spectacular, and to feel her glide through the water for the first time was unbelievable. As I took her helm for those first moments I had the strangest feeling that I had been there before, and it wasn't like a new experience – although I struggled to describe the feeling, it felt more like a re-acquaintance with an old friend.

The launch itself was a great occasion for everyone involved with *Kingfisher* so far. All four of her designers – including Alain Gautier who'd flown in from France – had joined us and I just hoped that they all felt proud of the beautiful boat they had built. Auckland was a great place to be at this stage of the America's Cup. The Italian team Prada had made it through to the final and were about to race against Sir Peter Blake's Team New Zealand – current holders of the Cup. There were onlookers everywhere as we tied *Kingfisher* alongside the pontoon.

Just before the launch we attached a plaque that read 'Built in New Zealand by the team at Marten Yachts'. It was carved out of a piece of Kauri wood estimated to be up to 800 years old. A Maori group performed a *haka* on the pontoon beside her. It was the first time I had seen this, and I think both Mark and I were overcome by the sheer power of emotion it conveyed. *Kingfisher* will always be a Kiwi to us, and it seemed appropriate to bring her into the world that way. Her naming was carried out by Lady Pippa Blake, wife of the most outstanding sailor ever – Sir Peter Blake. I stood nervously stroking my fingers over her as Pippa's words rang out powerfully and confidently over the crowds: 'I name this boat *Kingfisher*. May God bless her and all who sail in her – especially Ellen.'

Once the bottle smashed over her bow I climbed over *Kingfisher*'s pulpit and kissed her bow.

Chapter Fifteen

One month later *Kingfisher* left New Zealand for her 12,000-mile journey home. As we sailed away from Auckland, for the first time we watched the skyline we knew so well disappear into the distance. I'd loved New Zealand. It was the longest period of time I'd spent in one place for years, and it had really begun to feel like home, both through the great spirit we had amongst the team and the kindness and enthusiasm that the Kiwis had shown for the project. But the delivery trip would take us halfway around the world and I was desperately looking forward to it. We decided to stage the journey back over two legs; the first to Cape Horn, with a crew of four; then I would sail home to Europe alone. I was going to have the chance to really get to know *Kingfisher*.

The crew for the first part of our trip was Bruno Dubois, Martin Carter and Andrew Cape. Capey had routed me for the Route du Rhum and had sailed as navigator in numerous offshore races, including the Whitbread twice. He was a typical blond Australian and although without doubt he had their characteristic sense of humour he was outwardly quieter. He and I were going to discuss the weather in detail with a view to our Southern Ocean leg.

Bruno was from North Sails and had been working with us on the sails front since the beginning of the project. We were in the process of developing a relatively new type of durable offshore sail made in one piece on a mould, which many said would never work for the Vendée. Bruno was great to have on board, having competed and been involved in a whole host of racing events, including the Whitbread many years before.

We were a happy crew, and bar the tail-end of a depression where the wind piped up to 38 knots, we were treated very kindly on the first leg. I spent many hours talking to Martin about longer-term modifications and preparations. Not only did we have the Vendée start in ten month's time, the Europe 1 New Man STAR was in June, and even if all went well we would have just a couple of weeks to prepare for it once we arrived back in the UK. It was the qualifier for the Vendée Globe for most entrants too, so being there on the start line was very much a part of every skipper's Vendée preparations.

Life on board *Kingfisher* is pretty basic, with only an area about a metre square that you can stand up in. On her starboard side there's a tiny sink with two manual pump taps, one for seawater and one for fresh water. Opposite the sink is a gimballed camping gas stove, designed to stay level whatever *Kingfisher* was doing. As far as kitchen and hygiene are concerned, however, this was the lot – no toilet, no shower and certainly no hot water. I slept on the chart table seat for the delivery, leaving the pipe-cot bunks which we had fitted each side of her cabin to the guys and especially Capey! Apart from this tiny part in which we lived there was just storage for sails and food, and sacrificial areas which in grave danger could be isolated completely from the rest of the boat with water-tight doors. When we think of dangers at sea, icebergs spring to mind – they are numerous in both Arctic and Antarctic waters – but there are also plenty of other obstacles floating out there which can bring your race to an abrupt and frightening end.

Cape Horn was stunning, far more than just the rugged storm-swept rock one imagines. We had arranged to liaise with another boat, *Pelagic*, skippered and crewed by Hamish Laird and his wife Kate. Mark was on board along with Antony Lane and a friend of his plus a French electronics engineer who would hopefully fix our temperamental sat com dome. It was a while since I had seen Antony and his calming character was wonderful to have around in such a short-lived but potentially very stressful moment.

In the final moments of daylight we watched the high mountains in the distance, ice-covered and sticking jaggedly out of the fjords. That night we moored in a bay called Caletta Martial and were ferried over to *Pelagic* for a meal and a sleep in cushioned bunks! I was reluctant to leave *Kingfisher* but knew that before I left next day I would need to sleep. At daybreak the following day I climbed up *Pelagic*'s companionway to be greeted by one of the most beautiful anchorages I had ever laid eyes upon. The shores were a faded, weathered green and the water pure, dark and still, and *Kingfisher* lay silently just a hundred feet away as if resting on her perfect reflection. The cold air cut through my thermals as I perched in the cockpit pulling my legs close to my body with my arms.

I left that afternoon sailing *Kingfisher* alone for the first time – and only just in time too as a storm blew through, leaving the others to battle into 60-knot headwinds as I sailed away in the last of the lighter breeze to the north. We had several real tests on that trip, but the main thing was to learn. Weather decisions are crucial to the single-handed sailor and each day I would work out my weather strategy as if racing and e-mail my thoughts to Jean-Yves Bernot. Not being able to discuss things, particularly when you're tired, can be enormously stressful, and working with Jean-Yves helped my confidence. I was collecting weather information from the Internet using the satellite communication equipment I had on board, which comprised two satellite telephones, a Mini-M, which has a slow Internet connection speed that I used primarily for voice, and also a Satcom-B satellite connection with which I could log on to the Internet at ISDN speed. Although the Internet is a big aid to navigation, so much information is available that the real art is to decide what's useful and what's not.

As we crossed the Equator I felt obliged to follow King Neptune's ancient initiation rite. Tradition dictates that each sailor who passes the Equator for the first time is to be tied up and tortured. Generally this involves being dressed up, covered in disgusting food and often having bits of hair shaved off! I made myself a cardboard crown and trident, and wrapped myself in the European flag, talking to the camera as King Neptune. Then I changed roles to become the victim, mixing up an unappetizing blend of dried peas, stew and chocolate protein compound which I poured all over myself. I filmed it all and sent back footage. Mark and the rest of the team were sure I'd lost it!

I thought a great deal about them all while I was out there. I kept a picture of Marie, Pipo and the kids and another from *Kingfisher*'s launch with the team standing proudly on her afterdeck, one of Mum and Dad, and a card that Mark had given me. I had a tiny model of *Foncia*, Alain Gautier's trimaran, in the centre of the chart table he'd given me when he'd flown down to New Zealand for our first sail on *Kingfisher*. I had the hearts and souls of a great number of people on board with me.

I developed a very special relationship with *Kingfisher* during our time alone. We learnt to rely on each other. I could feel when she was unhappy with either too little or too much sail, or when she wanted to sail as close to 100 per cent as she could. I was continually cleaning her, tidying up any mess or minor damage. I knew exactly where things were and always stowed the ropes away meticulously in her cockpit, so they didn't lie on the floor. Down below we had fitted numerous storage racks on either side and underneath her side-decks so that we could firmly attach plastic boxes containing everything from spare winch parts to circuit board spares to dried fruit. And when I practised tacking and gybing, I'd run through the harder jobs like shifting these boxes from side to side to help keep her level and consequently more powerful. Physically, it's one of the toughest and most frustrating jobs on board. A dinghy can be tacked in seconds, but it takes about half an hour on a 60 racing yacht like *Kingfisher*: from preparing everything, and shifting the weight to physically tacking and then tidying up her lines afterwards, it's a mission which you certainly don't just undertake for the sake of it!

I also learnt a lot about myself. I saw that sleep had a large effect on my well-being and decision-making capabilities and found natural patterns within my sleep which helped me to recover more quickly from fatigue. I was happy on board and felt very much at home with *Kingfisher*. I had learnt about her and I knew more about my own tolerances and weaknesses. I had a funny feeling that that was going to be useful in the year to come – and I was right.

My first landfall was the Ile de Groix, just off the French coast, and it was there I met up with some of the shore team to go through the jobs list and discuss the work that needed to be done in advance of reaching UK shores.

Kingfisher looked immaculate as we made our way through the Solent, and I felt intensely proud of her. We were met by a host of people, including Mum, Dad and Gran, who waved from the Red Funnel Red Jet! Ashley Perrin was down in the main sitting area with Gran; I saw them both looking out and there was a third face in the window – Mac! Gran even came on board once we had finally tied up alongside in Southampton. It was a very strange feeling having sailed halfway around the world, and odd to think that the last time *Kingfisher* had been tied up alongside a dock it was in Auckland. Our good friend Eric the cameraman jumped aboard. Everyone loves Eric, it's people with character like his that really make others smile. Still, as he filmed, some of the first words I spoke were 'I don't want to get off.'

Plymouth will always remind me of my Round Britain trip, and we were moored in the marina, right next to the Royal Western Yacht Club where *Iduna* and *Elan Sifo* had berthed, during our final week of preparation for the Europe 1 New Man STAR across the Atlantic. I was acutely conscious that we were on display and nervous about how we would compete against the others. This was the first time *Kingfisher* had even been seen by her rivals and she was very much an unknown quantity. I hoped she would be fast, but the truth was I had no idea how she would fare. Above all, though, I had no idea how *I* would fare. From weather tactics to sleep management, we had the whole lot on our shoulders. I knew that I would be out there against the best skippers in the world and that the pace of the race would be fast. And although the Vendée Globe was fast approaching and all would want to make it to the start line, these weren't the kind of people who would just take it easy in the interests of self-preservation, whatever they might say to the contrary.

There were twenty-five boats in Class 1 and well over half of those were monohulls. There were ten boats in our class capable of winning. I was asked in successive interviews about my hopes for the race. I always replied that if I could finish in the top ten I would be happy, but deep down in my heart I knew that my goal was very definitely top three. I ran through plans in my head. What could we do to finish in the top three? What might help me get there? There were no easy conclusions. I knew we had a fantastic shore team – the best. After all, they'd turned *Kingfisher* round in less than two weeks after she'd sailed halfway round the world, which was amazing. Although there were definitely gaps in our knowledge we accepted that and just grunted up. I also knew that as soon as the ten-minute gun went it was down to me – I really would be on my own then.

On the morning of the start I felt sick with nervousness, and though I tried to put on a brave face, I knew I was struggling. Burdened by the pressure of performing well, I did not feel myself at all. We now had everything we needed and I was competing on equal terms with every other skipper – failure would be down to me now. I had a bad pain in my right knee that had been there since I ran along the dock on return from New Zealand, and though not too agonizing, it was still a concern, as I could not put all my weight on the knee when it was bent. I said goodbye to Mum and Dad, but I wasn't really there; it must have been like hugging someone who had already left. Dad was interviewed once I'd gone, and later, when I saw a recording of the interview, I could see from his face that he was worried, but his words showed that he'd reassured himself. *'It's a superb moment, because this time she has a really fantastic boat to attempt this race in. It's wonderful.'*

At the ten-minute gun the team jumped off. I headed away from the line, then tacked, building up speed to power across the start. *Kingfisher* and I were off. As soon as I was clear of the support boats I stuck her on autopilot and grabbed my mobile. I sent a text message to everyone in the shore team to say thanks. My eyes filled with tears of joy as I typed before switching it off.

At the Eddystone Lighthouse, the only mark of the course before America, it was *PRB* that edged ahead of *Kingfisher* to take the lead. At that point the fleet started to split, some choosing to head immediately inshore to get out of the worst of the adverse tide.

For Ellen, she will certainly continue to climb the learning curve in this respect – but learning has never been a problem for her! Her grin said it all as she raced *Kingfisher* for the first time out into the English Channel.

'It's great to be back at sea, its where we belong, *Kingfisher* and me. I'm relieved to have got away from the start line cleanly and she feels great. Its always an emotional moment – in particular the moment when the shore team got off – thanks guys, fantastic team effort to get us here. *A donf!*'

I have never felt as nervous in a race as I did in the 1 STAR. Each time I grabbed twenty minutes' sleep I would wake with the most profound knot in my stomach. I could never relax with the weather, continually worrying if I had chosen the right option, and whether the others had picked the same route. Every few hours we would receive the position reports and would know whether we had gained or lost miles on the others . . . Our lives on board revolve completely around these figures, and our hearts almost beat to their pace. If you lose miles for whatever reason, you can't allow yourself to be demoralized by it. It's as much a mental battle as a physical one and it's a fine line between watching too closely what the others are doing and calling your own shots.

Initially we had quite light breeze as we sailed along the South Coast of the UK to head out to the Atlantic, and we had dropped to sixth or seventh place. I fought on though, pushing hard and changing sails hourly at one stage to make it around the Lizard headland.

By the second day we had retaken the lead, which was an incredible feeling. *Kingfisher* was holding her own. But even though I was leading at these early stages I knew that we had a very long way to sail. I kept telling myself, just hang in there, don't do anything stupid and don't make mistakes. Leading brings its own problems and I had never led a fleet before. I felt the pressure mount massively. You are the 'tester' of the fleet, the others sit behind you and watch your every move – and those closest are perfectly placed to sail around you if you enter a windless zone or make a bad call.

We were soon into the Atlantic depression systems, as we had been with the Route du Rhum, and life on board was getting tougher, not only physically but also tactically. The wind changes direction quickly with the passage of the fronts, and if we weren't to lose miles we had to tack in response immediately. Every task meant twenty-five minutes of hard manual work, commencing with the shifting of the boxes, then her sails in the forepeak. Each weighed little less than me but was twice my size so it was a bit like trying to roll an unwilling body uphill in an earthquake.

It's blowing a *&^**?& right now. 35 knots almost consistent. hAHve spent a good hor on deck checking and re-checking to c if all is OK. Found a few small probs, but nothing too serious. life on board os incredibly testing, the motion is horrnedous, and the wind and seas seem to grow not only in size3 and strength, but also in their unpredictable nature! Felt hungry so made a mushroomn pate, cheese and tomatoe sauce sanwich. FElt bizarre balancing the bread in my soaked knees, trying to pur the tom suce so it didn't get thrown everywhere as anything elselooose in the cabin would be. I've spent a while sitting in thee cuddy in the past days . . though know it feels like a fairground log-flume. Ploughing into waves, with green water darkeneing the hiding hole every few minuters . . though unlike the log flume, the fun oif the spray has passed . . It's impossible to see out of the windows, continously under water, be it rain, sporay or solid waves. there is a rattle in the riggin of the halyrds . . I have minimised it by tyimng them back tight to the mast, glad mikey put those covers on at the spreaders . . Everything down below much drier since our mini-refit. greeat work guys . .

My knee is quite painful too, though has been the
least of my worries over the past days . .
    Hanging in here, quite literally,
Exx

Three boats were dismasted in that first storm, including two race
favourites, Thomas Coville on *Sodebo* and Yves Parlier, and I was
shocked to hear of their news. Yves had just fitted a new mast after
our problems the previous autumn. He must have been spitting
fire.

    Eight days in, we sailed through a vicious front. I was still strug-
gling to sleep. We were down to three reefs and the storm jib, and
her motion was violent, but to leeward I could see a sail with a red
square which I recognized as Bilou's (Roland Jourdain's). *Sill* was
the first boat I had seen since we cleared the Channel, and I imagined
what might be going on on board, whether he was sleeping or
nervous too. There is always a strong bond between single-handed
sailors and I felt it more strongly than ever on that stormy evening.
And while I would do anything in my power to finish ahead of him,
I actually really liked the guy. A funny, chilled-out character, Bilou
was also incredibly good at what he does best – race. I could see
from the weather pictures that the winds were likely to change
quickly on the other side of the depression, but I knew I could not
sleep until they had. I dozed in the cockpit, freezing cold but just
waiting for a tack which when the wind changed took us over forty
minutes. Afterwards I collapsed in the cockpit feeling cold, tired
and a bit desperate. I pulled myself out of it by making up my mind
to strip off, dry off and refuel – I knew I needed to try to switch off.
I finally climbed into the bunk on the leeward side, as it was safest,
and had a cup of Horlicks. As I lay there, deafening sounds echoed
through poor *Kingfisher* as she sailed on through 40-knot winds. I
reached above me to touch her deck, saying gently, 'Hang in there
lass,' and tried to sleep.

    With my eyes closed I still could not sleep; I thought of black
places, counted sheep lying in a field of grass, but nothing would
send me off. I think the general perception of sleep on board a boat

is far from the truth. Many people ask, 'How do you wake up?' but in fact the question we ask ourselves is 'How do you sleep?' When a boat is travelling at speed or often, even worse, when there is little or no wind, sleep is virtually impossible to grab. Waking up is the easy bit, it's trying to get yourself divorced enough from your circumstances to sleep, or even relax, that's the hard bit.

In the morning the wind dropped away and after studying the latest weather fax I realized we were in the centre of a secondary low-pressure system. I gambled on sailing at 90 degrees to the route but to where I calculated the breeze should be. Little by little the wind kicked in and within hours we were sailing at 10 then 15 knots. When the evening position report came through I was 75 miles ahead of Bilou. I was over the moon, though things were soon to go downhill fast . . .

POSITIONS IN MONOHULL fleet at 1038 GMT WEDNESDAY
1. KINGFISHER 871
2. SILL +5
3. WHIRLPOOL +71
4. TG4 +86

The past 24 hours saw a change of fortune for Ellen MacArthur, now hanging on to a very slender 5-mile lead over SILL (Roland Jourdain). A lot can happen in 24 hours at sea . . .

Yesterday afternoon, Ellen was awoken by the Raytheon radar alarm. Unsure of whether it was a ship or not, she quickly went on deck, only to find herself in thick fog. With Kingfisher steaming along at 12 to 13 knots at the time, this was a fairly nerve-racking moment! Then, fortunately, the fog began to clear, and there was the object the radar had pinged – a 'beautiful' iceberg. She even managed to photograph it whilst hand-steering around its windward side (less chance of 'growlers', the small lumps that fall off the main berg and are in many ways more dangerous).

A couple of hours later as she went to go down the fore-hatch to get the kite up as the wind freed, she slipped and went crashing down the hatch, hitting her hand, leg and head on the way. So now we've got icebergs around, it's just above freezing, the boat is charging along, blood on the spinnaker (which she wants to get up) and a bit of pain happening! Undeterred she got the kite up, sorted the boat out, and got back to the cabin to reassess her injuries. Looks like a potentially broken finger, gash and big swelling on her head (seem to remember this one from the Route du Rhum as well!), and the other leg to the one that already hurt a bit swollen as well. Her 'good news' in her call in to us was – 'at least I didn't faint!'. She's OK, but a little bit bashed about.

In amongst all this, the wind is moving all over the place, and Ellen struggles to get a grip on the weather situation, albeit with a lack of information to support her. The fleet heads further south, and Ellen puts some distance to the north – turns out to be the wrong choice and coupled with SILL's apparent performance advantage off the breeze, her lead is now down to zero . . . . the match race begins again.

After a very busy twenty-four hours we were just hanging on to our lead and the following night I had the spinnaker up and was trying to relax.

Suddenly there was a bang and to my horror on deck I saw the kite collapse and fall into the water signalling a 3-hour fight to recover it. I had to sail backwards, blow all the lines and then really struggled as it wrapped itself around the keel. I'm totally drained now, going to have to sleep. My body feels like its been through a mincing machine. I've no idea how I got it back on, once it was in the water the load was enormous so we're on course again at 11 knots. No idea how many miles I've lost though.

I was lucky that Bilou clearly had problems of his own. The following morning I found that rather than dropping into second place, I had actually increased my lead. I was exhausted but over-joyed. We were just days away, and had broken free into the light upwind conditions. I collapsed on the chart table seat and slept more soundly than at any time before on the trip.

The nerves refused to go away though, and even on the final day out there, when the wind stayed strong enough to help us in across the shallows and towards Newport, I was still uneasy. For the first time in any race I knew I wanted to finish. I was exhausted, and had spent every day of the race with a knot of tension in my stomach that had little to do with sailing but everything to do with what was riding on the race. I had pushed myself hard, and as a result *Kingfisher* had shown her true colours; but she was tired too – we'd sailed over 16,000 miles in three months, and we were both in need of a rest.

It was the quietest of mornings as the first signs of life slipped into view framed by a foggy grey sky, as a damp chilly breeze blew. I thought back to my first ever transatlantic with Alan when we left Newport exactly four years earlier. Those four years could have been ten for all that had happened. It took a while for reality to sink in on that morning, as suddenly but briefly the weight which had been on my shoulders for two weeks lifted as I thrust my fist in the air to the crack of a gun.

We had crossed the line in first place, after fourteen days, twenty-three hours and one minute at sea.

19th June 2000 – SHE DID IT!
Ellen MacArthur breaks record in Europe 1 New Man STAR victory . . .

In the early hours here in Newport, USA, Ellen MacArthur crossed the line to take victory in the Europe 1 New Man single-handed transatlantic race. After a tortuous final 36 hours in light and variable winds, the 23-year-old slid into Newport, Rhode Island at 1021 GMT this morning, to become the youngest winner of the race since its inception in 1960.

I was just about ready to drop after this race – I had been full on for over three months, and most of that was at sea alone. When I read the results from the sleep study we had carried out I learned that my average sleep per day over the previous fourteen days had been 4.2 hours – no wonder I felt completely drained. It's a difficult situation when you finish a race as you know you need to download as much information as you can to your team. When they are revving up, you are clapping out!

I returned to the UK where I gave more interviews, some in Derbyshire which gave me a day there to catch up with the family, then more in London. I spent a day in Cowes and took a two-day trip to the Alps to a place near Chamonix where Mark had lived in the past and which he frequented as often as possible. With a guide, Michel, we set straight off to climb in the mountains, each of us tackling ice climbing for the first time, which I revelled in. We spent the night high up in a hut roughly five hours' trek from the head of the cable car, and though I rallied, I remember feeling completely exhausted. I had pushed myself really hard, but knew that my will to go for it often concealed my fatigue.

Immediately after this I was back in Newport, where I spent my birthday for the second time. Then I set off with Martin Carter, and Eric Lindkvist, our awesome Swedish cameraman, to bring *Kingfisher* home after her refit over there. I was looking forward to getting out of the harbour and just being out at sea again. Although I had hoped the trip would be a respite, I was wrong. I developed a cough the day we left the States and did not manage to shake it off all the way across. It would be wrong to say that we didn't have a smile from time to time, especially as Eric took an instant dislike to the food we had on board and had an entertaining way of showing it. I think he found it hard to understand why we were eating freeze-dried. He's quite a good cook and on Martin's birthday he separated the peas, other vegetables and meat from one of the foil-packed dried meals and cooked each separately for a special treat. I warmed immensely to Eric during that trip, and we talked a great deal – he had a kind heart, and though he could be exasperating as he asked you to 'climb the mast just one more time' for another camera angle, he always did it with a persuasive smile that could have had a prime minister standing on his hands. Eric was an absolute perfectionist and a brilliant cameraman – the images he collected from that trip were stunning.

We were now in our final dash towards the Vendée start, with just two months before I sailed *Kingfisher* to Les Sables d'Olonne, and my schedule reflected it. Interviews, corporate sailing days and meetings filled the diary. I went to the South of France to take part in a catamaran regatta, visited a meteorologist called Pierre Lasnier in Nice for more weather training, then travelled throughout France and Belgium giving presentations about my life and the Vendée Globe. But although my life felt like a sleighride as I was carried

235

along by the momentum of the project, I was put firmly back in my place by another trip to France.

Shortly after landing back from America I travelled to Brest to sail with a group of kids in an event which had been part organized by Marine Crenn's brother Antoine. At a young age Antoine had suffered from leukaemia and now worked with a charity called A Chacun Son Cap which had started to bring kids who were suffering from the disease together with kids who had recovered, and take them out on the water. It allowed them to talk to each other about their situation – which must be something that is impossible for the majority of people to understand – but it also enabled them to forget their illness, albeit for just a few days. It was one of the best days' sailing I'd ever had, we laughed so much we had tears in our eyes, and the kids were just incredible. They were not interested in being treated differently in any way, and were unbelievably keen and competitive on board. I joined them on the second day, and it was staggering to see just how much they had bonded already. They made me feel like a novice on board! I was very sad to leave them – the experience hammered home to me how incredibly lucky I was.

It was a hard summer that year for all of us; the pressure was increasing not only for me, but also for the rest of the team. Mark's workload, in particular, was immense, and we called each other constantly to check all was OK. For a while, when *Kingfisher* was in Cowes, we actually managed to spend some time together. Ian McKay was around too and as the demand for promotional material for the Vendée grew, so did the time he had to spend producing it. Since I opened up to him in London we had remained very close friends; he understood the pressures that we were all under, and just having someone to talk to who was coming at it all from a different angle was a godsend. Ian treated me as an equal and it felt like a long time since I'd had such a good mate. Bar my early days with Merv, I'd relied pretty much solely on Mark.

Mark and I had virtually lived together for four years, trying to build the project, taking things forward day by day. But though I did not see it then, the circumstances of our coming together had shaped what followed. Mark had devoted his life to the project.

50 With Merv, working on the design of *Kingfisher*

51 *Kingfisher* takes shape in New Zealand

52 Sailing *Aquitaine Innovations* with Yves Parlier

53 Walking with Dad and Mac in Scotland during a life-saving short break

54 A dream come true as *Kingfisher* is launched

55 *Kingfisher* in her element. The swing keel is clearly visible

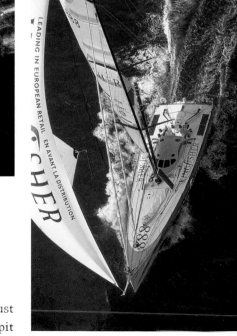

56 If you look hard you can just spot me in the cockpit

57 Ducking waves in the North Atlantic

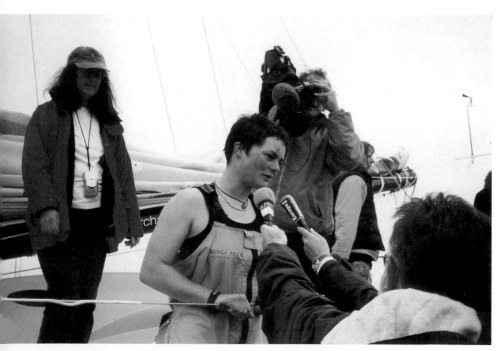

58 Just after winning the Europe 1 New Man STAR transatlantic race
– notice the cut on my forehead

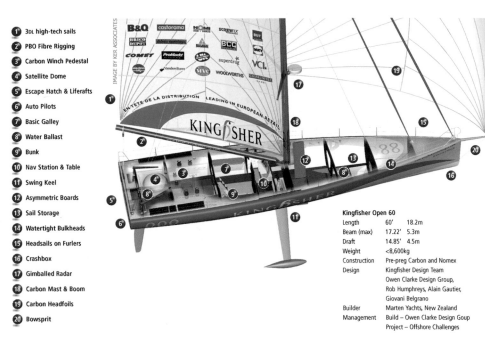

1. 3DL high-tech sails
2. PBO Fibre Rigging
3. Carbon Winch Pedestal
4. Satellite Dome
5. Escape Hatch & Liferafts
6. Auto Pilots
7. Basic Galley
8. Water Ballast
9. Bunk
10. Nav Station & Table
11. Swing Keel
12. Asymmetric Boards
13. Sail Storage
14. Watertight Bulkheads
15. Headsails on Furlers
16. Crashbox
17. Gimballed Radar
18. Carbon Mast & Boom
19. Carbon Headfoils
20. Bowsprit

IMAGE BY KER ASSOCIATES

Kingfisher Open 60

Length	60'	18.2m
Beam (max)	17.22'	5.3m
Draft	14.85'	4.5m
Weight	<8,600kg	
Construction	Pre-preg Carbon and Nomex	
Design	Kingfisher Design Team	
	Owen Clarke Design Group,	
	Rob Humphreys, Alain Gautier,	
	Giovani Belgrano	
Builder	Marten Yachts, New Zealand	
Management	Build – Owen Clarke Design Goup	
	Project – Offshore Challenges	

59 *Kingfisher*

60 Philippe Jeantot and the Vendée skippers the day before the official start

1 The Vendée fleet at Les Sables d'Olonne before the race

62 The *Kingfisher* team. From left to right, back row: Dana Bena, Mark Turner, Tanguy de la Motte, Martin Carter; front row: Amanda Carter, Marie Cairo, me, Pipo Cairo

63 Kids who'd taken part in the Castorama competition before the race enjoy a day out in Les Sables d'Olonne

64 With Mum and Dad before the Vendée start

65 Saying goodbye to Mathilde

66 Leaving Les Sables d'Olonne harbour on the way to the Vendée start. Ian's on board with the video camera filming the event

67 Racing the Vendée

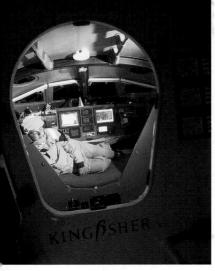

Asleep in *Kingfisher*'s cabin

69 Home! *Kingfisher*'s chart table

An unexpected
est on board

72 Mending broken shelves during the
Vendée. Hot work!

The monitor that recorded my
ep patterns during the Vendée

73 Mending a block during a
frenzied day of equatorial repairs

74 Marion Island, 1,000 miles south of South Africa

75 A wave rolls down the deck. The last picture the camera ever took!

We had known each other since I had been little more than an eighteen-year-old kid and though my future had been determined before the end of my first year with Mark and I had done a massive amount of growing up, I sometimes felt that our partnership had not moved on to reflect it. Although I knew that Mark respected me, I also felt he could sometimes still see that eighteen-year-old who had first spoken to him. Things had changed and the reality was that I was now a highly independent twenty-four-year-old professional sailor. It was always going to be a difficult transition to make, and though at times it was hard, in many ways it was Mark's nurture and support that enabled me to realize my ambitions. The reality was that it was a big step in the right direction; working like this we could make the sponsorship work, as it enabled me to have the time to go and train on the water, and give presentations when necessary. Leading a team, being its public face and competing for that same team was a huge responsibility. In just two years we had gone from struggling to find enough money to get a document printed, to winning a high-profile transatlantic race against the best in the world. I didn't allow myself to dwell on what we had achieved. None of us, especially me, could afford the tiniest trace of complacency. We needed each other, thriving on each other's determination and passion to get things right.

At this stage making a success of the project meant ignoring how tired we were. The diary was fit to bust and we had to keep going, both giving as much, or even more than we were really capable of and with the race just weeks away it was taking its toll.

We missed out on the family holiday that year. Mum and Dad bailed out of going to Scotland, having decided that I would be better off just spending three days at home – and they were right. But it was difficult to relax. There were always people to visit and people who visited whenever there was wind that I was at home, and however well-meaning, this added its own pressure, along with plans to make and a race now looming startlingly close on the horizon.

My final sail alone before we based *Kingfisher* in Les Sables d'Olonne was to be the delivery from La Trinité where we'd been filming with the BBC. Alain Gautier was going to join me on board for the first part of this. We sailed out together into the Bay of Biscay and even though we would only have twenty-four hours together, it was wonderful to share, however briefly, his experiences of the Vendée. At thirty-nine, Alain's experience was extensive, from the Figaro fleet to Open 60 trimaran fleet to three round-the-world trips on Open 60 monohulls, including two Vendée Globes, the second of which he had won. Having Alain as part of the team had been Mark's suggestion, and it had worked well. He was someone I could identify with completely and he was open and generous with his advice. Having Alain around had been fantastic and somehow he gave me a quiet confidence. I stayed out for one day longer once I had dropped Alain off outside Lorient, but with a forecast of little to no wind I decided to enter Les Sables early and try to get some rest.

Early on in our time there I got together with the team for a wild night out. Marie, Pipo and the kids had moved to the town once we returned from New Zealand, so they knew the lie of the land extremely well. We had a fantastic time; everyone relaxed and made complete fools of themselves and we danced the night away until close to dawn. We profited from the last of the summer celebrations with a few drinks in an almost Caribbean-style beach bar, and then finished the evening in a nightclub. None of us realized then how impossible reliving that kind of evening would become in only a few months' time.

Before the final countdown to the race I took a brief trip back to the UK during which Ian dragged me away for a couple of days to try to help me unwind. He'd been on a holiday on the Norfolk Broads some time before, and he suggested we spent a few days messing about on a boat with no pressure, anonymously and without fuss. Although it was not long enough, we had a wonderful time, leaving Horning on our first morning bright and early, with mist lingering over the water and amongst the foliage. We had hired the smallest sailing boat we could find so that we would not be restricted at all about where we went and it also happened to be the oldest available. Those three days reminded me very much of my time on *Cabaret* as a kid. We had visited the Norfolk Broads then, and even now, over ten years later, I felt the same excitement at the promise of adventure.

At the end of the trip I had to head home to Derbyshire to go through my Vendée medical kit with Uncle Glyn. Running through the lists of drugs was mind-boggling. Taking each one out of its packet and labelling it with its potency was a sobering reminder of what I was embarking on. There were drugs for serious infections to be injected three times a day, powerful painkillers, DIY kits for setting broken bones and ready-threaded needles for sewing yourself up. I thought again of what Alan Wynne-Thomas had been through and it hit home sharply that I would have to be completely self-sufficient out there. I even tested myself by injecting saline solution into the muscle of my leg. Once Glyn showed me what to do on himself I couldn't back out, but at least the two of us weren't caught as we stood there with our trousers round our ankles and syringes in our hands. I knew that if I had to repair myself thousands of miles from a hospital, as others had done before, I needed to be prepared, whether that meant coping with hypothermia or sewing something back on. There was also another possibility of which all skippers are aware – the responsibility of having to treat someone who we may have to rescue. As Pete Goss had shown in picking up Raphael Dinelli, we were going to places where we could rely only on each other; there was no one else out there.

While in Derbyshire, I went to say my final goodbyes to Gran, who we knew was not going to come to France to see the race start. She had never been abroad, and she felt that it would be impossible for her to come out in a boat to watch us all leave. I could sense her worry at saying goodbye, but she's a strong lady and I knew she believed I would get around safely.

Back in Les Sables, the change in just the week or so I'd been away was extreme. The whole town had been completely consumed by the Vendée Globe; as I drove past shops there were posters on the walls and pictures in the windows. The Cap Ouest restaurant had adopted the *Kingfisher* team and was already decked out in blue and yellow. The compound by the pontoons was a completely different place, with two-storey tents covering hundreds of square yards of ground. On the pontoons themselves was the most significant change – twenty-four of the most technologically advanced Open raceboats in the world were lined up there.

This was it. This was really it.

We were one of the lucky teams. Our boat was almost ready and raring to go. Other competitors were less fortunate; we saw boats with question marks on their hulls looking for sponsors and others still undergoing major work. The diversity of the fleet highlighted the fact that the Vendée was a unique race. There were some 50-footers among the 60s, and although their skippers were out there to race, they would leave the dockside without a realistic chance of winning. One was *Aqua Quorum*, the boat I'd raced in the Route du Rhum; ironically she was skippered by Patrice Carpentier, now fifty, who had raced Robert Nickerson's *Panic Major* in the first Vendée. *Elan Sifo*, raced by Catherine Chabaud last time, was there once again, now sailed by Joe Seeten; it seemed a lifetime since I had docked on this very pontoon with her four years before. There was the Russian Fedor Konioukhov, the ultimate adventurer. Starting with Everest, he had climbed the eight highest peaks of the world. His boat bore the number 8848, the height in metres to which he had climbed. In 1990–91 he had sailed non-stop around the world alone and now he was going to race around it. He was a shaggy-haired and bearded man, deceptively slight, with an unassuming personality. He spoke halting English, but with even less French it was hard for him to communicate with the majority of the fleet. I warmed to the spirit of this man who quietly goes out and just does things without a fanfare. People like him underlined that the Vendée Globe was still an occasion for adventure. We'd be passing through some of the most isolated and untouched areas of the world – this really was the Everest of sailing.

There was concern in the air though; the Vendée, a race historically known for its pioneering spirit, was now clearly more competitive than ever. There were twenty-four competitors in this fourth edition of the Vendée – more than the total number who had managed to complete the race since its inception in 1989–90. At least half the boats sitting on the start line had the potential to win. There was speculation around the pontoons about the pace of the race, whether we would be tempted to push ourselves and our boats too far ... the tension was growing each day. There were some incredibly experienced guys out there, many of whom I had raced either with or against before: Yves Parlier was now setting off for his third Vendée Globe; Marc Thiercelin, who had finished second in the previous Vendée and second in the Around Alone, was there with a new boat; Catherine Chabaud, who had a new Open 60 for this edition had finished sixth in the previous race; and of course there was Michel Desjoyeaux, dubbed 'The Professor', who had twice won the Figaro, and the AG2R transatlantic once, and had already raced around the world in the Whitbread. In my own mind before the start, he, along with Mike Golding in *Team Group 4* and Bilou, with whom I'd sparred during the Europe 1 New Man STAR, would be likely to be my biggest rivals. I also knew that the Southern Ocean would be a different ball game to what I'd encountered before, a big unknown ... We all had to sail safe, but judging from the noises being made before the start, it didn't sound as though any of us had any plans to be hanging around down there.

Time was in short supply in the weeks before the start and I spent a large part of the month of October in Les Sables d'Olonne, partly because I wanted to be with the boat and remain aware of what was happening on board, and partly because it was just less hassle if I could stay in the same place, because so much needed to be done in preparation for being at sea for three months. There was not only the weather planning and the technical side of the boat to sort out – obviously the major things – but everything else as well, from which kind of soap would work best in salt water to the number of tubes of toothpaste or sunblock to take. We even vacuum-packed my thermals and underwear so that there was no chance of them getting wet before they were needed.

As the days to the start counted down, the number of visitors increased. I found I couldn't walk anywhere without being stopped and asked for an autograph and it was humbling to see people's excitement when they spotted me in the street or when they walked past the boats. People travelled hundreds of miles to immerse themselves in the atmosphere at the start of this incredible race.

Home in Les Sables was an apartment block just across the water from the boats; we had taken several rooms on one floor to house most of the team. It was fairly basic summer holiday-let accommodation when we moved in there, with folding beds that also served as the sofa. I put up a few posters on the walls, spread my charts on the table and filled the cupboards with my bags. Everyone was busy in Les Sables, and once again it made a real difference having Ian around; we got on better than best friends, and I really felt that I had an incredible understanding with him.

The pressure felt immense, and in the final three weeks I was ill twice. Both times I was sick and felt exhausted. I was concerned about how prepared I was physically. I had tried to use the gym during the summer and had managed a few runs, but against what I would have liked to achieve I had done very little as I had simply not had the time. Now I was worried about living through the repercussions on the boat. I had still not completely shaken off the cough I'd picked up during our delivery back from America, and I was annoyed that after all we had been through I was not A1 for the start. I even had a massage, a first for me, and the masseur told me that he did not think I was stressed, which was a bonus of sorts.

Castorama, one of Kingfisher's store chains, had run a competition inspired by the charity A Chacun Son Cap. They had provided ten hospitals around France with models of *Kingfisher*, and the kids had designed and painted them. A small group from each hospital had come to Les Sables for the announcement of the competition results, and I got the chance to present the prizes and show the children around *Kingfisher*. Although I felt like death warmed up, it was a very inspiring day in the blur of nerves before the start, a moment which made me forget my superficial illness and think even harder about how lucky I was to be about to set out to achieve what I'd always dreamed of . . . those kids would be with me on board.

Satellite trucks and TV cameras from all over mainland Europe flooded in, although apart from some loyal regional TV stations, the Brits were conspicuous by their absence. The nights were the easiest time to be around the boat, when the majority of the public had gone home and I could get on with things without being stopped too much. Although the support was incredible, it could be tiring signing autographs during the day – I learnt quickly that you have to do it in short bursts, or you can't really 'give' to those you meet. It was always painfully hard to draw myself away, and I often relied on Mark, Dana or Ian to help me.

Each skipper followed the weather like a hawk. We all knew that in previous races one of the hardest obstacles to cross was the Bay of Biscay and that in the past many boats had been dismasted and forced to turn back within the first few days. The forecast for start day was horrendous – we were due to be hit with 60-knot winds on our first night – and did not improve. On the day before the start we all headed to the skippers' meeting. We went through the process of the start procedure and the problematic towing situation on the morning of the start, and as the meeting drew to a close the English voice of Richard Tolkien piped up, asking whether with such a forecast we should actually start the race. There was a deathly silence, then much discussion, after which the decision was made to postpone the start. With the atrocious conditions forecast, we knew that it would now be nigh impossible to leave for at least two days, which was one of the safety issues: if someone had a problem, they would not be able to get back in. The storm would make the entrance to Les Sables virtually impassable to the competitors, quite apart from the danger caused by the hundreds of spectator craft which would be likely to try to see us off regardless of safety considerations.

Like all the guys, I was psyched up to leave, but there was a sense of relief when the start was delayed. An odd mixture of deflation and anticipation marked the two days that followed, but they passed frighteningly quickly and they did give us the chance to spend a bit more time with our families. I felt sad for the thousands of people who had descended on Les Sables for the start weekend. It must have been very disappointing for them.

With the race delayed Mum and Dad had left on their original ferry booking with Glyn and his wife Steph, Fergus, Lewis and his friend Pete, and Mum and Dad's friend Wendy. I was sad that they couldn't stay to see us all leave, but as the day progressed and the wind worsened I was glad that they were not around to see the storm. That night I went bowling with the rest of the team, although after a few throws I found it hard to concentrate. It was wonderful to see everyone smile so much – in many ways their jobs were done now – but when everyone else went out for a meal afterwards I headed down to the boats with Ian to check all was well.

Outside the storm was howling, and as we walked down to the marina the wind was deafening as it ripped through the swaying masts and rigging. We wandered past the pontoons, shifting a few fenders on boats in danger of damaging themselves and tweaking a few mooring lines. The rain absolutely lashed down and the boats suddenly looked very vulnerable. I could not help but think what it must be like out at sea in this as the spray splashed our faces.

As we stood, two solitary wet figures, next to *Kingfisher*, we realized that we were going to be together for a long time. I held Ian's hand tight as we stood in *Kingfisher*'s cockpit, thinking about the three months to come. What we had was a deep friendship and the bond between us was a strong one. The time we had spent together during the year had been special, I had begun to rely on him in many ways, and despite the fact that I had been away at sea for much of the time, he was always there to encourage me, whether by phone, in person or by e-mail. Ian shared my joy that I was competing in the Vendée. He wanted me to go and he wanted me to do well, and when he told me that he would not worry while I was out there, I knew that he meant it.

The day before the start the storm assaulted Les Sables. Waves broke so high over the harbour wall that the lighthouse at the end of the breakwater disappeared under them. When I went to the base of the breakwater to film with the BBC crew, I was amazed at how battered the waves made the place look. The carefully attached banners all the way along the breakwater were like rags in the breeze. The wind whipped up the spray under the dark sky with an intimidating wildness. I was glad I could go back to my room, warm up, make a cup of tea and study the weather in peace.

I collected together my clothes and placed them in my bags. I laid out what I would wear on the start day and put it in a separate pile. I had bought a tiny waterproof case in which I placed a photo of Mum and Dad, my passport, mobile phone and two credit cards; I hoped I wouldn't be needing any of those, bar the photo until I was back in France again. I rechecked my bags, then my cupboard – that was everything. I took a final look through the latest weather fax that had been sent through, then crawled into bed beside Ian. My mind was full of a million things but I felt calm here. His hand reached over and stroked my head, and though I said nothing I felt a tear run on to the pillow. This was the last night I would be able to close my eyes and sleep soundly through till dawn. As I drifted to sleep I comforted myself with the thought of the sleep in a warm bed that would be waiting for me when I finished.

Chapter Sixteen

Dana had been fantastic and organized everything. In the end Mum and Dad flew out to Les Sables d'Olonne to see me off, even though we had already said our goodbyes days earlier. I knew that it would mean so much to them actually to see us leave. Soon after waking on the morning of the start I went to see them for a final chat. They were in the apartment at the end of the corridor, and as I walked along it I could hear the sound of my footsteps echoing. I knocked, and Mum opened the door; both she and Dad smiled, but I could see the expectant expressions on their faces as they waited to see first how I would react. I could not help but feel that they looked lost and almost vulnerable as I walked in. Their clothes were all packed away as if they'd been waiting, ready to be granted their five minutes. When you are concentrating so hard on what you're doing it's easy to forget what the consequences are for those around you. Despite their inevitable anxiety I knew that the last thing Mum and Dad wanted to do was hold me back; they were confident that I had it inside me to do it and were aware of how much I had dreamed of the moment about to arrive.

I wanted to say goodbye properly before we were on the pontoons and as I hugged each of them I held up a brave face assuring them that we really were ready. I thought it would be great just to miss out this goodbye bit and go as it would be less painful for everyone. I kept telling myself that I wasn't saying goodbye but just 'See you soon' – and somehow the tears stayed back.

246

As I climbed on board *Kingfisher* that morning the atmosphere was subdued. There were visitors everywhere, but no noise – almost an acknowledgement of what lay ahead, a kind of reverential feeling for those twenty-four boats. I wanted to see each skipper in turn to wish them a safe voyage and Mark had suggested I gave out stress balls, each one of which I signed along with a message to each skipper. I just knew that I had to make contact with all of them before we left. There was a heavy drizzle as I either dodged along the pontoons or ferried around from boat to boat in the RIB. I almost missed Catherine Chabaud, with whom I had a particularly strong connection, and when she spotted me just as her boat *Whirlpool* was heading away from the pontoons she yelled at one of the harbour guys to pick me up in their Zodiac. We hugged and wished each other the best for the months ahead before I was whisked back to the mêlée on the pontoons. There was obviously a special goodbye from the guys on *Aquitaine Innovations* and, with his stress ball in one hand, Yves looked me squarely in the eye and raised his index finger to stress his words: 'If I don't win, you have to win, and if you don't win, I have to win.' We kissed and I left.

When I handed the fifty-nine-year-old Pasquale de Gregorio his stress ball he smiled. I said, 'See you when you get back.' 'I doubt you'll be around,' he replied, believing I'd be long gone by the time he finished. But I knew that I would do everything in my power to see every skipper as they arrived back in Les Sables d'Olonne. I wanted to be there for each of them.

The emotion in the air was physical but the reactions among the skippers were different; although everyone was outwardly calm, each of us wished we were already out there. As Mark and I walked along the pontoon with our arms round each other I have no recollection of what was said. His eyes were red and sore, but like everyone, he was keeping his emotions in check – the finish would be the time to let them go. He held me tight beneath his arm, his head pressed against mine. We had been through so much together, just so much – and now we had reached that moment and felt numbed by its intensity. I knew as we walked that although we would be apart for the next three months, Mark would live every second of the race with me. His mobile would never be switched off and he would never take a night's sleep without thinking about how I was out there. I think he had the worst of it just waiting for that phone to ring, waiting for the voice on the other end, wondering whether it would be happy, worried, frightened or exhausted. At worst, there might be no voice at all. The waiting game would be a harsh one to play.

Marie and Pipo were there waiting by the boat with Mathilde and her little brother Pilou, and as I reached down to kiss Mathilde I realized she knew what I was about to embark on. She grasped her Barbie doll tight in her right hand, and a little tear ran down her face as she hugged me.

'A bientôt, Mathilde,' I said, 'See you soon . . .'

Without a doubt the most openly emotional goodbye was with Eric the cameraman. He hugged me harder than I think I had ever been hugged before, and sobbed into my shoulder. I tried calmly to tell him that everything would be all right, but though it remained unsaid, none of us knew for sure, and trying to reassure him nearly sent me over the edge. It was a stark reminder of how close to the surface people's feelings were that morning.

I climbed back on board *Kingfisher* and looked round, but there was no sign of Mum and Dad. Although we had said our goodbyes, I hoped that they would come down. I wanted them to know that I was OK and ready to leave. I popped below, scanning the cabin to check all was well and that we were ready to go and I stripped off my wet jeans and put on my thermals. I passed the jeans to Ian, who promised he'd wash them for when I got back. He pushed a boiled egg and an apple into my hand; I hadn't fancied any breakfast that morning and he knew I wouldn't have eaten anything since. The egg was still warm as I took it and popped it into my pocket. I wished it would stay that way until I saw him again.

Martin stuck his head round the cabin door and said that Mum and Dad were there. I'd been sure that they would come and that they would have waited until the last minute so that they did not get in the way. I hugged Mum first, wrapping my arms round her and losing myself momentarily as I buried my face in her long black hair. Dad then hugged me firmly, giving me a firm pat on the back as he always did. I looked up at his face and I could see that he was proud, but I could also see the pain and the worry. I had done well thus far not getting emotional, but as he kissed me on my forehead I knew it had to be for the last time. I gave him a firm squeeze and turned away. As I looked back to give them a final wave they had their backs to me, my heart went out to them – they were being so brave. I felt so proud of them too.

Things felt easier immediately we slipped our lines from the dock and headed slowly down the long channel out to sea. Most of the team were still on board, or alongside in the RIB. As we were towed along the walls were packed with people cheering 'Ell-en; Ell-en; Ell-en' – I could only hope that it would be a great race for them too. Ian was on deck with a video camera in his hands; he did not look up and I knew that his way of handling the situation was keeping himself busy. It was an unreal experience anyway. I felt that the crowds were there not just to celebrate our departure, but to share in it. It was their race too. There was a fascination with what we were about to do as if we were astronauts or explorers, only in the Vendée there was a subtle difference – we were going out into the unknown to race.

As I steered *Kingfisher* towards the harbour entrance my mind was on getting out to sea . . . and safely. I'm not sure that I actually allowed myself to think too hard about what we were setting off to do. With Mark, Ian and the guys still on board it was easy to pretend otherwise. I suppressed the thought that in an hour's time they would all be gone.

It became more peaceful once we edged our way out to the start zone. The cheering drifted away on the wind, and we could hear our own voices once more. Perversely, I was less focused then than for the single-handed transatlantic or any other starts – perhaps concentrating too much on spending the last few precious minutes in people's company had taken my mind off it. I gave Ian a massive hug and a kiss, which Mark captured on the boat's digital camera. It was a picture I looked at many times during the following months. The moment didn't last, though, as we were soon joined by the fleet of boats which had come out to see us off. The water was getting hectic, churned into a confused mess, and we had to take care hoisting the mainsail and stowing the lines away. As we did so, the RIB drew alongside and it was time for the guys to go. Only Pipo, Martin, Mark and Ian were still left on board, and as they walked in turn to climb over her rails for the last time I hugged them tight and felt the nerves really kick in. I think that the hour that followed their leaving was probably the loneliest of the race. They were all still close and I could see them, but I couldn't touch them and I knew there wouldn't be another chance to until we returned.

I just wished that they would disappear in a flash, so I'd never have to look into their eyes or wave for that final time.

As the start gun fired I was angry with myself. We had not had the code 5 up, as I had suggested earlier, before being encouraged to calm down, and it would have been the perfect sail to head off to our first mark with. Mich Desjoyeaux had led the fleet out of the start zone by heading north up the coast. I worked hard over the following minutes, hoisting the code 5, and sailed around our first mark. It was incredible – we had 23,000 miles to race and were already fighting for positions as if we were just racing along the coast. As the last waves and shouts came from the team, I was already thinking of rounding Finisterre . . .

That first night was a tough one, sailing in light airs, yet still with the horrible swell from the storm. I don't think any of the skippers slept much that first night, whether it was from the noises coming off the snatching ropes or the mixture of anticipation and apprehension at heading out into the open ocean for three months. During the night as I was working on the computer it finally hit me: this is it, I'm doing the Vendée Globe. Better get on with it, I thought!

There was sobering news in the morning as I called in to our first chat session with race HQ. Mike Golding, undoubtedly one of the race favourites, had been towed back into Les Sables. Late that night, he had just changed sails and was standing in his hatchway looking up when suddenly there was a loud crack and his mast came tumbling down. When I heard the news I felt numbed by it. Mike had been preparing for this race since I was working on the 50-footer in Cherbourg, when Merv had played such a big part in his early preparations. He must have been absolutely devastated – he had been out there to win.

We came out of the first night in thirteenth position, which I was disappointed with, but positions change quickly in these situations, particularly if you're rounding a corner as we were. I was astonished to learn that Bilou had also been forced to turn back. He had broken his halyard that held up the gennaker and at the same time smashed a tooth. He had been back for a middle-of-the-night pit stop with a dentist and halyard maker! By 5 a.m. he was out again and on a mission! My only problem had been squashing my finger beneath one of the ballast valve handles as I leaned my whole weight on it to push it down. It throbbed like mad and instantly begun to turn black – stupid.

I thought a lot about the team on our first day at sea. I knew that on the evening of the start they would have all been out to celebrate making it through stage 1 – a successful start. A few days later, though, by the time I was around Cape Finisterre, they would all scatter, returning to their different lives. Martin and his wife Amanda would return to New Zealand, Mum and Dad would fly home, Mark would go off to the French mountains. I hated the thought of them splitting up after all we'd been through together, but life had to go on and anyway, I thought, I would soon be closer to Martin and Amanda in New Zealand.

Martin had given me the Maori charm he wore around his neck and which he had never taken off since Amanda gave it to him before they were married; now it was around my neck and was going to stay there until we crossed the finish line. Marie had given me a tiny metal pulley which she had worn around her neck for over ten years, and I'd promised her I would bring it back as fast as I could.

I was having one of those mornings – as I opened my log book I found a long message from Merv. There was so much of him in

Kingfisher that I just hoped that for his sake and the entire design team's I could do justice to their efforts. His message ended:

```
In the background or the foreground I'm always there.
Keep safe and come back to all of us who love you. Sail
fast, sail hard, sail safe
Your best mate - always
Love
Merv xx
PS. And for f***'s sake clip on!
```

I knew that I was in no way alone on this venture. There were many hearts and souls with me, following each day. Things were going to be OK out there . . .

```
10/11/00 (ellenmacarthur.com/day2)
Position  44° 51.8N  006° 48.1W
Heading/speed  264  0
Wind from 219  at 13.1 knots
Pressure of  1016
Sea temperature  10
Sail configuration is  Full main  Genoa
Percentage performance  0
```

```
Tonight the moon is out, the sky close to clear -
glazing the deck with moonlight. We're close hauled on
Port tack, and with a wind shift in our favour we're now
heading towards finisterre.
    All is well on board, I feel very relaxed, happy in my
daily chores and dofeel glad to be out here ondce again,
even if this is for the big one.
    Spoke to Uncle Glyn today, to ask him if I should
stick a burning hot wire through my fingernail to
release a bit of pressure as it was black after I
trapped it last night. The answer was yes - although he
did point out that someone would normally do it for you
```

. . . oh well – not the first time! He was right though,
although a little sore it didn't hurt much – and the
blood spurted out, leaving a still sore, but less
painfullly hrobbing finger. THis morning I was alongside
Whirlpool, Gartmore and Solidaires. It's been a day of
tactical sailing – tacking on the shifts, and watching
the wind direction minute by minute. Our positions are
changing on an hourly basisright now – so I'm just
concentrating on the best speed in the best direction
. . . II've slept well today, and some tonight already.
THough an hour period with 4 or 5 dozes would be classed
as a great sleep!
 Looking forward to the sunrise tomorrow, and hoping
that the dolphins come past as they did when the sun
set . . .
 This is it kiddo.
 a donf!
ellenx

I surprised myself that after the first difficult day I really did feel
OK out there. I did not have that desperate feeling I'd had through
the 1 STAR, and felt on top of the decisions that were being taken
by the rest of the fleet. Yves and Mich had taken an early lead which
I was not surprised at, but after our magical night, the position
report came in to show that I was in third place. This was good
news, but I knew the boats that were further offshore would begin
to catch up quickly. It began to dawn on me as we prepared to turn
left for the first time how long we really would be out there, but I
was excited about it – it was a massive challenge, and I honestly
felt that I was as ready for the race as I ever had been, and was just
looking forward to putting all the skills I had learnt into practice. I
sent a short e-mail home to Mark to reassure him, and I thanked
goodness that I felt better than in the 1 STAR.

 But as the fleet rounded Finisterre we got a good old hammering.
The breeze increased violently as the front came through, and the
conditions were tough, with a freezing wind, and a fine rain which

felt like pins sticking in your eyes as you tried to squint ahead into the breeze. There was also a lot of shipping, which was always a background worry, and as I clung to the foredeck changing down to *Kingfisher*'s storm jib my world shrank to what was illuminated in the pool of light from my head torch. Several times I was hurled into the air so violently that I landed on her deck grabbing her grab rails. I made sure I was clipped on though, and was glad I weighed 9 stone, rather than 12!

I tried to doze in the cuddy waiting for the wind shift to come to allow us to plough on towards the south, but I was damp and cold, my only comfort being a pair of mittens I pushed my hands into to keep the chill from them. When the wind eventually changed, and just before it reached 50 knots, I had problems fighting with the daggerboards as with the hammering into the waves the down-haul line had jammed, which meant I had to go forward with a screw-driver to force it back into its conduit. When eventually we were able to tack I breathed a real sigh of relief, but we were sailing incredibly uncomfortably into the swell – and fast. If ever there was a break-boat situation because of sea conditions, this was it. The motion with the new wind direction was atrocious as we literally fell off each wave, and I felt sick inside as I heard one of the sets of shelves give way beneath the weight of the boxes stacked on it. I picked up the upturned boxes and took a quick look at the damage and saw immediately that it was going to be a nasty repair. Sorry, *Kingfisher*, I thought. Cape Finisterre was certainly living up to its tough reputation.

14/11/00 02:49Z (ellenmacarthur.com/day6)
Well it's uite beutiful out here, though the wind is
quite variable.
The moon orse at the begginning if the evening – making
the first our of darkness very black. THere are several
cargo ships around, one just passed behind me – heading
out into the midst of the Atlantic. Funny as he headed
west I felt a little surge of excitiement for him, that
he was off once agaoin on another passage.

The wind despite it's variability in strength has come round once more to the NW which I am pleased with. My course is much better, and my hesitation to put up the spinnaker was right. Just ahd the longest sleep of the race, feel a bit sleepy, but I think after the ahammering off finisterre my body needs to recover a little. My eyes are still sore, and my body aches, but inside I feel fine – just want to keep on trucking! Dissappointed at slipping back in the position reports, and after the light patch I just wen through I fear I shall have slipped back some more – though yesterday evenig things were looking much better – I was in 5th . . .

Oh well – time to send this, hope you are all well back at home. Funny it seems for a while now that time has stopped. It's wonderful to be here at the chart table litening to the water passing under her hull. The little red glow from her instruments, and a bit earlier, dare I say it. I had a 20 minute session of TOm Jones! Fantastic . . .

X

Conditions stabilized well once the seas had calmed down, and we began our gybing match down to the Canaries. Though we had to pass to the north of several points in the Southern Ocean, the Canaries were our only waypoint until we were in those freezing conditions. It was an opportunity to concentrate on the weather in that area. Behind the islands it's renowned – along with intense heat from Africa, you can find yourself starved of winds closer inshore. Things were still looking good though – we were powering along – holding 5th place, but the unthinkable happened. I was dozing in the cuddy for 20 minutes, and during that time a squall came over, I woke to feel *Kingfisher* accelerate, then broach and our world falling on its side. I blew the mainsheet and the code 5 sheet, whilst trying to bear away, but the sheet burnt its cover off, and my hands and jammed on the winch – and as I reached a second time

255

to free it, the sail blew out. I could have cried with anger and frustration. 7 days into the race – and already we had lost a sail. Without sails we go nowhere, and as they are so specialist these days, we can be hammered in certain conditions without one . . . I fought to get its skeleton down cursing to myself for having let this happen. Any self pity soon disappeared though with news of another competitor. Belgian Skipper Patrick de Radigues had been knocked unconscious during a gybe, and woke as his boat hit a beach on the Portuguese coast. Miraculously he'd managed to hit the only beach for miles along a rocky coast, but his dream for the Vendée was shattered.

```
15/11/00 22:58Z (ellenmacarthur.com/day7)
Position   28° 19.6N   016° 04.4W
Heading/speed  276   12.43
Wind from 52  at 15.5 knots
Pressure of  1014
Sea temperature  16.3
Sail configuration is  Full main   Code 5
Percentage performance   98.6
```

Well it seemed a bit strange to sail once again pst the canary islands. the lsat time I was here it was just over 3 years gao, and I was with my Mini Transat boat, about to turn into port. And now – once again to see those lights, butthis time to carry on. An incredible and exciting feeling.

I didn't excpect to be in 3rd either, especially after the previous nights problems with the code 5 – amazing what you have to sacrifice for a couple of places! The guys in the motor boat patrolling the waypoint zone were superb, They said so many wonderful things, and almost sounded more excited than I at my position! WOnderful . . .

Tactically I think I was lucky to get ahead of Marc THercelin, I would have favoured the offshore option too

at the beginning, but seeing the barometer fluctuate
wass good news, and did indicate that I wasn't about to
be becalmed with the hot African air!

Anyway - dont want to spend too much time below - as
there are a number of baots around. I just want to be
away from the land again!
night,
ex

There was more good news by this stage though. Mike Golding
had been able to ship his spare mast over from the UK and had
restarted the race. I thought a great deal about Mike during the
following days. For him the race was about winning. He had already
sailed around the world three times and it took real guts to do what
he did, to sail back out of a quiet Les Sables and an empty channel
to restart a week later – I respected him enormously for it.

On board the winds were getting stronger as we sailed into the
trade winds. Living on board became markedly more stressful, as
with each wave you flew down you held your breath. We broke a
batten in the main during the night – though I don't know how it
happened. The only remedy was drop the sail completely and repair
it. My to do list was getting longer.

16/11/00 22:17Z (ellenmacarthur.com/day8)
Position   23° 39.0N 020° 02.2W
Heading/speed 224 15
Wind from 78 at 24.3 knots
Pressure of 1016 Rough
Sea temperature 12.8
Sail configuration is 1st reef Code 5
Percentage performance 94.2

Hi - what a day!
Well the kettles on, and there's that gentle hissing
of the gas burning away .. Sounds tranquil if it
weren't for the violent motion, and screaming surfs!

257

Today has been a sleigh ride . . . Non stop surfing, averag ing speeds of over 15 knots, and surfs (even on the autopilot) at over 22!!

I was glad to be away from the Canaries and into open Ocean. It's funny how confined you feel when close to land . . . RIght now it is dark once more, and there is that constant 'shaking' motion as we hurtle down, across and through the waves.

I spent atleast 4 hours helming today. Not only as it it's faster, bt actually an amazing feeling. AS you ride up to the top of the wave and look over the next ti's like being pushed off the top of a hill on a brake-less bike . . . There's simply no stopping you. *Kingfisher* is handling fantastically, the autopilot struggles in the waves, but we're doing Ok. As I came down below I saw a avigation light on my port side. I believe it was Marc Thercelin, in Somewhere. He overtook last night aftert the islands, so if it is him, it's a great feeling to be back up there. It's both exhilerating and frightening (JUST SURFED AT 23,3knots!!) I have my legs jammed under the chart table to hold my self in, the whole boat feels like she is one of those fairground rides which show you a picture of a ski slope and shake you around – though here it's pitch black – there's a fire hydrant on you, and it's not over in 3 minutes! THinking very Much of Mike Golding and his problems right now. It seemed just so unfair . . . Losing your mast on the first night, Time to go – paella should be rehydrated by now – might be time for a damp nap in the cuddy!
night,
ex

Bar our negotiation of the Cape Verdes about 500 miles west of Senegal, we were pretty much now on the direct route for the Equator but I still wanted to make more progress to the west. Although the Equator is a fickle place, there is one rule of thumb that generally works; the further west you are on crossing, the more consistent the breeze will be. It was while approaching the islands that I decided to go for a more westerly option. Although in the final position report of the day no one had gone for it, I held my breath and gybed on to a course which was not far off 90 degrees to the route. News that day had been that Bernard Stamm, the Swiss skipper, had retired, forced to pull into the Cape Verdes after breaking his tiller. We were experiencing testing conditions on the way south, and although many feel that it is easier to go downwind, it is actually more dangerous. Although you sail faster, you are also closer to the edge – and the Southern Ocean could be the classic example of this.

I knew that the following morning the results would be painful, but at the end of the day I had already dropped to eighth position; whereas the others had gone for speed and sailed higher, I had tried to stay as deep as possible to stay to the west. The wind intensified during the night, and I hand-steered for a while, keeping the Code 5 up to sail deeper and faster to the west. My worries were confirmed though, in that when the positions came in we were sitting fourteenth. Now we were just going to have to sail for our lives.

The sea temperature was up to over 20 degrees, and life on board was getting fairly uncomfortable. Frustratingly, however, our gybe had shown that there was a 6-degree difference in the readings from the two temperature sensors – a bit of a problem as I knew how important sea temperature would be once we plunged into the south. It's not much fun sitting down below sweating, especially when you charge the batteries for a couple of hours. The cabin turns into a sauna, and you can't even open the hatches because of the risk of waves coming into the boat . . . rather unexpectedly when alone at sea, I was also living with the danger of being smacked in the chops! We were now well into flying-fish territory, and the frightened little things would leap out of the water, sometimes hitting the boat, and sometimes passing over. I'm afraid it is instant death for a number of them, and you find the odd eye which has popped out staring at you from the cockpit floor, but the majority land relatively unscathed on the decks and make the most terrible racket as they desperately flap their wings and slap their tails in search of water. I'm a sucker for wildlife though – every time I heard one flapping on deck, whether at night or by day, I would always lift the poor thing back into the water; I could not bear to hear them struggling. Many skippers actually ate them, and having tried them myself I knew they were good eating, but I couldn't bring myself to do it. Even though I knew I had to eat, my appetite was never that great!

```
19/11/00 01:54Z (ellenmacarthur.com/day10)
Position   15° 03.0N  026° 54.5W
Heading/speed   223   13.47
Wind from 79  at 17.8 knots
Pressure of   1012   Moderate
Sea temperature   15.4
Sail configuration is   Full main   Code 5
Percentage performance   104
```

Well we seem to be doing OK . . . I don't think we could be sailing any fast er in this direction anyway! THe wind seems to have shifted more into the east for the night, but progress is very good, and like this we will not be losing grond to the west. If in the morning our course is too westward we can reach back to the east – but once ground is lost to the west it's gybng to get back down there, and gybing is slow . . .

  Spirit's are up, as word from the others is of there problems to get further west. They are in a NEl'y flow of air, and will have to gybe down through it to get out to their west. Maybe my severe drop in the classement was not so bad after all. 4th to 10th could be getting better – touch wood. (IN fact I have several pieces of wood inside KINGFISHER. There is the piece of Kaori wood engraved with 'Built in New Zealand by the team at Marten Yachts' (thanks guys!!) and piece of oak tree from my gran's field which Dad has made into a pencil

holder fo me, with a hundered year old threp'ny bit
embedded in it - which was the name of my first ever
boat . . .)

The approach to the Equator is looking a little
complicated - though never a simple zone to cross. The
HP of the Azores and the HP of Saint Helena are both
weak (the main N ans S hemisphere HP systems) - which
leaves the Doldrums as a less concentrated band, with
several tropical waves rolling through, and large
disturbing cloud masses.

The game is to cross it at it's narrowest point - easy
to say, but harder to carry out, as this windless band
is drifting daily.

On board things are generally well. THe code 5 came
down for a couple of hours and I went into Genoa mode
shortly after sailing through the lee of the Cape
Verde's. Now though it's back to code 5 - whick -
excluding this two hours has been flying since the
disaster with the other.

I feel well, thoguh my hands are covered in tiny, but
incredibly sore little salt sores . . . Nothing seems to
be able to get rid of them once they're there, and the
hotter weather is not helping . . They need to stay dry
and cool - two impossible factors on a 60 foot baking
oven! THese boats (and it's begiinning now) do get
incredibly hot arunnd the equator . . THe hot sun above
us bakes down onteh deck, heating our airtight living
pods like a greenhouse . . .

ANyway - time to go and trim those sails - I sense a
wee change in the wind.
More later.
love
ellenxx

I made the most of the relatively stable conditions during the
day to attempt the repair of the shelving unit, though it was one of

the most miserable jobs imaginable. With no ventilation in the cabin the heat was sweltering. Merv had prepared a special repair kit but sanding and cutting carbon, with dust sticking to my sweat, was itchy and uncomfortable. And it took hours to complete. I was so black and sweaty afterwards that I looked like a coal miner. I would have preferred to attempt it at night, but with the frequent thunder and lightning clouds we were now seeing it would be too dangerous. The only bonus was that it took my mind off worrying about race positions. We were playing a lottery with the winds here in the Doldrums, and as I'm not a practised gambler, the strain was taking its toll. I cleaned up after fixing the shelf and rewarded myself by putting on a brand-new vacuum-packed T-shirt, and though I'm certainly not fussy about luxuries it felt great! I also thought I should try to do something about the sores on my hands; having spent five hours wearing tight rubber gloves had left them more swollen than ever. I called Uncle Glyn to ask for his advice and he suggested I scrubbed them with pure alcohol and a tooth-brush. As I scrubbed the skin split apart, draining the fluid which had built up inside. It stung like mad but it certainly seemed to relieve the soreness afterwards.

We were approaching the zone with little wind now, and I was aware that in reality there was little we could do other than try to get south as fast as we possibly could. We had picked our longitude to cross, and were beginning to pull up to the rest of the fleet.

```
22/11/00 01:49Z (ellenmacarthur.com/day14)
Position   05° 18.5N  026° 24.5W
Heading/speed   175   1.43
Wind from 113  at 4.5 knots
Pressure of   1018
Sea temperature   16.7
Sail configuration is  Full main  Genoa
Percentage performance  25.6


Well – another still night, but this time thw
horribleist swell, and a struggling 2 knots. Just seen
```

the mst astonishing thing . . . a satellite I guess -
coming hurtling sown to earth. It lit up the clouds like
lightning - before heading into the water - seemingly
becoming more and more orangy. Extroardinary - I thought
I was dreaming!

I have slept a wee bit tonight though Ithink I shall
have a few more 10 minuters . . . THe engine's on
charging, and I don't really want to stay in the cabin.
Feeling very relaxed - even despite several hours on the
deck tonight trying to get the girl going. Looking
forward to finding these SE trads . . . and pleased that
however briefly, we've moved up the fleet to 3rd. I
can't think that anyone has sailed more slpwly than us
in the last 6 hours!
night night,
a donf ! Ellenx

By morning the wind had lightened, and we really were heading
into the Doldrums. Although it was imperative to sail through here
as fast as we could, I also knew that it was a good opportunity to
make repairs if the wind dried up completely – there wouldn't be
many more chances before we entered the Southern Ocean. As if
on cue, once I had organized all the tools for the jobs that needed
doing, it rained, and the wind vanished. Go for it, I thought, and
lowered the mainsail. I worked frantically, scurrying across *Kingfisher's* decks, dashing below for bits and pieces. I melted three
extra holes with the tiny blowtorch in the sail around her third reef,
so that in storms water could run away rather than sit and collect
there. I replaced the batten, and put some extra patches on the sail
where it touched the spreader, and the second I had finished I set
about the ten minutes it took to rehoist her sail. On to the grinder
it was! Once I had finished I had the biggest grin on my face ever,
we had completed everything on the mainsail. I then set about
working on her mainsheet and jib sheets, changing a block over
and protecting others, then covering the working parts of the
ropes, where wear would be at its greatest, with spectra covers. It

263

was a wonderful feeling to complete the entire task list and I gave *Kingfisher* a great pat on her coach-roof as I packed away all our tools.

Now we were ready to head south and she seemed pleased. A few minutes after finishing up the wind increased, and we sailed from beneath that enormous rain cloud towards the Equator, crossing the line the following night. It was a special feeling charging along in a T-shirt and shorts in the middle of the night, the moon shining bright above us. I switched on the floodlight in her cockpit and talked to the camera. I had four tiny bottles of champagne on board for such occasions; one for the Equator on the way south, one for the Cape of Good Hope, one for Cape Horn and one for the Equator on the way north. I opened the first bottle, and as I tipped a little over the side for Neptune, a little on *Kingfisher*'s deck for her, and drank a little myself, I spoke to the camera: 'First of all thanks Neptune for letting us safely cross once again, thanks *Kingfisher* for bringing us this far and looking after me, and here's to every other boat in the fleet coming safely across this line going to the south and coming back from the south . . .'

But while we were going well, the second half of my wish had not been granted – the following day I received news of yet another retirement. Eric Dumont, who had finished fourth in the previous Vendée Globe, had serious rudder damage and had not managed to find a way to repair it. The fleet was already thinning out.

```
26/11/00 03:20X (ellenmacarthur.com/day18)
Position   08° 13.6S   029° 44.2W
Heading/speed   194   11.33
Wind from 117  at 13.2 knots
Pressure of   1017
Air temperature
Sea temperature   16
Sail configuration is   Full main   Genoa
Percentage performance   99.5
```

I've changed the way I sail *Kingfisher* today - trying
some thing different. THings feel a bit better on board,
mand my moral is a bit better than the last couple of
days. Not that I've been too gloomy - but things do seem
to be looking up. Hopefully in the mornign position
report we'll at least be holing or own. . . . TIme will
tell.

The sunset tonight was stunning - bright orange -
masked by a quite cloudy horizon - the clouds almost
becoming silhouettes . . .

Tonight - for the first time my salt sores are getting
better, and I've had a couple of good hour long sleeps
. . . THere are ship's around though, adn I'm only 300
miles from the coast of Brazil - so I'm keeping an
alarmed and physical eye out!
night night for the rest of it!
ex

We were now pretty much on the upwind motorway, and would
be on the same tack for almost 2,000 miles . . . I was hoping that
Kingfisher would excel in these conditions, as she had been competitive in the Europe 1 New Man STAR against the others. I was
lying in fifth position, with Catherine Chabaud ahead, and Bilou
just having taken third place. Behind me was a little more space
though – there was a clear 60 miles before Thierry Dubois, Thomas
Coville, Marc Thiercelin and Dominique Wavre, who were all,
incredibly, within just a few miles of each other. Tactics had been
very interesting crossing the Equator: Catherine had passed the
furthest east and encountered few problems, which surprised me.
Theoretically now through the equatorial zone and with it to her
east, she was in a great position to take miles from us all – it just
depended how close she would end up sailing to the centre of the
St Helena high pressure system. It looked like it had been a good
decision.

27/11/00 90:02Z (ellenmacarthur.com/day19)
Position 11° 58.1S 029° 56.8W
Heading/speed 208 13.79
Wind from 107 at 15 knots
Pressure of 1018
Sea temperature 16
Sail configuration is Full main Genoa
Percentage performance 104.9

Well it's been a very noisy and windy night. The wind
picked up to 23 knots yesterday evening - so at least if
nothing else we're sailing quickly, and are looking in
good shape for entry into the Southern Ocean . .

  Spent the whole day just about yesterday studying the
weather - reading more about he HP, the Southern Ocean
Lows etc . . etc . . The weather was very stable
yewsterday, and I went for a different combination with
Genoa and one reef in the main. She seemed much more
balanced, and I was pleased with my determination to
keep changing things. Yesterday it seemed to pay. In the
position reports last nihgt I seem to have closed in on
Bilou's latitude - so I'm feeling fiarly pleased . . .

  This moorning the wind seems to be dying a little -
but I shall come up in prder to passst o the east of the
Isle of Trinidade.

  Will work more on the weather again today, and try to
get some sleep. IT's already getting cooler down below,
which is a godsend, and makes everything on board much
easier to do. Better make the most of it though! Soon
there will be little chance of getting a tan!
exx

   Although we were still several thousand miles away from the
Southern Ocean, it's incredible how much of my focus was on it.
These days were the last we would have for over fifty in anything
like clement weather, with a relatively steady breeze. In the trade

winds there are squalls and sail changes, but on the whole things are more settled. It's essential to rest as much as possible before entering into the south. I was already adjusting to it, finding I was sleeping in longer bursts. It seemed to be a sub-conscious preparation for a phase of the race I knew was going to be harder than I could imagine. The south can be an incredibly beautiful place, with amazing long swells and surfing conditions, but you should never go there without total respect for it. Although those I have met who have been there said it is the most incredible place, I have also known people who have not, and nearly not, come back from it.

There is no room for error. Those who come out first will be the ones who can handle its harsh environment the best. But there will always be that element of risk down there. No one can stop a freak wave from turning a boat over, no matter how well it was prepared for the race. I wrote in my daily log:

This race shall be won by the most reliable boat . . . that which can push enough, for long enough – but keep things together . . .

We had already covered over a fifth of the race, but the pace at which we were running was hellish. We were not just pushing, but pushing hard. Just how long could it be kept up? I was critically aware that now was the chance to go over *Kingfisher* from top to bottom with a fine toothcomb, to make sure that everything was as OK as it could be for the south. Each day I would do general checks, but soon that in itself would be more dangerous. I did a lot of work during these days on the autopilot which had already let me down on a couple of occasions by simply cutting out, and although I tried various options to fix it, it was still a mystery. I was all too conscious of the fact that with a single-handed race the autopilot is everything, and losing it one of the biggest fears. Likewise, with no power you have no pilot, and without it you simply cannot carry on. On modern race-boats you cannot just lash the helm, they need computers to control them, especially as we sail at such high speeds.

There was also the rig check to do, scaling the mast to look for any signs of wear or problems. It was not the easiest of jobs but the sea was relatively flat, so I grabbed the opportunity. It's not easy alone as the boat never wants to sit still, and there's no one to winch you up or ease you down, so just getting up and down is tricky. Like climbers we use jumars, hand-held brakes that can be slid up a rope but grip tight when pulled down. These enabled me to climb while always attached, but they had their disadvantages in that they made getting down incredibly difficult. Not losing your grip on the mast is one of the hardest of tasks, but holding on to the mast as well as lowering a jumar is tough to say the least!

On my first attempt I discovered a problem with the genoa stay, which meant I had to go back up. As I was already tired from the first ascent this was frustrating, but things got worse when the wind rose while I was at the top and *Kingfisher* heeled – any more wind and I could have walked down her mainsail! Once on the deck I furled the genoa, unfurled the solent and prepared my tools for the second ascent. All was well and *Kingfisher* was much more stable, so I climbed up once more and attacked the job. The problem came when I was ready to go down, and realized that I had forgotten the second jumar so had to climb down from three-quarters of the way up the 90-foot mast completely unattached. I berated myself for being so stupid. I just could not afford that kind of carelessness.

I guess it was no different from what the old clipper crews did day in, day out, but at least there were other guys around to scrape them up off the deck if they fell. My body went into overdrive, my hands clenched white-fisted around the rigging. It was a huge relief to make it back down, and even more so five minutes later when the pilot cut out and I was right there to grab the helm – thank God it hadn't happened ten minutes earlier . . .

```
02/12/00 07:33Z (ellenmacarthur.com/day24)
Position   32° 11.7S  017° 44.0W
Heading/speed   200   9.84
Wind from 339   at 11 knots
Pressure of   1017
```

Sea temperature   12
Sail configuration is   Full main   Spinnaker
Percentage performance   98.9

Well the sun is rising once again, and unlike the
leading boats in the fleet we seem to have escaped for
the moment the front which is lying across the southern
Atlantic Ocean. A night with two gybes, though I am a
little concerned I have not gained enough to the south
. . . we shall see shortly.

    The front is in the stages of dissipating as a new low
forms to the west. Yesterday we had the beginnings of a
huge swell, which is asure sign that wind is on it's
way. The sea has changed once again - to a darker inkier
blue, the stars are progressively more and more the
stars of the SOuthern Hemisphere, and as if a symbol for
our entry into the SOuth the moon is back, each night
showing more and more it's beauty. Last night the
silvery flickers on the water were so incredibly gentle,
such a dusting of beauty on a sea which looks so
desceptively peaceful . . . like nothing could disturb
its steady motion.

    Yesterday was a day of work again. Several tactical
gybes on the wind shifts to try to edge our way into the
South - adn more checks. I checked all the compartments
for water and dried out the sail stowage area. Bypassed
part of the pilot system to try to solve our niggling
problem (so far good news!). I also cheked cabling for
chafe - and stowed away my second bag of rubbish!
Yesterday was a day of good spirits, with a few naps and
a bit of dancing to a Santana CD. Only days now before
the thought of dancing as the sun sets seems a long way
away.

    Soon we shall cross this dissipating area, and plunge
down into the south . . . where we shal stay for roughly
50 days. THe sleigh-ride round the South Pole shall not

be easy. Extreme care is needed to avoid icebergs; and
managing the storms as they hurl themselves over us will
be a 24 hr job. I am looking forward to the South,
though I am exrremely wary, and reespectful of it's
danger. In my mind the SOuth is almost the start of the
race. IT's the 'entrance' to home - and from here we're
off - we all hope - for Cape Horn.
Till tomorrow . . .
exx

Although I knew that I would never stop learning, I had also
learnt so much already. The previous night when I had gained miles
on the rest of the fleet by choosing my gybing time carefully I really
felt that I had a handle on what I was doing. I was watching the
satellite pictures like a hawk. When the model came through at
0000Z I knew what to do and it was a wonderful feeling, I just hoped
that I could keep up the good decisions. Although conditions here
were still relatively stable, we were sailing with our spinnaker, so
I always slept or dozed with my eyes half open, and when I woke I
would instantly jump up to check that the spinnaker was OK and
that we didn't have a wrap around the forestay. The spinnaker is
not the easiest sail to handle or get down in a hurry when alone, so
I had to be really careful, never sleeping far away from its sheets.

That morning I was startled by the flapping of sailcloth, and with
my heart in my mouth I ran to the bow to investigate. It was obvious
what had happened. The metal ring in the corner of the sail had
worked through the webbing straps which secured it and the sail
was now flying in the air held only by two corners, looking pathetic,
like a sheet hanging to dry in the breeze. I set about and changed it
as fast as I could. We'd gone into fourth place that morning, and I
sure as hell was not going to let those miles slip away. I took down
the wounded spinnaker, then put up the Code 5 and unfurled it,
relieved to feel *Kingfisher* pull away once more. I then began a tiring
six hours of sewing on the foredeck, finding new webbing and
sewing it into the corner of the sail. The cloth was so thick in the
corners that I had to push a bradawl through the sail first to prevent

270

the needle from breaking as I pushed it through. I sang to myself, and tried to keep myself happy as I worked away, the occasional droplet of blood dripping on to the deck as my finger was punctured by the needle. I had to do a good job on this one – the loads on the corners of those sails are immense, and I couldn't afford to do a half-baked repair which would break again. As soon as the repair was done I changed sails, and returned below.

Tactically it was complex now too. We were all, or so it appeared, trying to move towards the south-east, but it was a question of negotiating the best route between the systems, with the central aim of getting south into the westerlies first. There was definitely the possibility for some big position changes, and although Yves had stretched away a little, a lot could happen over the next days. In just a day and a half near the centre of the St Helena high-pressure system Mich took over 100 miles from Yves. It was as though we were all in the slip lanes of a motorway, and although there was not much room to overtake as we came into the slow lane, there was always someone who managed to accelerate out into the fast lane and make a gain.

Sadly, there was news of more problems with the fleet. Raphael Dinelli hit an unidentified object and damaged his keel badly. The Southern Ocean is the last place to be with suspect equipment and Raphael knew this better than most of us as in the previous Vendée his boat rolled and sank slowly in a horrendous storm – literally beneath his feet. He was saved by a life-raft that was dropped from an Australian Orion patrol plane and by Pete Goss, who turned back in that same storm to find him and pick him up.

I really felt for Raphael. He'd been pretty much as close to death as you can get in the last race, and now, having found the courage to try again, his race had been ended again. I hoped that he would make it round, whether in or out of the race. Mike Golding had now passed the Equator, and though just under 2,000 miles behind he was going strong. It must have been so frustrating for him as he was not in remotely the same weather system, but I knew that he would give it all he had. Fedor Konioukhov too was now a long way behind – though still a few hundred miles ahead of Mike – and as I plotted his position on my chart I hoped that he was enjoying his race.

Now almost in the Roaring Forties, we had a welcome reminder that we were heading down into the unknown – one of its inhabitants . . . the albatross.

4/12/00 12:20Z (ellenmacarthur.com/day26)
As I sit at the chart table I feel far from alone . . .
For above me hovers a friend . . Wings outstretched
almost as if resting, as he circles around and around
. . Inquisitive as I enter the cockpit he comes closer –
but almost as if wishing to be invisible to camera he
backs away as I try to film.

Af few hours ago we gybed . . A gybe heading amost due
south . . . THe gybe on which to enter the real Southern
Ocean. As the front passed this morning the sky cleared
for a while, the sun lighting the waves in what felt
strangely like a rare fashion, so quickly the feel of
this sea has changed. Right now it is colder, the air
and the water. THe waves are growing almost hourly,
physicaly picking *Kingfisher* up and releasing her down
the next slope . . . like pushing a toboggan at the top
of a hill. Incredible to thing that this is merely the
beginning . . . we have not yet passed the 40th parallel.

This morning I felt worse than I ever recall feeling.
My body ached all over – my head felt tired as
Kingfisher violently surfed endlessley down the
waves . . .

Yesterday evening I had been preparing her for the
South. Re-stowing all the boxes, checking coentents,
etc. I was under the cockpit floor happily stowing when
iheard a fluttering and felt the boat slow. Scared that
my hand stitching had parted form the kite, I leat on
deck to find that the cloth of the sail had 'peeled'
it's way out of the edges of the sail, with about 30
metres of cloth training in the water. THen recuperation
of the sail took the best part of an hour – which
involved retreiveing the halyard, cutting the sheets

off, hanging over the side with a boathook, and
eventually, once the sail had streamed out away from the
boat, pulling the whole shabang on board – not an easy
task as most of it then decided to take off and fly off
in a skyward direction .. Exhausted, I changed for the
gennaker, then an hour later the genoa ... I slumped on
the chart table seat – and woke 2 hours later ...
Exx

05/12/00 01:06Z (ellenmacarthur.com/day27)
Position 40° 05.9S 008° 17.9W
Heading/speed 175 13.9
Wind from 303 at 18.3 knots
Pressure of 1001
Sea temperature 18
Sail configuration is Full main Code 5
Percentage performance 98.6

well, our first nihgt in the 40s ...

Now in the Roaring Forties, our next objective as far as the rules
were concerned was basically to leave Antarctica to starboard, and
the various waypoints which are placed to keep us from straying
too far into the ice. Over five days the sea temperature had dropped
13 degrees, and I piled on extra layers of thermal clothing. The
Southern Ocean was upon us, and whilst we had not yet had a
particularly bad storm, I was to be the first in the fleet to witness
the other threat the Southern Ocean has to offer. It was the morning
of 8 December, and after an uneasy night of concern I had managed
to sleep for a while at daybreak. The wind had been getting progressively stronger over the previous twenty-four hours – it was now at
30 knots. *Kingfisher* needed constant monitoring as we were not
past the centre of the depression, and I was expecting a further
increase in the wind strength.

I had been watching the sea temperature, and although our
sensor was misreading I believed it to be about 4–5 degrees. I

had put the radar on with an alarm for the night, just as a backup to sticking my head out of the hatch as often as I could; though to be honest, in the dark you'd be pushed to see anything anyway.

I was glad that it was morning now, and on waking stuck my head up to peer ahead out of the windows. I could see little as they were covered in condensation, so I decided to wipe them. As I foraged for a piece of kitchen roll I saw that the radar was clear. The shock came as I wiped the cloth across the final window – rather than a grey sky, there was a tint of blue . . .

'Ice!'

With a surge of adrenalin I was out of the hatch. As I swung to look around I saw a very melted but still 40-foot-high berg slide past us. It had missed us by feet, quite literally, and luckily we had passed on its windward side where there were no growlers (the smaller chunks that have separated from the main berg). I felt quite sick and shaken inside, and for hours I seemed to be waiting for the splitting, thudding sound as we drove into yet more ice. We were surfing regularly at over 20 knots, and a collision at that speed did not bear thinking about. Although we were OK, we had been just a breath away from our world disappearing. There had been no freezing water flooding into our home, nor the splintering sound of carbon . . . for the moment we were safe. From then on, rather than rely on the sea temperature indicators in the hull, I collected a bucket of water and placed my watch in it in the cockpit; it had a temperature sensor on it and was a system which seemed to be far more accurate – I was relieved.

During the morning the wind shifted and we were able to sneak back further north. Yves had been maintaining a 100-mile lead on Mich and Bilou, who were further north than I, though Yves was as far down south as 52 degrees. There was no doubt that he was sailing a shorter distance down there, but what he didn't realize was that he was about to become isolated from the rest of the fleet, becalmed in the Southern Ocean. Catherine had fallen back in her more northerly position, sailing a greater distance – and on the other extreme – with slightly less wind. There are all sorts of things to get your head around in the Southern Ocean though: obviously the meteorological and ice hazards, but also the magnetic anomalies, which can result in over 40 degrees' variation in the reading on a magnetic compass. But the barometer was still dropping, and as it fell from over 1,000mb to 988 I realized it was going to be a big one. Time to go surfing!

```
10/12/00 09:53Z (ellenmacarthur.com/day32)
Position  45° 46.1S  027° 59.0E
Heading/speed  149  17.75
Wind from 279  at 31.6 knots
Pressure of  988
Sea temperature  4.3
Sail configuration is  2nd reef  Solent
Percentage performance  109.1
```

That's better! Ex

```
10/12/00 10:48Z
Position  45° 53.1S  028° 18.8E
Heading/speed  149  18.24
Wind from 280  at 34.7 knots
Pressure of  989
Sea temperature  4
Sail configuration is  2nd reef  Solent
Percentage performance  111.5
```

Ohhhh shit!

```
10/12/00 12:58Z
```
I'm not worried about positions, and told myself that this morning. I knoew I would be further behind. It's part of the cgame. Look at Yves! ANyway - had a mammoth camera sort this am, after seeing two whales 30 feet away! Now have the little BBC one working - I feel so damn lucky to be given all this fancy equipment toplay

with – Kingfisher herslef the cream on the cake! Better
go – wind rising agian up to 38 kn. Bloody hell we're
surfing, hit 29.3 earlier. . . . More later, Ex.

By this stage we had two reefs in the main and the staysail up
and were hitting speeds of over 30 knots . . . wow! It was amazing,
as we just picked up a wave and accelerated, getting faster and faster
with a speed that seemed to just keep on going. The motion was
violent and the noise overpowering as we shuddered to a stop after
ploughing into the wave in front. You could feel the pressure from
the weight of water as it piled across the deck. I couldn't leave the
cabin even for a second without being fully kitted up.

I had one pretty intense moment during that night when both
autopilots failed, meaning I ended up on the helm doing 25 knots
down a wave, unable to leave my station. I had to wait, find a good
wave, get her on a surf, then dive below to reset the instrument
system for it to kick back in. Pretty stressful, but we were powering
along still.

I wasn't the only boat that was smoking though: Dominique
Wavre with his boat *UBP* had just smashed the twenty-four-hour
record, which in fact Yves had set on entry into the Southern
Ocean. Dominique's record was incredible – a run of 430 miles in
twenty-four hours, which worked out at an average of 17.75 knots.

By this stage it really was freezing, and I thought I'd be lucky if I
ever managed to defrost my feet. The freeze-dried meals were a
godsend though – no matter what the variety, they slid down my
cold salty throat like nectar. But I was glad when the winds began
to abate slightly as this gave my heartbeat a chance to slow down!

We were approaching a pair of islands about 1,200 miles south
of South Africa, called the Prince Edward and Marion Islands; on
pulling out my Antarctic pilot I was quite excited to read that both
had been South African nature reserves since 1995. As usual, and
suffering from what seems to be a physical attraction between me
and any mass of rock which could remotely be called an island, we
passed very close. Though tactically it was far from being easy I
would not have changed it for the world. I had not even an image

in my mind of what the islands might look like, and when Marion Island appeared before us as a grey outline it took my breath away. As we got nearer I was amazed by the sheer volume of wildlife which surrounded it – petrels and albatrosses – and above all marvelled at its snow-capped mountains. Its slopes were green in colour, and though the vegetation was far from lush, I was overwhelmed by its beauty. Only a handful of people live on Marion Island, in a tiny research station, and as one of the few people who have actually seen it, I felt incredibly privileged. Even more incredible than the island were its feathered inhabitants which followed us for days and nights afterwards, never failing to be there in the morning as it got light. We were heading for the French Iles de Crozet, just under 1,000 miles directly east, and I wondered if the birds were perhaps simply commuting from one set of islands to the next.

```
13/12/00 18:09Z (ellenmacarthur.com/day35)
Position  47° 57.5S  048° 54.6E
Heading/speed  166  11.84
Wind from 305  at 14.2 knots
Pressure of  978  Calm
Sea temperature  -1.2
Sail configuration is  Full main  Spinnaker
Percentage performance  102.3
```

```
Well it's very strange when you're 1000's of miles away
from anywhere to suudenly see another boat. Yesterday
morning, as the first light drew itself from under the
cloud, there was THomas alongside. He's been there all
day, and I have to admit that I'd rather be physically
alone. It seems funny to look over to the South each
time I leave the hatch, to have someone else - as I know
will be looking at me. It's different when it's the
albatrosses. WHen it's the whales or dolphins for sure
they're not racing against me - and if so for fun ..
Well it's a start ... Feeling stressed - so will try
more later ... sorry ex
```

I am sure that many skippers in the race would have been over the moon to see another boat, and I still don't completely understand my reaction. I am sure it sounds ridiculous, but I felt cramped by it. Thomas called on the satellite phone too, as oddly it had suddenly begun to work here once more. So strange to hear his voice . . . I sensed that he was keen to talk and heard from his messages back to HQ press centre that Mark passed on that he was obviously really pleased to see another competitor. Funny really – Mark in the Mini with Thomas alongside him, then me in the Vendée. During that day we sailed within sight of each other, though in gradually changeable conditions. As soon as I saw Thomas on the horizon I could see which sail he had up. The wind was dying, and I quickly decided it was time to change my own. Before long I had switched through gennaker to code 5, then to my spare spinnaker, which I was very glad I had packed up in the sock after our disaster session earlier. I was so determined not to be passed by Thomas that it made it difficult to sleep, and with a new depression in the air sailing was testing as I knew that I needed to sail deeper and lower than he was, staying more to the north. I took bearings of him with my compass to see whether I was making on him or slipping back. As the day drew on we sailed towards, then below, the Iles de Crozet. Birds in the air and seaweed in the water provided visual evidence of our nearing land. Seeing the weed reminded me of sailing close to the Falkland Islands on our delivery trip from New Zealand and having enormous chunks of it caught on our keel. I'd actually prepared myself to dive in to remove it, though luckily, just as I was coming to terms with how cold the water was going to be, it miraculously slipped off. We had fitted an endoscope on *Kingfisher*, which allowed me to look down under the water and see her keel to be sure that there was nothing caught round it or around her rudder. There is nothing worse than thinking there is something there but not knowing. The procedure for removing the weed or object is not so simple either, especially when you are sailing with the spinnaker or code 5. You have either to furl the sail or sock the spinnaker, then turn head to wind and try to sail backwards for long enough for the culprit to come off. Frustrating to say the least, and not ideal as often it could be really quite windy with a risk of breakages to the sails – you use more sail area when sailing away from the wind than against it, so when you turn against with full sail and a good breeze you are always cautious. While within sight of Thomas I had to sail backwards twice but once I got back on track and was sailing at full speed again, this almost made up for the feeling of frustration.

```
14/12/00 04:09Z (ellenmacarthur.com/day36)
Position  47° 26.7S  051° 41.4E
Heading/speed  116  9.96
Wind from 33  at 9.3 knots
Pressure of  979
Sea temperature  5
Sail configuration is  Full main  Genoa
Percentage performance  95.1
```

```
Oh bugger!
  This mornings not one of the best of the race. It's
not Kingfisher, the weather nor technical problems – but
the skipper who's causing the upset this morning. From
being in a very strong position yesterday morning we
have slipped back – letting at least one boat through
ahead – and almost certainly losing rapidly the lead we
had. The option to be in the north was certainly the
best. Yesterday morning the weather info showed that the
wind would switch to the west more quickkly and for
longer, giving us more of a chance to make ground to the
north. But once we were trapped below the islands it wa
too late – and whether it was me tying my brains in
knots or not, we basically didn't gybe when we should
have, concentrating on sailing lower and faster than
Thomas. So this morning the wind has gone light. It has
turned as I thought it was due to earlier yesterday, and
despite sailign roughly in the right direction at 10
knots I knorw that those further north will be sailing
```

downwind in 25 . . . It's a real shame . . . I feel quite
deflated ans frustrated at having been so stupid . . .

 Despite all this life on board os good - the moon last
night was so so bright, and seemed to shne as strong as
the sun as it rose . . . Beautiful. There are hundred's
of birs around us once more, and as I took off the code
5 from the bow this morning, the tiny petrels were just
meters from me. CHeeky little things, they love to fly
above the mainsail, playing dare devils with the
updraught . .

 Sorry everyone - I feel right now I've let you all
down . . I promise we'll try our best to mae up the
miles . . . starting with trimming the sails right now!
later,
ellen

It was a stressful night of staring at the satellite pictures, just
waiting to see if there would be a slim chance we might make it to
the north of the depression. I could see that the front was long
and pronounced, but we simply had to get into the downwind
conditions again. A tiring eighteen hours followed which ended up
upwind for the most part, and near the front in 35 to 40 knots. We
held on to the staysail, but there were so many sail changes, and
during the approach of the front I only managed to get cereal bars
and some dried fruit down. We made it through the front, which
was a godsend, and although we were in the downwind conditions,
during the first hours the going was tough as we were sailing fast
into the old wave pattern – head on to the waves. On top of this we
developed a new problem; the Satcom C and B seemed to have
stopped working. Although the C was receiving messages, it seemed
unable to send them, while the B, which is the only form of telephone that works 'deep south', had begun to lose its signal. The C's
power supply also seemed to be malfunctioning. For some reason
it was turning itself on, then resetting itself, meaning that for most
of the time it couldn't receive anyway. We had tried to prepare for
all eventualities, but it was a massive concern not being able to get

on to the Internet via the B to pick up more detailed weather information. Knowing where the centre of the depression was and being able to see how a front lay was a huge advantage. In a race situation, equipment like this is not only a means of communicating with shore, but also a vital tactical aid. I knew that if I could not manage to get it working I would be out of communication with land until Cape Horn – at least forty days away.

It's not much good if you can receive on the Satcom C but are unable to let anyone know that you have done so. Eventually I got to the bottom of the problems – both had been caused by the reception in the area we were now sailing into – and had both systems working. While I was relieved to have them back I was annoyed that it highlighted a stupid hole in my preparations – I should have known to which station, or area, the settings needed changing.

But there was more stress, much worse than the issues with the antenna. During the passing of the depression I had really screwed it, and gybed too late. I should have gone much earlier, but I waited and as a result lost out, dropping myself into sixth position. Fourth had been better than that! It was incredible to think that after thirty-seven days of racing there were four of us with just 14 miles between us. Mich and Bilou were out there as the leaders, by this stage a good 300 miles in front. Yves was lying third but had been on a course that took him dramatically south; now, on his way back north, he had lost his lead but was moving again and was easily holding third position.

We were sailing in an intensifying depression, and I had completely messed up. For the first time in the race I climbed into my bunk and as I gritted my teeth together in anger, I felt my eyes beginning to fill with tears. The Southern Ocean was starting to wear me down. I knew I was tired, and that had probably led to my mistake in going too far north. After an hour's rest I felt stronger, which was just as well as the depression was deepening on top of us.

The following day I was on better form and decided I would make the fastest progress I possibly could. I held the genoa up to 40 knots of breeze but hand-steered so as to keep it full. The wind felt incredibly powerful, and *Kingfisher* just seemed to rally, sailing faster and faster, and surfing for longer and longer as the waves built around her. It was magic sailing; even the sun was out and the blue water seemed to shine as its crests began to break in a starkly contrasting white. *Kingfisher* felt alive as I held her helm in my hand, and was loving every minute of it. Our speed went up – 15 knots ... 20 knots ... 25 knots – incredible, almost like slalom skiing through the waves. I grinned from ear to ear – this was the best sailing anyone could imagine. This was what we had come down here to see, the enormous breaking waves, the wildlife and the feeling of being in the largest open space that exists on earth. I closed my eyes as we surfed down the massive waves, trying to feel *Kingfisher*'s position, the wind cold and fresh on the side of my face though through it I could still feel the sun. I could hear the humming as her keel flew through the water, probably with a piece of weed on it. After a few hours, I changed down to her solent, then went below to check the weather and sleep a little.

Below, every sensation of speed seemed amplified, and the sounds were deafening as she screamed down the waves. I found myself repeatedly holding my breath as we took off over the crests of the waves, and with the power in her sails and her lightness, we accelerated faster and faster. I braced myself in place against the violent motion by jamming my knees beneath the chart table and I gripped the edge of it as we became airborne, hoping to goodness that the pilot would not let go. If we gybed in this we'd be in desperate trouble.

We were approaching the Kerguelen Islands at about 50 degrees south and midway between South Africa and Australia. I was trying to cross as far to the north as I could. There is a massive patch of shallow water just to the north of the islands and as a result the sea was building. Shallow water means breaking waves – and big ones if it's blowing 45 to 50 knots. If at all possible I wanted to avoid gybing in this; with this wind, I risked breaking battens in the mainsail. I decided to change sails to allow me to stay deeper, using a system we'd developed whereby we could attach the tack of the staysail out to a pad-eye on *Kingfisher*'s gunwale. Worth a try, I thought, and battled forward to set the sail.

```
17/12/00 09:47Z (ellenmacarthur.com/day39)
Position  47° 50.1S  077° 19.3E
Heading/speed  158  14.87
Wind from 295  at 19.3 knots (remember 50 degrees W
varn.)
Pressure of  1002
Sea temperature  3.1
Sail configuration is  Full main  Code 5
Percentage performance  95
```

As I sit here now I feel worse than I have ever felt in my lofe before. Physically i am totally exhausted, and mentally – not so far off. My whole body aches, and feels drained. My mind feels like it's been frozen, and is trying to wake. Yesterday was the hardest challnege of my life, though funnily this morning feels 10 times owrse. It started when the tack of the staysail blew off. THe sail had been set to windward, as teh wind waswell over 40 knots. THe day had been fantastic – surfing at over 30 knots, and really feeling we were catching the others, amter our stupid course to the north. I am learning so much – sailing the boat one of those things – and only yesterday did we seem to have got it roght in strong downwind conditions. AS the sail felw into he air I bore away quickly to hide it behind the mainsail. I dropped the halyard immediately and went on to the foredeck to sort out the mess, not easy in 45 knots, but we were slower without the sail – I just had to holsd my breath as the waves plughed overthe bow. It was then theat she started to go – to gybe, and before I could make it back to the cockpit her deck was vertical, and we were lying helplessley on our side. In itslef this is a fairly bad situation to be in – but what was

to come was far worse. As she lay on her side the
mainsail lay crookedly on the runners – I fought to get
the other runner on to release her from this agnizing
position – bt it was dfficult climbing up the deck. We
did it – tthen gybed over – but had to go back as the
runners were caught around the top battens . . By this
stage one of the battens had broken – in fact the car it
travels on too – and alhtough annoyed I know this does
happen – a nd is not so bad to fix . . . or so I thought.
On further inspection, and about 20 mins to srt out
the mess I realized that I couldn't get the mainsail
down to fix the problem. IN fact the broken batten had
slid out forward over the second spreader – and neither
love, money nor the best will in the world was going
to let me lower that sail with out going up there to
remove the batten. GOing up the rig is generally the
solo sailor's worst night mare – but going up in 40
knots plus just doesn't bare thinking about. I knew I
had to do it. I kew that if the wind rose further I
would be unable to get the sail down. In my mind I had
no option – I just went into autopilot, put on my
harness, rigegd up a taut halyard and climbed. It was
bitterly cold, the biting wind cutting into the bare
skinon my hands and face, the first passtrt to the forst
spreader was OK – not too much movement, and I still had
engy – but the second part to the second spreader was 10
times harder with each inch I climbd . . . I was
beginning to get tired – as each wavae we surfed on
(which were about 10 meters high) was trying to throw me
off the mast. As I got to the second spreader I had just
two feet to go, but it felt those were the hardes towo
feet of my life. I struggled to inch my way up, adn hung
there a while banging away at the mast, trying to
recover. I found the energy from I don't know where –
and made it on to the spreader. THe batten was in
front of me, and if I timed it on the sufrs I could pull

284

it out. Relieved it would come, I dropped it to the deck.

I was now quite cold, and shaking with the effort, you'd think getting down is the easy bit - but in fact it took me forther to the edge than I wished to go. I had to take each jumar in turn and lower it, taking the weight of the owrking one to dit on the lazy one. Eash few inches I descended I had to take my weight with my hands - or legs - which proved exhausting still . . . I arrived at one point with a slack jumar and an unattatched one, with all my weight on my right wrist in one of the webbing loops n the sail. I hung tere - banging into the mast - trying desperaltely, and unsuccessfuly to get my foot thruogh the gap between the sail and the mst. I started to hurt badly - still no joy. GOodness knows how I managed to get thtat other jumar on - but i think that the hospital kids had a fair lot to do with it, and the want to get back home again. It took over an hour to get down - just 15 metres . . . a painful hour. Once on the deck I was shaking but overjoyed and set about fixing the issues . . . The batten I changed - anothter I thgihtened and sewed a part of a spreader patch on. I barely had the energy to put the sail back up again, then cllapsed in the cockpit. A I dashed about the deck working my vision went funny - I was seeing stars permanelntly, as if I was about to black out. Bizarre - i didn't but wonder if it's something to do with adrenalin or haiing been close to the edge . . . or then again maybe I was just frozen. I was so glad to have made the repair, but till this morning really didn't realize how much it had taken out of me. THis morning was worse . . . I saw a rip in the genoa . . . along the foot. I tried to sleep last night - but was worried about it - so at forst light tried to fix it. It was impossible - even with the sail sheeted hard ebind the main it flapped and flicked in my face, and ripped the stitching out that I was trying to put

285

in. Hence this morning is one of the owrst. I cannot
sail at full potential . . . the sail I need is out of
action . . . SO frustrating. And now – to top it all –
after putting up the gennaker in 17 knots of wind – it's
now blowing 29 and on the limit. After trying to fix
that sail I was at my lowest point tin the race. I cried
out loud to the heavens . . . just sometimes you have
those moments – and that was one of them . . . After
almost killing myself yesterday to keep going and fix
the problems whilst hanging in with the flleet, today I
am losing miles, because of a stupid tear in a sail. So
frustrating, I cna't sleep, or switch off. Something
else I guess I have to learn. THe good news is though
the sun has come out. Maybe I'll get a chance to dry out
that sail . . . Thanks so much for following me,
everyone. THe support e-mails are fantastic. They really
change my days, and give me more than just a reason to
be ot here. SHaring this challenge is one of the most
important things for me. Second to, though I have to say
– making it back home to France!
till tomorrow . . .
exx

Oh Mark. I just want to thank you with all my heart . . .
I could not or would not ever wnat anyone else there as
my number 1. You're the best, I have tears in my eyes as
I wrie because I am so glad you're there. I really have
been close to the edge – and I want you to know thatyou
played a very big part in carrying me back.
Love ex

That evening as I charged my batteries I fired the C up to find
two messages, one from Mark, and one from the race organizers –
they were flagged Urgent; something had happened to Yves. I felt a
sickness in my stomach.

The French message required me to divert my course to Yves's position, confirmed that his speed had dropped to less than 5 knots and that there had been no contact. I checked his position – we were less than 100 miles away. My heart raced as I switched on the breaker to activate the Satcom B. Thankfully it was working again, although it still seemed like an eternity waiting for it to connect to a satellite and find a signal. All sorts of things went through my mind. Had Yves fallen off his boat? Had he been dismasted? Was he injured? Still I waited for a connection. I dialled Mark's number. He always answered. His voice sounded surprisingly calm and he had more news – Yves had sent a short message to say that he had been dismasted but was OK – that was it. I threw my head back in relief. Thank God.

I had still been requested to continue to his position by the race organizers, so I changed sails to remain on a more northerly heading. Mark and I arranged for a rendezvous call when I was 20 miles away, so I switched off the B – it was just before midnight when I called back. Mark told me that my diversion had been called off. I felt for Yves – his third Vendée Globe, in a boat he knew so well. His last had been halted by a broken forestay and rudder; now by a broken mast. But I did think back to his words before the race: *'If I don't win, you have to win, and if you don't win, I have to win.'* I felt determined. The race was on.

The following day Mark sent on Yves's statement about his problems as a result of what had happened out there in the storm. We knew from his speeds that he had been pushing very hard, and after he'd dropped to third due to his too southerly weather option he'd been really going for it.

```
Everything happened very quickly. The wind climbed very
fast, and very strongly under a storm cloud. My boat
took off, gybed uncontrollably and wiped out on its
side. As she came back up, the shock loads were so big
that the boat gybed a second time and I was thrown
across the cockpit. The boat took off again on a surf,
but nose-dived with the water coming right up to the
mast – and it was that that brought the mast down. Now
```

all is well, and I confirm that I do not require
assistance.

Yves surprised everyone the following day with the news that he would not abandon the race. As he had 6 to 8 metres of his 25-metre mast remaining, he intended to continue under the jury rig, permitting him to sail with a fourth reef in his mainsail and he believed he might be able to attach the broken mast for the remaining part of the Southern and Atlantic Oceans. He would have to find a quiet spot from which to work – not easy as he was miles from anywhere – but this said a great deal about Yves – his determination and his nickname of the Extra Terrestrial! It took him fifteen days to sail on to a beautiful, remote, natural harbour in Stewart Island, New Zealand. Vendée Globe rules allow the sailors to stop to repair their boats if they need to, but only anchoring the boat – touching any part of the land above the high-water mark is not allowed. He spent two weeks in the bay repairing and rebuilding his mast, using light bulbs to build a makeshift oven in which he could 'bake' the carbon, and having re-rigged his sails was able to continue his circumnavigation with his extraordinary jury rig. Throughout his amazing experience one of the biggest issues was food. He had only bargained for 100 days. So while making repairs he'd eaten shellfish plucked from below the waterline and he then had to collect and dry seaweed for his long trip home. His repair job was incredible and although he no longer had a chance of winning the race, his spirit was intact. Awesome.

18/12/00 16:23Z (ellenmacarthur.com/day40)
FOund the tinkling noise . . . it was the pin from the
hinge on the two doors into the back storagea area.
Today I've re-spliced the vang, whipped around a few
ropes. FIxed the genoa, re-fixed the camera housing.
fixed the car on port side outobard, found wheree the
carbon piece came froem . . it was the winch on mast . .
smething caught arouund the tailer, and damaged it . . .
It's useable though. Have refixed the piece inside the

tailer, and seems OK . . . gennaker went up on it - no
probs . . even had a nap!

I'm sorry the last few days were so hard, I know it's
as bad at your end too. Maybe give you a call later . . .
not looking foraward to those lost miles . . . though
looking at the last few reports - miricles can happen!
later, ex

I was sitting in fourth position by this stage and was intensely
frustrated that I was not sailing faster than Thomas who was ahead
of me at the time in third. I was further south than him, though,
which for the time being was good news as I was sailing a relatively
shorter course. There was one issue though. The depression to the
south of us was slowing and had virtually stopped, and the two
headings I could take were either just south of the direct route
(which was by far the fastest) or further north and away from the
ice and the Antarctic convergence zone. I was tired, but still having
to make these crucial decisions. We were out of the ice zone for the
time being but were approaching it, and while I wanted to keep
away from the bergs I also desperately needed to stay out of the
centre of the lingering depression. We had 25 to 30 knots where we
were, but those to the north had 40 to 45 knots. To the south though
there was less still, then nothing.

I grit my teeth as I open the fore-hatch, as the frezing
handles seem to 'bite' my cold, hard hands. Feeling
stupid, I use my feet, frustrted at myself for making an
unhealed knuckle bleed once more. For this is not the
Atlantic, here it is cold and remote - the nights movng
in - with a feeling that the icy Antarctic winds slowly
place their arms around you . . . the cold seeping
through to your bones.

The days at the moment are better - the sun rises and
sets - which seems extrardinary for the south. I always
imagines an endless grey - but it has proved to me that
it has many faces, many moods and many seasons. It is

unpredictable and as I sit here there is a massive band
of dark clouud to windward. As always it approaches us
slowly but surely – with the rain clearly visible as it
pelts down to the sea below.

Ex

The hardest part out there is assessing the weather, especially when you're cold and tired. The pressure never goes away, and each time I made a decision, I felt an apprehension, followed by painful hours worrying whether it would pay off. The sheer exhaustion just seeps into your bones, and miles gained or lost against rivals become the core of each day. Win miles, and morale soars. Lose them, and you have to try to harness that frustration to fuel further decisions.

On day 44 of the race there was fantastic news: we had leapt into third position – our southern route had paid off, we were down below 55 south – but with the most fantastic reaching winds coming up, we had made a spot-on decision. That day things really seemed to be going our way.

The night came in and the winds were no stronger than 20 to 25 knots. The sailing was fast and the waves were building. I helmed that evening, enjoying the feeling of *Kingfisher* just sliding over the waves; I was comforted by the feeling of being in control, knowing when she would turn as I gently pushed and pulled her helm – a feeling I missed when the autopilot steered her in its own impersonal way.

As we sailed I thought of Thomas. If we just sailed fast and safe we could keep him there. Then, with an agonizing silence and cruel lack of drama, the Code 5 sail came away from the top of the mast and floated down into the water. *Kingfisher* slowed, and I instantly ran to drop the main halyard to stop her completely so I might have some chance of recovering the sail. Shit! My fingers worked overtime, opening clutches, loosening sheets. I looked up, and there swinging from the top of the mast was a metre of halyard; the rest had come away with the sail. I just couldn't believe it – we'd lost our third sail.

An hour later I felt wretched. My knee burnt red hot from being dragged down the deck as I struggled to hold on to the sail, and my clothes were wet and cold as, hanging on the end of her bowsprit, I was repeatedly plunged into the freezing water as we wallowed without power.

I couldn't believe we'd lost another sail, not here, not now. Things seemed so bleak. I was forced to cut the sheets to stop the sail from acting as an anchor under the water, then left myself with no choice but to drag the sail out from the sea by hand. It took all the strength I had to get just an inch or so over her guard wires, and often I would lose five minutes of work as an unusually large wave swept over the boat and mercilessly dragged the sail back with it. As I edged it up over the guard wire I prayed that there would be no damage, but my heart sank as I saw a massive rip, then another. Our sail was well and truly destroyed.

I was relieved that the wind was increasing though. At least we were able to sail with the genoa and not feel that we were painfully under-canvased. That night I lay on the chart table seat with my head back on my fleecy pillow and called Mum and Dad to let them know what had happened – this was something I had begun to do after each disaster we had so that at least they knew that I was OK. The last thing I wanted was for Mum and Dad to hear a story on the news which worried them. At least this way no matter how bad it was they would hear my voice first to know that I really was OK.

Now I had dried out I felt better, but I knew what was to come. It was blowing 30 knots, and I was going to have to climb the mast to replace the halyard. I called Mark to tell him of all that had happened, and felt some relief to have described it to someone else. I said on the phone, 'I will guard that gennaker with my life!'

I climbed the mast on Christmas Eve, and though I had time to get ready, it was the hardest climb to date. I had worked through the night preparing for it, making sure I had all the tools, mouse lines and bits I might need, and had agonized for hours over how I should prepare the halyard so that it would stream out easily below me and not get caught as I climbed.

When it got light I decided that the time was right. I kitted up in my middle-layer clothes as I didn't want to wear so much that I wouldn't be able to move freely up there. The most dangerous thing apart from falling off is to be thrown against the mast, and though

I would be wearing a helmet it would not be difficult to break bones up there.

I called Mark. It was evening in France where he was living in the mountains, and he was just about to sleep. I told him not to worry if he tried to contact me and I did not reply as I would be up the mast for the next couple of hours. Though his words were reassuring I could sense his concern.

I laid out the new halyard on deck, flaking it neatly so there were no twists. As I took the mast in my hands and began to climb I felt almost as if I was stepping on to the moon – a world over which I had no control. You can't ease the sheets or take a reef, nor can you alter the settings for the autopilot. If something goes wrong you are not there to attend to it. You are a passive observer looking down at your boat some 90 feet below you. After climbing just a couple of metres I realized how hard it was going to be, I couldn't feel my fingers – I'd need gloves, despite the loss in dexterity. I climbed down, getting soaked as we ploughed into a wave – the decks around my feet were awash. I unclipped my jumar from the halyard and put on a pair of sailing gloves. There would be no second climb on this one – I knew that I would not have the energy.

As I climbed my hands were more comfortable, and initially progress was positive. But it got harder and harder as I was not only pulling my own weight up as I climbed but also the increasingly heavy halyard – nearly 200 feet of rope by the time I made it to the top. The physical drain came far less from the climbing than from the clinging on. The hardest thing is just to hang on as the mast slices erratically through the air. There would be the odd massive wave which I could feel us surf down, knowing we would pile into the wave in front. I would wrap my arms around the mast and press my face against its cold and slippery carbon surface, waiting for the shuddering slowdown. Eyes closed and teeth gritted, I hung on tight, wrists clenched together, and hoped. Occasionally on the smaller waves I would be thrown before I could hold on tight, and my body and the tools I carried were thrown away from the mast; I'd be hanging on by just one arm, trying to stop myself from smacking back into the rig.

292

By the third spreader I was exhausted; the halyard was heavier and the motion more violent. I held on to her spreader base and hung there, holding tight to breathe more deeply and conjure up more energy. But I realized that the halyard was tight and that it had caught on something. Damn! I knew that if I went down to free it I would not have the energy to climb up once again. I tugged and tugged on the rope – the frustration was unreal. It had to come, quite simply the rope had to come free. Luckily with all the pulling I managed to create enough slack to make it to the top, but now I was even more exhausted. I squinted at the grey sky above me and watched the mast-head whip across the clouds. The wind whistled past us, made visible by the snow that had begun to fall. Below the sea stretched out for ever, the size and length of the waves emphasized by this new aerial view. This is what it must look like to the albatross.

I rallied once more and left the safety of the final spreader for my last hike to the top. The motion was worse than ever, and as I climbed I thought to myself, not far now, kiddo, come on, just keep moving . . . As the mast-head came within reach there was a short moment of relief; at least there was no giving up now I had made it – whatever happened now I had the whole mast to climb down. I fumbled at the top of the rig, feeding in the halyard and connecting the other end to the top of *Kingfisher*'s mast. The job only took about half an hour – then I began my descent. This was by far the most dangerous part and I had my heart in my mouth – no time for complacency now, I thought, not till you reach the deck, kiddo, it's far from over . . .

It was almost four hours before I called Mark back and I shook with exhaustion as we spoke. We had been surfing at well over 20 knots while I was up there. My limbs were bruised and my head was spinning, but I felt like a million dollars as I spoke on the phone. Santa had called on *Kingfisher* early and we had the best present ever – a new halyard.

MERRY XMAS!!
Well it seems incredible to think that just 12 months
ago we were not so far fro the Southern Ocean . . . It's

also inredible to think that since then *Kingfisher* has been finished – launched, delivered – double-transated and now globe-ing it! Once again a Christmas alone – though last time it was up in the Whatekeri Mountain Rnge in New Zealand. I don't really kow why I chose to be aloe last year too. I guess it was subconcious preparation for now. I was sitting in the cuddy the other day thinking . . thinking about how much time *Kingfisher* and I have spent together . . Well we've sailed over 35 thousadn miles – and providing all goes well and I finish the Vendée we'll have spent over 6 months at sea in th past 12. That shocked me when I though it! THe past six years seems to have come into focus over the past weeks. In a weeks time we'll be about half way round, again, incredible to think that the trip is passing so quickly. Because the Vendée is quickening its pace I think we're finding time is flying by – though there are still those days where it seems like home is a long, long way away (which it is!) About 8 thousand 200 miles as the crow flies from here. It would have to be a very brave crow though – because settingoff a journey from 50 degrees south could be a chilly affair – he would certainly need additional fuel tanks and a very warm scarf! Navigation though would be easy, as there are plenty of seabirds to ask diections from!

I pause to find something warmer to wear as I type, and I can't help thinkigng that if I dry out this jacket one more time I shall have a salt-crystal garden hanging from each of the sleeves!

This whole project has been one of the best experiaences of my life. I have learn't more than I ever believed possible – worked with the best team I could ever imagine, and have travelled the world – much of which under sail.

In a way that makes this all sound very easy . . . but in fact it's been the hardest thing I've ever done too

. . . Part of that out here, because for the forst time i my life I feel I've found y limit, an the decision-making, and sheer number of jobs we had to get through to be here right now. I have to thank the team for basically dedicating their lives to the project. An awesome effort.

So we're here – thanks to everyone, and it's my turn to get round quickly and safely. I a m finding the race to be the most inredible experience. It's dificult but rewarding. Hte pace of this race is like no other. THough we have a long way to go, we are racing liek a transatlantic. Incredible pace, crazy speeds and – with every one of us a will to get to the finish – a difficult jobto balance. The hardest thing of all is the constnat decision-amaking, the relentless movement . . . It's not like we get a chance to relax. Tactically a small mistake can cost us hundreds of miles . . Errors just can't be made . . It would be a very diffierent situation of it were not a race out here!!

Finally; like to wish every one of you out htere a happy Christmas. It shall feel strange opening my presents alone, and as my heater's broken there's little chance of Santa popping down the chimney – the exhaust's got a bung in it now anyway! Thank you all so much for your thousands of messages. I cannot thaknk you enough – I just hope you can feel what a difference they make to life out here. WHen things are tough I really feel like I'm not alone – and your energy and support shines through every time . . . thankyou. I just hope that we can hang in here, and catch those others up before we get home! Now that would be the prefect gift for Xmas. Take care, Merry Christmas,
love ellen

It was odd being so far away from the rest of the world on Christmas Day, but I did my best to do things properly. I was lucky

295

with the weather, the wind stayed reasonably steady, and we were able to sail all day without major sail changes. I had everything from a miniature Christmas tree to tinsel and plastic farm animals, and even a tiny lantern with a small supply of candles which I hung from the cabin roof at night. It brought tears to my eyes to see the kindness and amount of thought that each person had put into the gifts that I'd stowed away on board before the start. But the best thing that happened on Christmas Day was a conference call where Mark had organized for all my friends and family to call in and have a chat. It was an odd feeling having people drop in and out of the conversation, coming and going as if they were literally dropping in for a chat! It was only after twenty minutes that I discovered Mum and Dad had been there the whole time but just not said anything! Ian was there too, and contributed his usual funny comments and dry wit, and the team from the office also joined in. Although I could not have been physically much further away from them all, I felt very close to everyone that day. A real Christmas.

I scattered the tinsel in our chilly cabin and put the tree above the chart table. I heated Gran's Christmas pudding which I had on board as pretty much my only weight concession, then sprinkled the tiny bottle of rum I'd been given on to it. Dad had even included a sprig of Derbyshire holly in the parcel, and I lit it, just as he did each Christmas . . . I blew up a balloon and wrote on it in indelible pen, *Happy Xmas everyone, luv you all xx*, then threw it over the side into the Southern Ocean.

I sat down to reply to some of the festive e-mails that I'd received, including one from gardener Alan Titchmarsh. He'd been following the project and we'd become friends. I needed his advice!

```
Dear Alan . . .
    Hello there - and thanks for your Xmas e-mail. Xmas
here was a little strange - though I was lucky with the
weather, and got a bit of a break. I neded it after my
Xmas Eve nightmare of the mast ascent. Above all the rum
custard and Gran's Xmas pudding warmed the cockles -
which since our 3 hour airobatic's session were still a
```

little chilly! Today is a great day . . . we are in 3rd (though you probably know) – and now – just 36 miles behind Bilou. I am so pleased, and just hope that we can hang in here without getting into trouble . .

Now back to Xmas . . . I recieved a whole host of small and light presents which ranged form crochet dog hair charms to spare pants from Mum (as always), the good old chocolate penny, a few glo in the dark dolphins, and a tiny candle lantern which hangs in the cabin, to remind me of sailing when I was a kid with the paraffin lamp. THere was one present though – one which would interest you the most.

It's a tiny pot-your-own bonsai tree from Helen (who you breify met at the ferry terminal before we sailed in Cowes). Now Helen is very keen on nature, and has a degree in Environmental Science – so very apt on her part, and great to be able to rekindle those memories of harvesting and planting runner beans in the old Ski yoghurt pots with Dad when we were kids.

So, being the forst person to spring to mind, I'm writing to ask you for asdvice on the finer matters of seed cultivation! I though the wee plant might be a little confused if I plant him in the summer – in the Southern Hemisphere – and a little bemused as he fries as we cross the Equator . . Will he have a sense of where he belongs – or will he – for the sake of argument remain a bit of a wanderer – like myself – who lives his life dashing from season to season? Might it be that I will be obliged to travel the word with this tree . . . ?

The instructions say to moisten the compost with water. Now I have only water-maker water – mineral-less I guess, and wondered if this would make a big difference to his growth – should I dissolve a vitamin tablet in his compost . . . ?

Mmmm . . .

I guess that it must seem a little strange being asked

for gardening advice from a boat about as far away from
soil as you can get . . Well there you go, funnier
things have happenned!

Hope this message finds you well, and that you've had
a great Xmas, and all the best for 2001.
Best Wishes!
ellen
(and samuel the Carob seed, obviously, as a bonsai with
small aims in life)

28/12/00 05:13Z (ellenmacarthur.com/day50)
Position 53° 36.9S 167° 48.5E
Heading/speed 66 15.52
Wind from 290 at 25.6 knots
Pressure of 976
Sea temperature 7.3
Sail configuration is 1st reef Gennaker
Percentage performance 93.3

Again I sit . . THe wind has dropped after a alrge
cloud. already I have taken the reef i and out of the
mainsail 6 times. t's frustrating, as after 20 minutes
had passed the wind always seems to pick up . . thogh
you never know. The sun shines between the squalls
around us, and the seabirds play, swoop and swim as we
chundle past. It's been a good morning for progress –
though frustrating as always with the squalls. I've
never seen squalls quite so violent as here . . Going
from 15–30 knts in one hit. I' afraid for the gennaker,
and it's our last! THough there is no option but to fly
it if we are to make progress . . .

It's great to be a little ahead right now, and I feel
more thanbefore now I am away from the others that I am
sailing my own race . . No longer in quite the same
weather as those ahead – or behind, I feel – for the
want of a better phrase – a little freer!

We are just sailing under the most western part of New Zealand as I type, and in just over 24 hours time we shall be on the same longituse as Auckland. I thik *Kingfisher* is feeling she's close to home right now, though we've had a talk, and I've told her that we might stop off the *next* time round.

The wind continues to die . . . just 14 knots now . . CAn it be that the wind will stay so light, maybe I'll wait another 10 minutes . . yes 10 minutes. THen shake out the reef. It's a hard one to take in and out is the frst, as I have to pull up the whole sail. Frustrting, long – but rewarding as we speed off after.

There we go . . . 24 knots of wind. I knew it was worth waiting! Today I have checked for oil in the generator – pumped out water that was kicking around in the forepeak. Changed the rubbish bag (always a great one!) and generally checked around down below. Oh yes – I've wired the Sat C into the 24V transformer to see if I can kick it into life. So far – i seems to be working better anyway.

I'm a bit worried about a depression which is due to form ahead of us. I don't feel like getttiing trapped beneath it as it streaks to the SE – but it looks like it'sll be hard to stay to it's north. It seems to be developing earlier than we think which is good news though – so maybe it'll drop south ahead of us.

Better pop up and ease out the sails a little.
ellen
xx

We were approaching the International Dateline where we would enjoy 29 December twice! We were sailing between the Bishop and Clerk Islands which lie several hundred miles to the south of New Zealand and it was here that I saw my first boat since Thomas, a massive Australian fishing vessel called *Austral Leader*. She called up on the radio and it was fantastic to chat with the lads on board.

They seemed quite fascinated by what I was up to – so much so that they came over for a look. There were thirty-two guys on board, all off for a three-month trip. But somehow, while it was exciting to see land and another vessel on the same day, there was also the same familiar feeling of claustrophobia – so it felt good to leave those final islands behind us en route for Chile.

The leading boats were sailing into the most remote waters of the world – the South Pacific Ocean. The next land we all hoped to see would be Cape Horn itself – still well over two weeks away. We were lying third and I was over the moon about our position, we were catching Bilou fast – and Mich was being reeled in bit by bit . . .

Further back, Mike Golding, who was slowly creeping up through the fleet, got caught in 58-knot winds. He lost one of the battens in his mainsail, and eventually decided just to go below while the autopilot steered his boat and sit it out. The deck is a dangerous place to be in a Southern Ocean storm.

There was news that Frenchman Thierry Dubois was to pull out of the race due to a complete electrical failure. Thierry had also been one of the casualties of the last Vendée, and had incredible strength of character to return to race in those same waters again. He had built his boat largely himself, and had been a friend since those early years in La Trinité.

```
29/12/00 07:20Z (ellenmacarthur.com/day51)
Position   54° 25.2S   178° 30.2E
Heading/speed   64   14.58
Wind from 312   at 19.5 knots
Pressure of   981
Sea temperature   7.9
Sail configuration is   Full main   Genoa
Percentage performance   103.5


Well we're flying right now . . great wind angle, and
eay sailing. A bit frustratinig at times as the little
gusts come, and we fall over a bit, but all in all we're
```

76 Christmas aboard, 2000

78 Halfway up the mast,
removing the broken batten

Preparing to climb the mast

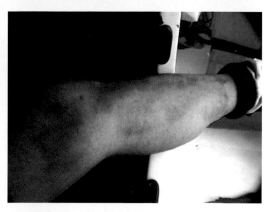

79 The side-effects of a trip up the mast

80 Inside the iceberg zone. The bigges' one I saw – the size of an island

81 Sailing *Kingfisher* in a swe'

82 Mum and Dad were flown out by helicopter just hours before the Vendée finish. They saw first-hand how I'd been living for the previous three months

83 The finish line

84 Celebration

85/86 (left) Saying goodbye for the last time

87 (above) And all alone just minutes later

88 The first interview in Les Sables d'Olonne

89 Mark and I share a post-Vendée interview – a very emotional occasio

90 Backstage at the Vendée prize-giving. In the foreground is Mich Desjoyeaux, the winner

(above) With Ian, Mum and Brian
Pilcher, an incredible six years after my
round Britain sail

(right) Yves Parlier, whose Vendée story
was amongst the most extraordinary of all

(below) With Alain Gautier, a great
friend and sailing companion in 2001

94 Back on the water – aboard *Kingfisher Foncia*

95 *Kingfisher Foncia* doing what she does be[st]

96 At the EDS prize-giving. The first time I raced *Kingfisher* with a crew – an incredible team

97 Euphoria: celebrating with the *Kingfisher Foncia* crew after winning the Challenge Mondial

98 With David Beckham, Sir Alex Ferguson and Michael Owen at the BBC Sports Personality of the Year awards

99 (above left) Accepting an honorary degree from the University of Derby, where my Nan finally completed a degree at the age of eighty-three – an incredible achievement!

100 (above) At Buckingham Palace to receive my MBE with Mum, Dad and Gran

101 (left) Nan's graduation

going well now. Today has been a day of sleeping, weather study and spilicing. The weather study reveals that there is one mother of a dpression heading over us around the 31st – Happy New Year! For *Kingfisher* it will be the worst yet – so I'm trying to position myself for it in the best place. Difficult – as the weather information here is not so accurate. Had a good splicing session, and repaired the old gennaker halyard to re-use if ever the new one breaks. It was a long job, and a very difficult and tight vectran splice . . Lots of pulling and squeezing, feeding and fidding! after an hour and a hlaf the job was done – so pleased I was a t cracking it I went straight on to make a new spare jib sheet . . . again – in case. I was quite chuffed at havigng completed the whole job in the cuddy withought a oilies on – I just dodged the torrents of water as they sluiced over *Kingfisher*.

During tonight we're lined up to cross the Date Line – so roll on once more the 28th of december. Very strange – though it helps keeping theboatsclocs in GMT. At least we don't completely lose the plot. We've passed under Auckland now – so we're more in known territory, it feels a little comforting to know KF has sailed this bitbeofre, though I am quite sure that the Pacific will not be wearing the same face for us this time. Prudence is the key word.

I heard yesterrday that Marc Thierecelin is saying that hee 'is fed up with sailing behind the little ellen' . . . well I could throw that one back by saying that I'm missing sailing with Bilou. So I'm hurrying along to enjoy some company!

Take care everyone. Ellen

I always felt much better for having repaired things; finding it an almost therapeutic way of taking my mind off the immense stress of the decisions. It was something that was always burning away inside me; looking after *Kingfisher*, making sure she was always repaired as soon as possible and ready to face whatever was coming next. This involved not only repairs though, but scores of checks, from the oil in the engine to the amount of food we were consuming, to each fixing on her deck, and the lashings on her rigging. It was easy to tire yourself out, but at the end of the day you had to do what you had to do. It was now approaching New Year, and there were yet more difficult decisions to make. Spirits were high once again, I had caught up to just over 100 miles behind Mich . . . we were on a roll. But all was not straightforward, there was an enormous depression roaring up behind us, and for Bilou, still less than 50 miles away, and myself it was looking as though we would not make it to the north of it . . .

```
31/12/00 07:41Z (ellenmacarthur.com/day53)
Position   55° 15.7S   165° 30.5W
Heading/speed   106   10.3
Wind from 46  at 23.6 knots
Pressure of   972
Sea temperature   19.5
Sail configuration is   2nd reef   Solent
Percentage performance   86.7
```

I feel quite low roght now – akin to the weather system which has moved on top of us. I am very tired, and can't sleep. The motion of KF is horrible – nothing i seem to be able to do makes her feel more comfortable. we are between two wind ranges – where she'd be better off wiht the Solent – but i daredn't risk brreaking the sail – so we bounce and pound along with 2 reefs and staysail.

There are clearly two weather options . . . this morning I was hoping to stay with that of the north – t o pick up the westerlies and fire east – but the wind has turned earlier, and now we are heading to the south of SE – in a wind which is basically east. I am not sure if my chouice is th4e right one. the wind is fluctuating, and my emotions rn from laughter to crying as the wind swings, anent oh rain pours . . .

We stand to losee a gret dealif I am worong. we could get trapped in the south, not make the waypoint, and have to sail some stupid course 90 defgrees to the route to get there. I am very worried, northing ai can do makes m emfeel better inside, nothing relaxes me, - I ahevne't even managed a proper meal today.

This is hte harsdest part - it's harder than the breakages, and the problems. It's putting us in the right place. we wroked hard to get bac up the fleet, and now we stand to lose what we ahve gained, and that is eating away at me right now likke it wantsto engulf me. I find it impossible to put into words the anguish inside. The worry, the constant frey ness - the hors and hours staring at a computer screen analysing and reanalysing till your blue in the face, and after all your work could easily convince yourself that either opteion is the oene to go forl. I guesst hta' what I lack - the experience. The expxeriece of standing by a decision, and understanding it in a way different to I do now.

This for me is the hardest part.

At this point I was at my most tired in the race. Never had I pushed myself so hard before, and never had I felt so desperate. I had never forced myself beyond what I thought were my limits before, and now I was there it was the hardest thing ever to come back from. Reasoning was virtually impossible, the constant danger and stress of the race were taking an immense toll, and the sapping effect of living on the edge for over fifty days was for the first time becoming startlingly obvious. We were being pushed to the south, with no option as far as the race was concerned to head any way other than towards the ice. It's almost as if I had lost control of myself; when you reach this place you feel completely in despair as if things will never get better. It's hard to see anything but the dark side, and as you're physically thrown about, and desperately cold, you frustrate yourself more by going way below despair. *Kingfisher* was not happy, she was uncomfortable in the waves and it was transmitted through to me like a signal ringing warnings in my brain. There was nothing I could do; we were sailing slowly in a direction we did not want to go in, and the sea was horrendous. I slumped down in the cockpit on to my knees, banging my fists against my legs, I hurled my head back and yelled, screaming so loud that my throat was sore.

'Why? Why us? Please, just please give us a chance!'

But the dark sky wasn't listening and the torrential rain trickled down my neck, slowly sapping yet more of those precious reserves of heat from my body. Images of Mich sailing away downwind flashed through my head. I was angry and frustrated and felt that I was letting people down. We were losing miles to Mich, and losing them fast. It was more than just physical exhaustion, it was causing more pain inside than I had ever felt before. I clenched my teeth hard together and I threw my head down against the hard wet floor and wept. I cried like a baby till I was so numb with the cold the pain was dulled. Shivering and weak, I crawled into the cabin and slept in my waterproofs, curled up in a ball in the footwell by the engine.

On waking again I called Ian in a distraught and washed-up state. In the past he'd had an uncanny knack of picking me up and making me smile when I thought I couldn't, and I needed a hug right now. Mark had already said that I was lucky not to be in the same position as some of the other Vendée skippers who'd had to stop to repair their boats, but I felt he had totally lost patience with me. I couldn't shake off the feeling that I had made the wrong decisions in the last days and as a result let people down. In my weakened state I doubted my decision-making skills but Ian let me talk; I unloaded my worries and insecurities and everything just flowed down the phone. He knew I needed to be snapped out of this destructive slump and at the end of the conversation he told me something that really shocked me. He said that he had been told never to tell me this but felt that right then he had to. After finishing an interview before the Vendée, Mich was reported to have made an off-the-cuff comment in which he claimed that various skippers believed that I had received banned outside assistance when winning the Europe 1 STAR. Ian reasoned that comments like this would not be made unless I was doing something right. It was the biggest kick-start I could have had. I was furious, no one cheats and I sure as hell never had, and Mich would have known the impact of even suggesting it. The anger rose inside me, and fuelled by it, I refused to accept my position in this race. We still had 10,000 miles to sail and I was going to give my all.

Less than a day later we were heading straight into an iceberg field. The water temperature cooled, and I knew it was just a matter of time before we encountered the first ice. As morning broke I spotted the first berg looming out of the greyness of the sea and sky. I was in a state of expectant nervousness, laced with a thrill from the potential danger. You know that more than ever you are living on the edge, that you cannot fall asleep, and that profound dread of a splitting, crunching, gut-wrenching halt to your journey is ever present. You try not to think about the 'what ifs' of a collision with an iceberg weighing thousands of tons, you mustn't imagine how *Kingfisher* would react to an impact at 15 knots with a cliff of solid ice any more than you would think of a car crash each time you went for a drive. But you know damn well inside that it's not just the race that could end, but everything. The only other boat in the iceberg zone was Bilou's and his sobering remark was that was it was not a place for a father.

```
02/01/01 18:28Z (ellenmacarthur.com/day55)
F****** close and nothing on radar. Not exactly small or
melted either. I'll be glad to gybe to the North! I saw
it on the beam again . . . Bollocks. Deep breaths and
relaxing req'd. x
```

I sent an e-mail to race headquarters with the positions and sizes of the first bergs I saw, stating that the second was half a mile long!

I finished by saying that I hoped that was enough for one day . . .
it's freezing here!

```
6 iceberg seperate mais pas petite (500M par 200M
approx) sur une ligne 58 24.8S 143.03W et 58 07S 145 07W
.. Une a 58 35.85 143 19.3W (enorme - une demi mille en
longeur) Une a 58 32 28S 143 15W (avec beaucoup de
growlers sou le vent) Une petite a 58 09.5S 142. 41.5S
Une grande a 57 44.5S 142 00.1W...
    Voilà, j'espère c'est sufficement pour une journée! Ca
Caille ici! ellen
```

I felt completely trapped by the ice; each time a berg slipped
behind us into the grey gloom I would make out another before us.
There seemed no easy way through as although there were gaps
between the bergs they were strewn with growlers, often still the
size of cars or even houses. Most of the larger bergs looked like
sections taken from the cliffs of Dover, hundreds of feet high and
jagged with crevasses. Even sheltered from the icy wind outside,
the cabin felt like a freezer. It was only after the seventh berg that
I felt it was safe to gybe out of the zone to the north. Gybing is a
long job on an Open 60 – swapping the sides of all the boxes below,
preparing the runners, rolling up the gennaker – then that horrible
moment where the mainsail flicks over and poor *Kingfisher* is
pushed way over on to her side as the wind fills in on the new side
of the sail. It's a fantastic feeling easing the mainsheet off and
feeling her accelerate away before unfurling her gennaker, bringing
up her swing keel, and tidying away all the lines scattered throughout her cockpit.

After the gybe I saw a further three bergs, the first quite small,
but the second gigantic. From a distance it looked like an island,
long, and sloping gently into the ocean. Its sheer mass became more
evident when it seemed to take hours before it felt that we were
any nearer. I took pictures and a video of it, in complete and utter
awe at the beauty of this massive block. I could see families of birds
on top of it as we grew closer, and clearly see and hear the waves

breaking around its base as on a rocky shore in a storm. The wind was up to 30 knots by now, a rise of 5, which was pushing us closer and closer to the side of the berg, and though we made it safely round we passed at well within a mile. As we rounded its most northern point I was stunned to see two enormous ice caves, perfectly arch-like in shape and sinking away to darkness deep within the berg itself. Each was large enough to sail *Kingfisher* into – a trip, though, from which there would be no coming back for sure. Its sides were tinted with an aqua-blue colour, and it looked so white against the inky-grey sea and darkening sky. There was an aura around this berg, a feeling of complete and utter isolation. I knew that it was highly unlikely that human eyes had even seen it before.

The next and final berg though was the one which posed the greatest problem. It only became visible a couple of miles ahead as dusk was approaching – I had no option other than to go below it, past its leeward face, which is the dangerous side. Growlers are guaranteed on the downwind side of these bergs, and though I had seen a few scattered around, they had been car-sized and visible. But ahead of me I could see more growlers, and though I sailed as low as I could to miss the berg, and was over a mile from its position, there seemed no avoiding what was ahead of us. The dark sea was strewn with ice, almost like ice-cubes floating in a glass. Shit.

I punched OFF on the autopilot and grabbed *Kingfisher*'s helm, lifting it so that I could steer standing up to see over her bow. I found myself slaloming between these lumps, just hoping that there would not be a cluster close together.

That evening I dozed in the cuddy and made hot coffee to keep myself awake. I never normally drink coffee from day to day as in this way its effects at sea are more dramatic, and it did the trick this time, warming me too. It was even colder at night, and I used the discomfort this caused as another aid to keeping myself awake. I pushed a pair of mittens firmly on to my numb hands to try to protect them so that they might work if they were needed in a hurry. The wind was strong now, between 28 and 30 knots, and with the driving rain I knew it would be almost impossible to see a berg even if it were only a few hundred feet before us. The dark clouds scared me a few times, fooling me into thinking that there was a berg looming before us, but as my heart raced, my eyes managed to pick out that for the next ten minutes at least we would be OK. I felt strong during that time in the ice fields, it was a wake-up call, something to concentrate hard on and take my mind off the pressures. I joked at the camera and spoke to it with obvious concern but amazement on my face. That was one of my strengths – just digging in when the going got tough – but then, as often as not, suffering the consequences of overdoing it afterwards.

I had been in touch with Mark several times that day, keeping him up to date with what was going on. He had been having dinner with friends in Chamonix during my day, and now, my evening being the early hours of his morning, we were talking as he lay in his bed. We'll never know if it was just worry, but Mark was violently ill throughout that night as he lay awake waiting for the next phone-call, just to be reassured that all was OK.

Although I did not know it at the time, I was not the only one who had had a bad start to the New Year. There had been tough times on all of the top three boats. Mich had broken the starter motor on his engine and, unable to charge his batteries, was in trouble. It's always a judgement call to decide how many spares you should have on board, how many backups to backups, and part of the learning process is knowing what to take. So far I felt we had been lucky bar the breaking of the halyards and the losing of our sails, but Mich was definitely facing a major setback, which if not resolved would have a massive impact on his result in the race. Bilou too was in a desperate situation; he had ripped a section of track off his mast which meant that he could only put up his mainsail with two reefs in. Not being able to increase sail was of crucial importance – especially in light airs. When Mark told me the news I could not stop thinking about Bilou all day – he is the nicest guy you'll ever meet. He had had this problem since entering the Southern Ocean, but had chosen to keep it quiet till now. It's a very different type of emotion when you are exhausted and thousands of miles away from anywhere . . . you are not driven to cry because you are feeling upset, but you are simply driven to your instincts; there is nothing inside you to fight with any longer, no reserve left to draw from.

I found that I was encouraged enormously by contact from other people. Ten or so e-mails would be filtered through to me each day from the thousands which were flooding into the website. We had everything from families in Germany, to classes of kids in schools all over France, to the Swallows and Amazons group at the Alverstoke Junior school. There were always messages which stood out though, some which cheered me up, some which made me realize how lucky I was. One of the most memorable was about a young girl called Chiara.

Dear Ellen,

Our daughter Chiara is five years old. She came home from hospital this afternoon. Her treatment for leukaemia has produced new side effects and, once again, given us a real scare.

Still, Chiara amazes us a little more each day with her sense of humour, her ability to laugh at her condition and at her mother and me when she senses our concern. Her remarkable courage and perseverance give her great beauty and radiance.

The reason for my writing to you today is that I know that you support sick children, and this has moved me greatly, especially as the long journey that you have undertaken alone in the Vendée Globe bears some resemblance to Chiara's own journey. You are crossing areas which you alone can explore but which you allow us to glimpse. You alone can win your race. Dear Ellen, I wish you to win this Vendée Globe. Your victory would send a fantastic message of hope to our daughter Chiara as she too hopes to transform her solitude into victory, with all the strength and perseverance that she is able to muster.

If the whims of the ocean were to frustrate your
efforts before you reach the Sables d'Olonne, we would
remain extremely grateful and attached to you for the
exceptional journey which you have been sharing with us
over the last two months and for the beauty that
emanates from you.

05/01/01 22:35Z (ellenmacarthur.com/day58)
Oh Bilou
I saw your news this morning. I am very sad for you.
I've been thinking a lot during to day . . . I hope that
you will find all the energy to repair it. It must be
hard, but we are with you . . . becareful up there, I've
been up several times, and it's not easy – the best is
on deck AT THE END! You must come back, I'm missing
you! We must stay together till the end . . . Wish I
could help . . .
Kisses,
Soon Ellen.

Sent: Sunday, January 07, 2001 04:08Z
Subject: Thank you
Thank you so much for your message Ellen

I'ts not easy at the moment . . On top of everything I
broke my gennaker halyard attatchment yesterday, I'm
sailing with two reefs and the genoa half unfurled! I't
been hard since the 16th December to have this mainsail
2 reefs from the top, without being able to do anything,
but well, that's racing.
Your are racing a great race, and I too find it superb
to be once more in contact with you. I wish you all the
best for the next stage, continue how you know you
should.
Kisses Bilou

Shortly after our communication with Bilou we passed ahead of him into second place. I now had Mich in my sights, but still had a lead of around 400 miles to overhaul. When Bilou and I had been pushed south of the weather system, Mich had jumped into the next and had a lead which was extending day by day as he surfed along within the next one. When a boat ahead is in a different system it can have a concertina effect – they can get into better and better weather and just eat away the miles while you're stuck in the light airs between two systems.

```
06/01/01 08:09Z (ellenmacarthur.com/day59)
Position  53° 42.7S  118° 34.8W
Heading/speed  59  10.28
Wind from 279  at 12.9 knots
Pressure of  995
Sea temperature  4.4
Sail configuration is  Full main  Spinnaker
Percentage performance  95.7
```

```
Wel all I can manage to say right now is Wow . . .
    As I type there is less movement in Kingfisher than we
have had for a long time. She slides gracefully along
under spinnaker in a lght downwind breeze. The moon is
out, and is getting close to being full, and there are
stars filling the sky – a site that I have rarely seen
down here. An cloudless sky, and a very thin mist
filling the air – giving the world tonight outside my
little hatchway appear alost magical .. Spirit's are
high on board after a constructive day, and again a
reaonable amount of god recuperative sleep. . . .
```

The pressure was on during our crossing of the South Pacific, and I was pulling out a clear lead on Bilou as the days passed. He was sailing wounded without his full main and now above all his gennaker. Poor Bilou needed at least 30 knots of wind before he had a hope of sailing his boat in the way she wanted to be sailed. Having attempted a mast climb once to replace the halyard he had been forced to give up – it was too dangerous. I recalled the days in the Jacques Vabre Race with Yves when I spent the best part of three days up a similar rig – his boat, like Bilou's, had a wing mast and it was a nightmare to hang on to. This had certainly been one of the deciding factors for us in fitting a classic, smaller-section mast. But I was in second place, and though 500 miles was a long way behind Mich we still had a long way to go. I was running my race looking ahead more than behind now. It was going to have to be a fairly flash move to catch those miles up but I felt nothing was impossible.

The stress and anxiety of the last few weeks had eaten away at both me and Mark, however, and things had definitely frayed around the edges. Like Mark, I had a tremendous amount of respect for Mich, but I felt that Mark's view was that he was unbeatable. I had to believe he could be beaten, but I didn't feel that Mark shared this view with quite the same conviction. I felt so strongly that it wasn't over till it was over. Mark was shattered too, but at the time when I was at my lowest ebb I needed to be able to turn to him without worrying about how I'd be received. It had to be an uncomplicated relationship and I vented my frustration in an e-mail.

```
I'm not goning to beat about the bush - but you're
really upsetting me at the moment.
    I hat hearing youso down. I know you've been, and
you're tired and exhausted> please try to get some
f*****g rest.
    When I'm stressed and tired and worroied I know you
are too - so please appreciate that it works both ways!
    I feel awful right now. I feel shit, and all I can
think of is haveing upset - or upsetting you. Don't tell
me it's stupid, and to get on with the race because I
can't - because I'm ellen - and I need to know you're OK
- in a tone of voice that reallymeans it. And if you're
not OK then TELL ME - beaciauae I can see that, and I
haven't just been born!
```

Now please GO TO F******G BED, and be better
tomorrow because I need you more than you realize, I
need to talk bullshit on the pohone, and explaiun things
you reallydon't want to hear, because we're sailing this
race together - and I needyou with me till the very end.

After I wrote to Mark I sat on the bow and watched the water
swish past for at least half an hour. I was worried about what I'd
said and I knew he would reply that same night. We'd cleared the
air, but I still felt I needed to emphasize one thing.

Michel Desoyeaux is NOT the best in the world. He
simply isn't he's not perfect, and I refuse to believe
he is. Yes he has more expereince, but i refuse to be
phased by him. The best in the world is that little kid
CHiara in hospital. ANd if she wants me to win - then
I'll do everything in my power to do that for her, even
if it nearly kills me, because Christ, i'm achieving
very little compared to her . . . When Iread her e-mail I
cried, because I know that I can beat Michel - and I
have to. Please understand that. I will not let him
cross that line first - I WILL NOT!
   And yes there will be tears, I know that, it's not
easy. But I want to beat Mich more than anything else in
the world right now. ANd I dont' want to win this race
for me. Far from it. I honestly and truthfully want to
win the race for everyone that's fololowing this project
- for all those kids, and for you lot. Mark, that's how
I get my energy . . .
   I know I've said it before, but the thought of ringing
you when I got down from that mast was one of the things
that really pushed me on. I'm not joking. I was so glad
to hear your voice, because I know you understand, and
when you said to me 'Don't worry you'll be fine' I knew
that you were pretty much shitting yourself as much as I

was – beacuse we both knew it was going to be far from
fine . . .

   . . . My final word is that i've changed my keyboard,
and am amazingly impressed by it's ease of typing . . . I
can almost touch type now.

**I knew Mark would notice and appreciate my switching straight
back to business. No nonsense. I hoped it would raise a smile.**

08/01/01 05:48Z (ellenmacarthur.com/day61)
Position 53° 23.0S 103° 43.0W
Heading/speed 63 12.95
Wind from 170 at 15.4 knots
Pressure of 994
Sea temperature 6.3
Sail configuration is Full main Genoa
Percentage performance 97.1

It's been a quiet, and a busy day really. THis morning
we were gybing under gennaker in a wind which came
predominantly from the NW, and then now – to be sailing
in a wind basically southerly – as the front of the
small depression which has formedto our South passes.
The wind had been very inconsistent in strength, and
patches of clesr sky have been mixed with several hours
of a kind of gentle but squally drizzle.
   Even as I write the wind has risen to 20 knots . . .
the sun has set, and there is a very delicate light
shimmering arornd the skies before the world around us
is hushed into that almost-darkness by the strengthening
evening breeze of the Southern Ocean. A solitary
albatross flickers through the air, as if trying to hide
before the clouds, as he glides away from his silent
visit to our little world.
   Cape Horn beckons, nd as the hours pass we become
closer and closer to htis ancient amaritime monument.

How diferent it feels to be approaching this time - very
much in the middle of an adventure, as oppose to our
last passage - very much the beginning. I remeber
vividly the feelings which flowed through me as we
rounded the horn last April. THe emotion of 'turning the
corner home' with the most beautiful Open 60 I could
imagine in the world. THe tears of thanks shed for
everyone who had helped - an whatever way for this dream
to become reality.

    And now, once again to be nearing this point . . . Who
Knows what emotions will flow. ut one thing is for
certain, and that's that we'lll be heading home. Each
mile bringing us closer to that finish line. I promise
you all that I shall sail this next chapter of the race
with all theskill and energy I have, and can muster. Its
not long now, and we're going to do our level best
through and past that final mile . .

    AsI finish this message something catches my
attention through the window abave. The moon is beaming
it's prescence through the tiny openings in the clouds
. . . Round and beautiful - it's not often I have seen it
down here . . . A gentle reminder that it's that very
same moon that you can all see in your hours of
darkness . . .
exx

   Things were going well on the race front, and although Mich was
540 miles ahead by this stage with a repaired engine, I was now
maintaining a 100-mile lead over Bilou and Marc Thiercelin on
Active Wear. It was a lead that I was having to fight for though as
the leech of our gennaker had split quite badly, and this being
our last furlable sail I was scared of the damage getting worse.
Reluctantly I decided that I would have to take it down to make
repairs. The wind was not too strong, but the motion of the boat
was horrible as she wallowed in the massive swell of the approaching storm. I tried to unfurl the sail by hand, which was hard as it

was over 80 foot long and contorted on a 60-foot deck. The more I unfurled, the harder it got as I worked each twist all the way down the sail to the bow. I knew I was sailing slowly and I was desperately frustrated at our speed. 'Come on, kiddo', I kept urging, 'come on.' But after an hour of struggling my patience was stretched and finally snapped when I slipped as a wave threw us sideways and smashed my face, causing a streaming nose-bleed. Wiping the blood away, I swore at the camera. Once again I knew that I was teetering on the edge of my limits, but finishing the job of unfurling the sail was a proper tonic. Then, once up again, I made myself turkey and chestnut, one of my favourite freeze-dried meals, to celebrate with. There was a very fine line between joy and despair: it was only afterwards that things felt good on board again. Conditions were fractionally more stable and for the first time in days the weather situation remained fairly predictable and I was able to get at least some sleep. But by the following evening the wind had filled in and the new depression was well and truly in contact with us . . . we were back to the unpredictable winds of the south.

09/01/01 09:30Z (ellenmacarthur.com/day62)
As I sit here and type I am cold and wet – wet with my
oown chilled sweat. It was a busy day once again . . .
weather study, and many many sail changes as the wind
slowly turned, and fluctuated in int's normal Southern
Ocean way. By suset I had the gennaker, and was asailing
in about 15-29 knots of breeze. There were squall clouds
around, and as I had the gennaker up I was worrled that
if I slept inside for a while I may be to slow to get to
the opilot, so iI piled on the lyers of clothes, and as
best as I could tried to keep warm and dose in the
cuddy. I put a spare oilskin over me to try to keep
warm, te water temerpture here is warmer, so it wasn't
as cold as it has been. Iwas just drifting through a
plethora (is this the right word?) of dreams, when
the heart-stopping slowing of the boat happenned, and
the grim realisastion that we had once again blown the

halyard . . . no suall, nothing – just a chafed through
halyard. The gennaker – our only gennaker was lying over
the waters surface, I immediately blew the main halyard,
and her driving sail came slithering down into an
unnaranged heap on the boom. I had to work out the best
plan to save the sail in the water – at least when we
were stopped we bought ourselves some time. *Kingfisher*
wallowed around over the waves, and as I stumbled back
across her rolling deck, seeing her sails down I could
not help but feel she resembled a wounded bird, I felt
for her. An hour later the sail was on the deck – a
fight and a half as it's covered in a film which is like
trying to drag a plastic sheet which is tuggingaway at
you. As I gingerly but forcefully dragged it over the
guard wire my worse fears were realized as I swa the
leech was damaged, and on further hauling huge rips were
present . . Myu hear t sank, I hope to god we can fix it
. . . Again up the mast, and a repair which I'm not even
sure is possible. Tha hardest part of all I think was
geyying the sail through the forehath – it's not quite
the same when i'ts' rolled up. It took all the energy I
had left to jump on it till it wast rhough – it tikk at
least 20 minutes, and everything at that stage ached.
Obly got the mainsal to get back up now I thought to
myself . . .

It was yet again a gut-wrenching situation to be in. I felt once
more like my world had crumbled around me. Why, oh why did
this have to happen again? The sail was badly ripped, but I knew
that I would simply have to get on and repair it. It was going to be
a hellish job – and one that I would have to do as soon as possible. I
was also going to have to climb the mast once again. I drew small
consolation from the fact that at least I'd repaired the broken halyard and it was ready to go. With up to 35 to 40 knots of breeze and
just over 500 miles from the Horn I was not ready to climb it, plus
with the wind we would see, between now and the corner, it was

not worth risking a change now. We shouldn't need it till we were round.

But the frustration and disappointment were fuelled by other news: Mich had just rounded the Horn with a 536-mile lead.

```
11/01/01 04:32Z (ellenmacarthur.com/day64)
Just trying to think of everything whilst I try to sit
here yawning . . . Shit am I tired. Wind alll over the
place, and despite getting tinto sleep bag - can't
sleep. Back in oilies once again. Wind now coming from
070 at 27-30 kn. motion horrid - I am at 45 apparrent
and am trying to leave forward ballast out so as not to
load up mainsail too much. Speed is down to 11 kn, as I
try to keep N-ish. Hard going. Will be along wait for
front, as it runs NE-SW. Big risk that I'll not even
make it above centre, and willbe easten by it as it
moves SE. F****** hope not. Scat show that the wind
behind front is maybe less than 29 kn. We're in deep
shit if this is the case, as cannot sail deeoe enough to
make Horn. It will be a frustrating shambles. Wish I
cold stop yawning. Not lookingforwatd to all the media
stuff. Really don't feel like it this time. It's hard
with so many worries! talk later, WIll try tonight -
time for 3rd reef.
bye e
```

The rounding of the Horn was not to be how I had imagined in the build-up to the race. As I began to write my thoughts on the computer before we arrived I knew that it would not be the silent rounding we had wished for. I could not stop thinking of the other competitors, and hoped that they too would all make it safely round the corner. Of the twenty-four starters seven were already clearly out of the race and another five had either had to anchor to repair or had serious problems. There was Pasquale, the Italian, in his 50-footer *Wind*. With his long grey curly hair, cigar and small round spectacles, he was a real character. Since the descent of the Atlantic he'd been sailing with three reefs as he had broken a vital piece of rigging. For another competitor, Fedor Konioukhov, things were looking very bleak. He was over 8,000 miles behind *Kingfisher* and was not only suffering massive sail damage but also had a serious kidney infection. I felt sad for the shy Russian who had already climbed just about every peak in the world. As I spoke to him on the morning of the start he had had an almost childlike enthusiasm for the race. His eyes had sparkled, and he spoke of rounding the Horn in daylight, but his dream was not to come true. Fedor would not make the Horn on this trip but was instead forced to sail hundreds of miles north to Australia for urgent medical attention.

12/01/01 17:46Z (ellenmacarthur.com/day65)
Well I feel quite overwhelmed reallyu. The stress and difficulties of the last few days seem to be melting into emotion as I approach the horn. The second time for *Kingfisher* aND I TOGETHER . . . it's a great symbol for the two of us personally, as the very frost time i was ever alone on here, was just a few miles form this famous rock. I cannot helpl but feel moved deep inside. THe thoughts of the past storms and struggles off this point. This race has been hard, but when I think of those here huindreds of years ago I feel very humble sitting here. For then, the corner was literally life or death, and my heart goes out to all those who have struggled, survived and died on this piece of water. . . . Those memories shall never be forgotten here . . .
    The weather is misty, I strain my eyes to see, but I must wait till I'm a little nearer . . ECH TIME i think of where we are, and where we've been I find my eyes welling with tears. It's been a long haul since the launch in NZ, and the most incredible adventure of my life. Not one just of the story of A GIRL ALONE ON THE SAEA, BUT FAR MORE THATN THAT. foR ME IT's a stiry of

teamwork, friendship and love, the story of so many
people working towards a goal, and if not working –
willing us on . . . I feel there are so many others with
me on board, i've never been lonely – far from it – even
in times of stress. I've been haoopy here with my friend
Kingfisher, and am now looking forward to the atlantic
trip. Firstly so we can be on our way home, ands
secondly so we can get our repairs done in warmer
condioitns. I cannot help but feel wer are 'wounded'
rght now, and need the warmer weather to repair and get
our strtength back . . .

I was right about our rounding, which ended up being almost like keeping to an itinerary. I was glad I had had time to contemplate what an incredible place this was just hours before, and even more chuffed to have actually stopped there a year previously. From filming it, to doing live radio interviews about it, to being filmed by another boat, to talking with the guys on the rock itself was far from being the peaceful moment Fedor had imagined and was in fact a very stressful time. At one point I had a camera in my hand, a call on the mini M phone, one on the Satcom B and a French voice screaming out on the VHF radio trying to ask more questions. It was odd seeing the faces of people on the yacht which was filming us, something which I don't think I was really prepared for. It was 1845 GMT on 12 January 2001, and we were now in a similar time zone to Europe. And I was still two days behind Michel Desjoyeaux.

Within about an hour of rounding Cape Horn the wind died and we found ourselves in almost flat water sailing close-hauled. I grabbed the opportunity the calm presented, shinning straight up the mast to repair the halyard. In these conditions I had it done in less than thirty minutes – incredible to think that a few weeks before the job had taken me three and a half brutal hours.

15/01/01 13:18Z (ellenmacarthur.com/day68)
Position   47° 52.0S   056° 16.7W
Heading/speed   55   14.48

```
Wind from 318  at 25.8 knots
Pressure of  999
Sea temperature  5.1
Sail configuration is  2nd reef  Solent
Percentage performance  99.6


STOP PRESS
ONe of the seeds has sprouted!! exx
```

Life after the Horn changed dramatically as we headed north; from wind speed to temperature everything switches in an instant. The sky suddenly becomes blue, and the water takes on a green tint you never seem to see in the south. You remember what it's like to be able to sleep at the chart table without shivering and to look at the weather without constantly searching through the information for the next depression that is going to run up behind you and bite you. Five weeks is an awful long time to be down in those conditions, and the relief is certainly proportionate as you start the trek north and back home.

Our first obstacle was fairly substantial in appearance as we had to negotiate the Falkland Islands. I remembered from the delivery back from New Zealand that there would be a terrific amount of kelp in the water, so was not keen to take a route inside the islands. Each time I had looked at the weather I felt that the western option was best, though generally every weather book said it was best to stay outside to the east. The weather was up to its usual tricks, however, changing in speed and direction and making me really work to make progress to the north. I was still tired, and again felt the enormous pressure of making that vital decision: to the east or the west.

I finally sheeted in the sails, and rather than go for the faster-reaching conditions to head to the east I slowed down and stayed west. My plan was to get the new breeze more quickly and then have a better angle for approaching the Equator. As we had seen on our way down in this ocean, it paid to be in the west, and that was my plan. I had to do something very different from Michel. With upwind conditions things were more stable for a while, though I had to be very careful of fishing boats heading out from Stanley. After the island though the wind freed and built a little, and at last I had some chance to rest.

16/1/01/ 01:43Z (ellenmacarthur.com/day69)
Position 45° 51.4S 053°04.9W
Heading/speed 44 14.86
Wind from 310 at 23.4 knots
Pressure of 1001
Sea temperature 5.6
Sail configuration is 2nd reef Solent
Percentage performance 105.4

Well all is well n board, it's great to be eating away the miles, though hte situation ahead is lookking les than straight forward. *Kinngfisher* is fluying along, she seems nt olike the pooint of sailoing . . . The motion though is quie violent – the waves now building, and a NW swell meean we're pounding, and it's a fragile balance between sped and saffetty. This evening the wind has strengthened once again, though less than consistent . . it's gusting from 19 to 25 knots, so difficut to set the tight smount of sail. Glad to seethat one by one the fleet are rounding the horn, i don't know about the others but iyt'll be a relief for me when everyone is safely round. Its a wonderful place, but one in whih to be very cautious. Everything on board is quite hard with this motion . . it's ecen less predicatable that tnhe Southern Ocean surfs . . The god news is I've had a good while to study the wearthertoday, and have nhad large amounts of much needeed sleep both early this morning, and during the day. Feeliong much better of it, and really feeliong ready to wrk hard tillthe finish. It's easy tp relax after the horn as the weather warms, but it's just the astart of the journey home. . . . With just

322

under 6,000 miles to go, we're far from round the corner
. . everyone in media centre hot on story of gaining
miles on michel. i said that I waould sail kf how she
wnts to be sailed till the end, and not push her to 120
percent to ctch mich.\if we gain miles it[s greatl, if
not hat's life as we are not in the same weather
conditions . . . talk later ex

The seas were generally pretty horrible and we got really thrown around in those conditions. We were right at the wind limit for the solent too which meant going forward for constant checks. If it came to it, it was a big step down to the staysail, and we'd really stop moving. I lost count of the number of times I dashed up to the foredeck to check it was still OK. Each time I went there was the little challenge of seeing if I could get up there and back without being dumped on by a wave. It was really hard even to walk along the side deck with conditions like that, let alone get there and back quickly. I would get as far as the dagger board standing upright through the deck, wrap my arms around it and hang on for grim death. It was pretty full on but reassuring that we were OK!

Already, just a few days into our new regime and with the water temperature rising quickly, I was feeling the massive pressure of closing miles on Michel.

17/01/01 07:25Z (ellenmacarthur.com/day70)
Well it's been a very frustrating night . . Nothing i
seem to have done will make *Kingfisher* go! It's been a
struggle. I just hope that oour apparrent lack of speed
is a pure illusision, and the position reports show
this, though with the others in a different weather
system now it's doubtful it will eb a gfood indication.

I've changed from 2 reefs and solent to fulll main and
genoa. I've had ballast in and out, i've even lifted up
and down the daggerboard to check there was nothing
caught on it . . . THings seema little better now, but

it's been a long an dtiring period of darknes. Not
helped by the fat that i'm sailing in thick fog - so
despite it not raining, the seond you venture outside
you become soaked with a thin but penetrating mist of
chill! THe high point of the night so far has been the
dolphin which came too join us for a short while, his
smalll dark body leaping from the waves in the misty
darkness . . . It still amazes me each time one of these
creatures comes over to visit. . .

   Quite a contrast to yesterday as we had close reaching
and blue skies for the most part of the day, though
yesterday too started with fickle conditions as we had
30+ knots on the nose for a while. THe forecasts are
subtley changinf daily, and it's our job to be able to
spot each subtelytly as it subtley shows itself!
bye for now, ellen x

But despite the problems we were having with the wind speed
and wave patterns our progress was good, Mich was now less than
200 miles ahead, and stuck doing just 7 knots in the high-pressure
zone of St Helena. We were fairly clear from behind too, as Marc
Thiercelin was over 200 miles behind us. I was still being spurred
on by anger at Mich's remarks and it was the biggest motivation
ever to be gaining miles on him, and above all to see that it was
going to be some time before he could get away to the west. He
was sailing north to the centre of the St Helena high-pressure
system, and as I got closer, the system drifted to the east. He
needed to catch the wind shift to get out to the north, but that shift
was just not coming for him. There was no question of being
happy with the position I was in until that line was crossed; I had
a fire inside me which was pushing me on, and with each day as
we closed on our ultimate destination, it was getting hotter and
hotter.

   There was interesting news from Bilou though – he had anchored
the boat in the little anchorage we had stopped in on our return
from New Zealand and climbed and repaired his mast and was

324

celebrating the fact that he could put his whole mainsail up. It was four weeks since he'd been able to do this and he was hot on Marc's tail. For every skipper in the race, it seemed it was far from over. Even Yves was off once again from his adventure rebuilding his rig in New Zealand.

```
21/01/01 (ellenmacarthur.com/day74)
Position  28° 47.9S  030° 31.1W
Heading/speed  67  11.75
Wind from 357  at 16.1 knots
Pressure of  1013
Sea temperature  21.1
Sail configuration is  1st reef  Solent
Percentage performance  101.1
```

What a night . .
   This mornign the sky looks like a picture postcard – deep pastel-like clouds against a lighteneing blue sky. The night however was not so clement! A couple fo hours after sunset it started, the clouds grew, and suddenly we were surrounded by a group iof particularly ugly ones . . . 6 hours later it was sunriuse and we were out the other side – but what a battle. As the clouds grew nearer the wind increased – it turned through 90 degrees from one cloud to another – the wind went from 17 to 35 knts, and twice in between I had to unfurl the genoa just to keep us moving. I dozed in the cockpit – but many times jumped up like i was on fire as the wind blew like mad – as if from nowhere. Each cloud had it's own charachter – each cloud its own wind. Yesterday we had the same – but it seems different in the day time. THough being sucked under those clouds makes it often feel like dusk. The sky darkens – the horizon is lost in the rain – and the wind blows, and blows . . . The rain so hard that the waves are flattened, so hard you have to squint to see. Often the way is to bear away, adn

Kingfisher takes off like there is air between her and
the water . . . the waves flow away from her bow – almost
like they're unattaached . . Incredible.
   Manging to stay in front of the fornt . . . just hoping
the wind turns back a wee bit into the west. . . .
ellen xx

It was hard work just waiting for the weather front to come over. We had been sailing in grey, foggy conditions, but as the front approached it was possible to see the sky once again, and not only the clouds around it, but also the mass of grey on the distance behind us as the front in the distance crept nearer. Although the front was fairly ominous in its appearance it was a blessing in disguise – the longer we stayed ahead of it the longer we stayed in good breeze. None the less I was looking forward to it passing as we would then be in lighter airs and, more importantly, dry weather. I was still worried about the gennaker I'd been unable to fix and it would be crucial for our crossing of the Equator. I had tried just after Cape Horn, but failed because it wasn't hot enough to burn off the moisture from its surface, making it impossible to work on. The passing of the front was as ugly as ever with changing winds, lightning and just about every other condition you could imagine thrown in, but basically the weather was improving. I was now wearing just a single layer of thermals and even enjoying bare feet – a stark contrast to the Southern Ocean.

This morning feels like a new start, it's incredible
. . . I had a great sleep last night, and at about 0100
set about checking *Kingfisher* all over from head to toe
. . we've had littel wind – and now, thank goodness –
the wind has turned – and it looks like – if 24 hours
eraly we might be able to tack . . . The wind is unsteady
– but erring on the side of northerly . . . During the
night I busied around below emptying water out of all
her compartments (only a few bucketfulls) right up
before her watertight bulkheads, 1 and 2! The motion of

Kingfisher is more silent than ever before . . . the sky
was as open as ever shrouded by a delicate veil of
glittering stars. Despite littel wind we never stoipped
once, and she gently trod across the smooth ocean
surface. THis morning as the sun rose the sky went pink
in the west, and in the easy the striking orange glow
looked like it hid a million treasures as it peeked out
from behind the scattered clouds. Teh clouds themselves
suspended almost as if pre-arranged in the sky . . .
There were layers and layers of them, adn I could not
help but gfeel that there were towns ande villages
hidden among them . . . It really is so very beautiful
. . As I stood in the cockpit I watched in wonder . . .
My eyes began to fill with tears as I marvelled at this
intense beauty, an intense beaauty – which at that
second in time, had only I along wtith that rising sun
as onlookers.
ex

I made the most of the more stable conditions finally to carry out the repair to the gennaker. I dragged it up through the tiny forehatch – it weighed almost 50 kilos – and only then did I realize for the first time the full extent of the damage. There were rips up to 8 yards long, and threads which had broken and pulled out of the fabric fraying the edges like an ugly wound. It took me well over an hour to clean them up, carefully leaving enough fabric to be able to match the edges together, and removing the hair-like fibres that would stop both halves sticking to each other. I painstakingly dried each side of each tear, and began the long process of patching the two sides together, first with 'stitches' of sticky-backed cloth, then with larger pieces. The sun beat down during that day, making work uncomfortable, but I was determined to finish it before the wind increased and became too high to keep the sail on the deck, so I put every bit of energy I had into it. Thirteen hours later, as the evening dew was just beginning to settle on the deck, I was finished. I bore away from the wind, hoisted the sail and furled it.

The final part of the repair had been a large white patch on the leech at the bottom corner of the sail, and the words I had scrawled in capital letters on the fabric were still clear to see in the twilight: 'North Sails – Born to survive'. I smiled – we'd done it.

25/01/01 09:28Z (ellenmacarthur.com/day78)
Another hard night . . . the trades with the lack of consistency of the high pressure are fickle and frustrating, though I'm not complaiinig as it's great to have wind! As I type the wind is blowing from 13 to 17 knots – and though that doesn't sound much – it's the difference between being OK or not for the genoa – so there's little peace! The wind over the past 12 hours has swung iregularly through 50 degrees . . . it really is a full time job to keep her moving well . . . On the other hand it's a lovely mornign – the massive zones of storm clouds have mnelted away in the morning heat . . . Maybe today will be abetter for some sleep. . . .
X

26/01/01 04:14Z (ellenmacarthur.com/day79)
Well the wind has died right off tonight . . we sail along at 9-10 knot's . . . it's frustrating, but I'm hoping it won't last for too long . . maybe the temperature change has brought this on . . . Im not sure. Today has been a day of varied winds, and again – many sail changes, the temperature has increased forther, and sleeping – especially during the day is difficult. It's hard work pulling out and putting in the reefs . . . The 1str reef especauilly as it has the most friction, and incolves lifting the weight of the whole mainsal . . . it's a big reef – the biggest of the three – so takes the wind out of you every time . . . Not made esasier by the heat. It really is a grind, and if the boat isn't bouncing to ease the reefing ennanats through it's almost achieved by half-turns with the pedestal . . .

Despite the exhaustion iin this heat of atually shaking
out the reef - it becomes well worth while as *Kingfisher*
once agiain begins her mission across the waves at her
full potential . . . a great feeling which makes the
breeze flow across her - taking away some of that
continuous heat . . .

It was hard work making progress in the fickle winds, and trying
to sleep in the heat was almost impossible. I covered myself in
cream to protect myself from the sun, but once below, I would
sweat so much I'd end up kneeling in a pool of milky perspiration.
My appetite disappeared as well, and though I am usually quite
good at feeding myself I found all I could eat in the heat was a bowl
of lukewarm couscous. With a seawater temperature of 25 degrees
even the water which came from the desalinator was already warm.
I was tired, and as the Doldrums were coming up was going to need
every ounce of energy.

Tactics were not so complicated here though, as basically the
further west you are, the more quickly you get through the Zone.
In the satellite images the way looked clear, I was 40 miles to the
west of Mich, and so things were looking fairly good. If ever we had
a chance to pass him it was now. I made a conscious decision to
hold on to my position to the west and keep those 40 miles between
us. Unfortunately someone else had different ideas. Two nights
before entry into the Doldrums I was sailing with the repaired
gennaker and full main. We were making great progress and trucking along to the north. The issue was that the nights were strewn
with squalls – and with our delicate gennaker it would no doubt be
one of these which could destroy our repair. I felt nervous, and
found it very difficult to sleep. But things went wrong for us in a
big way that night. The wind instruments at the top of the mast
started to malfunction. This meant that I could not use the autopilots to sail on an 'apparent wind angle' but only on a fixed compass
heading. It was a nightmare as it meant we weren't at all respon-
sive to changes in the wind direction. If ever the gennaker was
going to break it would be by being hit by a squall before I could make

it to the helm. I tried using the spare instruments we had on a pole on the back of the boat, but they were not sensitive enough for the light, changeable winds we were in. I would have to steer by hand.

I spent most of the night hand-steering and watching out for the demon clouds which bring strong breezes with them, and preparing for yet another climb up the mast. To the top once again, this time to replace her wind wand that held her anemometer.

26/1/01 16:15Z (ellenmacarthur.com/day79)
What better to take your mind off a race than a bit of early morning DIY? . . . Yes that sounds great, but what will it involve? Mmm. Now a bit of sanding, and quite a lot of drilling – oh yes, and a bit of wiring. Fantastic – when can I start . . . . Straight away, but unfortunately your workdshop is at 27 meters!
Yes ellen was once again up the mast this morning – will she ever shake this habit! During the night I expereinced problems with the wind instruments, the boat taxkeds herself due to a lack of wind data, and I quickly deduced that the anemometer was tired . . It's amazing how imperative that wind data is to us . . . Things have meoved on from looking at the wooly telltales and the clouds – wind speeds and angles are imperative to fast sailing, and sail limits – so it was change over the anemeoeter time . . As usualk a beautiful calm sunrise turned into a gusty bit of sea once I'd reached half way . . . I nmust have looked fairly silly as I had a long wand strapped to my back, and a massive bag of tools . . . (it's a bit far to come down if you've forgotton something!) It went OK other than the violent motion, and the amount of sanding needed to fit the wand. THe most frustrating part was the first time I fitted it – just to see how far it went in – and I couldn't get it out again! Once fitted I had to drill out for the retaining pin – quite a task juggling drill bt's and drills at 27m! THe painful part

was the slamming in the waves, causing the bag with
drill in poking into my leg . . the beautiful part was
taking just a second to galnce out over that orange sea
scape as the sun rose . . . The waters surface so
delicate as the waves texture it . . . Just stunning . . .
   Well its nice to be becak down again, and despit a few
holes and brusies we're on good form. Well Mark did say
it's about time I went back up the meast again . . .
Thanks mark!
love ellen

I was overjoyed to have new instruments, and had a great day
with the gennaker. But the worst was far from over. Just as I was
looking forward to my last real opportunity to sleep in the cool of
the night before the Doldrums, the instruments failed again. I was
distraught, and sick inside. This time it was not going to be so easy
to see the lighter side. I spent another tiring night hand-steering
with the gennaker up, forcing myself to keep my eyes open in that
hot breeze with the intermittent stars lighting our decks as the
squall clouds passed. Several times we were completely surrounded
by clouds, the wind dying and then hurling back at us, and the
thunder, lightning and cool rain helping enormously to keep me
alert. It is a strange feeling in those battles through the rain storms.
It's almost as though you are transported to another world with the
rain powering down on the water – the lightning and darkness and
the hot and the cold gusts of wind that pelt the rain at you. Then
suddenly, nothing, just the sounds of the water running off the
decks then passing the hull; no rain, just an agitated silence . . . till
that next crack of thunder.
   At first light the following morning I undertook yet another mast
climb. This time it should have been easier: I changed the circuit
board in the wind vane before I climbed, prepared my tools, furled
the gennaker, then set off on that journey taking me once again to
the furthest point I could get from *Kingfisher*'s deck in eighty days.
   The climb went well and the vane changeover was relatively
straightforward. But as I worked away I noticed a squall cloud

heading towards us. With it the wind increased and *Kingfisher* heeled over, her side-decks echoing with the sounds of the sea pounding along them. I had no option – I had to finish the job and get down. The rain began to fall, and I tried my best to keep the wires I was joining from getting wet, but it was virtually impossible. The stronger wind didn't cause undue problems though, what really sent my heartbeat racing were the light airs that immediately followed the squall. The less sensitive instruments on the back of the boat that were now steering us couldn't pick up the soft breeze and, confused, forced us to gybe. Although we had only a few knots of wind I knew that any moment the wind would come back strongly after the cloud, and the mainsail swung across the boat, jamming my legs between the runners and the sail. I forced the sail back over with my feet but each time it would gybe back again, trapping my legs. My mind went into overdrive, but I knew that I had no control over the situation; over 90 feet from the deck there was nothing I could do except just try to finish the job. The adrenalin was rushing through me, causing my arms to tremble as I fumbled to connect the wires. I tried to ignore the pain in my legs. If the wind came back now I would be in real danger – 20 knots of wind from the wrong direction would mean that the top of the mast would be pushed down to the water, and, though it didn't really bear thinking about, I would be underneath it.

I think that was the moment during the entire race when I felt the most scared, because my fate was entirely out of my own hands. Even when I was hanging from the rig with one hand in the south I was in control – either I let go or I didn't, but I still had a choice. Here I had none.

When I eventually got back to the deck I was shaking from head to toe, and black and blue as a result of two mornings thrashing around up there. I called Mark to let him know what had happened, then slept almost comatose for an hour or so before pulling out the gennaker once more.

As we approached the Equator I was catching up on Michel literally hour by hour, and watching the position reports eagerly, but while up the mast the day before and later recovering sleep, I had lost the 40 miles of longitude I'd had in the bag and was downright angry with myself for that. Why oh why did we have those problems now? Just a couple of days later and the outcome of the Vendée Globe could have been very different.

On 28 January I was just 26 miles behind Mich, and catching him. We crossed the Equator at 0907, and in light winds beneath an overcast sky I made my offering. I threw my second-to-last packet of ginger nuts over the side and thanked Neptune for letting us pass safely, finishing off my thanks with *'Thank you for putting Mich in a windless hole; I know that's not nice; but thanks.'*

That afternoon the wind died again and we began a forty-eight-hour fight to extract ourselves from the Doldrums. It was hot, frustrating sailing and I knew that I was absolutely worn out. I spoke to Mark.

It's so fluky. It's scary. I just want the wind to steady, it won't stay still for more than 3 minutes . . . oh @£!$%$ . . . the wind has switched, the genoa is flapping. I've got to tack again I think . . .

[several minutes later] This is so hard. I'm going 3 knots. When the wind changes the boat can't easily steer around it, even hand-steering, it's impossible. It's not easy . . . It's really not easy. There is no real weather information, we're just fighting for each mile, and hoping the Doldrums will move and let us through. You feel if you see the genoa flap one more time you're going to pull your hair out. The problem is we don't have any breeze to get anywhere, we've made our choice . . . the wind has swung again . . . unbelievable . . . it's been like this all night . . .

The following morning, and after what was probably the worst night, I took the lead in the race. I called Mark for the radio sched that morning not knowing the news. I was curled up on the chart table seat and when he told me I managed to smile, but I was so tired I could barely speak. I knew that I was slightly further to the east than Mich and that it would be a miracle if I popped out first, which was a real damper on the news. My comment to Mark was 'Sorry – you're going to have a busy day, aren't you?', then the wind shifted, and it was time to tack once more. When we left the Doldrums Mich had already pulled out a 40-mile lead on us, so *Kingfisher* and I made a pact together that we would sail just that bit faster and draw a couple of miles in each day. As long as the race was not over neither was our hope.

We had made our bed but we were not happy to be lying in it and now was the time just to get on with it, I kept telling myself. We were going to give it all we had to catch the white boat in front. Spirits were up, mentally I had thrown down the gauntlet and was pleased to be taking on the race again – it was as if we had just restarted it.

We were pushing on, desperate to make up the miles to Mich, but now, since popping into the lead, however briefly, the phone was ringing off the wall with requests for interviews and video chats via satellite – mainstream UK had woken to the race but we had not crossed the finish line yet, could we please get on?

We were making a reasonable fight of chasing Mich, and *Kingfisher* was fit and revelling in the breezes away from the Doldrums. I took a moment in the cuddy to rest as the sun went down, then my head was smashed violently against the bulkhead and the peaceful evening air was ripped by a horrific splitting sound. We had hit something hard and stopped dead in the water.

Looking behind from the cockpit I saw the tip of the rudder and the daggerboard floating away. My first reaction was fuelled by pure adrenalin, and I tore through the boat checking every compartment to check there was no water flooding in. I could hear my heart beating so loud that it was not even worth swearing to vent my fears. A quick check showed there was no water coming in. I grabbed the endoscope, fumbling to get it out of the box, and through the valve in the bottom of the boat – I pressed my eye to its rim – I could see no damage, thank goodness, and the keel looked OK. My mind switched from pure survival back towards racing. I could see one side of the daggerboard swaying pathetically from side to side below us and I knew I would have to get it out as it was slowing us down badly as it dragged through the water. I returned to the cockpit and tacked over, leaving the water ballast on the wrong side so I could check *Kingfisher*'s rudder. She heeled over erratically as her keel was to leeward, but I got a good look at the rudder – the tip was broken, but otherwise it seemed OK. As I tacked back, I slipped on a book full of photos of Derbyshire I'd been given for Christmas. Just few minutes earlier I'd been reading – transported to a very different world. I couldn't retrieve the last of the daggerboard, it seemed stuck, so I tacked back, and made a call home to tell Mark what had happened and to get the designers together in a conference call so we could discuss the best plan. I was worried for the rudder more than anything else. We had a spare but it would not be easy to change, and I wanted to hear the guys say that they thought it would be OK. It was a massive problem as we had several days of sailing upwind to the Azores high and although hopefully *Kingfisher*'s hull and structure were still sound we were definitely going to be without one of our daggerboards. Without it protruding vertically below the hull to stabilize us we would slide steadily sideways, losing miles on Mich, and maybe if things were really against us, let the others through on our inside. I was beyond frustration, I just had to deal with it.

The first task after we'd established that all should be OK was to get the damaged board out of its case. We were sailing a third slower than we should have been, which I had to stop as soon as possible. The problem was that each time I tacked over I was sailing at 90 degrees to the route I wanted to take, and would be losing miles to Mich, just as if I was standing still. When I tacked again to do the job I was on a mission! It took over an hour to remove the board as it had been rammed back into its case on impact, and by the time I had solved it I had sworn more than during the whole race put together! I had rigged a pulley on the front of the boat, and passed a rope around the board with a boathook beneath her. This allowed me to winch the board forward, but annoyingly the rope cut on to the damaged carbon and became almost impossible to move. Bit by bit I winched the rope out of the board and started again . . . we had to do this, there really was no option. Finally, after breaking the up-haul rope and attaching a halyard directly to the top of the board, I had loosened it enough to remove it from its case.

I left it in there for the time being – at least it was out of the water.

After tacking back it was already dark, and after a further chat with Merv I prepared my tools and set about trying to get some sleep. I was still exhausted from the Doldrums and I had to have my wits about me to get this done.

At first light I began the task of refeeding the broken ropes in the strut which is used to lift and drop the board – it wasn't easy poking fishing line and weights down a tube the right side of a pulley as it was blowing 25 knots and waves were washing down the deck, but I managed it. By far the hardest part though was removing the board from the starboard side and finding the emergency pulleys which were hidden in its structure. They had been designed so that they could go into the other case, but being asymmetric they would have to go in upside down. It was going to be a very nasty job but even so, little did I know how much it was going to take out of me.

I struggled for three hours trying to get the board from its case as each time I tried winching on the halyard it jammed just milli-metres from coming out. I jiggled it and winched, and tried attaching blocks to the mast – but all I succeeded in doing was destroying the bracket for the radar and driving myself mad! Each time I climbed 20 or so feet up the mast to shift the block or move the bracket. Conditions were horrible and I was tired.

It was taking my nerves well beyond where they wanted to go, it wasn't shifting, and I had the feeling I was continually taking steps back. I punched it, kicked it and shouted at it, and finally after at least five hours' work it popped out, spinning and whacking me on the side of my head in the process.

The first job was to lay it on the deck to find the pulleys, but even that was easier said than done as it was covered in a graphite compound which made it slide hopelessly everywhere and if it fell over the side I really would be in trouble. I lashed it hastily to the deck in a way which certainly would not have won me any prizes, then set about trying to shield the drill from the waves to find the pulleys. The two board ends were not exactly the same shape and in the repairing of them I had lost the small imprints showing the internal tubes. Drilling holes in the boards would undoubtedly

336

weaken their structure, so I was only going to get one shot at this. Each time *Kingfisher* went over a big wave I withdrew the drill for fear of breaking the bit as we hammered down into the wave, but it was a long task, and a frustrating one as it seemed to take forever to find the holes. Once I'd found the pulley I had to file away the remaining carbon and it felt like sacrilege just hacking away at this perfect and functional board. Meanwhile, the damaged one was lying on the foredeck where I had laid it, and I could hear it begin to wear away at everything around it.

I must have looked like a coalminer at this stage as I was covered in carbon dust and cuts, and my eyes stung, raw with the fibres that had blown into them. As I worked away I was hurting, suffering acutely each time I saw what a mess *Kingfisher* was in and how helpless she seemed. That helplessness was reflected by me too – I was shedding tears of frustration and physically there was little left inside me. I was fighting with a 12-foot board which weighs more than your average man and which refused to stay still while all the time crashing through 20 to 25 knot waves. I was struggling.

Finally, by sunset, I had the board back in the port case and we were sailing on it once again. The cockpit seats were covered with the drill, now taped into a plastic bag, files, hammers and tape. Poor *Kingfisher*, she'd been dragged through it once again. After all we had been through she didn't deserve it. She had looked after me so well, and then this happened. For the first time in the race we were faced with something we had no chance of ever fixing out at sea. It's amazing what can be fixed, but this was a solid piece of her which was smashed to bits, and we were going to have to finish the race like that. I felt as if I had let her down, I couldn't repair her, we had worked so hard together to look after each other, and we'd arrived at this point where nothing I could do would really help.

As for our distance from Mich, I was livid. We were now 76 miles behind . . .

I feel very sad to see the damage. It breaks my heart, I've tried so hard to look after her, and to win the race. The rudder, there is nothing I can do about, its out of sight and out of mind really. But lying on the foredeck is a very broken dagger board, and there are black marks all over the deck where the board was crashing around when I was trying to move it. I know the board which is down now isn't working 100 per cent because it is the wrong way, and that's pretty hard . . . you have to try to put it out of your mind and race like before but . . . it never really goes away. Something like that will never leave for the rest of your life. To hit something so hard. After all the energy we have put in, it's just pretty frustrating . . .

I will just try to do the best that I can. I promised that . . . can I still catch PRB? Big question. I don't think there's much chance of hitting something. Anything can happen, absolutely anything can happen. For sure with the problems we've had there is a loss of performance, but very much in my own mind, the race is still on. I'm looking ahead at Mich and at the guys behind, and I promised myself I wouldn't give up until we passed that finish line . . . am I allowed to swear?!!

I was glad that we were in the trade winds now to give me some chance to catch up on sleep and try to prepare myself for the breeze we would have after the high. Things were relatively simple tactically: we had to sail into the Azores high-pressure system, then out on to the sleigh ride back to France. During our repairs we had lost 25 miles to Mich, and it was frustrating to see wild speculation as to why we had lost the miles on Mich flying around. We had simply decided not to make our collision public until I knew that the repair was achievable and completed.

01/02/01 03:34Z (ellenmacarthur.com/day85)
It has been a bit of a 24 hours, and as I sit here I'm glad that it's over. Today was one of the hardest in the race for me, fighting — when you're struggling to find what's in you to fight. The good news is that the starboard board is bow in the port side, after a nightmare 9 hours of battles with pulleys, lines, drills and files! The board weighs more than I do, and shifting it around in 20 knots upwind wasn't easy — nor dry!

Oh Mark, as I reached the end of your mail I had tears in my eyes. The last 4 years have been the most

incredible adventure I could ever have wished to
expereice. When I thihnnk how much I have learned I feel
so very grateful to you .. THinking back to the first
time we really talked in your office seems like a
lifetime away . . . it's incredible . . .

Thanks so much for supporting me over the past 2 days.
Solving that problem was I think the hardest challenge
so far in the race. And above all striking at a time
when we were below par, and trying to recover. Thank you
for being there, thank you for organizing everything so
clearly and coolly – when your head was probably in as
much of a spin as mine.

I know it's not long till the finish, and I know that
we'll have to dig deeper still and push harder, but
also, and we've known this from the first time we worked
together – that it will be more than worth it, and our
blood, sweat and tears (and those of the team) have been
some of the best spent ever – I just hope that everyone
will feel this, even partially as strongly as we do.

As far as Mich is concerned I know it's far from over.
Wc shall see – I may be ide of the mark. I shall not try
to do anything other than my own race. What shall happen
will happen, and I'm not giving up . . . I'm not ready to
gover up till I've crossed that line. We've all worked
to hard for giving up.

What ever happens I do know that the project has been
a success, that we havve touched millions. For the forst
time in my life the media thing sc ares me. TO have some
privacy is important to me, but I know it will be OK,
and in a way the baord probalem was a godsend because it
took my mind off worrying about the finish.

Though I know, that the moment you hug me, that you
will look after me, and Mark – that is one of the
biggest comforts I have right now. Thank you for
everything, for ebing the best friend and companion . . .
Never doubt yourself Mark, you're f****** awesome too

. . . And don't doubt that I am in a very qualified
position to say that. I'm looking forward very much to
being with you, laughing with you and almost above all
working with you once again. We make the best team Mark.
always exx

It was quite obvious from the vibes I was getting through from Mark and the interviews that I was already doing that things ashore were changing fairly dramatically. In France any finish of a Vendée Globe is big news, and I was half prepared for that, but I was increasingly aware of how the story was developing in the UK, and internationally too, and now, less than ten days from the finish, it was hard to prepare for it mentally. The e-mails coming in could not have been more diverse, and the encouragement that people were offering was just second to none. I was completely and utterly bowled over. It was a strange position to be in because although I knew damn well that life would be turned on its head in a few days' time, I still had to put 100 per cent of my efforts into getting to that line as fast as possible. The race was still winnable.

One of the few e-mails I received from home came towards the end of the race.

Sent: Friday, February 02, 2001 17:35
Subject: Home

Hope all is well there and you have managed to recoup
some sleep to build up some energy. Had a strange
experience today. There was a knock on the door and I
thought it might be another reporter wanting photographs
so I had my words ready. Standing on the doorstep was a
'lifelong sailor' wanting to show his admiration for
what you are doing and gave me some flowers. I had to
prize a name out of him which I have found in the
directory. Tonight I will ring him and thank him again
and send him one of your posters. There is a feeling of
tension, excitement and expectation here. Take care – I

can't express my feelings right now – I'm a bit full.
Love as always – will you thank the team for cushioning
me from the truth. Mum

04/02/01 07:29Z (ellenmacarthur.com/day88)
I had the weirdest experience yesterday evening – a sand
storm! Suddenly it was raining sand, the whole deck was
brown. It was on the sails, the ropes, everything.
Africa feels a long way away, but I guess this came from
Morocco.

I have been working quite hard on a long jobs list,
making sure everything is done before we attack the area
of light winds ahead. I've re-spliced the spinnaker
sheets, re-stitched a few strops and even cleaned the
deck. I wish I could get the black marks out though, I
hate it when she's not looking perfect.

Had the best night's sleep for a long time last night.
Lots of 70-minute naps, with a few 20-minute ones as
well. Fantastic! The wind was quite steady, on a clear
night, with stars everywhere.

This next 48 hours is going to be decisive – the last
chance for anyone to pass I think. We seem to have been
keeping our distance on Bilou though he's been climbing
slightly on both of us, but thats probably due to a
better wind angle out in the west. Tring get a bit of
separation from Mich by sailing a bit closer to the wind
– at least I'm not just following his tracks. We'll see
whether it makes any difference – this shouldn't be as
bad as the Doldrums, but in every unstable wind mass
there are always chances.

As we approached the Azores high-pressure system there was
more morale-boosting news. Once again the number of miles
between us and Mich was coming down. At the time he tacked to
clear the system we were just 15 miles behind – and although once
again he was going to get away first, the gap was now smaller. We

just had to hang in there and sail the best race we could. In the light winds I swapped the broken daggerboard from one side of the boat to the other, an almost military procedure which took a fifth of the time in the flat sea and with the knowledge I had gained. I then dropped the broken board into its old socket so that the decks were once again clear, and with out of sight being in some ways out of mind, I felt a lot better to see her looking more normal once again. I was going to be needing that board in the reaching conditions heading out of the Azores high, but in the meantime I was going to profit from the light airs to try to sleep and tidy *Kingfisher* so that she looked as smart as she could for the finish.

The following afternoon she was sailing beautifully in a very light north-easterly breeze. I spent an hour or so trying to remove the black marks from her deck and cleaning the marks from around her exhaust pipe. I put electrical tape around her broken board to protect myself from its serrated edges, and tidied any fraying rope ends. Each time I looked at her broken board I felt my stomach turn. At least we should not be needing it between now and the finish.

That afternoon I sat in the bow beneath the most beautiful blue sky and talked to the video camera, just thanking everyone for all they had done to get us out there for the race. I talked about the situation at the finish and how I did not know what to expect. I said that I wished the race did not have to finish, and that it had been the most incredible experience of my life. There was an unbelievable quietness and tranquillity about that whole moment – no breeze, not even wind blowing on the camera microphone – my words spoken softly but clearly to the lens.

Just twenty-four hours later we had left the high-pressure system, and the wind was already increasing as the storm which was about to propel us to the finish approached. Now, within a week of the finish, communications were more often by phone than by e-mail.

07/02/09 09:22Z (ellenmacarthur.com/day91)
I had the first good sleep for a while last night.
Yesterday was once of my worst days, I was so tired,
and I couldn't pull myself out of it. Every small thing

became a big problem in my head. But last night I reduced sail a bit, the sea state forced us to do that anyway, and sailed all night with two reefs and the small staysail. And managed to sleep a number of hours in total, although I woke every thirty minutes or so to check everything was OK.

The really good news is that I am on to a new chart – and it shows the finish and even the Shetland Islands! Even better, I'm nearly a third of the way up the chart towards Les Sables now. In my mind, we are on the last stretch now, but it's still 1,000 miles. I don't think they are going to be easy ones either.

I've had from 17 to 33 knots during the night, which makes for some pretty exciting and nerve-racking moments as the wind picks up and the boat just goes in to turbo-mode surfing, almost out of control at up to 25 knots. There is water crashing everywhere, and the noise is deafening.

Got to go – looks like my lashing on the radar, broken during the dagger-board removal exercise, has come loose . . . the radar is hanging down . . . got to try to save it. ex

It was physically hard going with the changing winds, and the ever-increasing pressure of Mich being ahead of us. It almost seemed that with each day as we neared the finish life on board got harder. But the strong winds were in many ways good news as I found myself absorbed in looking after *Kingfisher*, spending a lot of time on deck making sure there were no problems developing. It's very easy in the rough weather to sit below in the warmth of the cabin and let your boat hammer along in the waves, but I could never let myself do this. If *Kingfisher* began to feel uncomfortable, then so did I, and I would be out like a flash either to reef or down or change her angle to the waves a little to see if it made a difference. Often I would find myself giving her a pat on her coach-roof or crying out 'Go, girl! You can do it!' as she took off across the waves. We were

343

on a mission, sailing as fast as we could – Mich was 122 miles ahead – but we still had over 1,000 miles to go. The race was far from over and we were far from giving up.

The outside world was unaware of what was going on when at 1722 on Wednesday, 7 February, *Kingfisher*'s genoa forestay broke: one of two fixed cables which stop the mast from falling backwards, and crucial to its rigidity. Though less dramatic than the collision with the container, it was actually the biggest threat so far to our completion of the race. Not finishing at all became an appalling possibility and I was as wounded by the damage as *Kingfisher* was physically. This was about the worst thing that had happened as it removed the mast's structural integrity. It had not fallen down, but would remain a risk we were going to have to live with until we finished the race. The strength of the lashings on the sail held the stay in place, but the 90-foot carbon mast had lost one third of its forward lateral support and we would be unable to use one of our most important sails or sail at 100 per cent again.

I was completely devastated. With the ominous bang as the stay broke went the last of our chances of beating Mich in the Vendée Globe and barring something unbearable happening to him, we now had no choice but to limp across the finish line, preserving *Kingfisher*'s crippled rig in the hope that we could stay ahead of Bilou. But if the mast tumbled we would lose virtually all hope of hanging on to our second place in the Vendée Globe or of finishing the race at all. It felt as though someone had taken my feet away from under me.

Those final four days of the race were among the most draining mentally. For over twenty-four hours I sailed with two reefs in the main and the solent, with half the sail area we should have had up. We were sailing no faster than a boat of half *Kingfisher*'s size, as she wallowed in the waves she should have been surfing down. It was killing me.

I knew that it would be a risk to set more sail, and that if we unfurled the power of the gennaker, each gust could pose a fatal threat to the mast, but I just couldn't handle it any longer.

There was little rationale in my decision to go for the gennaker.

344

The new depression was on its way, which would take us into the finish line, but I was determined to be as close behind Michel as I could be. After a final call to the mast manufacturers I climbed up on deck and unfurled the sail, and as I sheeted it in to harness the wind *Kingfisher* took off through the water. I sighed and yelled out loud with relief and delight as she leapt forward again.

Those final days blended fairly much into one powering downwind past Finisterre and into the Bay of Biscay. There were ships around too, a welcome sight, briefly reminding me of my days up in Hull on the River Humber. There was an aeroplane too, which flew over to take pictures, a weird experience as we hurtled down the waves towards the finish – it dipped its wings as it flew over for the final time and I realized it had been a long time since I'd seen a human gesture.

During the final days I received a long and touching e-mail from Catherine Chabaud. She was lying in seventh position, and had said that she felt the pace of this race was extreme, but she was glad to have been out there again. Later on, she too broke a stay on her mast. Cruelly, she was instantly dismasted and though just a few hundred miles from the finish line was unable to finish the race. A pointed reminder of what could have happened to us.

I felt excited, but at the same time more and more claustrophobic as we closed the French shore. There was a pain that was hurting more and more inside me; mentally I was washed out, physically I was spent, and in a few hours' time Michel Desjoyeaux would cross the finish line, taking first place in the 2000/2001 Vendée Globe Race. There would soon be only one winner of the race my life had revolved around for the last four years, and no matter how hard we tried it was not to be us. I spoke to Mark about the arrangements, but we both pretty much avoided talking about Mich's finish – it was imminent, but it just seemed something that mustn't matter any more. When I called Ian later, however, I could not hold back my emotions any longer. I began angrily blaming myself for all that had gone wrong, and wishing that we could wind back time and start again from our position a few hundred miles south of the Equator. If only I could relive those moments with hindsight! For the first time in the race Ian just didn't seem to understand me, we couldn't connect, and as I ranted down the phone I heard the fireworks going off for Mich's arrival and realized that it was not just me who had lost the race – we all had. Ian's despair though put me back on an even keel because this time I realized *he* needed *my* support.

Somehow the pain disintegrated once Mich had finished the race. I was 243 miles behind him and now I was glad that I had those miles. Suddenly I felt all the richer for still being out there on this beautiful, wild ocean. Our battle was over, we just had to sail home. There were no tactical decisions to make, nor was there any competition close on our heels. Bilou was 400 miles behind us after a difficult crossing of the Azores high. We now had a light breeze coming in from the north, and a strikingly flat sea. I walked along *Kingfisher*'s deck checking everything and noticed that the starboard bow light was not working. I went below and dug out a bulb, taking the screwdriver with me to remove the waterproof cover. I wanted her to look her best for the finish. I was sitting there on her pulpit when I heard that familiar clicking sound, and looked down into the water to see the glowing shapes of a pair of dolphins. I squeaked with excitement and laughed out loud as they played so magnificently beneath *Kingfisher*'s bow.

As I sat there soaking in what was around me, I looked up at a beautiful starlit sky, a gigantic blanketed dome that was somehow protecting us as it had for the previous ninety-three days. I was sure I could see more stars than ever before in my life, and as I watched *Kingfisher*'s tall mast glide beneath them I leaned forward and laid my cheek against the cool, damp fabric of her furled genoa swaying unnaturally on its stay. If ever there was a moment which got close to summing up what we had been through, this was it.

To try to stop the tears I hung my head over her pulpit to watch the dolphins, but before their streamlined shapes appeared again I saw only the reflection of the most beautiful boat in the world. She felt more like home to me than any place I had lived in during the previous seven years, and of the past twelve months I had spent well over six at sea with her. I gave up trying to resist and cried with sheer pleasure, watching my tears fall to the water's surface. If ever there was a heaven then surely I must be there.

346

My feet barely touched the pontoon as we headed towards the crowds. I was packed in amongst hundreds of journalists, many of whom I knew, but the faces were too blurred to make out. I could see there were several large guys around me wearing Kingfisher jackets. I figured they must be the bodyguards I'd been forewarned about, though it seemed odd that I didn't even know their names. One of them was by my side and had his arm around me; he began to speak to me and although I don't remember his words, which were drowned in the madness, they were kind, and considering the situation seemed remarkably friendly. I could sense the tension in his voice, however, and realized that he was physically shaking. I turned to look at his face, and saw the stressed expression in his eyes which managed a brief glance at me before returning to their job. He held me so tightly that I could barely breathe as we were squeezed along those few hundred yards of pontoon. I had never been under close protection before.

As we hurried along I was acutely conscious that *Kingfisher* was behind me. When my hand slipped away from her cool, damp, rounded gunwale I knew it was all over. We had made it, but it was over.

I was suddenly immersed in a world which had clearly been racing along during my absence, but which I had grown away from. I saw *Iduna* tied up alongside and tried to stop, but this exodus of people was something I could not control. Within seconds I was whisked away once again. As we stepped on to dry ground for the first time, to be honest I did not even notice, my feet were hardly touching the ground as it was. We passed the gangways up towards the Vendée Globe village and I heard, then saw, the crowds of people collected along the railings. I was conscious that my eyes were still quite red, but I was comforted by the fact that I could still see *Kingfisher*. There were a few people around her, but most had left. I felt so sad that she was down there – how could I abandon her like that? She was alone.

As we walked to the stage people were shouting and screaming, then the crowd went wild as I was directed up the steps. All I could do was wave and smile – I felt completely out of place and quite lost as the microphone was passed to me. *Kingfisher* was not there with me. I could not hold a part of her, nor climb inside her for security. Here on the stage, waiting to be interviewed, I felt truly alone too.

The lights shining on me were so bright that I couldn't see the hundreds of thousands of people before me properly. There was a video wall behind me showing my face that must have been ten times my height, and every emotion I showed was there for all to see. As the questions began I thought about the welcome I had enjoyed. I felt indebted to everyone there, to every single person who had come to see me that night. We started in French, then I was asked if I'd like to say a word to the many English people present. As I talked I glanced at *Kingfisher*. I could see the tiny strobe light flashing on top of her mast, as if she was trying to tell me she was OK. My eyes filled with tears and my voice began to break. I smiled to the crowd, waved my thanks, then turned away back down the steps.

I now had my first chance to see my family, but we were behind schedule, and the press conference was waiting. It seemed bizarre to be spending so little time with those I loved after so long away, but although it was precious, it also seemed unreal. I realized how apart from theirs my life had grown over the previous three months. I stood there in my thermals, boots and oilskin trousers, with no wallet, money or mobile phone. My hands still had sores on them, and I had not really washed for three months. Mum gave me a letter from Gran which took me straight back to Derbyshire as I read it.

As I write this letter I do not know the winner of the Vendée Globe Race. In my heart there is only one winner – you, dearest Ellen. Your determination and courage have touched the hearts of the public worldwide. Sorry I cannot be with you on this memorable occasion. I will be with you in spirit and look forward to our hug and kiss later.

Just before leaving I got a phone call from the Prime Minister. Everything and nothing seemed odd at this stage, I seemed to be living in a bubble looking out at all that was passing before me. I was waiting on Mark to tell me when I had to be where; having no idea of what was going on, a stark contrast to just hours ago, I felt helplessly reliant on others. On the way to the press conference I asked if I could go to the toilet and remember sitting down, putting my head on my knees and taking several deep breaths. I sighed with relief at the momentary quiet I had found, and smiled at the alarming comfort; it was the first time I'd sat on a toilet seat for three months.

Two days later I witnessed my first ever Vendée arrival as several of us went out in our RIB. Bilou was storming towards the finish line, having just broken the single-handed twenty-four-hour speed record. I shall never forget seeing his tiny sail appearing over the horizon, then, as he neared, the look of pure joy on his face. There were boats everywhere to see him in, and the sound of Breton pipes blew out across the water. As he entered the channel in broad daylight you could see the sheer number of people lining the walls and cheering him on. He stood on the bow of his bright red boat with his son, each of them holding a flare. In the RIB with us was a French journalist, Yves Pelissier, who had headed up that first 'A donf' interview in Plymouth. He turned to me and said, 'You must look after Mark too.' At the time I'm not sure his remark really registered, but in hindsight I know that he knew how things were – he'd covered every Vendée.

Just before Bilou reached the pontoon, we picked up the family from the shore and pulled alongside his boat. Dad called to him and he came over to the side of the boat. Bilou leaned over to shake Dad's hand, and Dad reached up and hugged him as if he had known him all his life. I'm not even sure they had spoken before. He's a very special man is Roland Jourdain. Mich, an old friend of Bilou's, was there too, and as *Sill* crept along the channel we boarded her together and lifted Bilou high up on to our shoulders.

Since the finish, Mich and I had spoken several times and his words at his press conference when he was asked what he thought of the 'petite Ellen' were very touching as he pondered aloud that 'he was not sure what he had been doing for the past ten years'. The anger I had channelled towards him during the race was gone. And later in the year he approached me and apologized for adding fuel to the rumours that I'd had outside assistance. It meant a lot to hear it, although at the time Ian had told me the shock was probably the saving of me. It was something which had eaten away at me and I was glad to be able to put it to rest.

With the end of the Vendée, it wasn't by any means just my life which had been altered. The day after the finish two scathing and groundless articles about Mark appeared in the French press. The headlines implied that I was the innocent Ellen, who was basically being 'managed' by the 'monsters'. It hurt us all to read those words; and seeing the pain in Mark's tired eyes at a time when he should have been euphoric was tragic. Throughout the entire race and the years running up to it we had looked forward to the months after the Vendée when we could celebrate, laugh and have fun together without the stress of the race around us. But now that time had come Mark and I were not able to share in the success. Although for me this feeling was numbed by the constant stream of engagements and travelling, I hadn't had time to stop to think what the repercussions would be. I was fire-fighting, and for the time being far from pro-active in my thoughts or actions. For Mark though this was an unmistakably raw deal: his Vendée Globe had been taken away and he had been faced with an impossible mission – trying to cater for everyone, trying to do the right thing when twice the demands we could physically achieve were being made of us. He was speaking incessantly in two languages, and all this when like me he was totally and utterly exhausted.

I was amazed by the things which went on during those few days of media frenzy – we desperately wanted the world to know what was going on, but that undoubtedly came at a price. I recall a rare occasion out walking with him when for the third time he was trying to tell a film crew that they could not follow me round for the day. It was two days after my finish and I had spent no more than an hour with my family. They seemed not to understand that I needed time in private with them; surely that would go without saying? Suddenly I had the impression that my life, and increasingly the lives of those around me, were beginning to be at the beck and call of others. As from this moment life had well and truly changed.

Our arrival back in the UK with *Kingfisher* was a complete shock to my system. I had imagined a few boats might be there to meet us, but was aghast as chartered ferries, choppers and tugs came out to see us in. As we headed up Southampton Water the guys at the oil terminal let the sirens off as we passed, and waved from the jetties; I was really touched by that and gave them the biggest wave I could. 'Welcome home lass,' I said, and patted *Kingfisher*'s bow.

The sides of the marina were lined with people, many of them waving little Kingfisher flags. I stood on the foredeck, and as I had done in Les Sables, I lit a flare to say a thousand thanks to all who had come. There were many familiar faces, all smiling and cheering, and one of them I could not miss – it was Brian Pilcher, whose enthusiasm when I first presented my plans to sail round Britain had made such an impression. I jumped from the boat and ran straight into his arms. He was there with his daughter and three-year-old granddaughter who, despite the excitement on offer, was unimpressed by anything but my weathered yellow salopettes. Her only comment: 'Nice dungarees'!

During the next few days I could feel I was exhausted, fit to drop – a state I would spend most of the year in. I was living off adrenalin to fuel the smiles and the energy for the interviews and somehow managing to carry on, functioning on little sleep, and delivering my thoughts to cameras from Germany to the States. Ian was brilliant, travelling round with me and giving Mark a chance to try to cope with the immense pressures we were under to meet the demands on us.

Although I should have grabbed this time to take a holiday, I found it impossible to tear myself away. Every few days there were boats finishing, and I had promised myself to be there to see in as many as I could. Ian and I took more flights from Nantes to London than most people would take in a lifetime – it was madness. We saw a triumphant Mike Golding finish an incredible seventh after all he had been through, sailing up to the fleet and overtaking shortly before, two other 60s. There was Yves, who finished thirteenth with his impressive-looking repaired mast. As I climbed on board to sail up the channel with him, his family and team, he let me taste some of the seaweed he had dried for his trip back; it wasn't that bad – it was just the texture that was awful. An incredible story!

Each time I dropped into the office I would find another enormous pile of press cuttings. I couldn't believe that people were writing so much. The requests were flooding in, as was news of everything from beer to mountains being named after me – even a sweet pea which reminded me of my granddad who had taken such pride in his own sweet peas. There were all sorts of articles appearing in newspapers, from 'Ellen to be millionaire' to a surreal piece claiming I had been stalked by a man who had swum around the globe after me! I was asked repeatedly about Ian and my family, and Mum and Dad had to get used to having journalists calling the house and turning up on the doorstep. I have to say that they were very brave about it all, but my intention was never to involve them in this, nor to become famous myself. I am just very much in love with my sport, and want desperately to be better at it.

One afternoon I managed a quick trip to an edit studio to see a rough cut of the documentary being made by the BBC. There was silence as they ran through the first version of the edit and I sat cross-legged on the chair staring at the screen. For the first time I heard what the others had said as I left, and saw the expressions on their faces. I saw the moment when I hugged Mum and Dad good-bye, and realized that though we'd been surrounded by cameras, I had no recollection of them being there at the time. There was the all-telling glance between them as I walked away, Dad briefly looking down, then turning to Mum for strength. She gave him a supportive smile, but it was a far from happy one, as you can imagine. I was almost traumatized by the visible effect I'd had on everyone by sailing off in such a colossal race. There was a quote from Dad that was dropped over the footage at that moment: 'You can't prepare for whatever your daughter might do . . . You might disagree with it, you might support her, you might go along with it, but at the end of the day you can't prepare for it.'

I felt an overwhelming gratitude to Mum and Dad for encouraging me to go off and follow my dreams. It would have been far easier for them early on to have just said no.

Then, as I watched *Kingfisher* slip away from the dock, Mark was asked, 'What would be your goal for her in this race?'

'Come back, safely, finish . . .' I saw his eyes fill with tears as he looked away from the camera. 'Ellen belongs at sea, and the boat belongs at sea. The sooner they're out there the better, and I have a lot of confidence in that combination when they're out there.'

In May, only a few weeks after Pasquale, the last competitor, finished after 158 days at sea, we returned to Les Sables d'Olonne for the official prize-giving. I hadn't really expected a big event, nor one that attracted such crowds. As I turned up to do my first TV interview I cast my eyes over the beach and saw lights and speakers suspended from two enormous cranes, and a big stage on stilts. If you hadn't known otherwise you would have thought it an outdoor concert.

That evening after dinner we were summoned outside to the beach for the presentation. It was almost dark, and the set looked incredibly impressive. There were thousands upon thousands of people packed along the beach, though in the dark it was very difficult to see just how many were there. There were two massive screens on each side of the stage, on to which were projected 40-foot-high video images. The atmosphere was electric. As I stood looking up to watch the video my knees began to shake. Pipo, Mathilde and Pilou were there and came to say hello, Pilou grasping his football which must have been at least half his size, and Mathilde looking proud and happy. As I was ushered towards the stage, I kissed Ian and headed down to the beach. The crowds were behind barriers, reaching out towards us. A man thrust a photograph at me, taken just after the finish. I tucked it into the inside pocket of my jacket. I read it later: 'Ellen, thank you for helping us dream.'

All the skippers were asked to walk up on to the stage together. The video continued to play with images of each of us which we had taken during the race. I had only seen a few of these and it shocked me to hear the others' voices, so happy or so sad, so loud and overpowering. Sixty thousand onlookers were transfixed. As the video stopped, the music began to play and the lights dimmed. Every second person in that audience turned on a torch and gently waved it before us. The MC told us, 'That is for you, they're doing it for you.' It was a beautiful way to show their appreciation.

The most wonderful feeling, which I know was shared by all twenty-four of us, was that we were all there to tell the tale. However long or short the journey, we had made it, every one of us safe and sound. As we lit flares and held them above our heads the music crescendoed. Each skipper, whether finished or abandoned, first or last, held such strong memories of an extraordinary race. I was sad that I had not made it back to see every one of them in. I had missed Joe, Patrice in the renamed *Aqua Quorum*, Didier, Marc and Bernard in *Voilà*. I had also missed Raphael Dinelli and Thierry Dubois, both of whom had completed the course but weren't classed, but looking round those faces that last time on stage I realized that there was another arrival I had missed, one which in all honesty I could not have tried harder to see. As the last of the fireworks burst and showered above us with the powerful sound-track pumping out of the speakers I turned away from the cameras, overcome with emotion for the first time that evening. I had missed the arrival I shall always remember and always regret; that of the man sitting right next to me, Michel Desjoyeaux.

*

I found it difficult to cope with the recognition that followed the Vendée. I was particularly alarmed that people would ask 'How are you going to stay in the limelight?' However well intentioned, they just didn't get it – I had never done this to be famous, that was never the objective, I had just wanted to race around the world. Friends stopped phoning, under the impression that their calls would no longer be welcome, then seemed genuinely bowled over when I rang them to say hi. I felt very strongly that it was not me that had changed, but everyone else.

At no stage did I feel like reversing what had happened though. I just knew that I needed to learn to adapt, and have people around me who understand how hard it is sometimes. Few people realize just how hard it is to keep smiling and looking happy when you're tired and exhausted, and how intimidating it feels to go into a room knowing that it's filled with people who want to talk to you. I've seen at sea how critical state of mind is to the way we perform – now I seemed to be struggling just to be me.

The hardest part was coping with losing the freedom to act as I wished. After such a big race I wanted nothing more than to slide away and collapse but I was on duty. When I had crossed the finish line of the Vendée Globe I felt that it didn't matter if I didn't sleep for a month because the job was done – but the job was far from finished and in many ways it had only just begun. During the summer of 2001 I was being pulled in every direction but forced myself to carry on. I must have been hell to live with as I beat myself up, angry and unable to relax because I had so much to do and no time to do it. We'd put aside thirty-four days to write this book, which became one of the biggest causes for my frustration. I had wanted to write since I was a child, but now the task just seemed to be looming over my head. It became startlingly obvious that I didn't have enough time. A possible solution was to have the book ghost-written, but I couldn't do it – in fact in my own mind it had never been an option. Nan would have turned in her grave at the thought!

Everything was getting too much. I desperately needed to take a day away but found the thought of not using any spare time to write even more stressful. I needed to get back in control and be in a position where a day away from writing was not a day that I should torture myself about. One night at Ian's I snapped, so distressed that I begun punching the stairs and crying with sheer frustration. My life was out of control, and at that moment there seemed absolutely nothing I could do about it. I knew that Ian, after spending so much time with me, knew how serious things were and had been waiting for me to break. He too felt helpless as his warnings to others seemed to be lost with the constant pressure. He let me blow my top, but eventually I just felt I had to disappear and I left to walk the streets of London.

At the same time with each presentation or interview, as I recounted my experiences, I was digging deep emotionally. And while I found myself becoming more and more defensive, no matter how I looked at it, one thing remained clear – it had been my choice to be out there. I'd been lucky, but now I found myself in a dilemma – I wanted desperately to share what I had been through, but as I tried to do so I was beginning to suspect that soon there would be nothing left inside to give. So many people wanted a slice, and to deal with that I knew I needed to regrow because there was only the core left – the slices were gone.

Things got progressively worse with Mark too. The constant pressure we had both lived under for almost five years was for the first time getting the chance to reveal itself as our lives became more reactive than pro-active. Despite our tiredness, things had been easy before the Vendée; we had had a common goal which had allowed us to put aside whatever tensions developed, but our relationship had essentially remained the one first formed five years earlier. Now things were going to have to change in some way between us, and we were about to find out that the transformation would be a painful one when Mark left for a life-saving and well overdue holiday with Dana.

Although Ian and I had always hoped to go away at the same time, it simply wasn't possible. The book was not something I could just pick up and put down again, and though I was desperate for a break I had committed to it and opted to stay at Ian's house in

London. It was the first time I had stayed put in the same place for as long as I could remember.

On the surface everyone said they understood, but still the pace didn't let up, nor did the state I was in. I was trying to recover not only from five years of hard grind, but also from three months of the most profound fatigue imaginable. It just proved impossible to get off. There were requests pouring in each day, from interviews to prize-givings to awards, to TV programmes, to endorsements, and with each I wanted to give my best. Everybody stressed that they just needed an hour or two and that they'd do all they could to make it as painless as possible, but if you are asked to do ten things on the same day that all take just a few hours, you simply cease to function. It went against our philosophy, but the hardest thing for everyone involved was to say no.

One evening I even took my entire family to an informal evening event in the hope of spending some time with them. As soon as the meal was finished I was ushered into a corner and signed autographs for two hours. In the end my only escape was to go and sit in the toilet for ten minutes – at least there I was alone. I felt so dependent on others and it just wasn't me, as I'd always been so independent.

I knew that I could not carry on looking at every interview and event I had to do with the same positive outlook. It frustrated me immensely that I couldn't be in ten places at once, nor say yes to all of the opportunities which came my way. I wished I had all the time in the world – I could have filled it!

More than anything, I needed to get back on the water.

The week before the start of the Vendée Alain Gautier had come to Les Sables d'Olonne and we'd grabbed a meal together where we agreed that we would race the Transat Jacques Vabre together aboard his 60-foot trimaran *Foncia* – it was the same race I'd done with Yves Parlier less than two years earlier. I had a tremendous amount of respect for Alain; he'd already played a massive part in the Kingfisher project and it was great to have a goal for the year. Things weren't going to be quiet on the Kingfisher front either, with a programme that culminated with the EDS Atlantic Challenge, a five-leg race which included two transatlantics.

First of all though came the Challenge Mondial with Alain on *Foncia*. This was an amazing event, giving me my first truly competitive offshore race on a 60-foot trimaran. Alain had a great team and a boat he knew inside out, which bode well for the spirit we had on board. Trimarans are very different from monohulls, relying on their beam for stability and power, and on their lightness for speed. They are just over half the weight of a boat like *Kingfisher* but have a wing mast several metres higher, so it doesn't take an expert to work out that they are blisteringly fast. Life on board was very different, with the waves screaming over the decks as we fired our way through them, whilst living in an almost survival-like capsule in the central hull. Their concept originally came through the pursuit of a multihull design that could be sailed alone, and despite their massive increases in performance, they are still sailed alone in some races. The experience was one I will remember for ever; sailing at unbelievable speeds, with every one of the five of us aboard grinning with pleasure.

It was the closest finish imaginable as we sailed towards the line off the Spanish coast. *Belgacom*, the leading trimaran, was a mile ahead, but sailing a little faster and lower, we managed to pull off something a bit different, and with one tack crossed the line just minutes before them. The feeling on board was euphoric – the value and power of teamwork really hammered home. I shall be forever indebted to those guys. If I'd been asked straight after the Vendée whether I preferred sailing alone or with a team I would have undoubtedly said alone, but just a few months later my view had changed – sailing with these guys had been one of the best experiences of my life, and I was hungry for more.

At one precise moment in the race, as I sat alone on the windward hull looking at the arid shores of the Mediterranean, I realized that I wanted to sail more in the multihulls. The decision was to be a mental turning-point. For the first time since I finished the Vendée I felt I was exercising some control over my life. I could feel that passion inside me again, and smiled broadly into space. I remembered what my dad had said during an interview: 'Ellen wants to compete, she's always wanted to compete – she will fight to finish the race . . .'

He was right. The race was far from over.

On returning from Spain I decided that it would be impossible to finish the book in 2001. I was angry with myself for not having made the decision earlier but it was a massive relief not to have it hanging over me. It didn't mean I was comfortable with the decision though.

With the journey to France for the start of the EDS came another major turning-point – both the end and the beginning of my relation-ship with Mark. During the crossing we'd decided to spend an hour or so going through various things that needed discussing. We'd had little time together during the previous months and the ferry seemed to offer a good opportunity. We sat in the dim four-berth cabin and waded through the printed sheets and notes that we had each made. Already tired, I knew I was at my wits' end. I felt I just could not manage any more. The schedule was still frantic and after giving up on the book I felt like a failure. The comments after I had delayed made me more angry – I had never tried to write a book before, and it became clear that others thought I'd undertaken an impossible mission. It was pretty hard to swallow after I'd just worked myself into the ground trying to complete it. I'd always said I was OK when anyone asked but with hindsight I wish that people could have realized just how bad things were inside. By the stage when I actually admitted that things were bad, it was too late. I'd reached breaking-point and I did not know how to articulate it. That night on the ferry though the full force of the anger came out. Never before in my life had I hit anyone, but I snapped and laid into Mark as if I was trying to kill him. I think it was the only way I had left of communicating. He did not retaliate, just tried to protect himself, until eventually, feeling as though my insides had been turned upside down, I ran out of the room. I did not return to the cabin and spent the rest of the night either outside huddled in a corner on the cold decks watching England disappear or curled up in a ball beneath the seats in the lounge area. Wherever I was though, my eyes remained firmly open. I felt more mixed up than ever before. I was searching for the way out, trying to find something to grab on to.

The following morning I met Mark at the car in silence. We spoke very little on that short drive, but as we pulled into the car park by *Kingfisher* he said, 'I don't know what you'll choose to do, but I'll be there for you, even if it's just to be the punch-bag.' I forced a grin, which he returned. Then he opened the door and left. Though I had felt suffocated in the aftermath of the Vendée Globe, I could now see just how much Mark was suffering too.

I took off in the car straight away and parked up on the cliffs overlooking the sea. Just five years before as a twenty-year-old I had raced into St-Malo after my first transatlantic race, passing the very headland I was sitting on. I had passed it again in the Route du Rhum, when it was covered with hundreds of thousands of people shouting and encouraging us. As I sat there I began to draw up plans for the future in my mind, and though then I knew that I was pretty much as low as I'd ever been, that passion was still very much inside me, and I was going to do my damnedest to let it out.

I loved the sea, I was drawn by the sea, and my job and motivation were to race on the sea. My career was only just starting and yet here I was feeling as though I was at the end of the line. I tried to be pragmatic and thought through my options again and again. After several hours I finally began to drift off so I locked the doors and slept.

I think that it was during the race that followed that I set out on the road to recovery. Initially it was tough. The first leg to Germany from France was the hardest for me; I felt trapped on board as if I just did not fit in with the guys. But we had 45 knots on the second leg, which was a great settler-in, and things improved after that. Nick Moloney, an Australian, was on board. He'd looked after *Kingfisher* during the spring while I was writing and though few things had changed, it took a while for me to get to know her once again. It had been hard letting her go at all, but Nick was a great guy and a good friend – he'd even raced *Le Poisson* in the 1999 Mini

Transat. It was still hard being on a boat where I was used to doing everything myself, and having others doing things. Having an extra four crew putting things in unexpected places and having to stow their kit took a lot of getting used to, but we still pulled off a second in both those legs, our good friend Bilou taking first!

One particularly notable crew member was Mark, who had returned to the water with a vengeance. I think Mark began to appreciate the change in me during this race as he watched me take on the responsibility of skipper. It was as good for him to get back on the water as it was for me, and the race undoubtedly marked the beginning of the rebuilding of our relationship.

A couple of months before the Jacques Vabre I eventually escaped for a holiday with Mum and Dad. They had rented a little cottage on the Isle of Skye. It sat next to a loch with an island just a mile or so from the sea. Watching the countryside open out before my eyes felt little short of a miracle, and seeing the speed at which Mac's tail wagged when I climbed off the ferry had me smiling immediately. We were to have a wonderful few days together, discovering our family's past as we researched in the local Portree library, and found the circular remains of Dad's great-grandfather's croft. We discovered that on Dad's side of the family the MacArthurs' trade was fishing – at last I'd found a family link with the sea!

Looking out of the window here as I write I am amazed at the sheer beauty of the Scottish countryside. I see the golden greens, and waving branches, the depth of the landscape. As I walk across the grass I feel a spring in my step.

I'd felt recently that I was becoming myself again and Scotland hastened this. I would go running there, pushing myself as hard as I could. Life had changed for sure, but I was now looking forward again, and it energized me. The summer had been atrocious in lots of ways. Mark and I had hated each other and lost the understanding we'd had, but time on Skye gave me the chance to write up the next five years. It had been taking shape in my mind for a while but at this point I hadn't discussed any of it with Mark. For me the first real step into the future would be when we sat down together and decided if we would run with it. I needed to be sure, and I needed to know that Mark was with me.

The multihulls had challenged me enormously. Sailing with Alain was already proving to be the most incredible learning curve and I revelled in it. I wanted to learn more and test myself. I somehow knew that the Jacques Vabre would show the way ahead. Racing single-handed in a trimaran pushes human endurance to its limits. I was desperate to tackle the Route du Rhum in one of these incredible machines. But the next Rhum was in just twelve months' time and I knew that although I could be on the start line I wouldn't be ready for it. To give myself time to gain the experience I needed and build the right boat I would go for the 2006 edition, while racing the 2002 edition in *Kingfisher*. This felt perfect and I was glad it would present us with the perfect opportunity to race together once again. The Vendée finish now felt like a long way away.

And that was, of course the next big question; the Vendée Globe. It seemed the entire world was trying to encourage me to cross that start line again. I knew that I wanted to return to the south and to sail in the Southern Ocean but I was not sure that the next Vendée was the best way. Although it was a race in which I felt there was unfinished business, my gut reaction was that the next Vendée in 2004 was too soon. I had come back from the previous race wanting to attempt it again, but if I completed the 2006 Rhum in a trimaran, the next Vendée would still be two years away and I would still be only thirty. The Vendée in 2008 was looking like the one. In the meantime I would have to find another way to sail south.

Since I had won the Young Sailor of the Year award back in 1995 I had been fascinated by Sir Peter Blake and Sir Robin Knox-Johnston's Jules Verne record. In a catamaran called *Enza* they had made it non-stop round the world in just over seventy-six days. In 1996 that record was beaten by Olivier de Kersauson, and it stood at just over seventy-one days. I had seen the footage of these incredible boats, so powerful, monstrous and quick, crewed by around ten people; this was a very different ball game. I was beginning to understand the multihull way now, and for the first time I felt ready to take a team of people around the world. I'd made my decision. The Jules Verne was going to take me back to the Southern Ocean!

I typed in a frenzied state to get these thoughts on to the computer, my fingers hammering away as the words seemed just to flow from my fingertips. It was a wonderful feeling to be planning something concrete once again, and though unsure of his reaction, I was excited to be sharing it with Mark. I heard a rustling behind me from Mac, who lay on her pouf by my feet. There were hardly eighteen inches behind my chair, but she had slotted herself in, good as gold, without making the slightest bit of fuss. I reached down to stroke her and she looked up, her muzzle against my arm. Always there for me through good and bad.

When I left Scotland I knew I was ready to share my plans with Mark. There had been times since the finish that I just wanted to crawl away and hide, but now I felt revitalized. And, quite frankly, I couldn't wait.

We sat in a little French café at the ferry terminal in Southampton. Mark was almost speechless as I handed over the sheet which outlined the plan for the Jules Verne and the trimaran, but quickly that wry smile turned to excitement and his eyes began to beam at the prospect of getting stuck in again. All things considered, I thought he took the news rather well!

A few months later I received a card from Mark containing two photographs, one taken before the Mini Transat and the other after the Vendée Globe. The note read:

```
Two very different pictures . . . A world between the two
and another once since . . . I wouldn't swap the last 4
years with you for anything - and I hope that I can say
it again in 4 years time.
Mxx
```

On coming back from Scotland I felt like a different person and was simply desperate to get on board the trimaran for the Jacques Vabre. It was going to be a massive challenge, and I was raring to get out there and just go for it again. We would be racing against the best in the world, and it was going to be awesome. Though at just over four years old, *Foncia* was not a new boat compared to some, she was reliable, and Alain knew her inside out – so, inside, I think we were quietly optimistic. The most worrying thing about trimarans compared to the monohulls is that there is just no room for error. Just two years before, when Alain had in fact been racing the same boat with none other than Michel Desjoyeaux, they had capsized just six hours into the race. Unlike monohulls, 60-foot trimarans will never right themselves: they are more stable upside down than the right way up. As we had seen two years before, the dangers out there were real.

Each time I arrived at the docks in Le Havre and saw the magnificent row of fourteen of the most powerful 60-foot multihulls in the world I felt very privileged, and I felt so grateful to Alain for asking me to race with him. Since he'd won the Vendée I was sure he understood what I had been through: he had known how vital it was just to get back out on the water.

The Transat Jacques Vabre was without doubt the climax of my season subsequent to the Vendée. It offered a fantastic chance to learn. The route would take us to Salvador de Bahia in Brazil and, for the multis, via Ascension Island in the South Atlantic. But before heading south to the equator, we would first have to tackle the sail out of the English Channel with its busy shipping, then the ominous headlands of Ushant and Finisterre. Again I would tune myself into the ocean, and develop once more that awareness of all that was going on around me. Your instincts change on a multihull – they are centred even more on survival.

E-MAIL UPDATE FROM ELLEN ON BOARD KINGFISHER-FONCIA
06/11/2001

What a night . . . it's been incredible, feeling like you are balancing on a tight rope with the wind howling past

every part of you. Well we're past finisterre, and
though 200 miles off it, we knew it. I shall never
forget the feeling as i rounded in the Vendée - 45-50
knots on the nose, though this time it was behind us
. . . it was incredibly dark at the beginning of the
night. . . . The clouds seemed to come down touching the
water, and its blanket covered over everything but the
wind. *Foncia* became harder and harder to steer, as we
continued in 25-30 knots with gennaker and full main . .
bit by bit though we reduced sail - till this morning we
were flying along at 22-28 knots under 1 reef and
trinquete. The wave crests become your guide, as they
are the only thing you can make out at speed . . . Thank
goodness that after a few hours of the long night the
moon rose - though behind clouds it was a godsend. . . .
As you grip the side of the seat with your free hand,
and the tip of the tiller with the other, you think of
little but protecting that person who is sleeping below.
it is your watch, and you are in control of this mighty
machine which is eating up the miles towards the south
. . . each wave taken and passed there is a sigh of
relief, and each squall brings a newly held breath as
you hope that as the leeward bow digs in it wills lowly
lift and free itself from its dark descent into the
waves.

There was something quite strange this am, a bright
red sky at three am in the north, with a shimmering
light coming up from behind the clouds. Never have i
seen that before, it could neither have been sunrise or
sun set - they were hours away . . . You can't help but
cast a thought to those who are sleeping, and how much
they are missing. The night time is a special time.

After 3 hours on the helm your arms feel like they
will never bend again, and your concentration is
spent. . . . You never feel like sleeping though - the
adrenalin of keeping things together stops any hint of

wearyness . . . we have tried different lenghts of
watches and with this motion, it's almost impossible to
sleep at all, and takes at least half an hour to dry off
and drop off. Solid water has been breaking up through
the trampoene as we ride over breaking crests and the
spray flying off the windward foil continuosly flies
into the air like a tornado . . .
   On my last off watch i curled up in a ball pulling a
sleeping bag over my front. It's still quite cold,
especially at night, and when the water botttles fly off
the shelf above your head onto your face, you know you
must have planted quite hard into a wave . . .
Time to go, it'll soon be my steer – funnily enough, im
actually looking forward to it!
e&ax

As we sailed down towards the Equator we were in first position, then Mich, sailing with Jean Luc Nelias, overtook us in *Belgacom*. But in picking a point to cross further east we managed to creep ahead. Tactically it was incredibly stressful – particularly as you're sailing in a big area of unknown. But the feeling on board was fantastic once we had crept through and headed south. We were in first position once again, all was well on board, and furthermore we had a lead of over 30 miles. But as Mich sailed further west, a boat called *Groupama* had sailed further east and managed, due to finding wind there, to take over 100 miles from us.

Despite their proximity we held off *Groupama* until twenty-four hours before the finish of the race. In virtually the worst run of bad luck you can imagine we not only broke the bowsprit, but then found several hours later we had a dysfunctional hydraulic ram. Our night was spent switching the 8-foot-long rams which hold the mast up from one side of the boat to the other. We were covered in hydraulic oil, sad and exhausted.

Overall we did have a great race, though, and on that final night, once *Groupama* had finished, we sat in the cockpit eating pasta, coming to terms with the fact that we had not won. We both felt that there was little more we could have done, and that we'd had a great race regardless of our position. Alain and I knew that we had unfinished business and vowed that we would race in the Jacques Vabre together two years later. I felt more motivated than ever before.

Though we had not won, our result in the Jacques Vabre marked the end of a very successful two years of sailing. As a result, on our return to Paris I was summoned to attend the FICO Lacoste Offshore World Championship prize-giving. Over the previous two years I had accumulated a sum of points from offshore events which led to me winning the title. I could remember being at the presentation just two years earlier, just months before *Kingfisher* went into the water. I could not believe what had happened to me over such a short period – it had been an incredible two years. For me the winning of that world championship represented the hard graft of an awful lot of people both on and off the water. As I spoke on the stage with the trophy in my hands, I wished that a whole host of names could be marked on it.

But the reception of the award was not the usual affair I had seen in previous years. This time the atmosphere was almost one of reverence as just days before we had lost a friend and quite probably the most highly respected sailor this world shall ever see. Tragically Sir Peter Blake was killed on 6 December 2001 while on his boat, *Seamaster*, in Brazil. He was the man I had seen on the big screen when I was eighteen years old winning the Yachtsman of the Year award with Robin Knox-Johnston. He was a driven man and an inspirational leader, and at the same time he had the most gentle character imaginable. He'd won every title, from the Whitbread to the Jules Verne to twice winning the Americas Cup – but his second Cup win for New Zealand was not enough. He undertook an expedition to sail to each corner of the world on a mission to open the world's eyes to the state of its oceans; in brief, he wanted as many people as possible to fall in love with the environment. While in the depths of Antarctica on the expedition which cost him his life he wrote this log, which had been e-mailed to me during the Vendée.

Today is a perfect day.

The written part of the Log is brief – because I want
to sit on deck and take it all in. I want to kayak to
some of the ice floes and watch the seals; I want to see
the penguins still heading for home – to their hungry
families ashore; I want to get close to a large iceberg
that is heading our way on the current – a berg whose
design Disney would have been proud of. It is great that
we have time – time to look, time to take it all in,
time to indelibly etch the scene on one's memory –
because no camera can do it justice.

2000 hrs: The sun is still blazing out of a clear blue
sky – but it is about to disappear down behind the
knife-edged peaks just astern. There is a chill in the
air that probably heralds a very cold night.

This is Antarctica!

As Nan said, 'Life holds a lot of treasure.' I've made a promise to
myself never to forget that.

On a cold morning in January 2002, Ian and I drove north. We'd be visiting home and also Derby University. I'd had several offers of honorary degrees since finishing the Vendée but in Nan's memory I chose Derby, the university at which she herself had graduated just four years before. In her will she had set up a small trust fund to make an annual award of a few hundred pounds to a student who had also had to struggle to attain their degree. An important part of the day was to hand over the first of these awards. I felt very nervous about this speech and discussed it at length with Ian in the car. I always got nervous when I spoke, and that morning was certainly no exception. I figured that the day the nerves stopped things would have ceased to matter and that would be the day when I should stop.

As we pulled into the car park next to the Playhouse where the ceremony was to take place, we were stopped by the man on the gate to ensure that we had the correct pass. As he looked in through the window he smiled, recognizing my face, then in a broad Derbyshire accent said in a particularly touching way that he was 'reet proud' of what I'd done. It was great to come back. The last time I'd been to the Playhouse was when Mum had taken me to see Button Moon at the age of four to try to take my mind off the disappointment of not going sailing with Auntie Thea!

There was little time to spare on my arrival as the ceremony was about to start, so after a brief cup of tea I donned my cap and gown and was whisked away with the University Senate to take our seats on the stage. Everyone was so friendly, and even during those minutes when I was waiting to go into the hall there were many mentions of Mrs Lewis – my Nan.

I am often aware of people looking at me as I walk from place to place, but when I headed to the stage at the front of that room, I felt I did not see a single set of eyes. The cloaks and gowns were like a forest and I just looked ahead to the stage at the front where I would be sitting. I knew as soon as I walked into the hall that Nan was there with me.

I sat through the first part of the ceremony with emotions that were so high that I could not tell if I was trying to hold back the tears or stop myself from grinning. When I thought of Nan in her long gown with her cap that wouldn't stay on I wanted to smile, but that made me think of her more, which was painful. Mum, Dad and Ian were sitting in the front row, and I found it hard to look in their direction. I tried to see the sea of faces as the water, and concentrate on what I was going to say. I wanted this one to be a good speech – for Nan.

My name was soon called and I was invited to stand and listen to a speech of introduction. I was OK to start with, but as the speech went on I could feel myself swallowing hard. It was a thoughtful speech, which seemed to trigger feelings from within me. She finished by speaking of Nan and of the time she had spent at the University. My mind began to focus on her, and as it did so I could feel my emotions going through overload. I could think of little other than how much courage she must have had to fight the pain to achieve her goal after all she'd been through.

Just as I wished I could be sitting in a room alone, it was the moment for me to speak. I was standing before several thousand graduates and their families sitting in complete silence. I knew at that point that I would not be able to finish the speech; already I was choking and could feel the tears welling. Never before had I failed to complete a speech, but this time, after I'd said that I had come here primarily because of my Nan, I felt myself choking and knew that there was little more I could say. I could barely manage the words 'It was her wish' before handing over the envelope.

I stepped backwards into my seat, and as the weight came off my feet I felt almost dizzy. All I could do as I sat down was think of her face in the photograph taken on the day of her graduation, and from then on could do little but smile with her. Her face was beaming, her eyes were sparkling and her skin was glowing. Nan had proved that she'd been quite literally living for that moment; she had achieved the goal which throughout her whole life she had refused to let out of her sight.

I realized then what an incredible inspiration she had been and always would be to me.

Thank you Nan.

Love always,

Ellenxx

Vendée Globe 2000/2001 Final Positions

Position	Skipper/CTRY	Boat	Days	Hour
1	Michel Desjoyeaux/France	*PRB*	93	
2	Ellen MacArthur/Great Britain	*Kingfisher*	94	
3	Roland Jourdain/France	*Sill*	96	
4	Marc Thiercelin/France	*Active Wear*	102	20
5	Dominique Wavre/France	*UBP*	105	
6	Thomas Coville/France	*Sobedo*	105	
7	Mike Golding/Great Britain	*Team Group 4*	110	1
8	Bernard Gallay/France	*Voilà*	111	1
9	Josh Hall/Great Britain	*Gartmore*	111	1
10	Joe Seeten/France	*Nord Pas de Calais*	115	1
11	Patrice Carpentier/France	*VM Matériaux*	116	
12	Simone Bianchetti/Italy	*Aquarelle*	121	
13	Yves Parlier/France	*Aquitaine Innovations*	126	2
14	Didier Munduteguy/France	*DDP 6oième Sud*	135	1
15	Pasquale de Gregorio/Italy	*Wind*	158	
16	Catherine Chabaud/France	*Whirlpool*		
17	Thierry Dubois/France	*Solidaires*		
18	Raphael Dinelli/France	*Sogal-Extenso*		
19	Fedor Konioukhov/Russia	*Modern University for the Humanities*		
20	Javier Sanso/Spain	*Old Spice*		
21	Richard Tolkien/Great Britain	*This Time*		
22	Eric Dumont/France	*Euroka Un univers de Services*		
23	Bernard Stamm/Switzerland	*Armor Lux Foies Gras Bizac*		
24	Patrick de Radigues/Belgium	*Libre Belgique*		

Minutes	Seconds	Speed	Hours	Deficit (Hours)	Comment
57	32	11.95	2235	0	
	25	11.95	2260	25	
2	33	11.58	2305	70	
37	49	10.82	2468	233	
47	12	10.82	2522	287	
24	0	10.59	2527	292	
22	0	10.05	2656	421	
7	11	9.96	2680	445	
48	2	9.95	2683	448	
46	50	9.62	2776	541	
32	48	9.59	2784	549	
28	0	9.19	2905	670	
36	0	8.76	3047	812	Completed race under jury rig
17	0	8.20	3255	1020	
37	25	7.04	3794	1559	
					Retired dismasted
					Retired with electrical problems
					Retired because of collision damage
					Retired with illness
					Retired with rudder damage
					Retired with rig damage
					Retired with rudder damage
					Retired with steering damage
					Retired ran ashore

Abeam Perpendicular to the side of the boat.

Bilge The part of the hull that's below the waterline. It collects any water that's entered the boat.

Block A pulley.

Boom The spar that extends backwards from the mast to which the foot of the mainsail is attached.

Bow The front of the boat.

Bowsprit A spar that extends forward from the bow.

Broach A potentially dangerous situation when the boat spins out of control and lies on its side across the waves and wind.

Buoy A float that acts as a navigational aid.

Cabin Living area below deck level.

Cans Buoys.

Catamaran A twin-hulled boat.

Cockpit Where the boat is steered from. Most of the control of the boat happens here.

Code 5 A cross between a spinnaker and a gennaker. A furling sail making it safer to drop.

Cuddy The small roof-like shelter over the cockpit.

Daggerboard A retractable fin that extends vertically from the hull to prevent leeward drift when upwind.

Deck spreader A massive boom-like spreader which can hold the rigging far enough from the mast to allow the resultant aerofoil-shaped mast to twist.

Forestay A metal rod supporting the mast from the bow. *Kingfisher* had three.

Furl To roll up a sail around its stay, a bit like a vertical blind.

Gennaker A large sail that is a cross between a spinnaker and a genoa.

Genoa A large jib sail that sets in front of the mast, but extends aft of the mast.

Gunwales The upper edge of the boat's sides at deck level.

Gybe To change direction so that the stern passes through the direction of the wind.

Halyard A rope used for raising and lowering sails.

Hank Metal clips used for attaching a sail to a stay.

Heel When the boat leans away from horizontal because of the action of the wind.

Jib A triangular sail which sets in front of the mast.

Jumar An ascending device that grips a rope so that it can be climbed.

Jury rig A temporary, improvised repair to a broken rig.

Keel A vertical fin that extends downwards from the bottom of the boat. Ballast in the keel helps keep the boat upright.

Knot One nautical mile per hour.

Leech The trailing edge of a sail.

Leeward Downwind.

Luff The leading edge of the sail.

Mainsail A large triangular sail that hangs between the mast and the boom.

Mainsheet The rope that's used to control the mainsail.

Pad Eye A U-shaped bolt attached through the deck as a strong fixing point.

Port The left side of the boat.

Pulpit The metal guardrail at the bow of the boat.

Pushpit The metal guardrail around the stern of the boat.

Reach Sailing with the wind perpendicular to the side of the boat.

Reef Reducing the area of the sail in high winds by partially lowering it.

RIB A Rigid Inflatable Boat. A powerboat with a rigid hull and inflatable tubes around the top edges.

Rig The arrangement of the mast, shrouds and sails.

RNLI Royal National Lifeboat Institution.

Rudder A vertical fin at the stern of the boat that steers it.

RWYC Royal Western Yacht Club.

Sheet A line used to control the sails.

Shroud Wires/rods or man-made fibres supporting the mast.

Sole The boat's floor.

Solent The intermediate jib sail, between the staysail and the genoa.

Spinnaker A very large light balloon-like sail used when sailing downwind. Sometimes referred to as a kite.

Spreader A long horizontal fitting holding the shrouds away from the mast and creating a framework of strength.

Stanchion A post around the edge of the deck that supports the lifelines.

Starboard The right side of the boat.

Staysail A triangular sail similar to, but smaller than, the jib.

Stern The rear of the boat.

Storm-jib A very small strong sail used in rough conditions.

Tack The direction the boat is sailing in relation to the wind, or to change the direction of the boat so that the bow passes through the direction of the wind.

Tiller Attached to the rudder and used for steering the boat.

Trampolene Netting hung between the hulls of catamarans or trimarans.

Transom The flat part of the hull at the stern of the boat.

Trim To adjust the sails in relation to the wind.

Trimaran A three hulled boat.

Trinquete A staysail.

Windward Upwind.

Acknowledgements

First of all, to all those people whom I have not included in this list, a massive thank you. This was a difficult task!

Mum and Dad for never trying to stop me from doing what I had burning in my heart. Lewis for inventing cool things, and Fergus for being patient with me in your youth! Mac for your happiness and never-ending tail-wagging – wish I could see more of you! Auntie Thea for introducing me to the water, and sharing so many thoughts and ideas. The rest of the family for providing such wonderful support, and putting up with me. Sarah and Ben for being such fantastic and understanding friends. Everyone else at school who became friends during those years. Karl Stanley for making me just grit my teeth and get on with things. John Manning for donating so much of your time to teaching young people sailing. The girl who befriended me on the dinghy course at Rutland, thank you! Malcolm Stanton for commenting about my writing to Mum and Dad when I was sixteen. Simon Ashton for putting up with, and caring for an over-enthusiastic seventeen-year-old. Mr Law for giving up his time to take us sailing on Friday evenings. Simon Reeve for being such a great friend and giving me a weekend outlet for my energy – and being so generous with your pork pie! David for giving so much, and Maureen for providing Tunnock's and moral support, and of course for thinking to enter me for that eye-opening competition. Robert Nickerson – what can I say, Robert? Thanks for giving me the helm! Joe Sempik for taking me sailing on *Knippa*, buying me beers and talking boats. John Duckett for bringing friendship and food to my life at the nautical school! Darren, Mick, Pete,

Mike and all at Hull Marina for taking such an interest. Dave Anderson for your field, Dave's mate who towed *Iduna* over the bridge. The Infamous Steve and Shamus for your amusing stories and generosity. Alan Brooks for being as far from the ogre examiner as you can imagine! The *Yachting* journalists who voted for me back in 1995 for the YSOY Award. Karl Kanti for your stainless-steel work. Don Hayes for believing in me, then letting me spread my wings. Graham Percy for being the driving force behind my first press dossier. Brian Pilcher – what more can I say but thank you for being simply Brian. Keith, Nigel and all at Musto for your continuing support, and keeping me dry! James Flynn and Navico for taking the helm for such a large proportion of the trip! John Hurry and Yamaha – without you I think I'd still be sailing around Britain! Howard Anguish and Hull Marina for allowing me to sanely prepare *Iduna*. Cosalt for supplying those items that I hoped I would not be using! Paul Mills and all at Marinecall for giving me a 24-hour weather service to tap into. John Goode and James Stevens for giving me the chance to prove myself. Tony, his dog and everyone from Scarborough – great pie and peas! The crew of *Royalist*, Paul, JB, Howy, Dave, JP and Joe, for their acceptance of me and non-stop laughter! Mr S. Skene – St Abbs – for the *Olsen's Fisherman's Nautical Almanack* and advice. Harry the harbour-master from Montrose for all your help and the tea-shed key! Hamish McDonald and family for your words and the most incredible welcome. Ross Buchan and his friends for making me so welcome in Whitehills. (Thanks for the shackles, and hope you got your placement and your engineering is going well!) The harbour-master at Whitehills for those five fantastically fresh haddock! Keith, Ben and the team from RAF Lossiemouth for a great night out, and my first ever official flypast – awesome! Sebastian Naaslund for being another crazy person with different ideas, and teaching me that languages are not impossible to learn. Barry Mercer and the crew of *Sakhr-El-Bahr* – who'd have thought it, Kentallen Bay! John Fitzgerald for letting me use your mooring and running me across to Oban so early – hope you've managed to get your folkboat finished! Bernard on *Dulas Dragon* for buying *Iduna*'s stove and then supplying a meal on it! The fantastic company I had in Loch Feochan, and our night out to the pub. *Fulmoral* and her crew for sharing stories in the most beautiful anchorage. The family in Ardrishaig for their cruising guides, tea and oatcakes. Frank McAllum and partner for a short break from a stormbound journey. Gordon Azzur and his friends for having a laugh and showing me round *Excalibur*. Roddie Leech for his active welcome in Girvan – escorted by bicycle! The crew of *Dream Twister*, Timmy, Jeremy, Mum and Dad and little sister – thanks for the help and the late-night but very welcome Portishead curry! *Dream Twister*, *Kittiwake*, *Camelina* (thanks for the flag), *Scatha*, and *Balandra* all for collecting £22 in that brown envelope marked BEST OF LUCK WITH THE REMAINDER OF YOUR VOYAGE! The crew of *Morning Roll* for inviting me on board and introducing me to squirty custard! Gemma and the crew from *Lady of Penpole* for inviting me out. Iain Rennie for a great night of conversation – hope you're still designing bike bits! Jeremy from the island opposite Croabh Haven – your lifestyle still inspires me now. The harbour-master in Peel for the tyres, and the welcoming lot from the yacht club! Also the Girvan harbour-master. Marc Lawler for a great interview with a great photo – I still have the cutting! Dave Morton and crew for the bacon and eggs that morning! Derek and Carol Jones for their company and the most wonderful photo I have of *Iduna* (it's in the book!). Bill McGill in the harbour office in Pwllheli for advice on heading down the coast. Sion Edwards from Aberystwyth, thanks for all your help and for keeping in contact. The crews of *Hi-Jinks*, *Mac-y-Sol*, *Fly*, *Fidget*, *Sea Horse*, the RNLI inshore lifeboat, and *The Squib* which all sailed out of Fishguard to come and meet us in! John and Margaret Richards for giving me the best night's sleep ever, making me feel completely at home and introducing me to so many fantastic people like Emlyn! Paul Camen and family for the cider and mackerel, and the lifeboat crew from Fishguard for an insight into chart plotters, a tour of the engine room and a quick spin! The Sea Cadets for showing me around their base and taking me on board TS *Appelby*. Richard Davies for my first trip to Ireland and a new experience travelling on the bridge of a 'sea cat' (wonder if that inflatable crocodile is still out there!). Tony Rees and wife for the very early morning rescue, and the subsequent bed! Marcus from *Shebeen* for so many stories, and baking that wonderful loaf of bread! The crew of the boat I was alongside in Milford Lock – I couldn't find your letters! The lift in Newlyn to the petrol station – it was a long way, I'd have been in a fix! John Lewis from the RWYC for making me feel so welcome in the club during the Round Britain and for hosting so many fantastic short-handed races! Sam

Brewster for showing me round *Heath Insured II*, and checking *Iduna* out! The crew of the *Corribee Rubicon* for the race out of Plymouth harbour! Col Brooks and all at ICC for a berth alongside *Egremont* with such great atmosphere! Carol Newman and her father from *Skycatcher* for coming over to say hi. Jonathan and Jennifer Blain for their meals and company. Chris and Shirley from the SCOD *Aderyn* – shame we didn't meet up again in Poole. Steve Belasco for letting me go to work on your furling system, and the photos! Ruth Macai and family from Portland, thanks for having me to dinner! Norman Meech for sharing his passion and building such a beautiful boat in Arish Mell. John Bolter for the free berth, the chat and that fantastic bacon sarnie! The BMIF and everyone from the organizers' office at the boat shows – you made me feel so welcome, both then and now, I shall never forget my first official show! MDL – free berthing in Ocean Village. You made it possible for us to stay for the show. Everyone at the Southampton boat show who helped us out in any way at all! Mervyn Owen for sharing everything, and encouraging me to the ends of the earth. Jock Smith and crew for a wonderful meal out and keeping in touch ever since. (Who knows, maybe pigeons will come back in as a form of communication!) Adam Allan and the Sea Cadets for a fantastic week's sailing from Gosport. VTS *Humber* – your voices were so fantastic to hear after four and a half months! Charles Boot for bringing Mum, Dad and family out to see me in at the end of the trip. Any port who gave us free berthing – financially it would have been impossible without you all. I just hope there will be an occasion in the future to come back and visit! Finally, all those who helped me out on the way around Britain, I am sure I have missed so many of you, but that doesn't mean that your help, kindness and friendship did not make all the difference to that adventure.

James Grazebrook and Halyard Marine for your support at the LBS 1996. The guys from ISIS mouldings who took me under their wing in London that year! The man from the Citroen garage who let me change the brake pipe. Dick Saint, Kay and the boys at HYS – especially Jim, who went out of his way to help! Led Pritchard – you were one of the few people in Hamble who gave me confidence. The guy from Hamble who talked to me in the pub. Trog, for that fantastic sail from Brighton to the Solent, and for being so funny! Nick Butt for being my crew for that delivery to Guernsey and for chatting in Hamble. Darren Wills for your help on *Elan Sifo*. Alex and Darren for a mad Irish sea trip! Wolfgang Quix. Alan Wynne-Thomas for having the guts to take me on, and for sharing so many of your Vendée experiences. You gave me so much confidence in those months. Bob and Carole for going out there and doing it, and housing us after the Ostar. Will from Portway for taking Mum and Dad out. Mike Golding for commissioning me to do that painting. Vittorio and the boys for inviting me along, becoming such great friends and showing me the North Atlantic and her icebergs for the first time. Giovanni Soldini, Andrea Tarlarini and Enrico for a fantastic trip to Italy on the 50. The crew of the *Matthew* in particular James, Luke, Richard, David and John the Bowman – for tales and malt loaf!

Ashley for the hours spent discussing projects, for your meals and floors in several countries; and of course, more than all those, for your friendship. Martin and Steve from Bowman Yachts for being such great friends in a tough year. Len the dog and his owners! Ed Gorman for giving my first ever national newspaper interview. Nigel Irens for your deep love of the sea, inspiring boats, and for being such a solid and wonderful person. Nigel from Hampshire Trailers for bringing a little sanity to a crazy situation! Mark Orr for lending part of that crucial money which allowed me to buy *Le Poisson*. The Silk Cut Boys for your friendship and kindness. Dick and Steve at Airwaves, especially for burning the midnight oil on our sponsorship video, and taking Reima and me off in Martinique just to see a little of the island. Thierry Fagnant at AMCO, the Guru of Minis, the master of roll-ups, teacher of French and all our suppliers and friends in La Trinité sur Mer (not forgetting Louise the dog). Thierry Martinez for sharing your house with us for so long, the perfect place to be! Nic LeMarchand, our first, and dedicated, preparateur. Richard Vass of Burland Solutions, you made a massive difference. Charles Dunstone and Carphone Warehouse, our first major sponsors for the Mini Transat in 1997. But not forgetting the many other players in that project. Royal Solent Yacht Club, IOW Council. G. Askew, Musto, SP Systems, UKSA, Simpson Lawrence, Mel Sharp, Nautix, Autohelm, Regis Electronics, Suunto, Ian Terry Engineering, Spinlock, Andrew Bishop, Marlow Ropes, Whale, Westaway Sails, Relling Sails, Tony Bertram and Bainbridge, Riggarna, Tim Dean and

Formula Spars, Ocean Safety, Ratsey and Lapthorn, Navico, DG Wroath, Simon and Reb Rogers, Johnny Caulcutt, Vix, my mum and dad, Mark's mum and dad. Hugh and Financial Dynamics for making the difference to Mark's chances. The Foundation for the Sports and Arts for sending the letter of support that transformed 1997! It couldn't have arrived at a better time. The Honda salesman who gave me a lift to Portsmouth. Woolfie for coming over to fit that pilot just days before the start for free. David Gown, Jim Doxey and Peter Halliwell for their help in the run-up to the Mini. Peter Bentley for getting stuck in helping me to leave with 'some' clothes! And to the organizers and skippers in the Mini Transat for the most passionate race with the closest-knit community among skippers I have known.

Our 1998 Route du Rhum campaign was supported by a number of suppliers and individuals. Without them, that project could never have succeeded. There are many personal supporters, friends and workers who make up the team to get a single-handed racer to a start and finish line.

Skandia Life, Peter Nicholson, John Caulcutt for inspiring everyone else to contribute as well, Royal Southampton Yacht Club (for a bed in their launch!), Royal Southern Yacht Club, Hardwick Press and Publicity, Acorn Maintenance Systems, PC Maritime, A. McIrvine, A. Chilvers, N. Hodkin, D. Moore, S. Hobday, R. Parker, Jock Wishart, S. Gordon – you all made the impossible seem possible.

Christian Stimson, our first office space, and one of the Rhum voluntary preparateurs. Nick our first student employee, and Marine our first real one! Hugh Morrison for your boundless energy and unwavering enthusiasm for the project, we would not be here without you, Hugh. Liam and Chris, your energy, jokes and patience got us to the Rhum in '98. Bitzy and Cannon Ball for being the kindest and friendliest faces in a foreign port. Herb for your life-saving weather information as we were crossing the Atlantic. Stuart and Angela in Plymouth for looking after us, feeding us and entertaining us! (Not forgetting that incredible home-made ketchup and Paddy's visits.)

383

Mike Hingston, the master of all-night working, and the real driver of *Kingfisher*'s sponsorship in the early days, supported by Jo Bootle, dedication beyond the call of duty! Geoff, for putting his faith in us, against the odds as others would see it. Jean, George, Lydia, Andrew, Gwen, Jerry, Graham, Patrick, Arvind and everyone at Kingfisher plc since 1998, and in the operating companies around the globe, who have supported me for every single mile. It's been a pleasure working with you all!

In addition to our primary sponsor Kingfisher, and our supporting sponsor Big Blue (Colin Campbell from National Boat Shows), we were actively supported by: TMI Atlantic Foundation, Marlow Ropes, AIRX by Bainbridge International, Osen Sails of Plymouth, Botalo Shoes, McMurdo Ocean Sentry (radar target enhancer), Pains Wessex Safety Systems, Nautix Antifouling, Anne Whitlock, PR Works, David Zorab, Spinlock, TT Designs, North Sails (UK), Northern Star Insurance, Aura Fabric Engineering. And many others who gave their time and energy to support us, including the committed shore crew of Liam, Jude, Sam, Emma, Jim, Nic, Christian, Marine, Tanguy, Capey and Andy from Goss Challenges who prepared the 50 in record time, and many voluntarily! James Boyd for being dedicated to his sport. And Ed Gorman again – that front page was timed perfectly! And all the other journalists from France, the UK and all over the world – without you no one would ever have heard of these incredible races. Tony Banks for being such an avid supporter, and momentarily taking your mind off football!

The Kingfisher Vendée preparation and shore team of Martin, Amanda, Pipo, Marie (Pilou & Mathilde), Mikey, Tanya, (Matthew), Marc and Tanguy. A dedicated team, and a very special and emotional time. Wonderful job, guys. You were the best! The Kingfisher Design Team of Merv and Allen at Owen Clarke Design, Rob and Nick at Humphrey's Design, Giovanni Belgrano and Alain Gautier. For designing the most beautiful open 60 ever. You brought her alive from that first sketch. Thank you. The BMF for your support and your counterparts in France and New Zealand. Yves Parlier, an important teacher for me, and his great team at Aquitaine Innovations of Stephane, Michel, Romaric, Agathe and co. Mick and Keep Safe Self Storage for staying late to let me in on my whirlwind missions!

Paul Brotherton for being so patient in teaching me everything I needed to keep dry! Gael Le Cleach for a patient introduction to a different type of sailing. The Bourgnon brothers for an unforgettable Fastnet experience, Pierre Lasnier and Jean-Yves Bernot for teaching me so much about the weather of the world. Audrey, James, Mary, Dana and the team back at home in Cowes, thank you for everything. Bruce Guthrie from 3M New Zealand – you went completely out of your way to help! Steve Marten, Allan and the great team of guys at Marten Yachts, Auckland NZ. Moët Chandon, Bruno Trouble, Marcus, Maria Ryan and the team at the Louis Vuitton Cup Media Centre, Auckland – it was a dream come true to even launch *Kingfisher*. Lady Pippa Blake, your blessing of the boat and even me has brought immense luck. Sir Peter Blake, tragically lost in 2001, the best professional sailor the world has ever seen and a great leader who was an inspiration on and off the water both personally and for the team at Offshore Challenges. Pat Ashworth for 'true grit', Darren from York for your great news, Dennis Skillicorne for those fantastic minidisks of your favourite radio programmes! The kids from A Chacun Son Cap, Sargent and the hospitals in France I visited, your smiles, gifts, and incredible energy – if anyone has been a hero to me, it is you guys!

As well as a great team of suppliers, our Partners for the Vendée Globe project: Kim and the team at BT (communication services) – it seems a long time since we first met back in 1995! W S Atkins (R&D using Computational Fluid Dynamics), Raymarine (Autopilot technology and radar), Bainbridge (Titan winch handles, Tylaska snaps, Sailmaking kits and all canvas work material), B&G performance instrument system, Volvo Cars UK, Red Funnel, EP Barrus (Yanmar engine), Marlow Ropes, Musto (technical Clothing), Future Fibres, Stratos, Wolfson Unit, Oceanair Marine (blinds), Pains Wessex McMurdo (marine safety equipment), Nautix antifoul, Harken winches, Bruno and his team at North Sails France and Bill at 3DL – 'born to survive', Ocean Yacht Systems (standing rigging), Bananas and Southern Spars, Suunto wrist top computers, TBS, Will and T&G, Facnor, Titan Australia Pty, TMI, UKSA, Team McLube, Richard Butcher, Travelwell, Debbie@Global Travel, Peters & May, Diverse, and TOC Scotland.

The thousands of people who came to Les Sables d'Olonne, who made the atmosphere what it was and showed such incredible warmth towards the team and myself. Philippe Hutcheon for the work Castorama did with the 'Castokids Programme'. Steve, Llion, Hugh, Tim, Gwynfor and the team at BBC Wales Extreme Lives. Howard and Pete for being such skilled rib drivers with a sense of humour! The team on shore during the Vendée that helped us share the story with millions, including Andrew, Richard, Erik, Lou and the team at APP, Rick, Jacques, Thierry M, Green Design, Gwenola, Marie, Ian, Windreport, Jean, Rachel and the team in London. Mark, Helen, Josie, Dana, Rosie, and the team in the office in Cowes, you guys lived and breathed that race with me – quite literally. There was not a moment in any day when I did not feel you were with me. It was 'your' race and your success – awesome! Bjork for taking on a mission cleaning after us lot! Sue, Wendy and Debs, Matt, Munners, Rhidian, Bob, Nobby, Max and the others, for your contributions in all sorts of diverse areas – awesome job, thank you. Philippe Jeantot and his team in Les Sables and Paris – thank you for such a great race. Dana's parents for building shelves and housing so much of our equipment! Every skipper who took part in the Vendée Globe, for your spirit, friendship and passion. Thanks also to the previous skippers of the Vendée, those who returned and, tragically, those who did not but shall never be forgotten. The 52,500 people who have e-mailed during the Vendée and other races, I only wish I could reply personally to you all! You have always kept me going – don't stop! Ian for your unwavering support. Paul Peggs, Brian Meerloo and Rice and Cole's Yard – for taking the time to bring *Iduna* back to life for my homecoming. Mrs Gration for being such a good friend to Nan and for your dishcloths and news!

Alain Gautier in particular for understanding and helping me through 2001. Loick, Ewan, Nico, Florent, P-Peche, Kiki, Xavier, Kinou, Mammouth, Frank, and Mick for some of the best times and best sailing ever! Ça part de la les Gars!! Nick Moloney for being such a great friend, sharing everything with us and being such a motivated guy. Hendo, Adrienne, Brian, Antony, and Mark for being the best guys ever to sail with anywhere – that EDS was a very, very special race. Ayy! Daphne, Steve, Jonny the Wylester, Adrian, Breeny, Nobbers, and Little Richard for your care and time spent looking after, preparing, sailing and improving 'The Fish'. Every single person who voted for me in the Sports Personality of the Year Award! Mark, Helen, Josie, Jonny, Kate, Lou, Mike, Charles, Kristie, Nick, Little Richard, Ant and Hendo. Wow, looking forward to the next one with you all! Natasha Fairweather at A.P. Watt, Clare Pollock at Penguin and Helen Campbell in Mallaig for being so patient. Rowland – well, what can I say! This is your book too, I cannot speak highly enough of your patience and dedication. Thank you for making this experience not just bearable but enjoyable. Once again the team at Kingfisher Plc, and Offshore Challenges Ltd. For the experiences behind us – and those before us. Thank you from the bottom of my heart. To *Kingfisher* for looking after me for every moment of those ninety-four days. I could not imagine ever having that same relationship with another boat. We grew up together. Finally, Mark Turner. There are few names on this list that you do not know, Mark, we really have shared so much. The future is always beckoning . . . let's never let that go . . .

Headings in italics refer to boats unless otherwise stated.

Following the project with

**Offshore
Challenges**

It doesn't have to stop here … when Ellen and her team are out racing, her company Offshore Challenges in collaboration with her title sponsors European Retailer Kingfisher plc, transmit her daily logs out to thousands of people by email.

If you would like to receive these emails from Ellen please sign up at :
http://www.kingfisherchallenges.com

or email to updates@kingfisherchallenges.com with your request including your name, full email address, country and frequency required

Updates can be sent daily, weekly or just when there is major news.

You can also receive a short text message update, again daily during a race, weekly during a race, or just when there is major newsflash. Email smsupdates@kingfisherchallenges.com with your name, mobile number including country code and frequency required

---

You've read the book, now check out the action on your TV, by purchasing the great video 'Taking on the World' online via http://www.ellenmacarthur.com

or by completing the form below. With this form it is available with a 10% discount

I would like to buy ____ copies of 'Taking on the World' video at £12.95 each inc. VAT in the following format
☐ English version PAL
☐ English version NTSC (USA)
☐ French version SECAM
Add £3.00 p&p in the UK and European mainland, and £5.00 elsewhere per order (of up to 5 videos)

☐ I enclose a cheque made payable to 'Offshore Challenge Ltd.' for
☐ I authorise payment on my Credit Card as follows
Name on card :
Address for card :

Type of card : [VISA] [MASTERCARD]
Card number :
Expiry Date :   Signature :
Address for delivery if different to above :

Email address :
Phone number :

Offshore Challenge Ltd. is registered under the Data Protection Act 1998. We do not share your details with any third party
Please write to: Offshore Challenges, Whitegates, Arctic Road, Cowes PO31 7PG, Isle of Wight, United Kingdom.